REIMAGINING

THE AMERICAN

PACIFIC

NEW AMERICANISTS *A Series Edited by Donald E. Pease*

REIMAGINING THE AMERICAN PACIFIC

From *South Pacific* to Bamboo Ridge and Beyond

ROB WILSON

Duke University Press   Durham and London   2000

© 2000 Duke University Press
All rights reserved
Printed in the United States of America on acid-free paper ∞
Typeset in Scala by Keystone Typesetting, Inc.
Library of Congress Cataloging-in-Publication Data appear
on the last printed page of this book.

CONTENTS

Searching for "the Local":

Hawaiʻi as Miss Universe?

Long ago, in the age of European discovery, when such explorers as the Florentine merchant Amerigo Vespucci roamed the waters of the New World, a wondrous island was discovered west of England and Portugal where labor was said to be a joy, where the will to profit was unknown, where the drive for grandeur, gold, and greed had been sublimated into care for the common good. Nowhere to be found on any earthly map of colonial possession, of course, this island was called Utopia by Sir Thomas More in a satire by that name in 1518.

True to Western forms of colonial settlement, this fantasy island of earthly possession, it is more accurate to say, was not so much discovered as made, in a raw act of state power, real politic, and cultural-political imagining, shaped into existence as some "brave new world" of otherness by *distancing* itself from some unnamed continent, some "mainland" of power where the civilized customs of early-modern capitalism were otherwise installed. "Utopus," so it is narrated by More, "brought his rough and rude people to that high point of culture and civilization whereby they now surpass practically all other men. As soon as he had landed and conquered the place, he caused the part where it was joined to the mainland to be cut through and let the sea around the land."[1]

Nobody has gone quite that far in recommending that modern-day Hawaiʻi be totally cut off from the "mainland" of the United States superstate or seek some form of economic autarky via complete delinkage from

---

1. Sir Thomas More, *Utopia*, trans. Peter K. Marshall (New York: Washington Square Press, 1965), 43.

the uneven flows of culture and capital emanating from the Pacific Rim (especially such sites as California, Taiwan, and Japan) and elsewhere. But, at times in this paradox-ridden era of primordial bullying and postmodern weightlessness at the global culture mall, it does seem fair to say that this new brand of cultural localism (and the "local literature" movement, as we shall explore) sought for in Hawai'i during the past twenty years has turned back from mongrel exploration and self-invention into a kind of utopic dream of bounded possession, willed imagining, decolonized fortitude, and reified belonging. These localist strategies are mistaken, if understandable, as I shall explain in the pages to come, especially given the global heritage of imperialism and the two-hundred-year-old national tendency to a historical obliviousness and a kind of tourist-driven U.S. transcendentalism immune to critique.

Riddled with ethnic tensions and racial battles that go far back in history, at least to the contact of Captain James Cook's untimely three explorations (cum apotheosis) in 1778 and the American Board of Commissioners of Foreign Missions' offshore project in white cultural redemption (cum indigenous demonization and racial abjection) in 1820, which dragged Hawai'i into the battle of imperial nations, postmodern Hawai'i is still struggling with these (uneven) global/local dialectics (ongoing) dependency syndromes à la some Pacific Caliban seeking for a blessed pidgin voice, and searching for some capable theory, economic sufficiency, and path to counterimperial survival as people and place.[2]

Nowadays in "postlocal" Hawai'i, at least within the tormented cultural politics of the literary scene, a dream of first possession, cum local entrenchment in ethnicity and place-based identity, at times refuses to join in the global flow; resists (understandably) national assimilation of self and culture; wants to start over (as it were) by going back to a time when the island economy was not so much caught up in the flows, mongrel mix, and struggles of imperial powers. "Hawai'i," as Joseph Balaz has written in an uncanny poem reversing the power flows of center and periphery and

---

2. The story of the Native Hawaiians' push to global nationhood and struggle to survive the onslaught of U.S., European, and Japanese imperial outreach into the Pacific (which resulted in the unconsensual if not forced annexation of Hawai'i in 1898), is documented in Tom Coffman, *Nation Within: The Story of America's Annexation of the Nation of Hawai'i* (Kāne'ohe, HI: EpiCenter, 1998).

colonizer (settler) and colonized (native), "is the mainland to me."[3] This book is an attempt to understand these localist drives and place-based orientations as part of a complex Pacific and Asian affiliation that does not fully fit the Eurocentric and/or "exceptionalist" model of American studies as it is now obligated and (as "field imaginary") installed.

For other cultural producers in our contemporary moment of U.S. global cultural domination, however, Hawai'i is simply an *easy* place to write about, to laze and gaze around in for a week or two, to tour, and thereby to work up into a narrative, genre piece, or fantasy with global staying power and (alas) media clout.[4] In a recent AP wire story entitled "'Baywatch' Posse Adapting Fast to Hawaiian Locale" posted in the *San Jose Mercury News*, we learn that David Hasselhoff, the beefcake lifeguard hero of the TV series *Baywatch*, in a one-week visit to the islands (*sic*) had already come up with *five* episodes that would "play off Hawai'i's culture and beach characters," as this No. 1 world-syndicated adventure show moves production from Santa Monica to the Aloha State's alluring North Shore.[5] It is no wonder locals in Hawai'i still insist on calling Hollywood the land of "Haole-wood" (*haole* is the Hawaiian word for Caucasian foreigner to the islands and can be an insult depending on tone and context),

---

3. Joseph P. Balaz, "Da Mainland to Me," in *Asia/Pacific as Space of Cultural Production*, ed. Rob Wilson and Arif Dirlik (Durham, NC: Duke University Press, 1995), 175.

4. I have nicknamed this glib genre the "747 poem" after the U.S. mainland poet David Smith, who came to visit the island for five days (around 1979) and wrote a poem gazing back on his experience (as writing tourist) in Hawai'i from a 747 jumbo jet window, then published his poem in *The New Yorker* within three months. *Honolulu Magazine* journalist Bill Harby later heard me shout out this critique at a local poetry reading at Che Pasta in Kaimuki in 1986, "Hey, that's a 747 poem!" and began to use it in his cultural descriptions of the literary scene. Also see the mock-tourist poem by Terese Svoboda, "The 747 Poem," in *Asia/Pacific as Space of Cultural Production*, ed. Rob Wilson and Arif Dirlik (Durham, NC: Duke University Press, 1995), 250.

5. *San Jose Mercury News*, 22 April 1999. I thank Lisa Weiss of the Ph.D. program in literature at UC Santa Cruz for forwarding me this news item. As she writes in her letter to me of 15 May 1999, "Mr. Baywatch seems to have adjusted quite nicely to his new surroundings, but what about the 'locals'' adjustment to him???" Lisa was part of the countercultural posse I helped to form, as it were, at UC Santa Cruz while teaching a graduate seminar in the fall of 1997, De-Orientalizing the American Pacific, which dealt with the racialized and banal heritage of U.S. Orientalism as applied (still) to sites of Asian/Pacific cultural mixture and racial tension.

for its ongoing racial obtuseness to local culture, Asian locals, and (above all) the indigenous Hawaiian plight.

Still, with my own blessing, Governor Ben Cayetano went out of his way to render a $3 million sweetheart deal plus free airfare, hotels, and car rentals to the eager *Baywatch* producers. Even as Hawai'i is undergoing an economic turndown (more on this below) in the wake of the Asian real estate and currency crisis and a massive tourism slump, this site of cultural (and film) production needed badly to win out over its competing Pacific site, Australia, in order to capture this tourist-friendly "Babe Watch" show (as it has been mocked in letters to the editor in Honolulu newspapers) now seen by a hundred million people in 148 countries. The semiotics of "South Pacific" scenery and the eros of bodily bliss still serve as tourist-flow allure, even as the place of Hawai'i (actually situated in the North Pacific) is not just feminized but localized and scarified into recalcitrant and sulking male locals (as in the ill-fated ABC drama of 1994, *Byrds of Paradise*, or the even more bungled and rude surfer-initiation movie, *North Shore* of 1987, in which a Hawaiian *hui* [club] bullies the poor little rich white surfer dude from Arizona, Rick Kane, into leaving his local girl, Kiani, tearfully behind).

"When I heard Hawai'i, I immediately said, 'No contest. Make the deal,'" Hasselhoff said, adding with entrepreneurial Pacific Rim creativity that somehow wants to be "politically correct," "I want to get into the folklore of Hawai'i—the real life stories. I want to play off the people." The visitors go for tapping into such local stories and indigenous myths, even as Hawai'i's culture-rich residents are a bit more wary of the *kapu* (system of obligations and restraints) and the *mana* (spiritual power emanating from person, language, object, and place) that goes on embedding stories into place, and island and place into larger myths and legends coming down from the spirits and from the past.[6]

The globally successful (and presciently multicultural) detective drama that ran from 1968 to 1980 on CBS and is still being syndicated around the world, *Hawaii Five-O*, had once localized (and even indigenized, as in Hawaiian land struggle episodes) its plots, characters, and languages,

---

6. For a richly archival and culturally respectful approach to the primordial legends and historical stories ("orature") coming down from the Native Hawaiian peoples to impact on contemporary literary culture, see Dennis Kawaharada, *Storied Landscapes: Hawaiian Literature and Place* (Honolulu: Kalamakū Press, 1999).

drawing on a wide array of Asian and Pacific locals in its stories of an embattled crime force (including, to be sure, the sinister "Oriental" agent connected to communist cartels from Hong Kong, Red China, and Singapore named Wo Fat, played by Khiegh Diegh, who conjured up a similar Maoist secret agent in *The Manchurian Candidate* of 1962). Longing to be the new Jack Lord of the bistros, tourist resorts, and beef-laden beaches, at least Hasselhoff's instinct for story was in the right place, if a bit naïve as to the lurking problems and tormented history of Hawai'i (as U.S. outpost in the Pacific) that cannot be gleaned in a tourist's week skimming books and videos on his new Diamond Head verandah.[7]

As the U.S. state of Hawai'i now undergoes its ninth year of economic turmoil in the 1990s, it yet again searches for a (lost) sense of place and (fleeting) vision of the future. This remains a difficult feat of cultural-political imagining, to be sure, because this quest for an affirmative sense of place-bound identity has long been, and still is, deeply tied into the complex global/local dialectics of jet mass tourism and U.S. exoticism projected in the Pacific. Where Hawai'i stands in the year 2000, in this swirling mix of image, slogan, and dream, we can hear a new localism being voiced (as I have suggested) within the larger economy of U.S. globalization. Tourists and locals alike can gather items of this new turn toward an entrenchment in place each day in the morning papers, where a tale of doom and gloom has continued to emerge in this year of expanding Starbucks, "nihilo-capitalism," and the contorted weathers of La Niña and El Niño.[8] Hawai'i, hobbled and ill at ease in its own desperate image-mongering in the Pacific Basin, is entering the so-called Pacific Century of the New Millennium kicking and screaming, crying out for more cultural air.

Waikīkī Beach, once called Honolulu's most "beautiful and dreamy suburb" by King David Kalākaua in the empire-crossed final days of the Hawaiian nation as he sought (like the poet-king that he was) to revitalize the legends and mobilize the native traditions of the past, has become the

---

7. The telling motto of *Hawaii Five-O* was "Filmed entirely on location in Hawai'i," and for the most part it was. See Luis I. Reyes, *Made in Paradise: Hollywood's Films of Hawai'i and the South Seas* (Honolulu: Mutual Books, 1995), 318–20.

8. On the creative destruction of "unregulated" capitalist globalization as it dismantles nations, see William Pfaff, "Gambling with Nihilo-Capitalism," *International Herald Tribune*, 18 May 1998.

site of Viagra tours for aging Japanese males seeking to find some fountain of youth in a blue virility pill.[9] Amid an array of mounting business closures and layoffs afflicting the state, Liberty House, the oldest and largest department chain in the state, declared a Chapter 11 bankruptcy in March 1998. This globalizing strategy of appealing to upscale Japanese and resort-minded tourists had failed, many claimed, and, humbled into downsizing, labor cuts, and debt restructuring, Liberty House was said to be "returning to its roots" by rekindling its old appeal to "local customers."

"The focus is going to be on being the local department store" it once was, Liberty House president John Monahan said; it will stock items "based not on what (New York's) Seventh Avenue tells us, but what Kapiolani Boulevard tells us."[10] We will stock American brand-name goods interpreted "for Island lifestyles," the Liberty House president said.[11] (A local bumper sticker reads "New York, Tokyo, Paris, Waimanalo," mixing and matching the global/local, but Liberty House's brand of localism would remain linked to Waikīkī's boulevard of transnational flows and sexpots and not tied to the rusting Hawaiian backwaters of Waimanalo.)

Architects of local affiliation now lament that Waikīkī (if not Hawai'i more generally) has lost its own "sense of place," the distinctive ingredients of place, language, and cultural attitude (the vaunted "aloha spirit" as it is overcalled) that once gave it a special feel and aura of distinct belonging. Some now would search the cities of Asia-Pacific (such as Taipei, Hong Kong, and Auckland) to see what Honolulu might do to

9. King David Kalākaua, *The Legends and Myths of Hawai'i: The Fables and Folk-Lore of a Strange People* (1888; Honolulu: Mutual Publishing, 1990), 64. "Viagra Lures Japanese to Isles for Special Tour," *Honolulu Advertiser*, 2 June 1998, A5. On the Pacific as site of Japanese sexual exploration on the beaches and in the neocolonial bedrooms of Waikīkī, see Karen Kelsky, "Flirting with the Foreign: Interracial Sex in Japan's 'International' Age," in *Global/Local: Cultural Production and the Transnational Imaginary*, ed. Rob Wilson and Wimal Dissanayake (Durham, NC: Duke University Press, 1996), 173–92, and "Gender, Modernity, and Eroticized Internationalism in Japan," *Cultural Anthropology* 14 (1999): 229–55.

10. Greg Wiles, "Liberty House Returning to Roots," *Honolulu Advertiser*, 18 May 1998, A1.

11. *Local*, in this case, means the self-imagery and marketing niche situated somewhere between the glamorous cultural capital of Neiman Marcus (oddly, in this time of state budget crisis, coming to Hawai'i in 1999) and the more ordinary wares of JC Penney and Sears: an aloha shirt or running shoes that might appeal to a teacher in Hawai'i Kai, a broker on Bishop Street, or a tourist from Iowa.

discover this sense of place amid transnational development and tourist blight. Even the huge shopping mall of Ala Moana, once the pride of Honolulu, no longer feels local or caters to local clients and customs. The Japanese mega-investors are pulling back and pulling out, as did Daiei Corporation in the spring of 1999 when it was forced to sell Ala Moana Mall for close to U.S. $1 billion to liquidate its huge transnational debts. Even the local mall at Pearl Ridge and Kahala Mall have gone upscale and feel lacking in the essential ingredients of that mystery quality, the "local culture" as such.[12]

Bamboo Ridge, a literary journal and innovative small press on Oʻahu that has supported the self-conscious affirmation of "local literature" as rallying cry and a symbolic terrain worthy of narration and figuration since its founding by coeditors Eric Chock and Darrell Lum in 1978, received National Endowment for the Humanities funding for a "growing up local" special issue of the journal.[13] This tactic was nothing new, but indeed expressed the main focus this journal has supported and nurtured all along, as the local writing scene has "grown up" in pidgin ways and mango days to receive mounting national attention and support.[14] This Bamboo Ridge affiliation toward preserving, affirming, and expressing "the local," as this drive can be affiliated to U.S. national identity dynamics and, by

12. For a poem on this missing "sense of the local" even at the shopping mall (where you would expect to buy at least a taste of the local, such as a piece of semisacred jewelry), see Rob Wilson, "Five Late Capitalist Haiku," *Hawaiʻi Review* 9 (1995): 10–13.

13. See Eric Chock, James R. Harstad, Darrell H. Y. Lum, and Bill Teter, eds., *Growing Up Local: An Anthology of Poetry and Prose from Hawaiʻi* (Honolulu: Bamboo Ridge Press, 1998), which has already become a text of local affirmation and pidgin-based literatures widely used in high schools and college courses in the state.

14. This attention can be signalized, in brief, by the enormous coverage the post–Bamboo Ridge work of Lois-Ann Yamanaka has received in national journals such as *The Atlantic Monthly* and *The Nation*, whose reviewers have defended her novellas against more local-driven charges that she recurrently scapegoats and humiliates her local male Filipino characters and all but ignores the deeper call of Hawaiian culture in her turn to U.S. pop cultural mixtures. For local rumblings, see Nadine Kam, "Writer's Blu's: Yamanaka's Award for 'Blu's Hanging' Is Yanked, Igniting a Hot Debate about Literature versus Social Responsibility," *Honolulu Star-Bulletin*, 3 July 1998. For a more national take on this controversy, see Jamie James, "This Hawaiʻi Is Not for Tourists," *The Atlantic Monthly* 283 (February 1999), which is a liberal polemic for freedom of literary speech based around a review of Yamanaka's "trilogy" novel, *Heads by Harry* (New York: Farrar, Straus, and Giroux, 1999). I will return to discuss Yamanaka's work in chapter 5.

contrast, to more indigenous Hawaiian decolonization dynamics, will form a key part of this study. For now, I want to set up the "tourist gaze" a bit more in this preface, to situate Hawaiʻi within the mixed makings of an Americanized Pacific.

Prior to World War II, Hawaiʻi was one destination of choice for a more wealthy, upper-class clientele, who typically came by luxury cruise passenger liners such as the ss *Lurline* and stayed at such sites as the Hawaiian, the Royal Hawaiian (which opened in 1927 and had its own *mele inoa* or name chant suitable for Hawaiian royalty written in its honor by Mary Keliiauka Robins), and the Moana hotels in Waikīkī. The meandering and self-divided short stories of Jack London such as "The Kanaka Surf" and promotional pieces for "globe-trotters by profession" such as "My Hawaiian Aloha" reek of this royal and upscale tourism, mingling London's racial and class claims to superiority and comfort in America's own outpost in the Pacific with a more long-wrought Anglo-Saxon sense of imperial masculinity.[15] London's Americanized and multicultural short stories tried to take enterprising possession of place at the same time they rooted for the dying aboriginal Hawaiians in confused stories such as "Koolau the Leper," which Hawaiians hate to this day.[16] Ever quoted in tourist blurbs and bylines, London helped to evoke this "aloha spirit" of

15. Although he stops short of reading London's Pacific and Hawaiʻi short stories as part of his drive to take literary and imperial possession of American frontier outposts (as London did in the Pacific Northwest with his Yukon tales of Darwinian possession), Jonathan Auerbach offers a superb reading of London's literary and cultural politics as coded with U.S. imperial masculinity in *Male Call: Becoming Jack London* (Durham, NC: Duke University Press, 1996). In fact, for Auerbach, London underwent a kind of self-dispossession of such U.S. macho codes in the Pacific: "Hawaiʻi and its people offered London an alterity powerful enough to resist the author's appropriation [of the territory] by way of autobiography [as he did in Alaska, which made him famous as an American writer]" (282 n).

16. See the hard-hitting critique of this famous London short story by Kuʻualoha Meyer Hoʻomanawanui, forthcoming in *MELUS*, who faults London for his misuse of indigenous history, racial abjection, and cultural ignorance of the Hawaiian codes he claimed to love and understand. This Pacific-based story of aboriginal resistance to their confinement as lepers exiled to Molokaʻi during the Annexation era, in short, is a local and racial mess. It can only be taught as a schizoid-text symptom of the U.S. will to take imperial possession of the islands so beloved of tourists (and writers) like London. Or, for that matter, consider Mark Twain laughing at his "Fellow Savages in the Sandwich Islands" on the lecture circuit, making a small killing on the mainland, and becoming a U.S. canonical author by doing so.

Waikīkī that once reeked of class aura, racial exclusion, and resort status as sporting site for the white corporate yacht set and Hawaiian royalty. The American male could laze and gaze at will in the native-pacified Pacific of the Royal Hawaiian Hotel, and the sovereignty call was (seemingly) dying out as the hula skirts and aloha shirts multiplied and spread across the globe.[17]

But, with U.S. statehood achieved finally (despite communist labor scares) in 1959 and the arrival of United Airlines and the technologies of space-time reduction, cheaper airfares and packaged tours brought large numbers of Americans and Japanese to Hawai'i. Along with Maui, Honolulu, "which [for tourists] is basically Waikīkī," became the major destinations of choice, the places of imagery and commodity aura.[18] Hawai'i called to the U.S. mainland via music, image, hula skirt, and resort hotel, and American paradise-seekers came in droves like the Brady Bunch looking for some lost aboriginal treasure, some fun and sun in the surf, or just a good tan to boast about back in the suburbs of California or New Jersey. Hawai'i, fetishized into United Airlines' sign of erotic longing and bodily bliss: "She was my little deuce coupe," if you know what I mean.

Tourism, for Hawai'i if not for Pacific sites more generally, depends on the globalization-of-the-local into a marketable image with lasting appeal, with enduring charm and mysterious claims to uniqueness, what Walter Benjamin termed the "aura" of the commodity form. Some 6.8 million tourists come to Hawai'i each year looking for that special something out there in the remote-yet-near Pacific. In this era of the declining yen and mounting financial crisis in Asia/Pacific, tourism remains the state's largest industry, largest source of jobs, and biggest generator of tax revenues.

Caught up in these pro-tourism, antilocal dilemmas, Hawai'i not only hosted the 1998 Miss Universe Pageant, in effect it became Miss Universe, saying to the global market (reached by telecast to seventy countries around the world), Visit me, love me, gaze upon me: I am yours and waiting with open arms in the spectacular Pacific. Like Bloody Mary in the

17. Matson shipping line, part of the local Big Five corporate oligarchy then as now, tried to revive the *Lurline* in 1948, even as the base of the U.S. tourist influx was changing and fading into the packaged paradise of the mass market.

18. Mike Markrich, "What Ails Tourism: Marketing Continued but Assets Weren't Protected," *Honolulu Advertiser*, 17 May 1998, B1–4.

cold war musical *South Pacific*, Hawai'i was singing the seductress song of Bali Hai to the tourist gaze: "Come to me, I am your own special island."[19]

Brook Lee, Miss Universe of 1997 and a multicultural, mixed-race product of Hawai'i, gave this appeal personal personification in her own charms; her efforts (along with $3 million put out by the state and the marketing prowess of Al Masini) were instrumental in persuading Donald Trump and NBC to bring the event to Hawai'i for the first time. Lee, who is one-fourth Korean and an ethnic mix of Hawaiian, Chinese, Portuguese, French, Dutch, and English blood, remains *local* at heart and in value. "I've never thought of myself as Asian," Lee said. "In Hawai'i you're just local." She added in pidgin English, "I never had Gucci bags before. I was so Arakawa's, it's not even funny."[20] Globally imaged, but paradoxically remaining local at core like a good used aloha shirt, Lee projected an endearing multicultural self-image much like the place of Hawai'i itself as situated in the global marketing of cultures.

Richard Kelley, chairman of Outrigger Enterprises, which controls Outrigger Hotels and Resorts, boasted of the globally circulating Miss Universe images, "We are all counting on the Convention Center to become a significant source of new business, and hoping that the images from the Miss Universe pageant compel viewers to plan a Hawai'i vacation." This goal of *compelling* the global tourist flow is couched, then (in London's era) as now (in the era of Paul Theroux), in masculinist terms of alluring possession: "to provide us with the muscle to market Hawai'i [as beautiful woman, one might add] on an international scale."[21]

This renewed focus on "the island lifestyle" and the push globally to market Hawai'i's special appeal as a beautiful, multiculturally appealing, and world-class Pacific *woman* was happening at a time when many (not just local writers) were beginning to feel a lost sense of place, a disturbance of the codes and myths. Indeed, place-bound consciousness was being lost in the simulacrous circuits of global imagery, where iconic value

19. I provide a larger critical genealogy for this white mythology of Bloody Mary and the appropriation of Asian/Pacific locals and locales in chapters five through seven of this book.
20. Quoted in Esmé M. Infante, "Brook Lee: Home and Happy," *Honolulu Advertiser* special report, 26 April 1998, 2.
21. Richard R. Kelley, "Groundwork in Place for More Industry Growth," *Honolulu Advertiser*, 17 May 1998, B1.

is repeated until it displaces or replaces the actual with its own semiotic connotations.

But what is the appeal of "Hawai'i" to the global tourist who would come here after seeing the Miss Universe contest or a Hooters Aloha Bowl football game? Mike Markrich, decrying the "declining appeal" of Hawai'i in general and the deterioration of the Waikīkī core in particular, where hotel development has been restricted since 1977 and the image "has gone down-market," argued that the "real draws" of Hawai'i have never changed: "the allure and charm of the unique Native Hawaiian culture, the warmth of Hawai'i's people, and Hawai'i's spectacular beauty," in that order.[22]

Again, the appeal is to Hawai'i's being somehow "true to its roots," meaning not just natural scenery and the much vaunted aloha spirit, but the "unique" native culture that is under threat and (to be sure) resisting incorporation into the tourist apparatus. Hawaiian culture is not just abjected and demonized, as it was by the earlier U.S. missionary generations, but preserved and pampered as a source of market appeal and state revenue.

Tourism—as a vast global apparatus—encompasses not just the marketing of places and cultures, but the whole infrastructure of transport, accommodation, catering, recreation, and services for tourists; growing in scale, tourism has become one of the largest of the world's transnational industries. If, by now, "tourism is to Hawai'i what automobiles are to Detroit,"[23] then what we produce and market in this post-Fordist climate is some intangible compound of material reality, exotic desire, and symbolic need: an image of place as well as that cultural-material polity itself in its appeal as a place and culture worth traveling to; a globalized image of locale and local place that hovers over the place itself and resignifies its meanings and events.

Recuperation of the local is perilous by now, in the globalized economy of cash flow and cultural mix. The turn toward "radical localism" is not necessarily a progressive move within the globalizing economy. In the state of California, to name an affiliated site on the Pacific Rim, the Sierra Club came close to approving a resolution calling for restricted legal immi-

22. Markrich, "What Ails Tourism," B4.
23. Ibid., B1.

gration into the United States. The resolution reflected not so much U.S. economic nationalism as a resource-protective environmentalism (advocated by scholars such as Paul Ehrlich, E. F. Schumacher, and Donald Worster), with its "roots not on the nativist right but on the green left, among population-control advocates."[24] The goal is a kind of static society that will not make excessive demands on the environmental resources. Sierra Club president Adam Werbach (while opposing the antiimmigrant resolution) puts the case for a "radical localism" this way: "We should demand that the Safeway in Iowa carry only native potatoes. And we should draw the line when department stores bottom out prices, muscle out local businesses and eradicate local culture."[25]

This kind of eco-friendly localism can be used to oppose the unpredictable dynamism of the capitalist transnational system, with its emphasis on liberalized freedoms of choice, competition, and mobility; it can also become the rallying cry to restrict the impact of technology, trade, and immigration across the borders, enclaves, and limits of what is taken to be the local community. This kind of place-bound and bounded localism, as Virginia Postrel claims, can promote a "slippery green slope to nativism" and, in effect, preserve a racialized hierarchy of social and environmental goods for those who already have plenty and want to keep others out. The line of creative flight is broken by state fiat or ideological will to power.

Hawai'i does not need more racism and a greater imbalance of cultural capital and goods, given the unstable postplantation and tourist-centered economy that is now emerging. Instead, as I hope to show, connected to diverse and thickened lines of flight, risk, and cultural innovation, Hawai'i needs some different strategies and newer tactics of symbol making, needs a broader or more global vision of the local plight ("plight of the local") as it were. This book is my own small yet affiliated attempt to provide such a study of a mixed place and culture long situated in the troubled yet promissory waters of Asia/Pacific.

An earlier version of "Bloody Mary Meets Lois-Ann Yamanaka: Imagining Hawaiian Locality, from *South Pacific* to Bamboo Ridge and Beyond" appeared in *Public Culture* 8 (1995): 137–58. The essay has been expanded

---

24. Virginia Postrel, editorial, "Slippery Green Slope to Nativism," *International Herald Tribune*, 14 May 1998.
25. Quoted in Postrel, "Slippery Green Slope to Nativism."

and revised, and is used with permission. An earlier version of *Good-bye Paradise*: Theorizing Place, Poetics, and Cultural Production in the American Pacific" appeared in *New Formations* 24 (1994): 35–50. It has been revised and is used with permission. An earlier version of "Blue Hawai'i: Bamboo Ridge as 'Critical Regionalism'" appeared in Arif Dirlik, ed., *What's In a Rim: Critical Perspectives on the Pacific Region Idea* (Boulder, CO: Rowman and Littlefield, 1999). It has been expanded and revised and is used with permission.

"How Did You Find America?"

On Becoming Asia/Pacific

When the forms exhaust their variety and come apart, the end of cities begins. In the last pages of the [Great Khan's] atlas there is an outpouring of networks without beginning or end, cities in the shape of Los Angeles, in the shape of Kyoto-Osaka, without shape.
     —Italo Calvino, *Invisible Cities*

We set our sails for Mao's China, and ended up in Southern California.
     —Regis Debray, quoted in *Another Tale to Tell: Politics and Narrative in Postmodern Culture*, by Fred Pfeil

"How did you find America?" an intrepid British interviewer once asked John Lennon in the pop-culture euphoria days of *Hard Day's Night* (1964): "It was easy," the Beatle responded deadpan. "You just turn left at Greenland." The cultural-political entity that was declared "America" is not so easy to find anymore; it will not suffice to retrack the late-imperial crossing from England, across the white Atlantic, to the *Ed Sullivan Show*. Forces of transnational production, immigration, cash flow, and transcultural interface have only accelerated since the New Frontier years. These transformations of space and national identity have spread, as Calvino's Italian explorer of global cities and early opener of Asian markets Marco Polo puts it, "an outpouring of networks without beginning or end" across the globe. In effect, confronting our disorienting transnational/postcolonial era, the United States of America goes on being restructured (and, at the level of writing culture, *reimagined*) into the impurity, flexibility, mongrel becoming, and disunity of the postmodern condition.[1]

The globe itself is now "awash with American cultural icons" that are taking on a more local face and striving to affirm traces of a more "local" or "regional" voice in their transnational outreach.[2] Paris, Hong Kong, Mexico City, and Tokyo are flowing, as it were, through the neogeo frontiers, borderland becomings, and Asian/Pacific contact zones of California.[3] This brave new world of Asian and Pacific becoming belongs not so much to nay-saying Governor Pete Wilson nor to the monolingual corporate-speak of Microsoft, but to the affirmative, mongrel, and mixed-language poetics of Gloria Anzaldúa and Lois-Ann Yamanaka in the process of becoming what he or she writes.

One need not invoke the stark forces of white cultural reaction at home (such as Allan Bloom) or economic ratification abroad (such as Kenichi Ohmae) to claim that many signs are already urging that modes of *transnationalization* and tactics of *regionalization* have transformed the contours of the U.S. national imagination with amped-up forms of geopolitical interaction, hybrid acculturation, and global exchange. Nations (or, on a connected if larger scale, "regions"; see chapter 1 on "Asia-Pacific" as such) are not just "imagined" into being by acts of political consensus, they are shorn from the past and all but dragged (singing) into the future by forms and forces of social restructuring, downsizing, cultural transfusion, willy-nilly abandonment, and political dissension. As David Reiff has remarked of these transnational changes now effecting the molestation of Los Angeles into a Pacific Rim interzone of heteroglossia, street rage, and

1. On the globalizing "aura" of American culture and mass media celebrity during the Kennedy era as measured against Soviet-style socialism, see Wayne Koestenbaum, *Jackie Under My Skin: Interpreting an Icon* (New York: Penguin, 1996), e.g., on "Jackie's Sublimity" (245–50).

2. Paul Maidment, "Pax Mickeyrana?", *Newsweek*, 14 August 1995, 32. As Jay Leno joked of the global spread of American culture and values via media empires and blockbuster genres such as *Evita* and *Armageddon* in the 1990s, "We're going to ruin your culture, just like we ruined our own."

3. In *The Borderless World: Power and Strategy in the Interlinked Economy* (New York: Harper and Row, 1990), Kenichi Ohmae boasts of this "global culture" of commodity consumption, "Young people of the advanced countries are becoming increasingly nationalityless and more like 'Californians' all over the Triad countries—the United States, Europe, and Japan—that form the Interlinked Economy" (3).

cultural fusion, "The only part of the daily newspaper that made any sense at all was the business pages."[4]

What I will here be calling a "global/local" dialectical optic is needed to understand these strange new forms of contact culture emerging inside America, especially in such sites of Asian/Pacific and settler/indigenous interface as California, Texas, and (to be sure) Hawai'i, sites where transnational and postcolonial tensions are daily aggravated, written about, and policed.[5] "[President Bill Clinton] is not an American—he's a *globalist!*" one disgruntled male caller complained on a right-wing talk radio show in Honolulu (May 1996), fed up with the influx of transnationalism and multiculturalism he saw deforming the United States into a mongrel maze. As the crazed ex-Soviet cosmonaut in *Armageddon* (1998) puts it, frustrated as well by the transnational makeup of his makeshift crew and spaceship trying to protect the earth from collision with an asteroid "the size of Texas," "American components, Russian components, what's the difference? They are all *made in Taiwan!*" These days, the United States of America, as will be explored here early and late, is being remade in Taiwan, as Taiwan itself is being remade by contacts and flows from California and New Zealand as well as from Hong Kong and the Bronx.

As U.S. trade and cultural exchange across the Pacific at times surpasses that with Europe, much of this amped-up activity of transnational dynamism and global-cultural mix can be located in the area now being signified in neoliberal discourse as "Asia-Pacific" (see chapter 1): a region of globalized space and "transnational imaginary" the United States has pushed westward toward and helped shape through the "frontier" mediation—and, in 1898, outright annexation—of Hawai'i as linkage to the vast markets and labor forces of Asia.[6] The production of Hawai'i into an

4. David Rieff, *Los Angeles: Capital of the Third World* (New York: Simon and Schuster, 1991), 22.

5. On transnational dynamics within "postcolonial" ambivalence, see Arif Dirlik, "The Postcolonial Aura: Third World Criticism in the Age of Global Capitalism," *Critical Inquiry* 20 (1994): 328–56, and related essays on the global/local dialectics of transnational encounter in *The Postcolonial Aura: Third World Criticism in the Age of Global Capitalism* (Boulder, CO: Westview, 1997).

6. On the Asia/Pacific region considered critically and affirmatively as a "transnational imaginary" of global capital and Asian American immigration, see the probing speculations of David Palumbo-Liu in *Asian/American: Historical Crossings of a Racial Frontier*

American outpost of commerce and culture in the Pacific took place throughout the missionary and geopolitical dynamics of the nineteenth century, as I will trace from inside the conflicted space of Hawai'i itself in chapters 2 and 3, stressing as well those "local motions" of contestation, mimicry, and resistance taking place via a willed reaffirmation of cultures of the local and indigenous national (chapters 4 through 7) that has been ongoing since the early 1970s.

These cultures of the local remain, given such a dialectical optic of global/local space, both conjoined and delinked from older imperial formations of continental nationhood and liberal modernity, in complex and changing ways that demand particularized articulation (see chapters 5, 6, and 7), in writers such as Lois-Ann Yamanaka, Eric Chock, Juliet Kono Lee, Barry Masuda, Rodney Morales, Carolyn Lei-Lanilau, Kathy Dee Kaleo-kealoha Kaloloahilani Banggo, Justin Chin, Joseph Puna Balaz, Wendy Miyake, and John Dominis Holt. This conviction of globalized space unhinging U.S. national from "local literature" identity is not just my own crazed attempt at cultural jeremiad. Even postmodern cities, by turns animated with the downsizing rhythms of postindustrial creative destruction and offshore dispersal, such as Los Angeles, Long Beach, Honolulu, Taipei, and "Kyoto-Osaka," have become fluid spaces of federal abandonment and transnational confusion dripping with the terror and wonder of street life in *Black Rain* and *Blade Runner*.[7] It would take a Jackie Chan to find pleasure and achieve compass in this urban maze, or an Ackbar Abbas to find sublime distraction in the Hong Kong city life.

Transnational and postcolonial dynamics now interact in ways we have yet to come to terms with inside contact zones and overloaded sites of U.S. culture. A hypernetworked India and market-oriented People's Republic

---

(Stanford: Stanford University Press, 1999), chap. 10, which builds on and extends the "Pacific Rim" discourse work of Christopher Connery, Bruce Cumings, and Arif Dirlik, which I myself am deeply indebted to and will respond to throughout this study. "Asia/Pacific," as Christopher Connery has suggested to me in an analysis of this study, represents a step beyond "Pacific Rim" discourse into something less haunted by cold war othering and the heritages of binary "oriental" codes; for a more detailed analysis, see my chapters 1 and 8.

7. For an affirmative analysis of this "global cultural economy" as crisscrossed by disjunctive transnational/local flows, see Arjun Appadurai, "Disjunction and Difference in the Global Cultural Economy," *Public Culture* 2 (1990): 1–24, as well as the darker *Post-Fordist* special issue of *Socialist Review* 21 (January–March 1991).

of China have ended up, so to speak, flowing through the global-popular culture pores and computer industries of Southern California and North Carolina. Still, at any point, the cold war phobias threaten to return, and the Yellow Peril discourse of binary othering so attached to by canonical writers such as Jack London and W. Somerset Maugham (writing in the late-imperial Pacific) can be dragged out to police and spook the racial/geographical borders between "us" and "them."

If the financial turmoil of 1997 and 1998 has suddenly resulted in currency attacks, IMF interventions, shaken optimism, and a palpable decline in tourism flow of some twelve million tourists, this may have (seemingly) given the lie to the up-with-transnational-capital teleology that was trumpeted in the fairly recent formation of the region as such (see chapter 1). But the flows, exchanges, and dependency patterns have not abated in the contact zones (e.g., Hawai'i) of Asia/Pacific: only the worries, and the promises, linger on the regional horizon as we enter these semiintoxicating waters of the "Pacific Century" and wander like baby Adams into the New Millennium.

Moves to contest prior and entrenched narratives of U.S. identity as dominantly Euro-American in makeup have proliferated inside borders of the national community as well. Forces of white reaction have only intensified the countercanonical recognition of Asian and Pacific, Latin and African movements toward recuperated identity and Native American constituencies working through, claiming, and contesting postcolonial terrains of "cultural hybridity." From a transatlantic perspective that goes on shaping the United States from Eastern and Caribbean shores, economic linkages and cultural migrations across the creolized diaspora and postnational hybridity materialize the disconnection of the United States and Great Britain from projects of nation-state modernity. Triangulated spaces such as those of "the Black Atlantic" or "the Asia/Pacific" can suggest the impossibility of shaping a *white* national identity fitted to some "morbid celebration of England and Englishness" or U.S. selves eternally tied to retrospective narratives of monolingual/monoracial unity.[8]

---

8. On discursive textures of these various postnational narratives and reimagined communities, see Homi K. Bhabha, "DissemiNation: Time, Narrative, and the Margins of the Nation State," in *Nation and Narration*, ed. Homi K. Bhabha (Routledge: London, 1990), 291–322. More specifically, see Amy Kaplan and Donald Pease, eds., *Cultures of United States Imperialism* (Durham, NC: Duke University Press, 1994); and Lauren

When the ambiguously transnational—Hungarian/English/German—count-hero of Michael Ondaatje's *English Patient* remarks, "I came to hate nations. We are deformed by nation-states," his sentiment of cosmopolitical detachment reflects not just a belated romanticist's love of vast desert sublimity and disgust at the dehumanizing horrors of World War II, but the rootless disorientation, political trickery, and denationalized cosmopolitanism we are now living inside—postmodern nomads, as it were, on the other side of Dresden, Anzio, and Hiroshima (and, I should add, after our failed U.S. imperialism against such sites as the Socialist Republic of Vietnam).[9] To find "America" today—if you were John Lennon returned to be interviewed about his own afterlife on an MTV chat room—you might say, "Turn left at Asia-Pacific," or "Find the dirty, magical waters of the Pacific Rim and just keep flowing."

As those prior narratives suturing "American" identity tend to break down and implode into politicized mazes of centrifugal heteroglossia, internal cultures of mongrel mixture, minority becoming, and local spaces have begun to fragment, disorganize, and become mixed even as they are fast circulated and stimulated (at another, more global level of image conquest) through the "hyper-geographical mobility of capital."[10] As David Harvey points out, in his skeptical analysis of ongoing global/local patterns that are changing the nation-state into a disorganized transnational entity, the U.S. production system can no longer function as it did in the cold war framework of Pacific Rim discourse, that is, circulating within the global financial imaginary as "in effect the guarantor of international value" and nation-state power.[11] The dollar and yen seem, at times, to be

---

Berlant, "The Theory of Infantile Citizenship," *Public Culture* 5 (1993): 395–410, on "American" (utopic) versus "USA" (liberal statist) forms of national identity within forms of post/transnationalization.

9. Michael Ondaatje, *The English Patient* (New York: Vintage, 1992), 138; Paul Gilroy, "Cultural Studies and Ethnic Absolutism," in *Cultural Studies,* ed. Lawrence Grossberg, Cary Nelson, and Paula Treichler (London: Routledge, 1992), 187–98. The result is what Simon During calls the spread of "the global popular," as he anthologizes the transnational (and interdisciplinary) growth of "cultural studies" to capture and express this new sensibility; see Simon During, ed., *The Cultural Studies Reader* (London: Routledge, 1993), introduction.

10. David Harvey, *The Condition of Postmodernity: An Inquiry into the Origins of Cultural Change* (Cambridge, MA: Blackwell, 1990), 190.

11. Ibid., 296.

coming unglued, even as the eurodollar tries to tie a mess of forces and codes into one system.

Still, the superpower status and financial power of the United States cannot at this moment be glibly denied or, on the other hand, reified into some archaic imperial emporium spreading its "postmodern global culture." Even George Soros, the global currency entrepreneur and Hungarian immigrant who has been instrumental (with all too cynical reason) in bringing "the Asian way" of capital expansion to its dollar-beholden knees in 1997, has begun to worry that, perhaps, "the international financial system appears to be suffering a systemic breakdown" immune to moral censure, global intervention, or deregulated fix.[12] At times, the socialized capitalism cum multiracial cultural hegemony of Singapore can look like a humane option of consensual control in relation to our own self-blinding theology of the free market as exported and installed under the global ideology of democratic consumption and profit expansion.[13]

Situated globally or locally, what we still can mystify and glory in as "American" products in culture, origin, and design may now need to be interrogated as plural, impure, and entangled objects of national identity calling attention to their own more *transnationalized* construction and *local* contention. In effect, the U.S. national imaginary will have to be remapped as a conjunction and becoming of global/local forces, as I hope to show in some detail. If American writing as such is forever in the breakdown process of "becoming minor" and expressing its multilingual entanglement in forces and peoples of geographical becoming, as Gilles Deleuze has claimed (in a tactic I will return to, embody, and examine), then this Asia/Pacific writing is a becoming other and elsewhere that is tied to a "becoming [that] is always 'between' or 'among'" energies and forces in the contact zones and borderlands.[14]

---

12. George Soros, "Avoiding a Breakdown," *Financial Times,* 31 December 1997, 1.

13. On the cultural politics of national identity construction in Singapore, see Beng-Huat Chua, "Culture, Multiracialism, and National Identity in Singapore," in *Trajectories: Inter-Asia Cultural Studies,* ed. Kuan-Hsing Chen et al. (London: Routledge, 1998), 186–205. On the deformations of New Zealand under the uneven global deregulation regimes of the Thatcherite 1980s, see Noam Chomsky, "Free Trade and Free Market: Pretense and Practice," in *The Cultures of Globalization,* ed. Fredric Jameson and Masao Miyoshi (Durham, NC: Duke University Press, 1998), 356–70.

14. Gilles Deleuze, "Literature and Life," in *Essays Critical and Clinical,* trans. Daniel W. Smith and Michael A. Greco (Minneapolis: University of Minnesota Press, 1997), 2–4.

This movement of "becoming Asia/Pacific" is fluid and palpable in what I call and will explore with some polemical irony and will to imperial decreation "the *American* Pacific." My aim, thus, in "reimagining the American Pacific" is both to dismantle stable U.S. hegemonic notions of identity, place, and region, and to create a kind of fluid and Deleuzian counterpoetics along lines of Asian/Pacific flight, place-based languages, and alternative imaginings. The culture of "America" may not be where it was located even a few decades ago. The "denationalization" of the world is not a fait accompli, as it seems to be on the business pages of the daily newspaper or *Forbes* magazine. But a transnationalized cultural studies must come to more fluid (and *critical*) terms with these dismantled territories of place, identity, and community. "America" needs to be found, as well, offshore and over the ocean, where identity flows and deforms and creativity takes place along a line of flight across the older world-system geographies of New England and Canton province.[15]

Culture is not just rooted but rerouted, as James Clifford, Karen Kelsky, Arjun Appadurai, and others have shown, by the new media that extend our sensory apparatus and flow across our borders of identity. What is good for post-Fordism may be leading toward the makings of some "post-America," for to be transnationalized American-style now means to become post-Fordized as cultural subject of the nation.[16] A nagging question remains on the U.S. cultural studies agenda: How does one find this (more borderless and impure) "America"?

Boundary zones, peripheral spaces, and local enclaves of cultural production and identity location—that would affirm forces and sublanguages of social contradiction, impurity, and ethnic difference—are emerging as powerful new spaces of national reinvention. This is palpable in the cultural formations underway in the Asia-Pacific region, where "local" and

15. On "global" flows of poststructural theories of decentered identity as well as technologies of virtual space and financial speculation impacting on "local" spaces as a "postmodern" cultural formation of global capital, see Vincent B. Leitch, *Postmodernism: Local Effects, Global Flows* (Albany: State University of New York Press, 1996), esp. chaps. 1 and 12.

16. As Antonio Gramsci reminds us about industrial regimes of hard labor cum Puritanism in "Americanism and Fordism," "The 'subaltern forces,' which have to be 'manipulated' and rationalized to serve new ends, naturally put up a resistance" (279). See *Selections from the Prison Notebooks,* ed. and trans. Quintin Hoare and Geoffrey Nowell Smith (New York: International, 1985).

"regional" cultures of reconstituted postcolonial "english," residual oral forms, and non-Western mythology, for example, have surfaced across ethnic barriers and disparate spaces to contest those canons of national oblivion and transnational hegemony.[17]

One sign of this altered ethnoscape of cultural location is the geopolitical assertion of "Asian/Pacific," to invoke the region my argument will substantiate from different critical angles, by means of articulating the "local literature" movement underway in the postcolonial state of Hawai'i, where English, despite its dominance since the 1840s as language of government command and since the late 1890s as language of public instruction, can still be considered by Hawaiians as ka ʿōlelo haole (the foreigner's tongue). Pidgin English has become the medium of center-periphery reversal and postcolonial flows. In "offshore" Taiwan, as well, English also becomes the language of transnational mixture and cultural flows, challenging and deforming the national hegemony of the KMT's Mandarin Chinese and the recent emergence of Taiwanese as lingua franca of everyday transactions in the "global city" of Taipei (see chapters 1 and 8).

At several key points, early and late, I will further this theorizing of the American national-local discourse by looking not at Hawai'i but at the complicated Pacific Rim space that is contemporary Taiwan, an island space and territory of cultural-political identity and creative flows perilously established "in the pores of the [three] empires" that are China, the United States, and Japan.[18] This emerging "Asia-Pacific" space represents a very contradictory region of entrenched multiplicity and mixture, reg-

17. See Asia/Pacific as Space of Cultural Production, special issue of boundary 2, ed. Arif Dirlik and Rob Wilson, 21 (1994), and the expanded book version by the same title (Durham, NC: Duke University Press, 1995); and Vilsoni Hereniko and Rob Wilson, eds., Inside Out: Literature, Cultural Politics and Identity in the New Pacific (Boulder, CO: Rowman and Littlefield, 1999). For a "historical geography" of the Asia/Pacific region that excludes Pacific islanders as agents in constructing the contemporary region, see David Drakakis-Smith, Pacific Asia (London: Routledge, 1992). On the Euro-American productions of the Pacific as a geographical and economic region contested from within, see Arif Dirlik, "The Asia-Pacific Idea: Reality and Representation in the Invention of a Regional Structure," Journal of World History 3 (1992): 55–79.

18. See Gilles Deleuze and Félix Guattari, "Geophilosophy," in What Is Philosophy?, trans. Hugh Tomlinson and Graham Burchell (New York: Columbia University Press, 1994) on Greece, especially Athens, as a space of creative flows and "a peculiar mode of deterritorialization that proceeds by immanence" on a peninsula close to the sea and between "archaic eastern empires" (87).

istering—and, at times culturally, resisting—the spreading neocolonial forces of transnationalization that have been christened by Akio Morita of Sony as a cheery process of "global localization," but that can be called, in dialectical fashion as well, the cultural space of local globalism.[19]

Ang Lee, the globally successful and locally problematic Taiwanese film director of *Pushing Hands* (1992), *The Wedding Banquet* (1993), *Eat Drink Man Woman* (1994), and *Sense and Sensibility* (1995), has captured the strangely rooted yet diasporic mixture of being Taiwanese yet becoming American, by default as it were. "In the process of Westernization," Lee claimed in an interview in 1993, "Taiwanese people have already done many of the similar kinds of work that immigrants would do. Although their bodies are not in the United States, they are immigrants psychologically. . . . What is the difference between living in Flushing, New York, and Taipei? Except that one knows America better and sees more Americans, there is not much difference."[20] Taipei, as "global city" of Asia/Pacific conjunctions, is always on the trans/national road to Mainland China, America, and Japan.[21]

Taking an expressly situated view of (trans)national location, Pacific islanders now emerge as cultural and economic agents constructing their past and contesting their future rather than succumbing to any neo-Marxian dependency model or the cultural neoromanticism of certain elites. The cultural nationalisms surfacing across the region, as in New Zealand and Hawai'i, need to be situated and assessed within the larger dynamics of the decolonizing Asia/Pacific region. The dynamism of global/local forces will intensify as Asian/Pacific cultures look inward for validation and sources of invention, remapping, and national fracture in such places

19. See Ohmae, *The Borderless World*, 93, 9.

20. *China Times Weekly* 65 (March–April 1993), 75. I thank Shu-mei Shih for this reference from her unpublished essay on the "problematic" nature of gender, race, and nation in Lee's films, "Globalization and Minoritization: Chinese Gender Politics in the Global Context." On mixtures of Taiwanese cultural identity and the flux of global technoculture, see Rob Wilson, ed., *Sailing to Ellis Island: Postmodern Poetry from National Tsing Hua University* (Hsinchu, Taiwan: Magajaros Press, 1997).

21. For two fine readings of national, transpacific, and transnational dynamics in postcolonial Taiwanese cinema, see Jane Yip, "Constructing a Nation: Taiwanese History and the Films of Hou Hsiao-hsien," and Wei Ming Dariotis and Eileen Fung, "Breaking the Soy Sauce Jar: Diaspora and Displacement in the Films of Ang Lee," both in *Transnational Chinese Cinemas: Identity, Nationhood, Gender,* ed. Sheldon Hsiao-pang Lu (Honolulu: University of Hawai'i Press, 1997), 139–68 and 187–220.

of uneven modernity as Hawai'i, Taiwan, and New Zealand, where what Arjun Appadurai calls the "Trojan horse nationalisms" of white settler states can threaten to implode with emerging counterclaims on nation-state identity and social formation by indigenous/multicultural national-isms linked to prior formations, symbol systems, and alternative lineage of cultural identity at once constructed yet more attuned to place forms and primordial attachments.[22]

Given these contexts of space-time compression, "localization" of global, regional, and national forms can be seen to take on two distinct yet inter-acting senses. First, *localization,* in the postmodern marketing sense of Sony's Morita and the *Harvard Business Review,* means the rejection of object uniformity and assumptions of product universality; instead, ob-jects and images will have to adapt to local communities and reflect re-gional tastes and subnational spaces to become "expressive." Simulation of the local can, in this global process, displace more authentic, mythic, or place-bound representations of cultural identity. In a counterhegemonic or more critical sense, as well, *localization* will here refer to the process of differentiation by means of which regional and local cultures can recog-nize the global design and world market and yet assert alternative spaces, sublanguages, and local identities grounded in the otherwise and else-where. This Pacific local cannot be all that easily consumed or customized by the outreach of global capital, as it links up with and deforms global products and designs.

Reflecting on the "politics of difference" being constructed in local/national sites along (and inside) the Pacific, Meaghan Morris inventively articulates postcolonial Australia as a complex space of cultural production in which the local, aboriginal, and regional pulls are implicated and acti-vated, rather than merely dominated and absorbed by Euro-American globalism or white settler nationalism: "If one is to act nationally and *regionally* while thinking internationally in the Pacific Rim today, there are gulfs of language as well as political, social, and cultural 'tradition' to be

22. On "Trojan nationalisms" of modernity ready to expand and *implode* into global/local contestation from Canada and the USA to Japan and India, see Arjun Appadurai, "Patriotism and Its Futures," *Public Culture* 5 (1993): 411–29, as well as speculations on the paradox of "constructed primordialism" and the global production of locality as identity space in Appadurai, *Modernity at Large: Cultural Dimensions of Globalization* (Minneapolis: University of Minnesota Press, 1996).

negotiated, chasms of ignorance and indifference, gruesome histories of imperialism and racism to be confronted, and the consequences of Australian and American unions' past complicity in the destruction of Japanese and Korean labor movements to be faced."[23] The local, articulated in Morris's grounded sense, as tied to national and regional forms of place-bound identity and political community, can still affirm the possibility of global difference and national contestation. The Pacific local, in this wary critical sense of situated articulation, can become a way of bringing historical countermemory to bear on the making of the Euro-American nation through its uniform narratives, mores, and seamless traditions. The local, projected as alternative space and registering those other (Deleuze: "minor") languages and countermemories to the "white mythology" or white settler imaginary of the nation, can become a strategy of multicultural affirmation and, at the strongest extreme of assertion, urge indigenous survival and forms of counternationhood.

Microelectronics, computerized technologies, and mass tourism will compress the globe through relentless interaction and cultural interchange. Still, at times, the staggeringly complex cultures in the Pacific Basin and Pacific Rim will push toward maintaining some measure of *local determination:* to preserve locations that offer, as David Harvey registers within the dynamics of postmodern capitalogic, "multiple possibilities within which a spatialized 'otherness' can flourish."[24] When Paul Theroux interviewed the king of Tonga, Taufaʻahau Tupou IV, for example, and asked the last monarch remaining in the South Pacific about his plans to unify Polynesia into a coherent region as the Hawaiian king David Kalākaua had once tried to do (and failed) in the neonativist 1880s, the

23. Meaghan Morris, " 'On the Beach,' " in *Cultural Studies,* ed. Lawrence Grossberg, Cary Nelson, and Paula Treichler (London: Routledge, 1992), 474. The oppositional regionalism and multidimensionality of cultural resistances as worked out in Pacific exchanges—"local appropriations for local ends [that] situate colonial dominance in part in the unforeseen consequences of [global] trade"—are situated flexibly as Pacific cultural practices in Nicholas Thomas, *Entangled Objects: Exchange, Material Culture, and Colonialism in the Pacific* (Cambridge, MA: Harvard University Press, 1991), 184. For an exemplary work in Asian/Pacific and counter–white national studies of popular culture, see Meaghan Morris, *Too Soon Too Late: History in Popular Culture* (Bloomington: University of Indiana Press, 1998); and, on a paradoxical and more tradition-oriented note, Nicholas Thomas, *In Oceania: Visions, Artifacts, Histories* (Durham, NC: Duke University Press, 1997).
24. Harvey, *The Condition of Postmodernity,* 273.

Tongan king answered by embracing the "politics of difference" of an Oceanic postmodernist. My aim in such a project, replied the king, "is not political. How could it be? The Cook Islands is a republic. Hawai'i is a state. French Polynesia is a colony. Tonga is a monarchy. There are too many differences."[25] At a time (1991) when France still went on testing nuclear weapons in the reefs of Polynesia and the USA was discarding its cold war arsenal in the Johnston Atoll and toppling Saddam Hussein in Iraq with Patriot missiles, rather than conjure some rival vision of political or economic homogenization, the king of Tonga said he would promote this Oceanic unity of Polynesia through the formation of a new magazine—of culture and the arts! (In using such cultural tactics, the king was mimicking a method of regional linkage and survival initiated by Albert Wendt of Samoa, Epeli Hau'ofa of Tonga, and Marjorie Crocombe and Subramani of Fiji, among others, in the 1970s.)

Given these very dynamics of transnational production within a postmodern / "postcolonial" world system that would consume, demobilize, and mimic resistance at the local level of culture, Arif Dirlik would give special weight to the significance of an emergent "critical regionalism" in its ability to forge local spaces of difference and social tactics of resistance. "The reaffirmation of the local that I am speaking of here is that 'critical localism,' " Dirlik argues, "which, even as it subjects the present to the critical evaluation from past perspectives, retains in the evaluation of the past the critical perspectives afforded by modernity. Excluded from this localism are romantic nostalgia for communities past, hegemonic nationalist yearnings of a new kind (as with the so-called Confucian revival in East Asia), or historicism that would imprison the past."[26] Given these *uneven* powers of postmodernity inside the global cultural economy and the political complications of "postcoloniality," we cannot go back to the future, that is, to preserving the culture of some nativist nation-state or to maintaining some precapitalist illusion of equality, racial purity, and cultural homogeneity.

25. Paul Theroux, "In the Court of the King of Tonga," *New York Times Magazine*, 7 June 1992, 42. Theroux's "tourist gaze" on the inferior Spam-eating natives of the Pacific in *Happy Isles of Oceania* is contested in Rob Wilson, "Paul Theroux's Venomous Views," *Honolulu Advertiser*, 8 January 1994, A9.
26. Arif Dirlik, "Post-Socialist Marxism: Critical Considerations," in *After the Revolution: Waking to Global Capitalism* (Middletown, CT: Wesleyan University Press, 1994), 108–10.

Still, even as stronger, virtual, and more devious versions of hypercapital command the contours of local space, time, and value, we do need to
hold out for some particularized places and enclaves of cultural production in which "the 'othernesses' and 'regional resistances' that postmodernist politics emphasize can flourish."[27] Stressing and *pressurizing the
local* as a site of "critical resistance" posits a more dynamic way of imagining the relationship of region, nation, and globe in which difference is not
subsumed nor reified but circulated and affirmed. Readings of "local
knowledge" that would ignore the larger macropolitics of context or suppress, at times, the neocolonial (or transnational) dynamics of uneven
development can all too unconsciously serve to ratify the market-driven
nation-state as space and goal of modernization.[28]

Within this globalizing economy, cyborgs of transnational Japan and the
"global city" of Kyoto-Osaka (or the Science and Industrial Park of Hsinchu, for that matter) can be intimately related to the local cultures and by-
products of Australia and Africa. Cyborgs across the Asia/Pacific help to
figure spaces of postmodern cultural production. Answering the question
of workaday and temporal disjunction, "How can I, toiling away in the
teeming city of Tokyo, have any true sense of relationship with a primitive
tribesman living in the wilds of Africa?", Masahiro Mori uses the creative-
destruction force of the robot to figure the global interaction of these
disparate spaces of production. Founder of the Robotics Society of Japan
and the Mukta Institute of transpersonal creativity, Mori writes in *The
Buddha in the Robot*, "When I start to make a robot, I have to gather

27. Harvey, *The Condition of Postmodernity*, 239.
28. For a critique of U.S. ethnography as insufficiently situated "local knowledge"
affiliated to a geopolitical misrecognition of Sukarno's overthrow in Indonesia, see
Vincent P. Pecora, "The Limits of Local Knowledge," in *The New Historicism*, ed.
H. Aram Veeser (New York: Routledge, 1989), 243–76. Pecora maintains that Indonesian "local culture," caught up in a postwar struggle for self-determination against
American intervention, needs to be situated "in the larger context of cold-war, East-West
geo-political conflict" (256). Regarding the dynamics driving "the local/global cultural
dialectic," James Clifford warns that the ethnographer of "thick description" should
beware of *localizing* narratives, that is, warding off into a historical essence "what is
actually a regional/national/global nexus" (100). See "Traveling Cultures," in *Cultural
Studies*, ed. Lawrence Grossberg, Cary Nelson, and Paula Treichler (London: Routledge,
1992).

materials: a motor or two, some aluminum sheet, steel bands, transistors, copper filaments, and so on. A robot is made by putting these components together according to one scheme or another, and if we are to understand the robot fully we must understand the parts. What are they? Where do they come from?"[29] Decomposing the robot's "Japanese" national identity into local/global subject, Mori deconstructs the *national* origins of this postmodern individual, the Japanese cyborg, as a process of economic interchange linking North to South, science to religion, body to spirit, technology to earth, global to local: "Where does the iron ore come from? It is mined in the mountains of Australia, China, and Africa, and brought to Japan in cargo vessels. Africa? Yes, Africa. Through the steel and the iron ore, the robot I am making is related to the home of the African tribesman I speak of" (28). Decomposed of national origin and unfixed of private identity, the robot/cyborg figures in Mori's reading, finally, as a *Buddhist transnational subject.* "I believe robots have the buddha-nature within them—that is, the potential for attaining buddhahood," Mori contends, theorizing this most postmodern Japanese subject, for whom imperialism and war are over (13). Interfacing human and animal, spirit and technology, physical and immaterial, cyborg workers break down the boundary of the local/global and dissolve the nation-state into configurations of the transnational future.

This *cyborgian future* is, in some respects, already spreading across the "Asia/Pacific" region of transnational production. Whereas earlier forms of nation making pushed the evolution of the nineteenth century toward horizontal solidarity and imagined community, it is becoming clear, in attempts to map the dynamics of postmodern spatiality, that the motions

29. Masahiro Mori, *The Buddha in the Robot: A Robot Engineer's Thoughts on Science and Religion,* trans. Charles S. Terry (Tokyo: Kosei, 1981), 28–29. While linking the cyborg-subject to the "contradictory, partial, and strategic" identities of American socialist feminism, Donna Haraway contends from a space of feminist/socialist mobility that "the cyborg is a kind of disassembled and reassembled, postmodern collective and personal self" (163). See "A Cyborg Manifesto: Science, Technology, and Socialist-Feminism in the Late Twentieth Century," in *Simians, Cyborgs, and Women: The Reinvention of Nature* (New York: Routledge, 1991). Theorizing the international division and "feminization" of labor forces and spaces ("homework" space) that the cyborg helps to install, Haraway contends, "Cyborg gender is a local possibility taking a global vengeance" (181).

and flights of transnational capital entail the *disinvention* of the bounded "nation-state" as we know it into a less stable, more fungible and hetero-glossic entity.[30] At least such a process is underway in countries situated in the First World of postmodern capitalist culture, such as the United States, France, Australia, Great Britain, and Japan. What some trans-national economists would now embrace as a *borderless*, open, decentered, and interlinked economy of Japan, the United States, and Europe has, in the upbeat Pacific Rim analysis of Kenichi Ohmae, "made traditional na-tional boundaries almost disappear, and pushed bureaucrats, politicians, and the military toward the status of declining industries."[31] "Almost" does not mean "already" here, to be sure: the process of installing this "global web," to support a *borderless* commodity culture liquefied in the First World economy of scale and speed, is complicated and contested, from Birmingham to Melbourne, at the level of everyday culture and space. Still, the transnational doors keep opening to the dirty waters and El Niño winds; spaces shrink and grow more porous, from Honolulu to Taipei and Auckland and beyond.

In the subject-formation of the United States of America that will inform (and deform) the argument of this little book, this big process of global linkage will suggest the disuniting of the postindustrial states and subjects of the American *e pluribus unum* polity into multicultural, racial, and neoregional forces of disidentification, discontinuity, reclaiming, and de-centering. As one precondition for the formation of democratic modernity as such, the political conviction of nationhood as an "imagined commu-nity" served, over the troubled course of two centuries, to unite diverse selves of linguistic, ethnic, religious, and territorial diversity (whom Bene-

30. On older and various Euro-American formations, see E. J. Hobsbawm, *Nations and Nationalism since 1780: Program, Myth, Reality* (Cambridge: Cambridge University Press, 1990), 23.

31. Ohmae, *The Borderless World*, xi. Given the interplay of the global with/against the local that Ohmae's work would ratify as a win-win process of transnationalism, eco-nomic and cultural forces rapidly feed off and back into each other. We see the rise of capitalogic models to explain these placeless and dehistoricized cultures of postmoder-nity (as in the theories of Fredric Jameson and David Harvey). Although such models are often accused of being reflectionist in orientation, it is now often difficult to differen-tiate the first set of global changes as strictly "economic" from a second or national set as purely "cultural."

dict Anderson calls the "creole pioneers" of populist nationalism in the
New World) into some teleology of shared power and collective purpose.[32]

As a master narrative for this tacit process of identity formation, "Americanization" of citizens implied not so much a stigma or a negation as a
utopic self-construction, in part dependent on a liberal discourse of democratic interpellation. Identification with national power and polity took
place for the democratic subject not only in the ballot box and at the
shopping mall, but, more variously, in the everyday and aesthetic practice
of identifying with the sublimating energies of the nation: some vast landscape such as Niagara Falls or the Western plains, some icon of technological might such as the moon landing or the transcontinental railway, or "the
people" itself seen as some intoxicating social glue of mass conglomera-
tion as in Whitman's "Song of Myself," secured a conviction of American
national subjectivity. As one such time-honored discourse of "Americanization," the cultural genre of the "American sublime" evolved through
the course of the nineteenth century in canonical authors of white settler
mythology such as Emerson, Bryant, Whitman, Church, and Stevens, as I
have argued elsewhere, to secure a conviction of national empowerment
and cultural identity as founded in the illusion of empty space, or a *terra
nullus* (as claimed in white Australia to displace aboriginal land rights) ripe
for the saturation of Euro-American power and representation.[33]

Democratic identification with the sublime power of nationhood, dependent on some trope of aboriginal legitimacy and first possession, is fast
coming apart at the cultural seams. Even the Grand Canyon, or what
Morton Kondracke has called the whole ideology of "Grand Canyonism"
invoked by the discursively inept George Bush reelection campaign in

32. See Benedict Anderson, "Creole Pioneers," in *Imagined Communities: Reflections on
the Origin and Spread of Nationalism* (London: Verso, 1991), chap. 4.
33. See Rob Wilson, *American Sublime: The Genealogy of a Poetic Genre* (Madison: University of Wisconsin Press, 1991), and chap. 7 below. On contentions against *terra nullus*
doctrines lingering on and debated in Australian courts, policies, and tastes, see *Aboriginal Australia: Land, Law, and Culture*, special issue of *Race & Class*, ed. Peter Poynton, 35
(1994). On transformation of the U.S. sublime in the transnational era of postmodern
financial capitalism, see Rob Wilson, "The Postmodern Sublime: Local Definitions,
Global Deformations of the U.S. National Imaginary," *Amerikastudien* 43 (1998): 517–
27, in a special issue on the American sublime as legacy of image and ideology spreading through forms of high and popular culture, from serial killings and romantic river
paintings back to the federalist landscapes of the Connecticut Wits.

1992 to shore up the national power of its disoriented and postideological presidential subject, can no longer serve as awesome instruction scene of national unity and self-transcendence to heal race, class, and gender divisions through sublime spectacles of American exceptionality.[34] Lawrence Kasdan's 1992 movie *Grand Canyon* gathered its characters at its closure before the Grand Canyon scene to heal, if only symbolically, the class and race divisions riddling Los Angeles before that same city, as paradigm of postmodern global space, erupted (later in 1992) into apocalyptic fires of local abandonment and international molestation. Ignoring the cynical reason of the Hollywood movie producer (played by Steve Martin), who used the Grand Canyon as a metaphor for the gulf that *separates* upscale white America from the black slums, the white lawyer (Kevin Kline) and black truck driver (Danny Glover) gather wives and children from the city to gaze in awe at the Grand Canyon as if sharing some primal ground of national conviction and cultural belief.

The "American sublime" as an aesthetic conviction of national empowerment for self/community/landscape, is supposed to work like this, the commonsense trope of primal natural infinitude in *Grand Canyon* implies, signifying our connection to the vast unifying wilderness of Arizona, a space unlike the tormented and terror-ridden ghetto of South Central Los Angeles. But, in an era of the decentered, flexible, and globally entangled production taking place across transnational cyberspace, when the "American company knows no national boundaries, feels no geographic constraints,"[35] can the appeal to a Fordist economy of scale, where size represents national strength and power is materially embodied in products of national identity, appeal with the same ideological conviction? Gone are innocent days of a postwar American movie like *Niagara* (1953), when the passionate (always excessive) body of Marilyn Monroe as phallic woman could compete, as semiotic image, with the power and treachery of the national falls (sublime wilderness) to embody the newfound hegemonic power of the United States as global force.[36]

Despite nostalgia for this nineteenth-century aesthetic of nationhood as

34. Morton Kondracke, "Gulf Wars," *The New Republic* 206 (20 April 1992): 46.
35. Robert B. Reich, *The Work of Nations: Preparing Ourselves for 21st-Century Capitalism* (New York: Knopf, 1991), 124.
36. For an analysis of the traumatic power of Elizabeth Taylor and "Marilyn heat" as American popular cultural embodiments in the 1950s, see Koestenbaum, *Jackie Under My Skin*, 66–82.

objectified in an imagined community and shared landscape, the local and the transnational will, in different ways and with distinct tensions, pull apart the "Grand Canyonism" of the American nation as we now know it, dismantle local regions, and forge transnational alliances that cut across traditional allegiances to place, group, class, and social community. This is not meant to proclaim postliberal prophecy nor to invoke transnational paranoia, but to register cultural description based on an investigation of social motions and cultural selves already circulating in the United States as these are displaced and transformed in national genres and, as regional forms, in the American Pacific.

Mapping the reformation of the "American Pacific" from within the militarized yet tourist-friendly sites of *South Pacific* and Pearl Harbor, as linked to ethnic and indigenous energies of Bamboo Ridge, I will focus on cultural conjunctions of global/local space as these impinge on the symbolic coherence of American national identity. To map the changing dynamics of *local culture* in the American Pacific, I will go on to theorize the emergence of the "local literature" movement in Hawai'i. This micropolitics of cultural identity will be linked to larger postcolonial and regional tactics of coalition in the Asia-Pacific region: a new regionalism imagined and contested, as it were, along a Honolulu–Taipei line of flight. In this large-scale or regional reframing, I will situate this local movement at Bamboo Ridge within the geo-imperial dynamics of the American Pacific, as this was constructed during the nineteenth century and as a reflection of decolonizing dynamics in the contemporary Pacific.

As such, I challenge (residually) "orientalist" representations or cold war productions of the Asia/Pacific as a *South Pacific* fantasy of the region through an analysis of American interactions with the offshore nation of Hawai'i. This particularized focus on the emergence of an *Asia/Pacific America*, via Hawai'i as space of multicultural mediation between California and Asia flows, will help to measure these motions of the local, national, and transnational imaginary. These "local motions" are conjoined in ways that reveal unequal flows of information and power. The Hawaiian indigenous movement demands a more complete hearing inside this so-called American Pacific. This is one way to answer the question, How do you find America today?

Epochal changes in postmodernist modes of production need to be linked to changes in modes of cultural reproduction within the political imaginary of America itself, and a discussion of literary and filmic cultural genres will allow me an entry into mapping these social dynamics. It was only two decades ago, during the struggle for Asian hegemony in the Vietnam era, that authors of Oceania and the Asia/Pacific could still be anthologized as so many "technicians of the sacred," that is, as mythic subjects expressing premodern communities, unconscious forces, aboriginality, and ancient language-games.[37] First World hunger for "techniques of the sacred" or for mythic transformation of everyday banality will no longer suffice as cultural description in the Pacific; in contexts of postmodern performance and constructed primordialism, even *hula kāhiko* (ancient hula, or "hula of old") can signify the resurgence of the Hawaiian culture within structures of state control, subaltern humiliation, and tourist consumption.[38]

There has been a more recent turn within the local literary culture of Hawai'i toward tapping into this deeper cultural resonance of place and language as willed ground of invented identity, sought after by renewing contact with the Hawaiian language and its archive of myths and orature, that "unwritten literature" as Nathaniel Emerson called *nā mele o Hawai'i* (the songs and chants of Hawai'i). At the same time, given global competitiveness and a nagging sense of cultural dislocation, as I have suggested in

37. See Jerome Rothenberg, ed., *Technicians of the Sacred: A Range of Poetries from Africa, America, Asia, and Oceania* (Garden City, NY: Doubleday, 1969; revised and expanded 2d ed., Berkeley: University of California Press, 1985). Even a liberal travelogue from this myth-drenched era provides a more historicized view of "Oceania" as site of decolonization, and argues that militarization has turned Hawai'i into "a sugar-coated fortress, an autistic Eden, a plastic paradise in which the militarism and racism of the American empire are cloaked by a deceptive veil of sunshine and flowers" (121); see Francine du Plessix Gray, *Hawai'i: The Sugar-Coated Fortress* (New York: Vintage, 1973), which also contains a portrait of the Hawaiian sovereignty struggle tied to protests in Kalama Valley as it was being suburbanized (125–45). Gray's claim that "the [Hawaiian] nationalist movement will grow in numbers and in identity" (128) will be supported in my analysis.

38. "For Hawaiian performers and audiences, *hula* and chant are now the strongest cultural links to a distant and glorious past" and, as such, are part of the "politicization of culture" in the sovereignty struggle; see Elizabeth Buck, *Paradise Remade: The Politics of Culture and History in Hawai'i* (Philadelphia: Temple University Press, 1993), 6–9. On the constructivist/primordialist debate over the forging of Hawaiian nationalist identity, see Jeff Tobin, "A Report from the Hawaiian Front," in *Asia/Pacific as Space of Cultural Production*, special issue of *boundary 2* 21 (1994): 111–33.

my preface, the Hawai'i Visitors Bureau goes on placing greater emphasis on the "aloha spirit" as a marketing device, which means, for instance, teaching hotel workers to smile at tourists, using real flowers in rent-a-car lobbies, and putting in free baggage carts at the Honolulu International Airport. As deeper resonance and gesture of reinvented Pacific authenticity, the local has become a contested terrain of Hawaiian cultural expression subject to strange appropriations, politicized reification, and multiple contestation, as I hope to make clear. One hundred years after the annexation of Hawai'i in 1898, very few in the U.S. island state are celebrating and many more are mourning an act of republican absorption that was protested by over twenty-one thousand Hawaiians to no avail in the era of U.S., European, and Asian imperialism in the Pacific.[39]

My focus, finally, will turn to tracking emergent spaces and genres of transnational interaction that would link the localism and indigenous nationalism of Hawai'i to the globalism and flows of the Asia-Pacific region, which goes on being constructed and redefined even as I write (chapters 4 and 5). In chapter 6, I invoke the shark gods of the precolonial imaginary of Hawaiian literature to contest the tacit makings of Hawaiian reality as (American) real estate. In chapter 7, I go on to read the locally produced movie rooted in the tensions of Hawai'i, *Good-bye Paradise,* as a social text from the American Pacific that reflects this interface of global forces and local resistance and, as such, refracts the micropolitics of a racially mixed and troubled Hawaiian polity. In chapter 8, I turn back to articulate what it means to "become global and local" while creating inside what is being called "the transnational imaginary" in such spaces of cultural production as Honolulu and Taipei. (My own identity as local writer and Pacific cultural critic will be dispersed, interrogated, and implied throughout this study.)[40]

Global, considered as a dynamic of the Asia-Pacific, here presumes (for

39. See Dan Nakaso, "Anti-Annexation Petition Rings Clear: Researcher Finds 1897 Document," *Honolulu Advertiser,* 5 August 1998, A1, on the discovery by Noenoe Silva of a petition in the National Archives signed by 21,269 Hawaiian citizens opposed to annexation, over half of the Native Hawaiian population.

40. I can only hope that two forthcoming works of poetry and poetics that I have worked on over the years while in Hawai'i, California, and Taiwan—*Ananda Air: American Pacific Lines of Flight* and *Automat: Un/American Poetics*—will help give the (tireless) reader a richer, affiliated, and stranger sense of the Pacific-oriented cultural production I have been a part of since 1976.

me) the uneven spread of capitalism as a world system, with shifting centers and peripheries and suggesting a new borderless geography of transnationalism undoing older configurations of place and the nation-state. Given an uncanny weight of situated articulation, *local* will here be deployed in three (overlapping) senses: first, local means the indigenous cultures of the Pacific not in pre- but in postcontact situations, comprising what anthropologists call "compromise cultures" that have come about as a result of long-term adjustments of Polynesian cultures to Euro-American contact and the influence of Western institutions, categories, and norms—the Pacific local in all its clamorous hybridity. Second, local implies the multicultural and polyethnic community that emerged in the U.S. Territory of Hawai'i around 1920 out of the plantation experience, when Asian/Pacific workers began to feel, in Ronald Takaki's analysis in *Pau Hana*, "an identity of themselves as settlers, as locals, and an understanding of the need for a politics that transcended ethnicity"—the multicultural local.[41] Third, local signifies the literary and cultural movement emerging in the late 1970s and 1980s, after the fact of Hawaiian statehood, that comprises an affirmation of ethnic heritage and regional ground and expresses minor languages of indigenous and subnational difference—the literary local.

The end-of-century United States, as I will be suggesting, will move toward implosive and impure ends: the end of "America" as a bounded entity/identity and its transformation, meltdown, and reimagining into a postmodern object of ideological desire in which the local, national, and global are more actively interfaced in "Asia-Pacific." Given the global web of American postmodernity, national products have become transnational composites; this will have to affect the very way we look at everyday American culture, cultural studies as such, and American studies in the era of the transnational imaginary.[42]

Although it may reflect a cultural conviction and linger on as sublime

---

41. Ronald Takaki, *Pau Hana: Plantation Life and Labor in Hawai'i* (Honolulu: University of Hawai'i Press, 1983), xi.

42. See Reich, *The Work of Nations:* "In such global webs, [national] products [and corporations] are international composites" (113). As Ohmae outlines this reorientation in *Borderless World*, "It is difficult to tell what an 'American' product is, because the very concept of an 'American' or a 'Japanese' or a 'French' or a 'German' product doesn't make sense" (140).

object of ideological desire, "America" is not so much the fixture of a national government or bounded cultural space as it is a transnational corporation with local roots.[43] It may not always be so, but this is how it feels to create "America" today from an angle of vision rerooted in the Pacific. Mark Twain warned, while writing up Hawai'i as a good plantation investment, missionary outpost, and tourist site fit for American readers from California to take over, profit by, and enjoy as we set out to tread these expansive, dream-laden waters: "It was such ecstasy to dream and dream [in the Pacific]—till you got a bite. A scorpion bite."[44] Writing a kind of ad copy for the islands, Twain poked fun at "our fellow savages in the Savage Islands" as he made a killing on the national lecture circuit doing so, at the same time supporting missionary and commercial forces that were mounting toward U.S. annexation of Hawai'i as blessed tourist isles full of sugar money and Edenic dreams of bodily bliss.

The superpower market-state that is the United States of America is, by now, fully immersed in the contemporary construction of "Asia-Pacific" as a post–cold war and globalizing region. "Asia/Pacific" represents an advance beyond "Pacific Rim discourse" (as described by Christopher Connery) in that it bespeaks a transnational community of liberal porousness and space-time compression, where market-driven coprosperity and democratic nation-states will have come home to coexist; where North/South colonialism, orientalizing binaries, and world war are said to get washed away forever in the magical waters of the Pacific. (The slow "rise" and sudden "fall" of "Confucian capitalism" during recent years, aggravated by our neoliberal policies, suggests how much of a scorpion the market-driven and web-drunken system of transnational globalization can be, turning back to bite its strongest proponents.)[45]

---

43. On "postnational"/transnational transformations impacting on the cultural economy of national identity and "American studies" as field imaginary, see the two special editions of *boundary 2, The New Americanists*, ed. Donald Pease, 17 (1990) and 19 (1992); and Paul Bové, "Notes towards a Politics of 'American' Criticism," in *In the Wake of Theory* (Middletown, CT: Wesleyan University Press, 1992), 48–66; "American" is placed, to be sure, in wary scare quotes.

44. Mark Twain, *Roughing It* (1872; Berkeley: University of California Press, 1972), 406.

45. See Christopher L. Connery, "Pacific Rim Discourse: The U.S. Global Imaginary in the Late Cold War Years," in *Asia/Pacific as Space of Cultural Production*, ed. Arif Dirlik and Rob Wilson (Durham, NC: Duke University Press, 1995), esp. 47–56, on the decline of "Rimspeak" boosterism in the wake of cold war logic and the binary spatializa-

On lines of flight westward to China and Japan, the United States of America has for two centuries flowed and fractured into "Asia-Pacific," where the ancient Orient dissolves into primordial Oceania and surges beyond into the new fanged prosperity of the Pacific Rim. Let us not get too drunk on the discourse of Rimspeak or a kind of neo-Pacific booster-ism! But, nonetheless, new and multisited mappings of this U.S. cultural imaginary are called for, fluid ones that can be tied to social movements and mixed languages and creative flows, tracking domineering territories and tactics of the neoliberal capitalist state and booming region while, at the same time, tracing emergent "lines of flight, movements of deter-ritorialization, and destratification."[46] My assumption is that such a "line of flight" need not be just an Ahab-like enactment of imperial dynamics and will to power over the native and other, but instead can mime, deform, and critique the statist project of Manifest Destiny as this trajectory of frontier expansion alters and dissolves in "Asia/Pacific."

It is to these by-now-emergent modes of "reimagining" space, cultural polity, identity, and national language—that go on, in effect, "shrinking the Pacific" from a post-"American" trajectory—that I now turn.

---

tion of the region. On the mythic and willed "Confucianization of Asia" as a regional challenge to forms of occidental modernity and liberal capitalism predicated on the American model, see Beng-Huat Chua, "Confucianisation Abandoned," in *Communitarian Ideology and Democracy in Singapore* (London: Routledge, 1995), 147–68.

46. Gilles Deleuze and Félix Guattari, *On the Line*, trans. John Johnston (New York: Semiotext[e], 1983), 2, 43, 64. On the poetics of creating culture and deforming "Anglo-American" geopolitics and settled territories "through a line of flight," see Gilles Deleuze and Claire Parnet, *Dialogues*, trans. Hugh Tomlinson and Barbara Habberjam (New York: Columbia University Press, 1987): "American literature operates according to geographical lines: the flight towards the West, the discovery that the true East is in the West, the sense of frontiers as something to cross, to push back, to go beyond" (36–37). For a more personally articulated and situated take on this, see the coda below.

CHAPTER 1

Imagining "Asia-Pacific" Today:

Forgetting Colonialisms in the Magical Waters of the Pacific

South Seas, turquoise green skies, the archways of a bazaar, the mysterious house—all of this Oriental scenery surrenders to the fairy-tale wish [for some imagined utopia] with great affinity and absorbs it. . . . the land of wishes from the [European] medieval South Seas, so to speak, has remained.
    —Ernst Bloch, *The Utopian Function of Art and Literature*[1]

James Clavell, who just died, made the Far East a less mysterious place.
    —National Public Radio reporter, on the death of *Shogun*'s author,
    6 September 1994

COURTING THE ASIA-PACIFIC YACHT PEOPLE

Nobody quite knows what "Asia-Pacific" means these days in terms of its specific ingredients or future directions, but one thing is clear: many forces are trying to court and construct it into an identity as metageographical "region."[2] To cite one local example, the Democratic governor

1. Defending the utopian function of wish and dream as projections of the narrative imagination worth preserving, even within the bleak dialectics of late capitalism, Ernst Bloch saw the "oriental" South Seas, from the medieval carnivals to the imperial fantasies of Rudyard Kipling in India, as a key site of Western dream projection and social wish; see "Better Castles in the Sky at the Country Fair and Circus, in Fairy Tales and Colportage," in *The Utopian Function of Art and Literature: Selected Essays*, trans. Jack Zipes and Frank Mecklenberg (Cambridge, MA: MIT Press, 1988), 176–79, 158.
2. As substantiated below, "region" in my usage means less a self-evident unit of geography or civilizational culture than some kind of (imagined) mutual coprosperity

of Hawai'i, Benjamin Cayetano, in May 1997 led a delegation of busi-
nesspeople, realtors, and Pacific educators on a ten-day trip to Taiwan
to promote business and investment opportunities in Hawai'i. As self-
appointed base of the Asia-Pacific Regional Operations Center (APROC),
Taiwan seemed a very likely place to make such a pitch as a site that is
competing with Hong Kong and Singapore to become "the space of [trans-
national] flows" across the Pacific.[3] Going beyond his upbeat pro-tourism
rationale, Cayetano sought to inform Taiwan's people about Hawai'i's Immigrant Investor Program, which has become one of the most popular
programs for immigrant investors seeking permanent residency in the
United States. "This program gives immigrant investors the opportunity
to stay in the U.S. with an investment of one million dollars," Cayetano
boasted, adding that it has already been implemented throughout the
United States.[4] Cayetano's mission is interested in luring not just Taiwanese investment from the Pacific Rim; he has already led similar trips to
the Philippines, Korea, Japan, and China. (Canada and Australia are also
making money-for-passport offers and, at the same time, trying to fight off
backlashes of "white only" nationalism and the reactive rise of Hanson-
ism.)[5] The call to Asia these days is not so much to the "boat people" but to

---

zone of our U.S. transnational moment. A historically informed approach that makes
for critical wariness about the way the world has been divided into "metageographical"
constructs drenched in power and ideology—"East" and "West," Europe and the Orient,
"North" and "South," First, Second, and Third World, and so on, down to this quasi-
deconstructive era of "civilizational" thinking—is offered in Martin Lewis and Karen E.
Wigen, *The Myth of Continents: A Critique of Metageography* (Berkeley: University of
California Press, 1997), esp. chaps. 2 and 3. ASEAN, for example, is seen to construct
Southeast Asia into a "residual and artificial category" that will give the regional players
a better sense of "coherence" than it ever had in the past, and thus a better grip on the
future direction of the region as such (176). APEC, a larger-scale area projection of
cultural and economic "coherence," is not dealt with in this important study.
3. I speak here of the "informational" or "global" city of transnational capitalism in
which money, information, transportation, media images, and commodities can flow
with maximum speed in a site of space-time compression. On Hong Kong's materialization of this fate in the 1980s and its threat of "disappearance" under Chinese rule in
1997, see Ackbar Abbas, *Hong Kong: Culture and the Politics of Disappearance* (Minneapolis: University of Minnesota Press, 1997), 2–25.
4. "Hawaii Seeking Investors," *China Post,* 23 May 1997, 5.
5. After years of stressing how its future was linked to the growth of Asia-Pacific as a
capitalist region, Australia is reversing the geopolitics of Labor Prime Minister Paul

the "yacht people" of some vast—and, at times, threatening (see below)—"Greater China."[6]

As a U.S. literary scholar, I could only recall the gloomier "Asia-Pacific" region portrayed in Maxine Hong Kingston's memoirs of the modern Chinese diaspora, *The Woman Warrior: Memoirs of a Girlhood among Ghosts* (1976) and *China Men* (1980): generations of uprooted stowaways contracted to years of labor in Cuba, New York, Bali, and Hawai'i; plantation workers, railroad men, day laborers working long hours in restaurants, clothing factories, and laundries, struggling for livelihood while surviving on mythic self-constructions as they confront social exclusion among the taunting "ghosts" of Gold Mountain.[7] Or recall as well Joy Kogawa's portrait of generations of Japanese Canadians in *Obasan* (1981), three generations unjustly uprooted from the Northern Pacific Coast region and forced to relocate several times in remote areas of Canada as wartime Yellow Peril discourse on the coast (as in California) reached phobic extremes: their property confiscated, citizenship questioned, families broken, long ties to the land, language, and nation denied.[8] Kingston, interviewed in Taiwan in 1995—in her own uncanny words, "a country made up of exiles, misfits, and outsiders" and, "like America, a country where immigrants have taken over the land and dominate the indigenous, primal people"—revealed the *traumatic* nature of her own family's U.S. immigrant experi-

---

Keating and beating a hasty retreat from the crisis of Asia. "Australia is geographically part of the Asia-Pacific region, no doubt about that," Treasurer Peter Costello recently said in New York, "but that doesn't mean our economy follows the paths of East Asian economies" ("Australia Distancing Itself from Asia Woes," *Honolulu Advertiser*, 26 May 1998, B6).

6. On the Canadian version of this ambivalent call to Hong Kong—"We want your money, but we may not want you"—see Katharyne Mitchell, "The Hong Kong Immigrant and the Urban Landscape: Shaping the Transnational Cosmopolitan in the Era of Pacific Rim Capital," in *Asia/Pacific as Space of Cultural Production*, ed. Rob Wilson and Arif Dirlik (Durham, NC: Duke University Press, 1995), 284–310. On Koreans as insiders and outsiders to the "American dream" of social mobility and capitalist trajectory across the transnationalized Pacific Rim in Los Angeles, see Nancy Abelman and John Lie, *Blue Dreams: Korean Americans and the Los Angeles Riots* (Cambridge, MA: Harvard University Press, 1995).

7. Maxine Hong Kingston, *The Woman Warrior: Memoirs of a Girlhood among Ghosts* (New York: Vintage, 1989), and *China Men* (New York: Ballentine, 1980).

8. Joy Kogawa, *Obasan* (Boston: David Godine, 1982); Kingston, *Woman Warrior* and *China Men*.

ence and the necessity to distort it by means of mythic imagination: "Now that my father has died, I can tell you that he actually came to the U.S. as a stowaway on a ship from Cuba, and he made the journey not once but three times. He was caught twice by immigration police and deported twice. I had to tell many legal and magical versions of my father's entry in case immigration authorities read my book and arrest and deport him again, and my mother too."[9]

Kingston's memorable portrait of such a *traumatized* Chinese immigrant is that of her dreamy middle-class aunt, Moon Orchid, who comes from Hong Kong to the United States in the 1970s looking to meet her by-now-diasporic family and connect with her doctor husband, who has illegally taken a second wife in Los Angeles and does not want her to interfere with his prosperous medical practice or new family. To quote *Woman Warrior:* "Brave Orchid [Kingston's quite worldly mother] looked at this delicate sister. She had long fingers and thin, soft hands. And she had a high-class city accent from living in Hong Kong. Not a trace of village accent remained; she had been away from the [Sun Woi, Canton] village for that long. Brave Orchid would not relent; her dainty sister would have to toughen up. 'Immigrants also work in the canneries, where it's so noisy it doesn't matter if they speak Chinese or what. The easiest way to find a job, though, is to work in Chinatown. You get twenty-five cents an hour and all your meals if you're working in a restaurant.' "[10] Moon Orchid cannot adjust and slowly goes crazy imagining that Mexicans, Filipinos, and Washington, D.C. "ghosts" are coming to take her family and turn them into ashes (156–60), multicultural immigrants and white immigration officials merging into one paranoid vision of North America as a land of symbolic disintegration, harm, language loss, death. For Kingston's aunt, crossing Asia-Pacific had become a space of fractures, disjuncture, traumas, confusion, and disappointments; this is quite another vision of exchanging money and labor for the passport to the "Gold Mountain" the United States is supposed (by diasporic Chinese) to stand for.

What is this "Asia-Pacific" region anyway, who gets to define it, in what language games, and toward what ends? In effect, here I will be worrying into discourse what it now means *to regionalize a space:* that is to say, to

9. Shan Te-Hsing, "An Interview with Maxine Hong Kingston," *Tamkang Review* 25 (1995): 6, 9.
10. Kingston, *Woman Warrior,* 127.

make it more porous to the cross-border flows of information, labor, finance, media images, and global commodities; to shrink the distances of space, culture, and time; and to cross and fuse the older national borders of the dirty, yet somehow vast and magical Pacific. To use Lawson Fusao Inada's title phrase from his parodic mock-tourist poem "Shrinking the Pacific," what does it mean *to shrink the Pacific,* that is, to compress and fuse (displace, confuse, disorient) these various and diverse Asian/Pacific cultures and peoples into an imagined single or unified zone of "space-time compression"?[11]

Such questions of construction and purpose in Asia and the Pacific region have taken on greater and boom-and-doom urgency since the currency and "asset bubble" crisis of 1997 and 1998 has now caused many U.S.-based economists and their journalist pundit allies to heap recriminations on the so-called Asian way of capitalist expansion and, thus, to question the whole process of state-driven liberalization regimes that had seemingly failed to protect the region and its nation-state players (especially Indonesia, South Korea, and Thailand) from high volatility and the global dynamics of boom-and-bust investment.[12] Even advocates of transnationalization and the patchwork liberalized economies in the Asia-Pacific region have recognized "the perils of globalization for small open economies" in the wake of the Asian currency (called in the U.S. press, in a metaphor laden with yellow-perilous implications, "the Asian flu") since the plundering and disorienting summer of 1997.[13] To be on the (uneven) road toward transnational globalization still remains a perilous task for the makers of materials, forms, and outlets affiliated to national culture.

11. See Lawson Fusao Inada, "Shrinking the Pacific," in *Asia/Pacific as Space of Cultural Production,* ed. Rob Wilson and Arif Dirlik (Durham, NC: Duke University Press, 1995), 80–81, on the huge problems of displacement that result as Japan flows back into Oregon. The Pacific Northwest region (as in British Columbia) is where Japanese citizens were racially marked as outsiders during the relocation and internment traumas of World War II. (Inada's poetry continues to come to terms with this via narrating his own family's experience of internment and relocation, his own traumatic and resymbolized version of Pacific Rim "regional" culture.)

12. For a reading of this "Asian crisis" as global in its characteristics and interlinked solutions, see Manuel F. Montes, "Global Lessons of the Economic Crisis in Asia," *Asia Pacific Issues,* no. 35, East-West Center, Honolulu, March 1998; and, more specifically, Richard W. Baker, "Indonesia in Crisis," *Asia Pacific Issues,* no. 36, East-West Center, Honolulu, May 1998.

13. Lee Kuan Yew, "Fix the Global Financial System," *Time,* 1 February 1999, Asia ed.

To mean anything trenchant, these days "Asia-Pacific" has to be situated and unpacked from within distinct cultural-political trajectories to disclose what this signifier stands for in its present ambivalent implications. Aiming to provide a U.S.-situated national and overtly politicized notion of "imagining" as an act of wary social fantasy, I want to play the dominant APEC-like (Asia-Pacific Economic Cooperation) constructions of Asia-Pacific as region of imagined capitalist coprosperity and market-driven bliss, as measured against the region as it is now being imagined in literary and cultural works by American, and Asian American, novelists (and, in other chapters, poets) that would challenge these neoliberal formations and suggest a different cultural-political way of reading "Asia-Pacific" as a space of identity construction. Doing cultural studies against the grain, as it were, *inside APEC.*

More specifically, I want to examine and provide a critical genealogy for the term "Asia-Pacific" as a cultural-ideological signifier, especially as this sign/banner has been constructed from a distinct U.S. trajectory, looking into its power-laden connotations as the U.S. Pacific goes on emerging from more overtly "orientalist" images of vast Asian markets and Yellow Peril threats, through the phobic sublimity of Melville's whale and Jack London's social Darwinist slime; down into the neofrontier of global cyberspace, where a tousle-haired Seattle multibillionaire, Bill Gates of Microsoft, would welcome the global village with open smiles and innocent American arms to what he rather naïvely enthuses is the system of "friction-free capitalism" taking place these days in what he calls (recalling the Gold Rush fury of mines and rails that built up California in 1849) "the Internet Goldrush."[14] As a point of contrast, I later evoke the way that a lesser and ever mobile regional power, Taiwan, is thickening this "Asia-Pacific" cultural-political imaginary into its own loaded signifier of promises, goals, and dreams inside the global/local city of Taipei, where capitalism is not so unregulated and not by any means friction-free.

14. See Bill Gates, *The Road Ahead* (New York: Penguin, 1996), chap. 8, "Friction-Free Capitalism." To quote from David S. Bennahaum, who ironically sees a new East-West division arising along English/Cyrillic alphabet lines erupting cyberspace markets: "Cyberspace is the ultimate distillation of what the Information Age is meant to be—a home for 'friction-free capitalism,' the end of nation-states, and a state of being where matter is 'demassified' into bits and electrons, which form the bricks and mortar of a new world" of transparent free-market exchange ("Freedom's Just Another Name for WYSIWYG," *MEME 3.03*, Internet journal, June 1997, section 5, "The WYSIWYG Society").

The commonplace and taken-for-granted assumption of "region" implied by a signifying category like "Asia-Pacific" entails an act of social imagining that has had to be shaped into coherence and consensus in ways that could call attention to the power politics of such unstable representations. To be sure, the everyday imagining of "Asia-Pacific" reeks of the contemporary (transnational/postcolonial) situation we are living through here and there on the Pacific Rim and Basin, so to speak, and can barely conceal the uncanny traumas and social contradictions that haunt its very formation. All but replacing warier cold war visions of the "Pacific Rim" as the preferred global imaginary in the discourse of transnationalizing and denationalizing corporate Americans, that is to say, "Asia-Pacific" has become a discourse of liberal sublimation that has surfaced, in the late 1980s and throughout the 1990s, to trumpet neoliberal market forces and regimes and thereby to forget cold war traumas and get beyond the stark geopolitics of imperialism and colonialism that had marked the region's long history.[15]

"Asia-Pacific," I want to say, is a utopic discourse of the liberal market, an emerging signifier of transnational aspirations for some higher, supra-

15. On U.S. discursive framing of the region circa 1970–1990, see Christopher L. Connery, "Pacific Rim Discourse: The U.S. Global Imaginary in the Late Cold War Years," in *Asia/Pacific as Space of Cultural Production*, ed. Rob Wilson and Arif Dirlik (Durham, NC: Duke University Press, 1995), 30–56. On the mythic poetics of U.S. geopolitical imagining in the post–cold war framework, see Connery, "The Oceanic Feeling and the Regional Imaginary," in *Global/Local: Cultural Production and the Transnational Imaginary*, ed. Rob Wilson and Wimal Dissanayake (Durham, NC: Duke University Press, 1996), 284–311. Also see John Eperjesi's probing study of Asia and Oceania's formation into a region of policy concern by the American Asiatic Society in 1898, in the context of U.S. imperial entanglements with Japan and China, in "Imaginary Circulation: The American Asiatic Association and the Creation of an American Pacific," which forms part of his doctoral dissertation being written in the English Department at Carnegie-Mellon University. On the rival imperialisms and economic expansionist visions that generated Japanese and U.S. outreach into the Pacific region in the late nineteenth and early twentieth centuries, as well as countertraditions of antiimperial nationhood that such social Darwinist visions evoked, see the powerful diplomatic histories of Akira Iriye, *Pacific Estrangement: Japanese and American Expansion, 1897–1911* (Cambridge, MA: Harvard University Press, 1972), and *Across the Pacific: An Inner History of American–East Asian Relations* (Chicago: Imprint Publications, 1997), as well as his edited collection on phobic and enchanted images, policies, and discourses, *Mutual Images, Essays in American-Japanese Relations* (Cambridge, MA: Harvard University Press, 1975).

national unity in which global/local will meet in some kind of win-win situation and the opened market will absorb culture and politics into its borderless affirmative flow. But, instead, the postwar Asia-Pacific region is still haunted by the "race hates" and "race wars" that deformed the prior vision of inter-Asia as a region of mutual coprosperity and coexistence just half a century ago, and we need to guard against the emergence of "provocative racial and martial idioms" in a new, transnational key.[16] Northern and Southern tensions, as well as lurking racialized binaries of residual orientalist frameworks, haunt the region and continue to return in uncanny ways on the U.S. home fronts.

As interlocked global players in the region, at least since the late 1970s if not throughout the cold war era of East/West demonization and in relation to the Japanese entanglement in imperial expansion during the 1890s, the United States and Taiwan have been caught up in the (neo-liberal or "postnational") *Asia-Pacific restructuring game*. Still, who best shapes and defines this "Asia-Pacific" region these days, and toward what ends? What does this discursive fusion of region into a higher unity imply for the diverse cultures, spaces, and "identity politics" of this region? Does "Asia-Pacific" mean anything more than the utopic dream of a "free market," that is, the post–cold war trope of First World policy planners and market strategists, all doors flung open to the free flow of the commodity form? In short, can this signifier of "Asia-Pacific" be wrested away from the discourse of APEC (for more on this, see below) to serve other functions and to open different cultural and critical possibilities? My own reading of Asia/Pacific will here be doubled, situated yet ambivalent, skeptical and utopic by turns, miming the language of imperial expansion and the capitalist state but turned back on itself. For, as I now see it, "Asia/Pacific" is

---

16. See John W. Dower, *War without Mercy: Race and Power in the Pacific War* (New York: Pantheon Books, 1986), 314. As Andrew Mack and John Ravenhill remind us, in a collection they have coedited titled (against evidence supporting the instability of any long-term "hegemony" in the Pacific region) *Pacific Cooperation: Building Economic and Security Regimes in the Asia-Pacific Region* (Boulder, CO: Westview, 1995), "For four decades following the end of World War II, the politically divided Asia-Pacific was the principal battleground on which global cold war rivalries were fought. Wars first in China, then Korea, Vietnam, and Cambodia pitted the United States and its allies against nationalist movements that, assisted by the two great communist powers, fought under the banner of revolutionary socialism" ("Economic and Security Regimes in the Asia-Pacific Region," 22).

not *just* an ideologically recuperated term, but represents those situated aspirations and shared promises of mixture and contradiction worth exploring as these go on clamoring into (uneven) existence.

"IMAGINING" ASIA-PACIFIC AS REGION

By *imagining* Asia-Pacific as region, I am working with the idea that imagining is not just an act of liberal consensus, cosmopolitan expression, or the shapely postcolonial construction of transnational "hybridity" discourse.[17] In the wake of anticolonialist cultural critics of mongrel "contact zones" such as Edward Said (*Orientalism, Culture and Imperialism*) and Mary Louise Pratt (*Imperial Eyes*) and creative cultural authors of "minority literature" inside English (such as the above-mentioned Kingston and Kogawa, the critically diasporic Japanese Brazilian postmodern novelist Karen Tei Yamashita, and the transpacific revolutionary Korean Pacific novelist from Hawai'i, Gary Pak), the verb "imagining" means articulating *a situated and contested social fantasy.* Imagining Asia-Pacific thus involves ongoing transformations in the language and space of identity by creating affiliated representations of power, location, and subject, in effect, expressing the will to achieve new suturings of (national) wholeness within "the ideological imaginary" of a given culture. In our era of transnational and postcolonial conjunction, that is, the very act of imagining (place, nation, region, globe) is constrained by discourse and contorted by geopolitical struggles for power, status, recognition, and control.[18] What cannot be imagined, as Wittgenstein once urged, cannot even be discussed, or in my terms, worried ("reimagined") into the language of political negotiation and affiliated spaces of social embodiment.

The "sublime object of ideology," as Slavoj Žižek fetchingly formulates it (in theorizing from a Lacanian-Marxist perspective the imagining of "sublime objects of desire" as diverse as the *Titanic,* capital, the dead body of Stalin, and the cold war psychodramas of Alfred Hitchcock), is haunted

17. On the dialectics of imagining a new cultural geopolitics beyond national or interethnic frames, see the probing collection of Pheng Cheah and Bruce Robbins, eds., *Cosmopolitics: Thinking and Feeling beyond the Nation* (Minneapolis: University of Minnesota Press, 1998).

18. *The Woman Warrior* is such a contested and politicized imagining: the despised Chinese daughter becoming "woman warrior" and "American-femininist," to free herself from stereotypes and her family from social disintegration.

by *lack* and riddled with traumas of incompletion and pained social struggle, antagonisms of class, gender, and nation in the (all-too-"phallic") language of imagining: "Ideology is not a dreamlike illusion that we build to
escape insupportable reality; in its basic dimension it is a [social] fantasy-
construction which serves as a support for our 'reality' itself: an illusion
which structures our effective, real social relations and thereby masks
some insupportable, real, impossible kernel."[19] Imagining is thus an act
of semijoyous signifying that both props up ("structures") and distorts
("masks") the materials of social reality, and works (through the production of some symbolic "excess" to cover up the holes) to conceal and reveal
(via sublimation, displacement, and other defenses) those social traumas
and antagonisms haunting its very creation.[20] (Uneven and unjust, the
memory of *immigration* and *war* is just such a traumatic Asian-Pacific
kernel being worked through in Asian American fiction as in other genres
of cultural criticism.)[21]

When reading a time-honored nature poem by Wordsworth or a self-
drenched essay by Emerson, we need not just admire the tropes, but work
to resist the layers of romanticism that would claim autonomy for the
transcendental "identity" of the U.S. poet for whom, as Emerson puts it in
"Self-Reliance," during the expansionist moment of Manifest Destiny on
the continental frontier, "Vast spaces of nature, the Atlantic Ocean, the

19. Slavoj Žižek, *The Sublime Object of Ideology* (London: Verso, 1989), 45.

20. Strong claims to aesthetic autonomy (as in the "pure poetry" of Poe or Mallarmé)
reflect a willed version of social abnegation and the all-too-romantic delusion by the lyric
artist (whom bourgeois society desperately needs) of "having escaped from the weight
of material existence" and having achieved freedom from reigning practices of utility
and commodity exchange. See Theodor W. Adorno, "On Lyric Poetry and Society," in
Notes to Literature (New York: Columbia University Press, 1991), 1:39.

21. In Kingston's narrative, "talking story" is a way for the immigrant to master social
reality in "the terrible ghost country of America" (*Woman Warrior*, 99) via a skillful
mixture of revealing and concealing, infusing history with myth, and speech with "un-
speakable" silence: "There were secrets never to be said in front of the ghosts, immigration secrets whose telling could get us sent back to China" (183). On "exclusion acts"
directed against Asian immigrants, barring them from U.S. citizenship and assimilation, see Lisa Lowe, *Immigrant Acts: On Asian American Cultural Politics* (Durham, NC:
Duke University Press, 1996); David Palumbo-Liu, "The *Bitter Tea* of Frank Capra,"
positions: East Asia Cultures Critique 3 (1995): 759–89; and David Palumbo-Liu, ed., *The
Ethnic Canon: Histories, Institutions, and Interventions* (Minneapolis: University of Minnesota Press, 1995).

South Sea—long intervals of time, years, centuries,—are of no account."[22] For a social-historical reading of such poetic "imagining" to take place, as Charles Bernstein has written in defense of more identity-blocking poetic languages such as those of the Language poets, "absorption / of the poem's ideological imaginary must be / blocked."[23] That is, in confronting the U.S. poet's "artifice of absorption," the reader must *refuse* full absorption into the lyric trope (here), the Emersonian language of sublime transcendence by means of which Atlantic and Pacific spaces and peoples are mastered into ciphers and history into a diary of national (and private) self-empowerment. Simply put, the trauma or "lack" that Emerson is facing is his own professional and class diminishment, as literary scholar and theological heir, in an era of annexation, frontier expansion, mass immigration, industrial takeoff, slavery, and ongoing Indian removal—to mention just a few traumatic issues of his day. Emerson's poetics of the American sublime serve, in part, as his own majestic attempt to maintain illusions of self-mastery ("self-reliance") and democratic autonomy within this "joint-stock company" of a culture, staying at home and conquering his own Pacific, as it were.[24]

We can recall here the way the great novelist Herman Melville, following more skeptically down Emerson's Manifest Destiny expansionist path, turns the American Pacific whale named Moby-Dick into a creature not just of *economic* but of *symbolic* excess and, thus opening the Pacific for American commercial usage, shows the quasi-imperialist danger of such a symbolizing process in the nature-destroying language of Captain Ahab on the transnational whaling ship *Pequod*. Ahab's very ship is named to commemorate the destruction of the Pequot Indians in Connecticut in 1637, which

---

22. Ralph Waldo Emerson, "Self-Reliance," in *Self-Reliance and Other Essays* (New York: Dover, 1993), 29.

23. Charles Bernstein, "Artifice of Absorption," in *A Poetics* (Cambridge, MA: Harvard University Press, 1992), 21.

24. "Performing the immigrant" (immigrant acts of heterotopia or ethnographic self-fashioning, for example) also raises the tricky "postcolonial" ruses for Asian American immigrants of what Kuan-Hsing Chen (see below) has called "diasporic opportunism" as the threat of U.S. professional/class positioning of an elite self as a perpetual "subaltern" of racial exclusion yet class superiority. On Emerson's troubled relationship to the expanding U.S. market and its annexationist policies in Texas and Mexico, see Rob Wilson, "Literary Vocation as Occupational Idealism: The Example of Emerson's 'American Scholar,'" *Cultural Critique* 15 (1990): 83–114.

later led to the wholesale destruction of native peoples. To suggest its imperial globality, interestingly enough as well, this doomed multicultural ship
of American commerce named *Pequod* is also transnationally masted with
pine wood from "double-bolted" and "impenetrable" Japan, "cut somewhere on the coast of Japan, where her original ones were lost overboard in
a gale."[25] A piece of Pacific timber from pre-Perry and Dutch-influenced Japan, that mysterious nation of typhoons, racial phobia, managed ports, and
closed markets. As Melville puts it, via Ishmael's erotically delighting in the
opening of these same sleepy Asian-Pacific markets and "all the millions in
China" (77) to American commerce from Nantucket to Formosa (448) and
Japan, "Penetrating further and further into the heart of the Japanese
[whale] cruising ground, the *Pequod* was all astir in the fishery" (463).

Feminized "oriental" markets, slavishly asleep in centuries of feudal
tyranny, landlocked wealth, and modes of animistic pre-Enlightenment
superstition ("long Chinese ages" of predemocratic speechlessness [467]),
must be liberated for purposes of global commerce and, to be sure, American expansion westward (across the vast Pacific, which Melville maps) to
the mysterious Orient. At times in the text, Melville's pro-imperialist tone
is ominous, foreboding in the past (and read into the present moment of
APEC): "Let America add Mexico to Texas," he writes in chapter 14, praising
the enterprising whalers of Nantucket, "and pile Cuba upon Canada; let
the English overswarm all India, and hang out their blazing banner from
the sun; two thirds of the terraqueous globe are his. For the sea is his; he
owns it, as Emperors own empires; other seaman having bought a right of
way through it. . . . The Nantucker, he alone resides and riots on the sea; he
alone, in Bible language, goes down to it in ships; to and fro ploughing it as
his own special plantation" (77). Melville links and crosses the Pacific as an
oceanic American plantation, and evokes the whale ship as factory via an
international division of labor in which "native American [meaning New
Englander] liberally provides the brains, and the rest of the world as gener-
ously supplying the muscles" (127); such is Melville's ominous vision.

---

25. Herman Melville, *Moby-Dick* (New York: Signet, 1980), 82. In the Persian Gulf War,
the Patriot missile was constructed in the media and by U.S. President George Bush as
an icon of national might, but on closer examination it can be seen (like the *Pequod*) to
be a transnationally constructed and globally manned object. These same Patriot missiles now watch over the peace and security of the Asia-Pacific region, especially in
troubled sites such as South Korea and Taiwan with their unresolved cold war tensions
toward the north.

Disavowing more Spanish or French forms of overt colonialism in the liberal-commercial takeover of the Pacific region, Americans supposedly always come to liberate the frontier and save the peoples from their own worst enemy, themselves.[26]

As such literary passages can remind us, representing Asia-Pacific— not to mention the troubled crossing of the Atlantic Ocean into New World real estate or the "middle passage" into creolized creativity of the "Black Atlantic"—was never just an act of private freedom, but was loaded with imperial overtones, subaltern trauma, and spooky nationalist fervor. For over four hundred years, the "Pacific" region has been a contested construct from various sociohistorical angles, a site of trade, conversion, conquest, and an East-West and center-periphery struggle in which native peoples and sites have been rudely subordinated. As Richard Higgott has remarked, in a useful essay from 1995 in Australia (the early home of APEC) called "APEC: A Skeptical View," "Competing definitions [of 'the Pacific' or, later, 'Asia-Pacific'] are often inclusive or exclusive exercises in the politics of representation."[27] Whose "Asia-Pacific" is a question that always needs to be asked, especially as we enter the uncertain and uneven waters of the New Millennium.

"The sublime" remains an appropriate U.S. trope to represent *sublimated immensity,* not so much of the ocean as such but (in a displaced form of

26. Richard Drinnon summarized the wisdom of Melville to his own generation of empire-building Americans crossing the continent to confront, via Manifest Destiny, the natives of Asia and the Pacific with latter-day Puritanical visions of higher possession: "As the author of *Moby-Dick* well knew, such [frontier writers and explorers] as James Kirke Paulding and Charles Wilkes already had come to regard the Western Sea [the Pacific] as an extension of the American West. Melville had the unsettling gift of seeing that when the metaphysics of Indian-hating hit salt water it more clearly became the metaphysics of empire-building, with the woodsman-become-mariner out there on the farthest wave, in Melville's words, riding 'upon the advance as the Polynesian upon the comb of the surf'" (215). See *Facing West: The Metaphysics of Indian-Hating and Empire Building* (New York: New American Library, 1980).

27. Richard Higgott, "APEC: A Skeptical View," in *Pacific Cooperation,* ed. Andrew Mack and John Ravenhill (Boulder, CO: Westview, 1995), 68. For the foundational contradiction between Euro-American cognitive and commercial mappings of the Pacific region and internal Asian and Pacific forces of settlement and diaspora, see Arif Dirlik, "The Asia-Pacific Idea: Reality and Representation in the Invention of a Regional Structure," *Journal of World History* 3 (1992): 55–79.

desiring) for the transnational free market: sublime immensity, as an image of national self-identity, has haunted American culture from the era of Manifest Destiny and the movement westward across continental vastness, via frontier settlement and Indian dispossession, toward the "illimitable" Asian markets of the Pacific Ocean. The ideology of this American sublime at once suggests some continental vastness of resources in the land and ocean, and a transcendental selfhood and imagined national community, that frees up longings for liberal infinitude and democratic possibilities of freedom, but blocks closure and certitude with the *trauma* of some excess "savagery" that may be lurking at the borderlands or "frontier" and refusing easy representation. This conviction of the American sublime is what the mystical Emerson called in "The Over-soul" and courted as ground of personal (and national) self-identification "an immensity not possessed and that cannot be possessed."[28] The sublime is exactly that U.S. trope used to represent the postcolonial pursuit of global immensity and the vision of expanding markets that now haunts Asia-Pacific as a transnational frontier in which the local, paradoxically, is said to win a newfound share of hegemony, and the traumas of colonial occupation, regional fracturing, and world war will be washed away in the dirty, magical waters of the Pacific.[29]

SOCIAL DARWINISM IN THE ASIA-PACIFIC:
SEA-WOLF TO CYBERSPACE

Caught up in the racialized politics of the Yellow Peril era of imperialism he helped to popularize and invent, Jack London portrayed the American outreach into "the illimitable Pacific" as a space of vast natural resources, international geopolitics, and primordial struggle. The muckraking novelist staged a battle for commercial (and male psychological) possession of this frontierlike space of the Pacific by means of a power-crazed crew of

28. Ralph Waldo Emerson, "The Over-soul," in *Self-Reliance and Other Essays* (New York: Dover, 1993), 53.
29. See Rob Wilson, *American Sublime: The Genealogy of a Poetic Genre* (Madison: University of Wisconsin Press, 1991), for my semi-affirmative critique of this national ideology as it worked itself out in a romanticized cultural form of continental possession. On the "colonialism" of our transnational (and supposedly "postcolonial") era, see Masao Miyoshi, "A Borderless World? From Colonialism to Transnationalism and the Decline of the Nation-State," *Critical Inquiry* 19 (1993): 726–51.

seal hunters in *The Sea-Wolf* (1904). "And north we traveled with it [the great seal herd]," London writes with macho savor for the hunt, "ravaging and destroying, flinging the naked carcasses to the shark and salting down the skins so that they might later adorn the fair shoulders of the women of the cities. It was wanton slaughter, and all for woman's sake. No man ate of the seal meat or the oil."[30] If the Pacific proved to be the origin and end of Jack London as representative U.S. novelist, as the suicidal contradictions and longings for capitalist egress of *Martin Eden* (1909) exposed, this ocean was the "frontier" staging ground for an imperial virility London advocated and embodied in strange, new ways as the "American Kipling" of his era.[31]

London's *Sea-Wolf* is set in 1893 during the Open Door era of imperial annexation as the United States reached out "into the great and lonely Pacific expanse" (29) via an overextended Monroe Doctrine into the peripheral spaces of Hawai'i, Cuba, and the Philippines. In this hyperbolic novel, a seal-hunting schooner named *The Ghost* is commandeered from private yacht into commercial venture by a power-hungry force of imperial virility named Wolf Larsen. As his name suggests, Wolf is a domineering American who rules over lesser moral forces and compels submission of his motley English/Irish/Scandinavian/Pacific islander crew of international outcasts hunting seal skins from San Francisco and the Farillon Islands to Japan. A literary intellectual named Humphrey Van Weyden is forced into "involuntary servitude to Wolf Larsen" (26) as wage-beast laborer after being shipwrecked near the Golden Gate Bridge and bullied by Captain Larsen to undergo physical abuse and slap-punctuated lessons in Darwinian social survival until this scholar emerges into a macho Robin-

---

30. Jack London, *The Sea-Wolf* (New York: Tor, 1993), 128. On the 1941 "classic" Pacific wartime movie of crazed males, *The Sea Wolf*, directed by Michael Curtiz and starring Edward G. Robinson as Wolf Larsen, see Rocco Fumento and Tony Williams, eds., *Jack London's "The Sea Wolf," a Screenplay by Robert Rossen* (Carbondale: Southern Illinois University Press, 1998).

31. See Colleen Lye's superb study of London and related figures in "Model Modernity: Representing the Far East" (Ph.D. diss., Columbia University, 1998); and Donald E. Pease, "*Martin Eden* and the Limits of the Aesthetic Experience," *boundary 2* 25 (1998): 139–60. On London's self-fashioning as an act of market expansion and a form of masculine self-empowerment caught up in U.S. frontier expansions into the Pacific Northwest and Asian markets, see Jonathan Auerbach's (overprivatized) study, *Male Call: Becoming Jack London* (Durham, NC: Duke University Press, 1996), esp. chap. 2, "Between Men of Letters: Homoerotic Agents in *The Sea-Wolf*."

son Crusoe. Van Weyden's toughened ego becomes capable of founding and settling (colonizing in implicit battle with the Japanese in their part of the Pacific) his own island in the Pacific, as he defeats Wolf in the struggle for possession of woman (a shipwrecked poetess named Maud Brewster), ship, and deserted island (Endeavor Island, an "undiscovered" seal rookery waiting to be colonized somewhere between Japan and "the bleak Bering Sea").

Troped into a "terrible sea" (224) of struggle, cruelty, and relentless "awfulness" (29), London's American Pacific is portrayed as a traumatic element of ooze and slime and cold indifference, threatening the ego with domination, abjection, and death like so many seals: "And I was alone, floating apparently in the midst of a gray primordial vastness" (7), Van Weyden screams out like a drowning woman, shipwrecked and unable to swim. The Pacific is the arena of "the sea-wolf," meaning not just Wolf Larsen but all forms of power seeking to dominate or be destroyed on ship, land, or sea.

As "industrial organization gave control" of capital over labor across the region (53), there is already in place a vast "division of labor" (2), London argues, between the strong and the weak, meaning those who can control force and plunder profits and those who submit to such energy and are humiliated, exploited, and devalued by indifferent laws of supply and demand. In such battles, Emersonian self-reliance is counted as "a cipher in the arithmetic of commerce" (53), only later to be resurrected in the Defoe-like circumstances on Endeavor Island, where the American strong self of Van Weyden can assert itself in an "unpeopled" wilderness of seals and ocean. The Pacific region is portrayed, from the perspective of this death-dealing schooner, as a space of seal hunting, murder, mutiny, and plundering, with market endeavors "ranging from opium smuggling into the States and arms smuggling into China to blackbirding and open piracy" (87). "Force, nothing but force obtained on this brute ship" of imperialism (38), Van Weyden realizes, as he is turned from a literary gentleman of idealist pretensions into his nickname of deformed matter, Hump: "I was known by no other name, until the term became a part of my thought processes and I identified it with myself, thought of myself as Hump, as though Hump were I and always had been I" (32). The interpellation of the Pacific space into a symptom of Darwinist identity struggle is all but complete, as London himself came to be known by his predatory nickname, Wolf.

Rewriting Melville's vision of the Asia-Pacific as a space of transcendentalized commodities and romance quest, London enforces a more "brute materialist" vision of the Pacific region with metaphors of desublimated matter drawn from biology and zoology and applied to humanity, society, and the market. Thus, Wolf's vision of human "piggishness" and "the way of the wolf" is naturalized as a primordial struggle to survive via energy and will to domination over the maternal Thing itself: "this yeasty crawling and squirming which is called life" (67). "I believe that life is a mess," Wolf proclaims, and would prove it by becoming animal like pig or wolf, or even more so, becoming yeast: "It is like yeast, a ferment, a thing that moves and may move for a minute, an hour, a year, or a hundred years, but that in the end will cease to move. The big eat the little that they may continue to move, the strong eat the weak that they may obtain their strength. The lucky eat the most and move the longest, that is all" (42). Humphrey Van Weyden has become a battered Hump who realizes, fists and knife drawn, "I was becoming animallike myself, and I snarled in his face so terribly it frightened him back" (72). For London, writing from within the age of Yellow Peril and native overthrow, the Pacific is a region of deformity, brutality, and disease, the national ego moving down on the evolutionary scale toward savagery, force, and virus. As the Cockney cook Tommy Mugridge puts it, "I near died of the scurvy and was rotten with it six months in Barbados. Smallpox in 'Onolulu, two broken legs in Shanghai, pneumonia in Unalaska, three busted ribs an' my insides all twisted in Frisco" (104). Torn between socialist compassion and Nietzschean power visions, the Pacific became the space for projecting London's tensions: a "double Pacific," at once a space where white men regressed into savage beasts and where a paradise of instinct and primordial power could still be found.

In Alexander Besher's "novel of virtual reality" and cyberpunk business-as-usual, *RIM* (1994), the social Darwinism of the transnational capitalist free market, with all its lurid games of macho competition and corporate killing, has gone inward, the Asia-Pacific now internalized into the space-time compression of cyberspace. The year is 2027, and Sartori Corporation (owner of a virtual reality entertainment empire based in a kind of virtual neo-Tokyo inside Tokyo) is embroiled in cutthroat corporate warfare to preserve market share. The Asia-Pacific is the space of the keiretsu wars, white-collar crime and Tibetan mystical quests for the digitalization of consciousness and the discovery of a "new Matrix" frontier being the order of the day. Frank Gobi is the American romance-quest hero (Besher's idealized self-image as "consulting futurist on Pacific Rim Affairs for Global Business Network" in Japan?) trying to save the Japanese corporations from mutual destruction and "data muggings" and to free cyberspace for open libidinal usage.[32] A professor moonlighting as cybernetic Bogart, Gobi teaches a course in "transcultural corporate anthropology and organizational shamanism" at UC Berkeley, now a Tokyo University extension, of course (15). He studies "the business culture that was emerging in the region" and has written an interactive textbook called *TransRim Customs 3.0*.[33]

The scenery in *RIM* is sheer phobic and techno-orientalist Pac Rim (and, elsewhere in cyberspace, Tokyo, and Berkeley, much quasi-orientalist sexuality with Japanese corporate princesses): "Rowdy groups of wealthy Greater Chinese businessmen milled about in front of glitzy Hong Kong–style hotels with atrium lobbies, preparing to head down to the Grant Avenue restaurants in New Chinatown" (65). Hong Kong to San Francisco, Los Angeles to Tokyo: the Pacific Rim has merged into one border-fusing culture of cybernetic capitalism. As he notes an array of "Rim carpetbaggers and keiretsu types," the scenery gets even more ominous, suggesting the reign of gangsterism and warfare in the region: "There were a couple of Greater China arms dealers, noticeable in their sharkskin suits of gray shantung silk. Flaunting jade rings the size of Kowloon and Seiko-Rolexes loaded with the latest Hsinchu Park circuitry on their pudgy wrists, the GCS looked more like rich uncles on holiday than they did merchants of death. . . . One of the North Koreans on board, a traveling salesman from Pyongyang, judging from his Kim Jong Il memorial bouffant hairdo, was already drunk and getting red in the face" (131–32). You get the picture: a kind of neo-orientalism directed against the Greater Chinese and Third World peoples of Asia, while global Japanese and American corporate forces try to outwit each other to control Asia-Pacific cyberspace as a vast market of entertainment and profit.

32. Alexander Besher, *RIM: A Novel of Virtual Reality* (London: Orbit, 1994), 57. On the devious workings of transnational culture and "cultural capital" flowing back and forth across the cybernetic Pacific from Asia to the United States, see David Palumbo-Liu and Hans Ulrich Gumbrecht, eds., *Streams of Cultural Capital: Transnational Cultural Studies* (Stanford: Stanford University Press, 1997).

33. Besher himself is the author of such a business guidebook called *The Pacific Rim Almanac* (New York: Harper Perennial, 1991). On such "Rimspeak" works of corporate business culture, see the cautionary and rich analysis by Christopher Connery (see n. 15 above).

In *RIM*, the Asia-Pacific geography has turned phobic and regressive: the United States and Japan align themselves for domination of the Internet frontier and exclude the "invisible empire" of the Overseas Chinese who practice clannish forms of gangsterism and subterranean capitalism as they belatedly seek to become, as one British journalist of social science puts it, "Lords of the Rim": "Thousands of middle-class Chinese immigrants have returned [from North America] to work in Asia this [back-and-forth across the Pacific] way, earning them the sobriquet 'astronaut,' because they spend so much time in orbit. They have become Overseas Chinese in reverse—living overseas and sojourning in Greater China."[34] Indeed, these Overseas Chinese again threaten to become the masters of Pacific waters and offshore moneys, that space of transnational flows where mobility is everything and secrecy has gone cybernetic; back-and-forth astronauts and opportunists of instability—"financial pointmen of the new age of borderless global capitalism," as Sterling Seagrave puts it with all the loathing (and resentful admiration) this biographer of the Song Family (and KMT machinations) can muster.[35] The vast multitudes of Asia are coming again, this time not from Japan but from "Greater China." They have mastered the latest capitalist technologies and speculative regimes of the West, and their powers to become "Lords of the Rim" are as inscrutable, occult, and sinister as ever.[36]

APEC'S DREAM OF "ASIA-PACIFIC"

Mobilizing a range of ancient energies and new possibilities, "Asia-Pacific" is used in all kinds of ways as signifier. We speak of "Asia-Pacific cuisine"—it's a hit at gourmet restaurants like Roy's in Hawai'i Kai and Indigo in Honolulu, and on menus at the Lai Lai Sheraton in Taipei; and there is an array of "Asia-Pacific" art magazines, architectural symposia,

34. See Sterling Seagrave, *Lords of the Rim* (London: Corgi Books, 1996), 321, who offers a phobic-sublime image of the Overseas Chinese as an "invisible empire" in Asia-Pacific, a globalized community of up to fifty-five million expatriates with $2 trillion in assets and a vast network of influence, favor, and crime.

35. Ibid., 272. On Taiwan as a postwar economy compounded of dynastic intrigue and strategic measures of U.S. anticommunist support via global media like *Time* magazine, see ibid., chap. 17, "The Fall of the House of Chiang."

36. These are the orientalist aspects of the Yellow Peril syndrome that John Dower traces back through prewar American journalism, popular culture, and mass media forms in *War without Mercy*, 162–63.

fashion and interior design spreads, and literary journals to be found from Tokyo and Hong Kong to Los Angeles using the cachet of this term. Cultural styles of "Asia" and "the Pacific" promise to fuse into some expressive hybrid synergy called *Asia-Pacific,* and no harm will be done except to purists of cultural borders or canon-mongers, who refuse to dream fusion (and "shrink the Pacific") over the world's biggest ocean.

More than just stylistic promise or commercial slogan, "Asia-Pacific" serves as a signifier to bespeak the push toward the creation of what is called "an open regionalism." This trope of *Asia evenly yoked to Pacific* is used to mobilize economies in the region, which, without such a signifier, does not yet exist in anything like a coherent framework; spaces and lives inside the creativity of the Pacific are being shaped, coded, and reorganized under this "Asia-Pacific" banner, and this demands critical interrogation.

Started in 1989 during a ministerial meeting in Canberra, APEC serves as the most powerful shape this desire for regional coherence, shared direction, and unity as tied to a narrative of a coprosperity sphere now takes in the Asia-Pacific of the 1990s. Fearing a round of conflict between the USA and Japan and discriminatory arrangements between Europe and North America, APEC came into a kind of slow, ad hoc existence into what one political economist calls a "capitalist archipelago."[37] Uneven and fluid at the core, this disjunctive signifier of "Asia" and "the Pacific" threatens to unhinge concentric East-West binary visions of superpower governance and cold war teleology.[38] At the outset, the United States opposed APEC, but under Clinton, it is a strong promoter of its expanding formation. One of the earliest visionaries of a new post–cold war Pacific was Mikhail Gorbachev (at a speech in Vladivostok in 1986), but history turned otherwise,

37. Bruce Cumings, "Rimspeak; or, The Discourse of the 'Pacific Rim,'" in *What Is in a Rim? Critical Perspectives on the Pacific Region Idea,* ed. Arif Dirlik (Boulder, CO: Westview, 1993), 25. Japanese economists, speaking in international forums at the East-West Center in Hawai'i and other such sites in Australia in the cold war era, had formulated such visions of "economic and cultural cooperation" as early as the 1960s, and Australian and American policy planners in the region long cultivated these broad links to Asia and what came to be called the Pacific Rim.

38. Even as U.S. policies are being disoriented in the region and the East-West Center of knowledge/power is threatened with extinction, to give one example of institutional and conceptual *instability* in the region, an Asia-Pacific Center for Security Studies opened in 1995 in Honolulu, with substantial federal funding.

and Russia has yet to be included in APEC although it has a long Pacific coast and history of entanglement in the region.[39]

As the organizing frameworks for the current use of "Asia-Pacific," as this vision of region is circulated by the economies around the Pacific Rim, APEC refers to the Asia-Pacific Economic Cooperation. Linking North America and Mexico to the export-driven dragons of East Asia, Tokyo, and the Pacific ex-settler states of Australia and New Zealand, APEC was formed to ease trade barriers and to liberalize markets in the region in some kind of consensual, patchy, culture-conscious, quasisystematic way. At this point, though the dollar, yen, and nuclear weapons refuse casual governance, APEC gathers eighteen "economies" for regional forums and policy prodding: Australia, Brunei, Canada, Chile, Mainland China, Hong Kong, Indonesia, Japan, Malaysia, Mexico, New Zealand, Papua New Guinea, the Philippines, Singapore, South Korea, Taiwan, Thailand, and the United States.

If you wondered what "Asia-Pacific" means and what ingredients are to be included, this is *one* way of defining the will to regional unity. The user-friendly identity term used to describe these diverse APEC players—as so many loose "economies" linked around and within the Pacific Ocean—suggests a de facto way of overriding problems and bypassing political tensions without resolving them in such a market-driven forum. Imagined into shape by some user-friendly trope of Pacific "community," APEC would fuse disparate units small and large, from city-states, superpowers, and Third World entities, into a vision of coherence, teleological optimism, and regional "cooperation." This vision of "Asia-Pacific" is premised on some commitment to the mandates of free market capitalism and a vague sense of Asian-Pacific cultural heritage and the allure of a "Pacific Century" destiny.

Under the postorientalist regionalism of "Asia-Pacific," the complex Chinese polities of Taiwan, Hong Kong, Singapore, and Mainland China can talk. Big and small assume symbolic equivalence around the bargaining table, players smiling with President Clinton and President Ramos in Asian-Pacific shirts at the same photo sessions. *Pacific regionality* here suggests some postpolitical cultural bonding, or at least underlying geographical linkage, that can network across the politics of Asia-Pacific. As

---

39. See text of speech by Gorbachev in Vladivostok, 28 July 1986, reprinted in *The Soviet Union as an Asian Pacific Power,* ed. Ramesh Thakar and Carlyle Thayer (Boulder, CO: Westview, 1987), 223.

this trope of community would have it, colonial history, world wars, and cold war trauma may be washed away in this Asia-Pacific. "Everything flows toward the Pacific, no time for anything to sink, all is swept along," is how Marguerite Duras uncannily describes this quality of Pacific waters to dissolve the traumatic past of colonial memory and to loosen capitalist class suffering (in her case, growing up semipoor and white in French colonial Indochina) into some perpetually flowing oceanic present where the spirit of optimism might be renewed and memories of war and poverty dissolved in these (seemingly) postimperial waters.[40] Colonialism, imprisonment, and internment apparently can be erased in the magical waters of the Pacific Ocean.[41]

In the skeptical (if somewhat schizophrenic) words of Malaysian scholar-activist Chandra Muzzafar, which still resonate today for lesser powers (connected to ASEAN) in the region that fear U.S. encroachment on their common ("Asian") identity: "As a concept, 'Asia-Pacific' makes little sense. Unlike East Asia or South Asia or Southeast Asia, it has no shared history or common cultural traits. Asia-Pacific is not even an accepted geographical entity. The U.S. has vast economic ties with Europe but is not part of the European Community which jealously protects its historical, cultural and political identity. Similarly, Japan is deeply involved in the U.S. economy but it is not part of the North American Free Trade Agreement. It is only in the case of Asia, more specifically East Asia, that there is a concerted attempt to suppress its common identity and thwart its legitimate quest for a common identity."[42]

On the other hand, to invoke the postnational vision of Kenichi Ohmae,

40. Marguerite Duras, *The Lover*, trans. Barbara Bray (New York: Harper, 1992), 22. The globally successful novel/movie by Duras, *Hiroshima Mon Amour*, tries to figure this new post-Hiroshima utopia in the troubled love-match of the Japanese journalist and the French nurse who cannot forget the traumas of world war and the cold war legacies of military and nuclear terror.

41. Another such romantic dreamer of this posttraumatic Pacific is the American banker wrongly accused of murder in the Stephen King–based movie, *The Shawshank Redemption* (1994), played by Tim Robbins. He longs to escape the Maine prison where he has been placed for a life sentence and get down to a little blue hotel by the Pacific where he can finally forget the brutal humiliations, capitalist crimes, and hellish degradation he has been through in prison: *"This ocean, as the Mexicans say, it has no memory."*

42. Chandra Muzzafar, "APEC Serves Interests of U.S. More than Others," *New Strait Times*, 29 July 1993, 13; quoted in Higgott, "APEC: A Skeptical View," 91.

who argues for a new and expansive "borderless" regional order, "Nation-states are eroding as economic actors, [then] region-states [such as Taiwan, Guangdong, and Singapore] are taking shape," which now recognize link-ages with the global economy.[43] To survive, he says, these entities of bor-derless capitalism must "put global logic first" to interact locally and thrive globally: places of Asia-Pacific identity must retool their industry and re-shape their conceptual and social geography to fit the contours of this transnational push. In Ohmae's trilateral (Japan/USA/Europe) arrange-ment of the "borderless economy," to meet the mandates of globalized production, it is no longer the nation-state but the "region-state" that becomes the agent of political-economic change.

At least in today's liberal-popular vision of the inter-Asia Pacific, APEC is the most broadly circulated framework for this restructuring move toward open borders and social interlinkage.[44] Formed in the shadow of global capitalism, APEC's vision of the "Asia-Pacific" is, in truth, *culturally and politically naïve,* ignoring, bypassing, or suppressing the cultural complex-ity, historical issues, and symbolic profusion of the region in order to form this regional identity. One Filipina scholar has described the "Pacific com-munity" idea as "a baby whose putative parents are American and Japa-nese and whose midwife is Australian."[45] This kind of *regionalism* can be as dangerous as nationalist interpellation, even if taking place at a higher (and more sublimated) level in which the absent others in relation to which APEC is forging its identity (such as the economies and cultures of Southeast Asia and the Pacific islands) are silenced and bypassed. Kuan-Hsing Chen has warned about this will to Asia-as-region (whether under a Japanese or Chinese banner) in the forum Multiculturalism and Multi-lingualism—Critical Limits of the Nation-State held in Kyoto in July 1996:

43. Kenichi Ohmae, "Putting Global Logic First," *Harvard Business Review* 73 (1995): 125.
44. Portraying various versions of local and global regionality in the Pacific, Richard A. Herr notes the shift from decolonizing visions of Pacific islands regionalism to those today which are more transnationally driven: "The emerging international order is likely to propel the islands towards further engagement with the rest of the world, particularly the countries of the Pacific rim" (298). See "Regionalism and Nationalism," in *Tides of History: The Pacific Islands in the Twentieth Century,* ed. K. R. Howe, Robert C. Kiste, and Brij V. Lal (Honolulu: University of Hawai'i Press, 1994), 283–99.
45. Purification Valera-Quisumbing, "Towards an 'Asia-Pacific Community': Varying Perceptions," in *The Pacific Lake: Philippine Perspectives on a Pacific Community,* ed. Jose E. Leviste Jr. (Manila: Philippine Council for Foreign Relations, 1986), 81.

"One has to be extremely careful with the celebrating side of regionalism; the imperialist 'Greater East Asia Co-Prosperity Sphere' project launched in the 1930's was able to operate precisely under the name of regionalism."[46] If in this era of global culture, as Milan Kundera put it, the European is "one who is nostalgic for Europe," the Asian as well may be one who is nostalgic for Asia as a civilizational and cultural unity.[47]

The assumption of some Asia-Pacific regional unity is, after all, the invention and construct of those globalizing powers who stand to benefit most by the borderless circulation of peoples, goods, and symbols within its framework.[48] As a multicultural fate in more localized senses, the "Asia-Pacific" imagined by authors as diverse as Melville and Epeli Hau'ofa, Maxine Hong Kingston and Patricia Grace, Haunani-Kay Trask and Ang Lee, John Dominis Holt and Vilsoni Hereniko, Kenzaburo Oe and Lois-Ann Yamanaka remains a riddle and a maze, a rim and a charm, a struggle and a curse, both dream and slime, an ocean with ancient contents and cyborgian futures all cast into one strange regional poetic. It seems offensive to bring together so many cultural constructions under the same frame, "Asia-Pacific." For this *transnational* commitment of APEC's vision of "Asian-Pacific" unity reveals the future in which cultural and literary studies will take place in the Pacific. If disorganized by the flux, we must come to terms with this reconfigured situation in which nations and localities are coming unglued at local and global levels.[49] The one-way gaze

---

46. Kuan-Hsing Chen, "Multiculturalism or Neo-Colonial Racism?", *Ritsumeikan Linguistics and Cultural Research Journal* (spring 1997): 373. In this respect, see John Dower's exemplary discussion of racial and economic exploitation of Asia by Japan, "Global Policy with the Yamato Race as Nucleus," in *War without Mercy*, 262–90. In Yellow Peril discourse propagated by Jack London et al., "Orientals" are feared for their military-industrial potential challenging the West (Japan), their inscrutable antidiscursive mystique and kung fu ways (China), as well as vast laboring hordes threatening white labor and national purity (India, China, Korea).

47. Milan Kundera, *The Art of the Novel* (New York: Harper and Row, 1988), 128.

48. *Globalization* of the local into some higher-level regional configuration has become the mandate of the transnational cultural critic/class tracking transcultural cash in supple ways, as the news reeks of identity politics, racial violence, ethnic strife, religious antagonism, and gender suppression, not to mention structural imbalances of labor and profit all along the "global assembly line" from New Jersey to Manila.

49. For a related discussion of what cultural studies might begin to look like inside APEC in places such as Hawai'i, Hong Kong, and Taiwan, see Rob Wilson, "Towards an 'Asia/Pacific Cultural Studies': Literature, Cultural Identity, and Struggle in the Ameri-

and "the whole catalogue of colonial platitudes" that propped up and mapped the region (as did the British in "meretricious" Hong Kong, for example) are no longer adequate to the scene.[50]

Perhaps postcommunist Yugoslavia is a worst-case scenario for subnational fragmentation into ethnic heteroglossia and disidentification at this time.[51] And yet, in the Asian/Pacific Rim hub city of Los Angeles alone, city schools are already four-fifths nonwhite (with Mexican, Korean, Vietnamese, Samoan, Chinese, El Salvadoran, Filipino, Iranian, and others) and must teach kids who speak something like 150 different native languages inside deteriorating conditions of economic polarization, lost promise, racial backlash, lean-and-mean budgeting in which more money is going to build state prisons than to universities, and conditions of postindustrial deskilling.[52] Perhaps this is *not* what APEC intends to mean by its trope of Asian-Pacific peoples' "working together" inside some late-capitalist eternity of "Asian-Pacific cooperation"?

Isn't "the Asia-Pacific" emanating from the Pacific Rim tigers and Japan/U.S. superpowers just a more loosely hegemonic vision of the region taking shape along the following lines: *too much Asian dynamism unevenly hyphened together with too little Pacific content to beat the world system?*

I bring up these *extraliterary* matters haunting APEC's "imagined community" because, if there is to be an Asia-Pacific signifier worthy of its peoples, symbolic heritages, and cultures, then one of the tasks for such a cultural poetics is to challenge and critique these liberal master formations of the Pacific region. Cultural criticism needs to locate such stories and

can Pacific," *Studies in Language and Literature* 7 (August 1996): 1–18, a journal of National Taiwan University. On a localist/nationalist note, also see Ross Gibson, *South of the West: Postcolonialism and the Narrative Construction of Australia* (Bloomington: Indiana University Press, 1992).

50. See Richard Mason, *The World of Suzie Wong* (1957; Hong Kong: Pegasus Books, 1994), 188–89, who was at least able to risk miscegenation and an affirmative portrait of Eurasian offspring, despite his overall allegorizing of Hong Kong as a spunky, meretricious prostitute who remained occult and innocent despite her violations by sailors and an array of neurotic businessmen from China, England, America, and Australia.

51. See Arjun Appadurai on what he calls "the Bosnia fallacy" of reducing such ethnic and nationalist conflicts to "primordial" or "tribal" antagonisms immune to modernization, in *Modernity at Large* (Minneapolis: University of Minnesota Press, 1986), 21. He credits the American mass media with such misreadings.

52. Richard Walker, "California Rages against the Dying of the Light," *New Left Review* 209 (1995): 42–74.

master tropes within history, pushing to unmask and expose the contradictions of such representations: "Asia-Pacific" as a unified, user-friendly, antisocialist, and seamless region where the culture of global capitalism will come home to roost.[53] While contemporary cultural studies works to provide genealogies and critiques of dominant cultural forms and social frameworks of locality and national identity, propped up as they often are by literary canons and the spread of academic discourses such as that of postcoloniality, it can also study these competing traditions and put them in critical dialogue in the present rather than keeping them apart or confined to the past.

More positively considered, the invention of an "Asia-Pacific"-based poetics demands border crossing, conceptual outreach, nomadic linkages, and interdisciplinary originality; its birth at this moment is mired in cultural politics and the global political economy. Much needs to be done to intervene as well in contexts and genres that dominate the airwaves with APEC-like stories and Pacific Rising images: media events, international forums, daily journalism, and so on, nurturing alternative spheres and counternarratives inside public culture. We can begin articulating a "critical regionalism" in the Asia-Pacific region, respectful of Asian and Pacific heritages, diasporas, and communities but wary of hegemonic designs on these diverse localities and groupings, as well as begin interlinking globally these local struggles.[54]

53. Asian-Pacific cultural studies needs to nurture, support, and teach the literatures and narratives of those less powerful and subordinated in the region, I would urge, whose complex claims on the *Pacific* (many of whose contemporary works are written not in indigenous languages but in World English) and *Asia* (which, as we all, except for Samuel Huntington, know was not and will never be a *single* Confucian "Orient") have too long been tokenized or ignored in the interests of settler peoples and *their* nation-state.

54. On the forging of a locally situated yet globally interconnected cultural studies as critical knowledge formation, see the powerful and situated analysis of Kuan-Hsing Chen, "Voices from the Outside: Towards a New Internationalist Localism," *Cultural Studies* 6 (1992): 476–84; and "Positioning *positions:* A New Internationalist Localism of Cultural Studies," *positions* 2 (1994): 680–710. On the intensifying formation of Asia-Pacific networks wherein Britain and Europe are hardly as important as "East-West" binaries once implied, see Jon Stratton and Ien Ang, "On the Impossibility of a Global Cultural Studies: 'British' Cultural Studies in an 'International' Frame," in *Stuart Hall: Critical Dialogues in Cultural Studies,* ed. Kuan-Hsing Chen and David Morley (London: Routledge, 1996), 361–91.

The meaning of "Asia-Pacific" has to be struggled for in specific cultural locations and institutional settings. For definitions of "Asia-Pacific" will mean different things to rival nations, racial and gender groupings, and hegemonic class agents. Global dreams of the Pacific region must be situated to bring out their contradictory social meaning, bringing them down to earth and cultural politics, placing master narratives of the local and small in their social communities, nearer to what Maxine Hong Kingston once called "those little stories of Chinese culture you learn from your mother."

On his way from Washington to the APEC meeting in Manila in 1996, where he would be greeted with "APEC Go Home" and "Say No to APEC" protest signs, U.S. president Bill Clinton stopped in Hawai'i to play some golf, rest, and prepare for the trip through what his policy planners now call "Asia-Pacific." Why stop in multicultural Hawai'i? "Because he wanted to see what APEC people look like!" At least that is what Seiji Naiya told listeners to ICRT (International Community Radio of Taipei) on 28 May 1997 as he accompanied Governor Cayetano on his passports-for-dollars mission to Taiwan. "Hawai'i is a real Asia-Pacific state," an important "linking place between North American markets and the large Asian-Pacific markets," Naiya added, with all the wonder and missionary zeal of a Columbus or Balboa in the New World–Pacific.

Yes, Come all ye transnational citizens to the magical new waters of Asia-Pacific! You'll like it there; in fact, you are already there working the territory inside the heart of Asia-Pacific, so let us now begin to describe, critique, and analyze what it is as "region," or better yet, imagine what it could be as a different, nonimperialist future.[55]

TAIWAN'S ASIAN-PACIFIC IMAGINARY

Underspecified and full of utopic longing for regional power, "Asia-Pacific" has already become a code term for internationalization in the

55. During the 14–16 November 1997 meeting of APEC in Vancouver—at which point Russia, Chile, and Vietnam were added to the expanding roster of APEC players in the Pacific—the indigenous peoples of the Pacific issued a "Pacific Peoples Declaration on APEC" (representing twelve nation states, sixteen First Nations, and over fifty organizations present) resisting and eloquently countering policies of "trade liberalization and other mechanisms for economic globalization" in the region as "undemocratic," disadvantaging to many, dislocating, as well as culturally and environmentally damaging. In short, the statement goes, "APEC is not viable for Pacific Peoples."

transnational era. Used with a mobile liquidity that befits its oceanic origins, *Asia-Pacific* serves as an organizing frame to marshal the global dreams and local tensions of regional centers such as Taiwan into a dynamic trope refiguring the political economy in inventive ways.

The complex "Asia-Pacific" locality of Taiwan looks at once forward to the high-tech and culturally commodified market of Japan and backward to its own primordial Pacific inhabitants whose languages and tribal visions make new claims on the Han-based nation that emerged in differential defiance. In this sense it is truly *Asia-Pacific* in its tension and ties to Asia and the Pacific, torn between Hong Kong and Tokyo and Beijing and Washington, as well as called back by the conjuring of primordial memories older than the modes of urban modernity and the nation-state the KMT represented as collective common sense to its tribal inhabitants from mountain and sea.

From my own informal survey of the *China Post* and *China News* in the spring of 1995 and 1997, it is clear that "Asia-Pacific" is a frequently used signifier to express Taiwan's regional insertion in a furiously globalizing economy, although what it means seems to my Americanized ears *peculiar.* "Asia-Pacific" means the transnational capitalist culture of Asia for the most part, and dominantly Hong Kong and Southern China, perhaps Japan; but there is no mention of any internal or island Pacific country or location, and the USA seems to figure only as one huge export zone.[56]

"Asia-Pacific" is a much-used term in Taiwan and serves as a key organizing signifier for this borderless regionality, evoking the Pacific Rim location of Taiwan as some kind of hub or center of fluid spatiality, a region open to transnational flux and to local linkages. Exemplary of the Asia-Pacific dynamics constructing and reforming the Pacific Rim, Taiwan is

---

56. The slogan "Go South," used by President Lee Teng-hui's Taiwan government to mobilize and diversify investment strategies (in places such as Vietnam, where Taiwan leads foreign developers), takes on credible weight as an unfulfilled linkage with the other Pacific and not just the migrant labor of the Philippines. This focus on "North/South" dynamics thus can have disturbing potential and help to unhinge the often deceptive "East/West" colonial binary imagination. This is the complex terrain an emerging Asian-Pacific cultural studies must help to figure. Taiwan's "Go South" strategy was of course a way to divert investment from Mainland China, where Taiwan investors have poured some U.S.$30 billion in the past decade. It can be linked, as well, to a push toward economic (and political) independence in the long run, and this is also a threat to imperial imaginings of the region as a Chinese-bound coprosperity sphere.

envisioned (by political policy and in its own English press) as a regional hub of Asia-Pacific transport, business, media, and exchange. Liberalization and increased deregulation in the 1990s have led to a freer flow of goods and people into and out of the island, which competes with more established business hubs such as Hong Kong and Singapore for regional primacy as "Asia-Pacific center" of exchange.[57]

Island of complicated locality, caught between discourses of the fake and the essential, Taiwan remains an Asian-Pacific space of unresolved ambiguities, part nation, part "Asian-Pacific" region of transnationalization, part Chinese province; some have even called it the fifty-first U.S. state. The complicated name game of fixing/slashing together identity—is it independent and sovereign Taiwan, "the Republic of China in Taiwan," Formosa, or some other new compound signifier?—has crucial consequences for international, national, and local domains and for how the "Asia-Pacific" region will be imagined and installed at the everyday level.

This "Taiwan" of Asian-Pacific longings remains an *unstable* entity situated flexibly ("ambivalently," as they say) among region, nation, locality, and what the Mainland Chinese regard rather ominously as "renegade province" of the Rim. The undefinedness, fluidity, and multiplicity may be, at this point in the unstable global economy, an advantage.

SHRINKING THE PACIFIC IN TAIPEI: UNLOVABLE, CHINESE-MONUMENTAL, MULTILINGUAL, GLOBAL/LOCAL TAIPEI

The brief period of Taipei's existence [moving "from colonial backwater to world city"] has created a remarkably rich diversity of architectural styles and features. . . . the architectural mix of Taipei has been subject to frequent derision. For example, [Michael] Herr ["Taipei: Wicked Cities of the World," *Holiday* 43 (1968)] has opined that "no matter how you come to love Taipei, you will never think of it as beautiful." W. Glenn ["Growing Like Topsy," *Far Eastern Economic Review* 61 (1968)] has disdainfully referred to the built landscape as a "mongrelizing." He cites the negative

---

57. The regional context is suggested in the following news item on APROC within APEC: "The 'Asia-Pacific Regional Operations Center [APROC] Coordination and Service Office' officially opened its doors amid fanfare yesterday, marking a major step towards developing Taiwan into a major regional hub for multinational corporations," especially as "other hubs in the region [Hong Kong facing 1997, Singapore after the Barings fiasco] are losing their charm to foreign investors" (*China Post*, 7 March 1995).

aspects of Taipei's environment: its hills are too far off, it has no port, no spacious parks, and few imposing buildings.

—Roger Mark Selya, *Taipei*

Many accounts of the city point out that Hong Kong does not look very different from other Asian cities with its indiscriminate mix of drab and grandiose buildings. However, all we have to do is compare Hong Kong with a city like Taipei, which is quite as affluent, to see the difference. Taipei also displays a mixture of architectural styles, but the overall feeling is not quite the same. One of Taiwan's strongest claims to political legitimacy has always been to present itself as the true custodian of "Chinese culture." As a result, there is a kind of hesitancy in its employment of contemporary architecture forms, which stems from the implicit ideological interference of its image of Chinese identity. Hong Kong has neither a fixed identity nor the inhibitions that come from it. . . . The Chiang-Kai-shek cultural complex is a pastiche of Chinese architectural styles, while the Hong Kong cultural center is committed to contemporaneity.

—Ackbar Abbas, *Hong Kong: Culture and the Politics of Disappearance*

Taipei, the magic postnational center where all roads lead and crisscross: a maze of unlicensed buildings, unregulated traffic, hazardous sidewalks, unsightly this and unruly that, but alive with the energies of construction and labor, impure mixtures of languages, speeds, messages. Beyond zoning, beyond rules, postmodern if not postcolonial Taipei swarms and creeps, amalgamates, grungy and grimy and full of signs and textures, mixes business and pleasure, life and cash: this neosublime of mixed commercial-residential uses makes Tokyo and Seoul seem as tame as Hilo. There's that ICRT radio ad for Pacific Rim survival (partly in English and partly in Mandarin) when it's summer in the city: "It's gridlock in Taipei. Oh no, I have another headache. Take Bufferin!"

As a space of flows and textures perpetually under construction and increasingly open to the creative forces of democratization in fluid new ways, Taipei, to zoom in on this urban maze of off-the-shelf vitality, barrages the senses of the visitor as an impure, dynamic, and unevenly interwoven mixture of the traditional and modern, postmodern and primitive, high-tech and agrarian residual.[58] As a fate of transnational and local

58. To register a negative evaluation of same, from an international and local viewpoint: "Taipei, according to some people, is the least inviting city in Southeast Asia, if not the

intermixture, Taipei incarnates all the expressive synergy of the global meeting the local, meaning the unstable global/local dialectic. Thus, there is cultural substance to the claim of an English-language FM station in Taipei, "Here's your chance to think globally, while you tune in locally to ICRT, and find out what's really hot on a global scale!"

Pacific Rim hub of globalized/localized contact and mishmash fertility, the "global city" that is Taipei confronts the contemporary as a space of uneven modernity, uneven sidewalks of odd materials, overloaded textures of ceramic and textuality, where well-gentrified streets collide into Third World hovels, the clash of cultural capital and sheer trash and industrial grunge, "pigsty" to some Germans—modernity, premodernity, postmodernity all at once in some collage not clearly accountable to the colonial-to-transnational "global city" paradigm set up (on the London/New Delhi axis of European core/Asian periphery) by Anthony King, though the Japanese colonial legacy of built forms, bureaucratic infrastructure, and class-divided spaces is there as spatial palimpsest.[59]

Taipei floats along the Pacific Rim as a place of work, under construction, embodying a fetching swarm and maze of interconnected neighborhoods and Chinatowns not just made for sightseeing. The motorbikes stopping, starting, swerving, nearly colliding, accelerating at their own interactive unregulated rhythm track the nerves of this Pacific Rim city. As mentioned, from certain European angles of urban vision, Taipei has been described as "the pigsty" of East Asia, scorned and derided despite its

---

world. It is filthy, chaotic, and the argument says, like a huge garbage dump with its 2.7 million residents breathing seriously polluted air, and drinking contaminated water. . . . The city has been described as a 'pigsty' by the German magazine *Der Spiegel*" (*China Post*, editorial, "Make Taipei Livable Again," 14 February 1995).

59. Anthony D. King, *Global Cities* (London: Routledge, 1990). As King remarks of such imperial-to-global spaces of cosmopolitan mixture, "All cities today are 'world cities'" (82), but not all of them like their new face where global capital meets and defaces the textures of the local-nation, where some sense of cultural identity had been constructed in the pores of empires and global flows. On imperial Japanese construction of China and Taiwan as postmodern and nonwhite primitive spaces, see Leo Ching, "Yellow Skins, White Masks: Race, Class, and Identification in Japanese Colonial Discourse," in *Trajectories: Inter-Asia Cultural Studies,* ed. Kuan-hsing Chen et al. (London: Routledge, 1998), 65–86. As Chen warns in his introduction on "The Decolonization Question," if wary of neoimperialism in the region by financial superpowers of transnational outreach, we have to resist surrendering "the power of geographical imagination to the super sates" such as the regionalization project of APEC (5).

buildings of Mainland-like imperial grandeur, its sweepingly situated grand memorials and vista-strong hotels (the Grand Hotel still has the best urban feng shui overlooking the urban landscape of Taipei as it spreads outward, with cloudy rivers in front and green mountains in back), all somehow invoking the physical monumentality of the Mainland and its courtly sublime. You may get disoriented in Taiwan, but when you do you will know you are lost and turned around in an ever porous region of "Asia-Pacific," where space is shrunken and diverse cultures collide, as borders are flung open to the future of creativity and risk.[60]

60. Linkage between Taiwan and peoples of Asia/Pacific may not be all that capricious or merely postmodern. Recent high-powered DNA research suggests that ancestors of New Zealand's Maori and other Polynesian peoples (e.g., the Hawaiians) came from China, specifically from Taiwan: "The DNA study [of Geoffrey Chambers at Victoria University] shows that, starting from Taiwan, they island-hopped their way through the Philippines and Indonesia to West Polynesia, on into the islands of East Polynesia and then to New Zealand." Maori oral mythologies identify Hawai'i (Hawaiki in Maori) as the Pacific home from which ancestors of New Zealand Maori set out on seafaring voyages of discovery and migration to Aotearoa. Here are the makings of a diasporic, interactive, and inventive Asia/Pacific of precolonial origins and native feats of Pacific crossing. See "DNA Tests Trace Polynesians to China Origins," *Honolulu Advertiser,* 11 August 1998, A1. On the plight of Taiwan's Pacific "mountain people" and "ocean people" within the KMT Chinese nationalist hegemony, see Fred Yen Liang Chiu, "From the Politics of Identity to an Alternative Cultural Politics: On Taiwan Primordial Inhabitants' A-systematic Movement," in *Asia/Pacific as Space of Cultural Production,* ed. Rob Wilson and Arif Dirlik (Durham, NC: Duke University Press, 1995), 120–46. On the conflicted nationalisms of Taiwan, see Marshall Johnson, "Making Time: Historical Preservation and the Space of Nationality," *positions* 2 (1994): 178–249; and on diasporic linkages and opportunistic breaks of "Greater China" across the postcolonial Pacific, see Aihwa Ong and Donald Nonini, eds., *Ungrounded Empires: The Cultural Politics of Modern Chinese Transnationalism* (New York: Routledge, 1997).

CHAPTER 2

U.S. Trajectories into Hawai'i and the Pacific:

Imperial Mappings, Postcolonial Contestations

It [Kokovoko] is not down in any map; true places never are.
— Ishmael on Queequeg's Pacific birthplace, in *Moby-Dick*

Water-carriage . . . opens the whole world for a market.
— Adam Smith, *The Wealth of Nations*

More often than not cartographers leave Tiko out of their charts altogether because they can't be bothered looking for a dot sufficiently small to represent it faithfully and at the same time big enough to be seen without the aid of a microscope.
— Epeli Hau'ofa, *Tales of the Tikongs*

Object of mythic allure and regional projection as situated between vast lands of Asia and the Americas, indeed the Pacific Ocean covers one third of the earth's surface and, in physical scale alone, comprises seventy million square miles. Within what is often called (in a bad metaphor) the Pacific Basin, hundreds of island cultures and disparate polities lie scattered across the archipelagoes of Polynesia, Micronesia, and Melanesia and comprise the raw materials of what one of the first postwar theorists of Pacific regionalism, Kiyoshi Kojima, calls "a vast area with seemingly unlimited potential for economic development."[1] As the uneven meta-

1. Kiyoshi Kojima, "Economic Cooperation in a Pacific Community," in *Building a Pacific Community: The Addresses and Papers of the Pacific Community Lecture Series*, ed. Paul F. Hooper (Honolulu: East-West Center, 1982), 27. Regarded as a key economic regionalist, Kojima began to form his vision of an interdependent "Pacific Community"

geography of the "Pacific Rim" or the no less fabled "Oceania," this region ranges from the Bering Straits of Alaska to Antarctica, from California and British Columbia to Japan and China, from Tasmania to Southeast Asia and from Indonesia to Chile, though Latin America (which figured prominently in the formation of the early-modern Pacific, via the galleon trade between Mexico and Peru to Manila) is mostly ignored today as crucial Pacific agent.[2]

Since the early sixteenth century when European ships first crossed this vast space of precapitalist bounty/depravity in the Pacific Ocean, until the late nineteenth century when "the wealth of nations" had expanded into and territorialized its diverse cultural polities and places into what Adam Smith called the "whole world for a market," waves of Spanish, Portuguese, Dutch, British, French, German, Russian, and American explorers, missionaries, naval powers, and commercial interests traversed and sought to name, construct, and, in a word, claim for distant nations this vast and unruly region coined "Oceania" by Western geographers (and now used in very different ways, in a tactic writing back to Empire, by Pacific island authors such as Epeli Hau'ofa).[3] By the use of Europe-

---

at the East-West Center in 1964, and the idea received broader Japanese and international support through the Pacific Trade and Development Conference held in Tokyo in January 1968. For a local challenge to this framing, see Ratu Kamisese K. T. Mara's rejoinder based on Fijian traditions, "Building a Pacific Community," 38–48, in the same volume.

2. For an important and richly situated attempt to see Cuba and Latin America more generally as entangled in U.S. foreign policies toward Asia and the Pacific, as these have hampered and bypassed long-held ties to the West Indies, see Roberto Fernández Retamar, "The Enormity of Cuba," *boundary 2* 23 (1996): 165–90, who is partly responding to the work of the *boundary 2* collective to comprise a critical response to the U.S. version of "Asia/Pacific."

3. According to Martin W. Lewis and Karen Wigen, "Oceania" as a geographic container did not fully come into cartographic existence until French geographers, such as M. Malte-Brun in 1827, detached the insular realm of Southeast Asia from the Asian mainland and appended it to Oceania as some vast oceanic region anchored by Australia and forming a fifth portion of the world. See *The Myth of Continents: A Critique of Metageography* (Berkeley: University of California Press, 1997), 219 n. 71. "Oceania" thus came into being, as a European and Australian category of regional linkage, when "a set of incipient world regional categories developed in the Renaissance was largely

centered maps and chronometers linking "East" and "West," as well as other cultural technologies of representation, the Pacific was measured into sites and grids that allowed enterprise to fill in the blanks and integrate the island real estate of primordial belonging for other uses.

In O. H. K. Spate's summary of this imperial-era geography, "the greatest blank on the map became a nexus of global commercial and strategic relations."[4] Filled with Asian and Pacific motions, cultures, and "complex exchange networks" that traversed this region for centuries, "the Pacific" (as a region) was a Euro-American formation that had solidified into scientific cartography after the Polynesian voyages of Louis Antoine de Bougainville and Captain James Cook between 1768 and 1779 to serve the economic and national interests of London, Paris, Madrid, and Washington.[5]

No such cartography is total, of course, and there were always lines of flight, resistance, and countermappings bespeaking the indigenous and local cultures and quasitribal nations as these sought to voice precolonial namings and affirm distinct metaphorics of a place-based imagination. Still, from the Romantic era when Bougainville troped Tahiti into France's island of Nouvelle Cythère as a Venus of pristine beauty and erotic aboriginality, the island (typically troped as willing woman) was rising up from slimy, magical waters of the French Pacific to learn Catholicism, be painted, decked out, and troped (as, later, in Gauguin), and sip cognac. Western capital and affiliated forms of cultural capital and media icons tracked back and forth from Europe, as the vast Pacific willy-nilly emerged into Adam Smith's nexus of water-carriage and (later, in the age of expansionist anthropology) Malinowski's laboratory of cultural and eth-

---

displaced by political mapping in the era of European colonization," which the U.S. Pacific explorations and belated settlements in the age of Melville and Twain are heir to (162).

4. O. H. K. Spate, *The Spanish Lake* (Minneapolis: University of Minnesota Press, 1979), ix.

5. On cultural identity as place-bound yet interactive, see Jocelyn Linnekin and Lin Poyer, eds., *Cultural Identity and Ethnicity in the Pacific* (Honolulu: University of Hawai'i Press, 1990), 1. In *Paradise Found and Lost: The Pacific since Magellan* (Minnesota: Minneapolis University Press, 1988), O. H. K. Spate summarizes the formation of the modern Pacific: "The [Euro-American] outsiders named the Ocean, gave it bounds, and in a not trivial sense 'the Pacific' as a concept is a Euro-American artifact. But it was not just 'made in Europe'; the local materials were not inert" (211).

nographic speculation on the origins of primitive cultures and savage otherness.[6]

Motivated by fantasies ranging from visions of vast oriental markets and labor hordes to longings for an earthly paradise of eros, Western representations and economic projections of "the Pacific" as a region took control, at times, over more local conceptions and, in many respects, helped to shape the way these very regions and cultures thought about their own subordinated role within the world system. As the "South Seas" became locked into the big "Pacific," "Asian and Pacific societies provided the building blocks" of this new cartographic structure, as Arif Dirlik has starkly argued, "and the globalized interests of Euro-American powers provided the principles of organization."[7] From the matter-of-factual diaries of Captain Cook as British marine absorbing "Indian" customs in the Sandwich Islands, to the cinemascope Bali Hai in *South Pacific,* tropes and narrative compacts of the occidental imagination could take fleshly embodiment and play themselves out, grandly or ridiculously, in "fatal embrace" with these myriad cultures of Oceania.[8]

What Native Hawaiians had long called, for example, with a virtually aesthetic respect for cosmic space that extended local and native namings and myths into specific terrains of their myriad gods, "the dark blue-purple sea of Kāne" (*kai poplohua mea a Kāne*),[9] was to be reconfigured,

6. On the mixed motives and often lurid and self-interested tactics of this "becoming Pacific Man" quest, see James Clifford, "The *Mahu* Goes Native: Sexist or Subversive? Gauguin's South Seas Visions and Renegade Hybrid Style," *Times Literary Supplement,* 7 November 1997, 3–4, based on the study by Stephen F. Eisenman, *Gauguin's Skirt* (London: Thames and Hudson, 1997). On the colonial discourse of Pacific sites and peoples, see Rod Edmond, *Representing the South Pacific: Colonial Discourse from Cook to Gauguin* (Cambridge: Cambridge University Press, 1997), which, though helpful on authors such as Stevenson and London "going Native," all but ignores the ongoing cultural productivity (and, yes, literature) of the Pacific peoples themselves as "auto-ethnographic" objects of the white man's gaze.

7. Arif Dirlik, "The Asia-Pacific Idea: Reality and Representation in the Invention of a Regional Structure," *Journal of World History* 3 (1992): 66.

8. "Fatal embrace" is the trope of romantic degeneration used by Herman Melville in *Typee* (1846; New York: Signet, 1964), 40, whose poor white hero finally wants to beat a hasty retreat from the primitive scene of his own quasicaptivity.

9. Samuel Manāiakalani Kamakau, *The Works of the People of Old (Nā Hana a ka Poʻe Kahiko),* trans. Mary Kawena Pukui, based on newspaper articles from 1869–1870 (Honolulu: Bishop Museum Press, 1976), 11–12. During the troubled reign of Kameha-

after contact, and renamed "the Pacific" after the Spanish christening of *El Mar Pacificó*. This name was given by Magellan, working in the miscreant metaphor lineage of Balboa, who took possession of these waters "for as long as the world shall endure." In the wake of Spanish, French, and British explorations and representations, the Pacific came to signify (as in Melville, or his untutored U.S. Pacific heir to sweeping narrative, James Michener) the linkage of the New World Americas to crusty and silk-and-spice-laden Asian markets, mostly to the advantage of European colonizing powers. The impact of whaling, fur trade, sandalwood and guano harvesting, as well as the implementation of a huge plantation system agriculture in Hawai'i, had transformed the city of Honolulu by 1850 into a global port of call for ships and peoples from Asia, Canada, and the continental USA.

This Pacific was not place-bound or bounded, but served as mediating sea lane, trade center, and fueling harbor. In *Moby-Dick,* Melville's grand vision of "the Pacific as sweatshop" (as Charles Olson troped Melville's movement from the working seaport shores of Gloucester) and laboratory of erotic longing and savage projection (as in *Typee*) had all but displaced (at least in the Euro-American imagination) prior (and often first) convictions of Pacific local space namings as a continuum of land, sea, star, and community—thus renaming those "storied places" of rooted belonging, place-based imagination, and Polynesian outreach, as the Hawaiians had called them in their taro-laden islands.[10]

---

meha III when land reform was initiated, Kamakau was one of the brilliant Native Hawaiian historians, trained in "Pacific research" by Sheldon Dibble at Lahainaluna Missionary Academy, who began to record and reinterpret Hawaiian *mo'olelo* as a source of culture, legends, and history. In an earlier if somewhat rougher and more Enlightenment-influenced version of *Hawaiian Antiquities (Mo'olelo Hawai'i)* (Honolulu: Bishop Museum Press, 1951), David Malo gives a related sense of "the ocean and its parts" as sedimented with diverse names and functions: "Outside of this was a belt called *kai-uli*, blue sea, squid-fishing sea, *kai lu-hee,* or sea of flying fish, *kai-malolo*," and so on to the Pacific's remotest depths (26).

10. Charles Olson, *Call Me Ishmael* (New York: Reynal and Hitchcock, 1947), 23. This Hawaiian sensibility for space and land as " 'storied places,' *wahi pana* where 'the old gods walked,' the forefathers dwelt" and *mana* lingered is evoked, in a contemporary reindigenous measure, by George Hu'eu Sanford Kanahele in *Kū Kanaka, Stand Tall: A Search for Hawaiian Values* (Honolulu: University of Hawai'i Press, 1986), 188–201. Also see the learned ethnography of Martha Beckwith, *Hawaiian Mythology* (Honolulu: University of Hawai'i Press, 1970), and Dennis Kawaharada's application of such

After Captain James Cook had (fatally) accommodated himself to self-apotheosis as the harvest god, Lono, another Hawaiian god of the local Pacific, Kāne, all but dissolved into the language of rival mythologies such as Pan, Captain Ahab, Tomo, Pym, and Venus; such Greco-Roman namings all but dispossessed Pacific peoples of semantic priority in the naming of place and peoples.[11] As medium of space and capital flows, the ocean was instrumentalized and integrated into some vast Asia/Pacific medium bespeaking national knowledge, adventure, and imperial possession. With the arrival of Cook's ships on the horizon of the Big Island like so many "floating heiaus" or water-coursing altars, "all the gods of the ocean have been destroyed," said a Hawaiian commoner named Kila, as Samuel Kamakau reports in his history texts written for Hawaiian newspapers. The globalized Pacific of Western gods and commercial forces will (seemingly) rule over the myths and gods of local knowledge.[12]

Trying to move beyond the older romantic sense of the South Pacific "as a lecher's paradise or a wastrel's retreat," Michener in 1951, writing with a Rotarian and sprawling prose befitting the entrepreneurial spirit of the postwar global dispensation, captured what the "American Pacific" (that is, the U.S. vision of the Pacific as this had been won through commerce, missionary work, and war) had become as vast ocean route to Asia in the final essay of his mixed fact-and-fiction collection *Return to Paradise,* "What I Learned." The Pacific was becoming a vast "highway" to the enterprising spirit and commerce of Asia, as it was supposed to function since the eras of Columbus and Walt Whitman: "There is only one sensible way to think of the Pacific Ocean today. It is the highway between Asia

---

Hawaiian stories to local places and as primordial ingredient of Hawai'i's local literature scene, in *Storied Landscapes: Hawaiian Literature and Place* (Honolulu: Kalamakū Press, 1999). For my own take on this, see chapter 6 in this volume on the uncanny return of a shark god story to disturb (and enrich) the contemporary poetry of place.

11. On the displacement of Hawaiian as language of instruction and government in Hawai'i under American missionary and commercial hegemony, which came to a repressive peak in the heyday of annexation, see Albert J. Schutz, *The Voices of Eden: A History of Hawaiian Language Studies* (Honolulu: University of Hawai'i Press, 1994), chap. 16, "Language and Power: The Past, the Present, and the Future of Hawaiian Language Policy." Only in the 1980s have these colonial policies on instruction (and place naming) been partly reversed.

12. Samuel M. Kamakau, *Ruling Chiefs of Hawai'i,* trans. Mary Kawena Pukui et al. (Honolulu: Kamehameha Schools Press, 1961), 100.

and America, and whether we wish it or not, from now on there will be immense traffic along that highway. If we [Euro-Americans?] know what we want, if we have patience and determination, if above all we have understanding, we may insure that the traffic will be peaceful, consisting of tractors and students and medical missionaries and bolts of cloth." But the globalizing economy was entering the cold war era after all, and Michener went on to issue a warning that the "Pacific traffic" in missionary beneficence and capitalist commerce (where, for example, the Indians in Fiji played stinking Chinese "Jews" of the New Pacific) could turn back from a "two-way affair" into a traffic of "armed planes, battleships, submarines and death," as it was to do not so much later in Korea and Vietnam in our arms race struggle with the Soviet Union and Mao's Red China.[13]

Through a mixed nexus of ships, harpoons, holy books, plantations, mines, nails, microbes, muumuus, novels, guns, property laws, and the wealth of nations, the Pacific Ocean that "zones the whole world's bulk about" was conscripted from being a space of indigenous eclecticism and multiple mythology—what Kant termed so many "lands without owners" in the far-flung Americas[14]—into forming an interlinked region of Spanish, Dutch, French, British, and American dominion, only later to be challenged by the

---

13. James A. Michener, *Return to Paradise* (Greenwich, CT: Fawcett, 1951), 416. On the Indo-Fijians as the stinking and greedy "Jews" of the neocommercial Pacific ("It is impossible to like the Indians of Fiji" [122]), see Michener's racially abjecting essay, much derided in Fiji to this day by postcolonial authors such as Sudesh Mishra and Subramani, "Fiji," 122–38. On the sentimental "orientalism" of Michener as disseminated in such journals as *Reader's Digest* and bespeaking his Eisenhower-era conviction of U.S. liberal magnanimity and financial might, see Christina Klein, "Cold War Orientalism: Musicals, Travel Narratives, and Middlebrow Culture in Postwar America" (Ph.D. diss., Yale University, 1997); also see the race-and-gender hierarchy of Michener's "Made in Japan" novel (and, later, movie) as discussed by Jane Hendler, "Constructing Gender, Race, and Nationhood in the Fifties: James Michener's *Sayonara* and Cold War Politics," forthcoming in *boundary 2*. On Michener's *Hawaii* and *South Pacific* narrative works bespeaking U.S. national-popular culture, see chapters 4 and 5 below.

14. Immanuel Kant's comment from *Perpetual Peace* (1795) is discussed in Masao Miyoshi, *As We Saw Them: The First Japanese Embassy to the United States (1860)* (Berkeley: University of California Press, 1979), 4. Kant's Enlightenment rationale reads in full: "America, the lands inhabited by the Negro, the Spice Islands, the Cape, etc., were at the time of their discovery considered by these civilized intruders as lands without owners, for they counted the inhabitants as nothing."

maritime might of Russia, Japan, and China. Various genres of discourse, from the Edenic imagery of literary romance and the noble-savage fantasies of missionary history to the evolutionary schemes of natural and social science, helped to subordinate these cultures of the "Great South Sea" into sites and passages within Euro-American reference systems.

By 1900, all of the Pacific islands, from Guam to New Zealand, had fallen under the colonial authority of outside powers reflecting the tyranny of distance and the pathos of the subaltern polity and subordinated cultural language. In the march toward annexation in 1898, the archipelago of Hawai'i was transformed from being a sovereign and internationally recognized Pacific nation into what the U.S. reciprocity pact of 1875 confirmed (in the proto-imperialist rhetoric of President Grant's secretary of state) would prove "a resting spot in the mid-ocean between the Pacific Coast and the vast domains of Asia"; and, by 1887, Pearl Harbor (once an area of Hawaiian fish ponds and watched over by O'ahu shark gods) had been contracted as an exclusive coaling station and repair base for American ships.[15] Pearl Harbor was no casual site, of course, but a deep-water coaling station suitable for American designs of expanding commerce, military outposts, and missionary outreach into the Pacific and Asia.

Through the production of Hawai'i into its crucial spatial (and multicultural) link between Asia and Oceania ("Asia-Pacific," as it would come to be called), the Pacific was transformed from a nexus of competing European outposts and Asian ports into the extraterritorial space of what continental ideologues mused over as their "vast American lake." "Hawai'i," in the words of military historian Malcolm McIntosh, had become "the command center for American Pacific forces and acts as the center of the web for American Pacific basing involving nearly a quarter of a million personnel" and extending from the Aleutians to Australia and from Japan and the Philippines to California.[16] The U.S. Pacific Lake, as it were, was

15. I. C. Campbell, "The Politics of Annexation," in *A History of the Pacific Islands* (Berkeley: University of California Press, 1989), 136; Arthur Power Dudden, *The American Pacific* (New York: Oxford University Press, 1992), 63–64, 83. By "American Pacific" Dudden signifies that the entire Pacific, after World War II when "imperial supremacy passed to the United States" (262), is a region that falls within the ongoing domain of American self-interest. For a competing definition of the Pacific, see note 23 below.

16. Malcolm McIntosh, *Arms across the Pacific: Security and Trade Issues across the Pacific* (London: Pinter, 1987), 140. According to the Empire-based metaphors of historians,

not empty or disenchanted: postwar *nuclearization* of the Pacific Ocean (a prerogative of global power the United States shares with France) has only made extraterritorial dominion over this site of hula skirts and bikinis (and the Bikini atolls) more seemingly complete.[17]

On the level of cultural production, by means of which a non-West could be all but deprived not only of control over agricultural and industrial productions, but over the globally recognized productions of their cultural spaces and group identities as well,[18] authors of national culture (such as Melville, Twain, Henry Adams, Michener, P. F. Kluge, and Theroux) in prolific works of prose possessed these "Happy Isles of Oceania" as innocent isolatos of their own democratic-commercial empire. Such writers remained at times capricious and intoxicated by oceanic scale and humorous intercultural differences, yet intent (beyond the psychological baggage of personal misery such as Theroux's divorce or Adams's fin de siècle nihilism after the suicide of his wife) on interlinking offshore Pacific locales to the higher national purpose and time-honored binaries of Euro-American possession.

Belatedly searching, after nasty little wars in Korea and Vietnam, for his own "paradise" in the scattered islands of Micronesia, travel writer P. F. Kluge reveals the will to take sexual and commodity possession that still can drive this U.S. romance in the far-flung Pacific, as his grand country takes charge of it, like a benevolent father or a Gump-like sailor on holiday

---

the Pacific Ocean has gone from being a "Spanish lake" (during the sixteenth and seventeenth centuries, when Spain dominated the Pacific via colonies in the Americas and the galleon trade) to an "English lake" (during the eighteenth and nineteenth centuries via the geographic and commercial expeditions of Cook, Vancouver, and others) to an "American lake" (via the mediation of Hawai'i, Japan, and the Philippines). See Dirlik, "The Asia-Pacific Idea," 69.

17. William H. Goetzmann, *New Lands, New Men: America and the Second Great Age of Discovery* (New York: Viking, 1986), 332. On the post-Hiroshima buildup of the Pacific into a "nuclear lake," see Rob Wilson, "Postmodern as Post-Nuclear: Landscape as Nuclear Grid," in *Ethics/Aesthetics: Post-Modern Positions*, ed. Robert Merrill (Washington, DC: Maisonneuve Press, 1988), 169–78; Peter Hayes, Lyuba Zarsky, and Walden Bello, *American Lake: Nuclear Peril in the Pacific* (New York: Penguin, 1986); and Stewart Firth, *Nuclear Playground* (Honolulu: University of Hawai'i Press, 1987).

18. Rey Chow, *Woman and Chinese Modernity: The Politics of Reading between East and West* (Minneapolis: University of Minnesota Press, 1991), xxii. Bertolucci's *The Last Emperor* is read in terms of uneven ("orientalist") exchange based on maintaining Euro-American control over global "codes of fantasy."

from the Iowa corn fields: "I remember the days when I looked at the map of the Pacific and plotted voyages, when I collected islands, when it was important for me to see as many as I could. It was like a hobbyist's obsession, or—this embarrasses me now—like having a woman."[19] (Yes, the Pacific as a woman easily to be had by Euro-American takers, who were lining up to court, paint, write up, and count the blessed isles of loot.)

Entangled in the imperial politics of globalization, Hawai'i would serve to mediate these interchanges of the Asian/Pacific East and the Anglo-Saxon West: U.S. acculturation took place in disciplinary spaces of contract labor such as sugar plantations on Kaua'i since 1835, or in public schoolrooms of literary instruction on O'ahu, where state-ordered dramatizations of Longfellow's *Hiawatha,* for example, were staged by Chinese Hawaiians speaking their "bad pidgin English," so as to civilize them over into English-loving and Harvard-leaning U.S. mores.[20] The Pacific local, as site of imagined identity and enduring culture of place-belonging, was linked by such schooling and laboring to technologies of metropolitan representation. As the "local literature" movement that has emerged in Hawai'i since the late 1970s can only now begin to suggest, these battles for regional articulation and cultural survival in the Pacific are far from over, as Bamboo Ridge and more indigenous-based authors counter such spectacles of U.S. otherness as *South Pacific, Hawaii,* and *Blue Hawaii* (see chapters 4 through 7) with quite differently affiliated and situated works.[21]

19. P. F. Kluge, *The Edge of Paradise: America in Micronesia* (Honolulu: University of Hawai'i Press, 1993), 109–10.

20. On socializing powers of the American plantation system as introduced in Hawai'i as early as 1835, see Ronald Takaki, *Pau Hana: Plantation Life and Labor in Hawai'i* (Honolulu: University of Hawai'i Press, 1983). On the schoolroom as space of American indoctrination, see Genevieve Taggard's memoir, "Hiawatha in Hawai'i," in *A Hawaiian Reader,* ed. A. Grove Day and Carl Stroven (Honolulu: Mutual Publishing, 1984), 209–14. The Hawaiian-raised Taggard (1894–1948) was early considered "A Poet of the Pacific" (1928) by Edmund Wilson; see *The Shores of Light: A Literary Chronicle of the 1920s and 1930s* (New York: Noonday, 1952), 345–50. Because "the natives [of the Pacific] have months of unbroken sun, and they are comfortable, amiable and healthy" (347), the great critic Wilson wonders whether such natives might have any need or seasonal motivation to write; but, as a Euro-Pacific by-product linking the metaphysical mind of the West with the luxuriant body of the East, the poet Taggard is said to be "sensuous as a matter of course" (348).

21. This "local literature" movement, generated since 1978 around Bamboo Ridge journal and press in Hawai'i (and connected, in loose and at times opposed ways, to the

This movement to express an aesthetic of regional coalition must not only be linked to American liberal multiculturalism as such, but also articulated to the dynamics of what Albert Wendt, Subramani, Mudrooroo Narogin, Vilsoni Hereniko, and others have theorized as the decolonizing literatures of the Pacific. Though political decolonization has come late to the Pacific region, as first signaled by the independence of Western Samoa in 1962 and ongoing struggles in New Caledonia and Belau, this process remains unfinished, even in what appears to be just another democratic U.S. state thriving under global tourism, Hawai'i. The discourse of local culture, I am urging, played an active role in these resurgent formations of Pacific identity and goes on adding a cultural dimension to the renewed drive toward Hawaiian sovereignty that has intensified and seeks federal (if not United Nations) adjudication.

Such versions of the Pacific go on being constructed by the advanced market-driven economies of the Pacific Rim, which, in their tropes of economic integration, can bypass community interests and "local" voices of these Pacific island cultures altogether. Since the 1970s, when U.S. trade across the Pacific surpassed that with Europe, the United States has been recognized as a Pacific-oriented nation whose economic well-being is implicated in the dynamics of this region. Although U.S. involvement in the Pacific region has remained military, especially as the Pacific was instrumentalized to Asia during the postwar era, Japan at times (with Australia, the anchor nation of "Oceania") has taken the lead since the early 1960s in advocating the formation of a quasi-unified view of the "Pacific Community" and in trying to integrate these heterogeneous cultures and far-flung geographies into a coherent economic zone, as it was to be declared later in the policies and visions of APEC in the late 1980s and 1990s.[22]

Hawaiian sovereignty struggle), can help to explain the space I will be calling "the global/local," one that sees the local culture as engaged with and situated against existing national and global frameworks and systems of Pacific narration.

22. Even as the so-called Pacific Basin and Rim were being perilously shaped, by global forces and capitalist nation-state theory, into an interdependent region of "mutual understanding" and "economic cooperation," as the idealizing postwar rhetoric goes, in the discourse of policy planners from Japan, Australia, the United States, New Zealand, and Canada, local Pacific cultures have emerged and networked across the region to articulate more place-bound tactics of resistance and to express claims of ethnic and indigenous difference.

Later in this chapter I want to zero back in on the resurgence of cultural-political forces in Hawai'i as one such space of Asian/Pacific production. But before examining this polyvocal and diverse literature in its ethnic historicity, I want to sketch in a critical genealogy of the imperial involvement of the United States in the production/representation of the Pacific Ocean as region of national interest and international necessity. Above all, I want to stress here that I am focusing on the "American Pacific" as a distinct area of historical formation coming down from the imperial era of Pacific outreach toward China, India, Russia, and Japan; the "American Pacific" is just one of several *postcolonial* regions that (like other settled areas of the Pacific) remains, in Subramani's telling phrase, "oriented towards the power that colonized it" and would include the former U.S. Trust Territory of the Pacific Islands (the Republic of the Marshall Islands, the Republic of Belau, the Federated States of Micronesia, the Commonwealth of the Northern Marianas), Guam, and American Samoa.[23] By a broader political definition still, one I want to challenge in this postcolonial era, the "American Pacific" means *the entire Pacific* conceived as a region that, since the end of World War II when supremacy passed to the United States, has been dominated by this military superpower and its neoliberal ideology of installing democracy and free-market regimes.

This "American Pacific" had begun to solidify into a region that we could recognize as our commercial and tourist "own" only during the imperialist struggles for Samoa and Hawai'i, that is, between 1873 and 1900. To be sure, this expansive installation of "our serene Pacific" assumed sway only after World War II, when the United States had defeated Japan and took control, via "strategic trust," over Micronesia and related territories of military self-interest in relation to China, Russia, and Japan. On the Bikini atoll, of course, twenty-three nuclear weapons had been arrogantly tested between 1946 and 1958, including the Bravo hydrogen bomb in 1954; Bikini Islanders, relocated on Kili, are suing the U.S. gov-

23. Categorization of "Pacific literature" into six distinct cultural regions (Papua New Guinea, French Pacific, American Pacific, Spanish Pacific, Australia–New Zealand, and the English-speaking British Commonwealth countries around Fiji) based on the lingering effects of colonial orientation is argued by Subramani in *South Pacific Literature: From Myth to Fabulation* (Suva, Fiji: University of the South Pacific, 1985), ix–xii. On the "French Pacific" as a region still undergoing political and cultural decolonization, see Stephen Henningham, *France and the South Pacific: A Contemporary History* (Honolulu: University of Hawai'i Press, 1992), 236 and passim.

ernment to remove radioactive topsoil from their native island and to recover a sense of political and cultural agency.

The "French Pacific" in the Polynesian South Pacific comprises another nuclear-rich zone of experiment, beach pleasures, and quasiterror that has witnessed the resistance of indigenous political and cultural mobilization during the 1980s, as the counterorientalist scholarship of Robert Nicole on the French colonial production of the erotic romance of Tahiti makes clear.[24] The push to reclaim some claims of "aboriginality" as ground of symbol-making identity and communal dreaming within the nonwhite Australian theorizing and novels of Mudrooroo Narogin begins to suggest the multidirections of this backward-looking yet future-oriented search.[25]

Clearing a way for these prior cultures of Oceania to break with more colonial modes of "cultural dependency" that are "even more soul-destroying than economic dependency" and yet eschewing (at that time) the purity of any easy cultural nativism, the Western Samoan novelist Albert Wendt outlines this collective Pacific project in "Towards a New Oceania" (1976), as it began to proliferate at sites from Papua New Guinea to Suva to the fishing hole of Bamboo Ridge: "Up to a few years ago, nearly all the literature about Oceania was written by *papalagi* [persons of European stock] and other outsiders. . . . The Oceania found in this literature is largely *papalagi* fictions, more revealing of *papalagi* fantasies and hang-ups, dreams, nightmares, prejudices and ways of viewing our crippled cosmos, than of our actual islands."[26] As linked to oral mythologies and

24. Robert Nichol, "Extending Orientalism to the Pacific: The Myth of Tahiti Revisited" (M.A. thesis, University of the South Pacific, 1993), and "Images of Paradise," Nichol's afterword to Vilsoni Hereniko and Teresia Teaiwa, *Last Virgin in Paradise* (Suva, Fiji: Mana Publications, 1993), 59–64. On the Bikini atoll as contradictory site of nuclear destruction and erotic fantasy, see Teresia K. Teaiwa, "bikinis and other s/pacific n/oceans," *The Contemporary Pacific* 6 (1994): 87–109.

25. See Mudrooroo Narogin, *Writing from the Fringe: A Study of Modern Aboriginal Literature* (Melbourne: Hyland House, 1990): "Most of the dramas so far produced have a strong realist slant with intrusions of what may be termed *Aboriginal reality* or *Aboriginality*" (27). A recent work of Hawaiian drama, '*Umi a Liloa* (1994) pushes toward this same recovery of precontact mythic spaces and models via intrusions of dream-time into the social reality of a sullen Hawaiian adolescent.

26. Albert Wendt, "Towards a New Oceania," in *Writers in East-West Encounter: New Cultural Bearings*, ed. Guy Amirthanayagam (London: Macmillan, 1982), 204–13. The *UNESCO Courier* (February 1976): 4–12, initially published Wendt's important essay under the cautionary headline, "The Angry Young Men of Oceania." Based on prior

markers of place/culture and as means to a rehabilitation of indigenous and ethnic identity, this New Pacific literature in warped and localized "english" has emerged across the postcolonial Pacific region to break the sense that cultural production only took place elsewhere, in metropolitan centers of cultural capital such as London, Paris, and New York.[27]

Given the narrative scope and renewed cultural assertion in such authors as Wendt, John Dominis Holt, and Patricia Grace, local culture in the Pacific no longer seems irrelevant, substandard, or, as they say back home in New York City, merely local. The struggle of Asian and Pacific Americans to affirm Hawaiian "local culture" against its unwitting homogenization into national culture can be linked to this uneasy decolonization dynamic. In interrogating this literature of the American Pacific, Hawai'i will be invoked as the deformed ethnoscape it has become in the national/transnational era: a postcolonial space imbued with contradictions and social conflicts that can no longer be sublimated into palms, waves, pink hotels, or, in Steven Okazaki's Hollywood stereotype, "little kids in the cane fields and hula skirts."[28]

From a critical-feminist perspective within the United States, Cynthia Enloe critiques everyday mappings of this "Pacific Rim" as reflecting the U.S. superstate and its "assumption of military interconnectedness." The

---

colonial divisions of the Pacific, Wendt's culture of Western Samoa in some ways has more to do with New Zealand *papalagi* than with the Polynesian culture of Hawaiians, who remain an "indigenous minority" in the American state of Hawai'i. See Albert Wendt, "The Return Home: A Dialogue" [with Subramani et al.], in *InterChange: A Symposium on Regionalism, Internationalism, and Ethnicity in Literature*, ed. Linda Spalding and Frank Stewart (Honolulu: InterArts Hawai'i, 1980), 77–78, and *Sons for the Return Home* (Auckland: Longman Paul, 1973). For a transregional collection of resurgent cultures in the Pacific, see Richard Hamasaki and Wayne Westlake, eds., *A Pacific Islands Collection* (Honolulu: Seaweeds and Constructions, 1984).

27. Wendt's own shifting cultural positions toward Samoan native culture, authenticity claims, and Pacific tourism as well are quite ambivalent, at times, if not downright confused and self-incriminating in some complex and self-ironic way. See Robert Chi, "Toward a New Tourism: Albert Wendt and Becoming Attractions," *Cultural Critique* 37 (1997): 61–106.

28. Quoted in Vicki Viotti, "Big Island 'Paradise,'" *Honolulu Advertiser*, 22 May 1992, C2. For skeptical takes on the "nationalism" and "nativism" being produced within (and against) forces of capitalist transnationalization, I benefit from Kuan-Hsing Chen, "Multiculturalism or Neo-Colonial Racism?" *Ritsumeikan Studies in Language and Culture* 8 (1997): 347–76.

consequences of uneven modernization, erotic commerce, and the U.S.-powered circulation of guns, money, and a far-reaching culture of self-commodification across the Pacific region become all too clear: "When American military planners look at the world these days they imagine the territories encircling the Pacific ocean as part of a single security—or insecurity—chain. To be secure, this 'Pacific Rim' must be strung with a necklace of American-controlled military bases: from Anchorage to San Diego, Hawai'i, Vladivostok, Seoul, Yokohama, Cam Rahn Bay, Subic Bay and Clark, Wellington, Bellau and Kwajelein. Having created this mental map, this assumption of military interconnectedness, the American strategist is on the lookout for gaps and disturbances."[29] Tourism and its needs produces its own erotic and exotic haze in the ever-flowing Pacific. But the rise of Asian/Pacific feminism at sites of regional contestation, such as the prostitution-dependent military bases in the Philippines or South Korea and Okinawa, not to mention the Nuclear Free and Independent Pacific movement now being agitated from New Zealand to Belau, has helped to contest the production of the *Pacific-as-Americanized space* that allows this superpower state to imagine "South Pacific" as a weapons-disposal zone.[30]

"Could we comprehend, at a glance, the mighty surface of the Indian or Pacific seas," urged Jeremiah N. Reynolds in 1839, that advocate of the sophisticated national exploring expeditions conducted by USN Lieutenant Charles Wilkes from 1838 to 1842 to surpass the British Academy mappings of Cook, "what a picture would open upon us of unparalleled industry and daring enterprise."[31] Overriding local cultures of the Pacific, Reynolds evoked the American sailor's dreaded specter of some "Mocha Dick" lurking in waters off Chile and "scenes of toil along the coast of

29. Cynthia Enloe, *Bananas, Beaches and Bases: Making Feminist Sense of International Politics* (Berkeley: University of California Press, 1989), 85.

30. On tactics to resist intrusions of the West into the contemporary Pacific as nuclear power superstate, also see Lenora Foerstel, ed., *Women's Voices on the Pacific: The International Pacific Policy Congress* (Washington, DC: Maisonneuve Press, 1992). Struggles for political and cultural survival continue in this interior Pacific; in Vanuatu, or what was formerly called the New Hebrides, for example, France continues to obstruct the transition to political independence. The USA also depends on nuclear geopolitics and a residual assumption of extensive extraterritorial authority to undermine drives to political autonomy, via "free association," in the Republic of Belau.

31. J. N. Reynolds, "Mocha Dick: or the White Whale of the Pacific," *The Knickerbocker, New York Monthly Magazine* 13 (1839): 377–92; reprinted in Herman Melville, *Moby-Dick*, ed. Harrison Hayford and Hershel Parker (New York: Norton, 1967), 589.

Japan," but predicted that if the watery vastness of the Pacific, from Japan to New-Holland, could be "at a glance" surveyed and interconnected, it could soon be turned through commercial redemption into "the whaling-ground of the American seaman."[32]

These spaces and resources waiting to be sublimated into enterprise, by means of what Adam Smith (if not Karl Marx) legitimated as capitalist water-carriage, would generate an apocalyptic and fear-inducing *white* omen of American purpose in Asia/Pacific, the struggle for sovereignty between Captain Ahab and Moby-Dick. Melville recognized from his 1841 journey on the *Acushnet* that "the vast Sperm Whale grounds of the Pacific were thrown open" to the "civilized steel" of the American and European national will to open the market.[33] By means of geographical exploration and commercial enterprise, even more than direct military intervention (although there was that already by David Reynolds in the Marquesas, during the War of 1812), this "mysterious, divine Pacific" that "zones the world's bulk about" became another medium of national expansion and transformation. Through the commercial mediation of Hawai'i as linked to the Northern Pacific, Melville saw, those "new-built California towns" of the railroad and Gold Rush would be linked to Asiatic lands and "low-lying, endless, unknown Archipelagoes and impenetrable Japans."[34]

Pacific island cultures were mostly troped and engendered (via person-ification of *island-as-woman*) into a racially inferior, sexually submissive woman, nicknamed Bloody Mary or Venus or something like that. This is apparent, still, in Paul Theroux's musings in Tahiti, following Gauguin's discursive tracks in the archive of white mythology (see chapter 5).[35] From

32. Ibid.

33. Melville, *Moby-Dick*, 369. On linkages of New England as cultural and economic region to the expansion in the Pacific, see Charles Anderson, *Melville in the South Seas* (New York: Dover, 1966), and Ernest Dodge, *New England and the South Seas* (Cambridge, MA: Harvard University Press, 1965).

34. Melville, *Moby-Dick*, 399–400.

35. Nowadays, as satellite TV since 1995 filters images of *Melrose Place*'s lithe blonde Amanda and the spoiled little rich kids (with problems) of *Beverly Hills 90210*, the young women in the South Pacific, as on Fiji, are coming down with eating disorders in their quest to match the U.S. thin-is-in look. See "Fat-Phobia in the Fijis: TV-Thin Is In," *Newsweek*, 31 May 1999, 70. This article is based on a controversial study by Dr. Anne Becker funded by the Harvard Eating-Disorder Center, who, despite counterclaims by Fijian scholars, seems to be following Margaret Mead down the South Pacific path to national career recognition. See Margaret Mead, *Growing Up in New Guinea* (New York:

the time Lewis and Clark pushed the national borders westward to the Northwest Pacific, the trope of "the first white men to see," survey, valorize, and name the landscape attempted to take conceptual possession and displace more local knowledges of place; by such acts of transcendental authority and higher scriptural authority, American authors linked sublime possession of space to the manifest destiny of the national will, as elected to expand and redeem the main continent from shore to shore, in a "passage to India and beyond."[36]

By Emerson's era, the impact of European customs and American commodified desire on the "Sandwich Islands" was so strong that the French archaeologist Paul-Emile Botta could conclude of the Native Hawaiians in Honolulu, "But nowadays the products of our industry have lost in their eyes the attraction of novelty. They have, moreover, learned to know what property means; therefore, they no longer seek to steal, or to murder unfortunate Europeans in order to rob from them."[37] Dismantled of

---

Dell, 1968), for more "cultural" findings about tribal peoples (outback) by a scientific, concerned, if totalizing outsider.

36. On Jeffersonian rhetorics of American possession, see Bruce Greenfield, "The Problem of the Discoverer's Authority in Lewis and Clark's *History*," in *Macropolitics of Nineteenth-Century Literature: Nationalism, Exoticism, Imperialism*, ed. Jonathan Arac and Harriet Ritvo (Philadelphia: University of Pennsylvania Press, 1991), 24–28. A case in point of such a possessive rhetoric unconscious of its imperial genealogy is Paul Theroux, *The Happy Isles of Oceania: Paddling the Pacific* (New York: Putnam's, 1992), who evokes "first white man to see" ancestors as agents of Pacific dispossession: "Not only Samoa, but other islands and, in a sense, the whole of the South Pacific is a clear example of this sort of transformation [by Western imagination] because it has been used so effectively as a setting by writers as various as Melville, Stevenson, Somerset Maugham, Rupert Brooke, Mark Twain, Jack London, Pierre Loti, Michener, and even Gauguin in his only book *Noa Noa*" (322).

37. Paul-Emile Botta, "Observations on the Inhabitants of the Sandwich Islands," *The Hawaiian Journal of History* 18 (1984): 26. The impact of civilization on the "pre-*haole*" Hawaiian population, through the spread of biological disease and ecological imperialism, was devastating; see David E. Stannard, *Before the Horror: The Population of Hawai'i on the Eve of Western Contact* (Honolulu: University of Hawai'i Press, 1989), and O. A. Bushnell, *The Gifts of Civilization: Germs and Genocide in Hawai'i* (Honolulu: University of Hawai'i Press, 1993). On this problem, also see Bushnell's novel, *Moloka'i* (Honolulu: University of Hawai'i Press, 1975), an uneasy novel on the much-represented Father Damon rescue situation, where Hawaiians are infected with leprosy and the microbe-ridden diseases of empire, all but becoming tropes (as in the Hawaiian fiction of Jack London) of imperial miscegenation.

custom, land, and diet, "civilized into draft horses, and evangelized into beasts of burden," as Melville described hybrid and racially marked citizens of Honolulu in *Typee* in 1843, indigenous Hawaiians had (seemingly, to the white male gaze) become interlopers in their own land, using, as Botta claimed, "English words, which the islanders deform so as to render them almost beyond recognition."[38] Noting the Hawaiian people's elaborate irrigation systems to cultivate taro fields and use of freshwater aquaculture, Botta was indeed impressed with what he called "the industriousness of this people," whereas from 1835 on it would become a common complaint of missionary pedagogues and American sugar plantation owners that Hawaiians were too lazy, childlike, and shiftless to work and so would have to be slowly replaced by Chinese "coolies" and later waves of Asian immigrants.[39] During the course of the nineteenth century, the disciplinary, cultural, and biological displacement of the Hawaiian people led to their becoming a minority in their own land.[40]

By 1890, as the Native Hawaiians had been reduced to a protesting minority in their own nation, they soon were deprived of national sovereignty and the land base necessary to Pacific cultural survival, despite their collective protests in petitions to Washington.[41] An "Asiaticizing"

---

38. Botta, "Observations," 30; Melville, *Typee*, 222. Also see Melville's degrading portrayal of Hawaiian King Kamehameha III as a pimple-faced, "fat, lazy, Negro-looking blockhead," who "has lost the noble traits of the barbarian, without acquiring the redeeming graces of a civilized being," as well as Melville's analysis of how "the two classes [of Hawaiians] are receding from each other" under English and American influence (213). On the disruption of Oceanic forms of cultural fabrication by Western commercial modes that will lead ultimately to "airport art," see Adrienne L. Kaeppler, "Art and Aesthetics," in *Developments in Polynesian Ethnology*, ed. Alan Howard and Robert Borofksy (Honolulu: University of Hawai'i Press, 1989), esp. 236–40.

39. Botta, "Observations," 28–30.

40. On generational shifts from a "rhetoric of revulsion" used by the American Calvinist missionaries to a "rhetoric of preservation" used by their anthropological and literary offspring such as Nathaniel Emerson and Armine Von Tempski, see Houston Wood, *Displacing Natives: The Rhetorical Production of Hawai'i* (Boulder, CO: Rowman and Littlefield, 1999), esp. chap. 3, "The Kama'aina Anti-Conquest."

41. See Haunani-Kay Trask, "Kūpa'a 'Āina: Native Hawaiian Nationalism in Hawai'i," in *Politics and Public Policy in Hawai'i* (Albany: State University of New York Press, 1992), 245. Trask's claim, to me an incontestable one, is that "historically, the decline of Hawaiians and their culture is traced directly to land dispossession" (256).

labor migration (recruited to his own downfall by U.S.-dominated forces in King David Kalākaua's reign in the 1880s) would lead to an influx of Japanese, Portuguese, Korean, and Filipino workers. Reaching a total of some 61,000 immigrants by 1920, these Asian and Pacific migrant workers would energize the dynamics of the "local" multiculture still coming into literary expression three and four generations later if, in effect, at times undermining Hawaiian blood-based claims to cultural-national priority.[42] The mix of indigenous and settler imaginary, claiming symbolic and legal possession of place and cultural identity under U.S. liberal hegemony, is not always an easy one (as we shall see in later chapters).

Although Hawaiian structures and "indigenous schemes" were by no means inert in this global restructuring of place into a site of commercial and cultural capital (as in the vast real estate and corporate holdings of the Bishop Estate, which rival those of Yale, Princeton, and Harvard Universities), the Pacific Ocean was surveyed and locked into networks of literary and scientific Euro-American discourses.[43] Place names and ethnic formations can still bespeak this domination. "In addition to imposing ethnic categories on Pacific Islanders," as Alan Howard notes of the politicized search to articulate group identity in contemporary Oceania, "Europeans imposed the categories of Micronesia, Melanesia, and Polynesia on the region."[44] If Magellan's Spanish imparted the label "Pacificó," by Greek

42. See Takaki, *Pau Hana*, who summarizes the colonization movement: "By 1920, the industry was reaching beyond sugar to pineapple production and toward tourism, and the [largely Asian] laborers were beginning to feel a new consciousness—an identity of themselves as settlers, as locals, and an understanding of the need for politics that transcended ethnicity" (xi).

43. Marshall Sahlins, *Islands of History* (Chicago: University of Chicago Press, 1985), 76. On the give-and-take of contact mythologies in Hawai'i, also see the different claims of Gananath Obeyesekere, *The Apotheosis of Captain Cook: European Mythmaking in the Pacific* (Princeton, NJ: Princeton University Press, 1992), who argues that the idea of the European as a white god to savages is "a structure of the long run in European culture and consciousness" (123). With much care, Sahlins sees Hawai'i as a space where rival hegemonies and forms of symbolic domination came into fateful global/ local contact.

44. Alan Howard, "Cultural Paradigms, History, and the Search for Identity in Oceania," in *Cultural Identity and Ethnicity in the Pacific*, ed. Jocelyn Linnekin and Lin Poyer (Honolulu: University of Hawai'i Press, 1990), 277. These racial and geographical

christening the islands (*nesia*) were grouped in the Enlightenment era as small (*micro*), many (*poly*), and black (*mela*). This is not to imply that these cultures of Oceania were not already linked, in complex routes of language, race, and exchange, by their own social motions. The *Hōkūleʻa* voyaging canoe that sailed back from Hawaiʻi to Tahiti in 1976 and 1985–1987 serves to retrace these ancestral Polynesian journeys and can be seen as a belated attempt by native peoples to reclaim their own oceanic territory as one of spatial grandeur and heroic enterprise.[45]

Another instance of Pacific knowledge that might here be invoked is the recovery in the 1980s of the "Molokaʻi Diet," by means of which contemporary Hawaiians (who have the worst health rate of any race or ethnic group in the United States) are going back to "a 'pre-Cook' diet" of taro and fish to shed the high-cholesterol junk food diet that plagues them.[46] If "cultural-constructionist" anthropologists can now argue that colonial administrations and disciplinary formations of Pacific islander "group identity" are based on racial categories and fixed cultural boundaries (what Epeli Hauʻofa mocks in *Tales of the Tikongs* as "the Bureau for the Preservation of Traditional Culture and Essential Indigenous Personality"), these are being now turned back (by such writers as the witty Hauʻofa and in the

---

categories of Melanesian, Polynesian, and Micronesian were imposed on the diverse islands of Oceania in the 1820s by the French explorer Dumont d'Urville; see Campbell, *A History of the Pacific Islands*, 14. In *Moby-Dick*, the Maori chieftain, Queequeg, comes from the Polynesian island of Kocovoco; as Ishmael comments, debunking the reality of Western maps of the Pacific, "It's not down in any map; true places never are" (56).

45. It is fitting that this *Hōkūleʻa* voyage, repeated and imitated during the 1980s and 1990s, has emerged as summarizing symbol of cultural identity not only for Hawaiians and Polynesians but for all Pacific islanders and their subjugated knowledges. The *Hōkūleʻa* voyages are portrayed as a beneficial recovery of the seafaring heritage of native Polynesians (especially as rehabilitated in canny Hawaiians such as Nainoa Thompson) as well as a "joining of research and cultural revival" by the anthropologist-participant Ben Finney, in *From Sea to Space* (Palmerston North, New Zealand: Massey University, 1992), 43–57.

46. Susan Miller, "Health Talk," *Ka Leo O Hawaiʻi* 86 (29 June 1992): 1–5. For research supporting this contrast between the traditional Hawaiian and modern American diet, see Stannard, *Before the Horror*, 96, n. 3. On contemporary Hawaiian attempts to articulate national and cultural identity against U.S. statist forms of blood quantum and contract law, see David Baker, "*Ea* and Knowing in Hawaiʻi," *Critical Inquiry* 23 (1997): 640–59.

reverse Hegelian master/slave dialectics of Haunani-Kay Trask) upon their Euro-American makers to mobilize goals of autonomy and native sovereignty far from the alienation of Pacific identity intended.[47]

Whether retreated to as space of physical rejuvenation or politicoerotic community in Samoa (Robert Louis Stevenson); whether projected as a space of aesthetic deformation and amoral excess in Tahiti and the Marquesas (Paul Gauguin); whether domesticated into a theater of evangelical redemption across Polynesia and Melanesia (like John Williams, as vanguard for the London Missionary Society); or worked over into a quasi-Mormon empire on Lāna'i (as with the crazy U.S. scholar cum political con man Walter Murray Gibson), the Pacific served nineteenth-century writers not just as home or site of belonging, but as space in which to project unequal visions of religious, commercial, and cultural capital. The Pacific became a site in which writers and artists could leave the metropolis, like Prospero, to act out their subjective "voyages of self-discovery" if not to "verify their fantasies" of conversion on the natives and themselves. Paul Theroux's *Happy Isles of Oceania* and Julian Evans's *Transit of Venus* are only the latest works in the lineage of this time-honored cultural genre of Euro-American male fantasy. Such authors go on taking possession of a remote, mute, eternally feminized Oceania, as this space and body can be filtered (inevitably) through an archive of prior discourse (Melville, Stevenson, Adams, Malinowski, Adams, Daws) of aesthetic/political self-empowerment.[48]

47. On the attempt to construct a "pan-Pacific cultural identity" in the wake of Western colonization that cuts across indigenous and ethnic modes of group identity, see Jocelyn Linnekin, "The Politics of Culture in the Pacific," in *Cultural Identity and Ethnicity in the Pacific*, ed. Jocelyn Linnekin and Lin Poyer (Honolulu: University of Hawai'i Press, 1990), 158–68. For a critique of how "cultural constructionist" arguments of Pacific anthropologists can undermine nationalist movements and play into state discourses of legal and administrative colonization, see Jeff Tobin, "Cultural Construction and Native Nationalism: Report from the Hawaiian Front," in *Asia/Pacific as Space of Cultural Production*, special issue of *boundary 2*, ed. Arif Dirlik and Rob Wilson, 21 (1994): 111–33. For Hau'ofa's debunking of postcolonial regimes in Tonga and Fiji as these administer indigenous culture and identity, see "The Glorious Pacific Way," in *Tales of the Tikong* (Auckland: Penguin, 1983), 83–93.

48. Portraits of these male Westerners and their dreams of possession are discussed, if not recuperated, in Gavin Daws, *A Dream of Islands: Voyages of Self-Discovery in the South Seas* (Honolulu: Mutual Publishing, 1980). Related texts are Theroux, *The Happy Isles of*

U.S. national interest, at some level of cultural unconsciousness, remained paramount. Observing that "the whole east exists for Europe to trade with" and that the Pacific stands already in that relation with imperial powers of Europe, Henry Adams made this all too clear when he concluded after an extended stay in the renewal zones of Japan, Hawai'i, Samoa, Tahiti, and Fiji, that America must be more selective in asserting hegemony within the Asia-Pacific region. "As financial investments," Adams wrote to Henry Cabot Lodge in 1891 from Sydney, "none of the Pacific islands, except the Sandwiches, are worth touching. . . . Nevertheless Germany, France, Australia, New Zealand, and the Lord knows what other countries and governments, are squabbling for the possession of these wretched lava-heaps."[49] While Adams scoured the Old Pacific to fulfill his vision of gazing at the "old gold" woman and rescue his ironical New England consciousness from sexual guilt and disgust at the market economy where morals belonged to a distant era, U.S. economic self-interest and geopolitical force still dictated the discourse of imperial geography and underwrote the purpose of the globalizing nation. Maritime power presumed imperial extension, even for a republican state, as Admiral Alfred Thayer Mahan would best incarnate for these same pro-imperial U.S. interests in the Pacific and the Atlantic, by making the Caribbean into a U.S. lake and Cuba and Puerto Rico (along with the Philippines) into pacified U.S. regional outposts.[50] By 1900, given the same imperial dynamics, Henry Adams would get his wish for U.S. national possession in

---

Oceania, and Julian Evans, *Transit of Venus: Travels in the Pacific* (London: Secker and Warrburg, 1992). As Evans writes, these white male voyagers "wanted somewhere to bring their psychological baggage and dump it" because, in the Pacific, each "longed for some sudden paradise to flower there, some sudden liberation from neurosis and desire" (198). For Evans, "Espiritu Santo was beautiful and enigmatic and rich, like the neurotic perfect woman" (148).

49. Henry Adams, *The Letters of Henry Adams, Vol. 3: 1886–1892,* ed. J. C. Levenson et al. (Cambridge, MA: Harvard University Press, 1982), 519.

50. On Mahan and Adams viewed as quasi-imperial U.S. agents, see Richard Drinnon, *Facing West: The Metaphysics of Indian-Hating and Empire Building* (New York: New American Library, 1980), 270–80, on policies of the "Adams-Seward-Hays Empire" as it expanded and interlinked the Atlantic and Pacific Ocean spaces and peoples; as Hay remarked of the Open Door policy to China in 1903: "We have done the Chinks a great service, which they don't seem inclined to recognize" (277).

the Pacific, as the Sandwich Islands became ratified (against Native Hawaiian protests) into the U.S. Territory of Hawai'i.[51]

Brevity of stay did not disqualify such writerly Westerners from such summary perceptions because, in many cases, the narratives of Hawai'i as a sensory Eden and/or fall-from-Eden staging space had already been created in the Western anthropological imagination of Pacific islanders as primitive Indians (as in Cook's journals), or, worse yet, as a primordial vista of vastness (as in the opening pages of Michener's *Hawaii*, which empties Hawai'i of Hawaiians via sublime description). The utilitarianism of Western historical consciousness could here seek (a) material fulfillment and/or (b) pastoral release in some contradictory third space.[52]

On the one hand, these metropolitan citizens of late empire were looking for fresh new spaces of commodified bounty: fur trade between North America and China flourished by means of Honolulu; whaling boomed in Honolulu and Lahaina in the 1840s; sugar plantations proved crucial to the white American takeover of the islands to integrate into the Western capitalist system (as crudely manifest in Twain's *Letters from Hawaii* and *Roughing It*, as we shall see later in chapter 3).[53] On the other hand, Hawai'i could be differentiated and distanced from the mainland USA, disconnected from the mainland as some timeless primordial paradise fit to preserve

51. Henry Adams, letter to Lucy Baxter, 30 September 1891, and letter to Henry Cabot Lodge, 4 August 1891, in *The Letters of Henry Adams, Vol. 3: 1886–1892*, 550 and 519. On turn-of-the-century imperial discourse and the global politics of industrialization that Adams, for all his irony, was subject to, see Gore Vidal, "The Day the American Empire Ran Out of Gas," in *At Home: Essays, 1982–1988* (New York: Vintage, 1990), 107–12. Although heir to a U.S. presidential family involved in what he mocked as "empire building" for over 150 years, Adams was struck by imperial and counterimperial dynamics in Tahiti as in Hawai'i, and tried to invent counterlinear forms of historical ethnography and subaltern biography in his *Memoirs of Arii Taimai*, in two distinct texts of 1893 and 1901, to express these Pacific-based dynamics he felt entangled in. See Daniel L. Manheim, "The Voice of Arii Taimai: Henry Adams and the Challenge of Empire," *biography: an Interdisciplinary Quarterly* 22 (1999): 209–36.

52. On the staying power of "pastoral" fantasies in the literature of Hawai'i as well as the hegemonic threat of representations of Hawai'i as "pastoral" island endemic to the tourist industry fantasy, see Stephen H. Sumida, *And the View from the Shore: Literary Traditions of Hawai'i* (Seattle: University of Washington Press, 1991), esp. chaps. 3 and 4.

53. See Dudden, "The Hawaiian Islands," in *The American Pacific*, 49–77.

nature as pastoral enclave. In this latter U.S. fantasy ripe for mass tourism, Hawai'i came to be released from this system of capitalist corruption and teleology of modernization (an image undercut by Melville in *Typee*, who by 1842 sees the Hawaiian royalty as the most corrupted and Europeanized natives of the Pacific) and became a site of leisure and letting go.

In 1867, at the request of the Pacific Mail Steamship Line, the U.S. nation purchased Midway island to establish a coaling station in the vast Pacific, and thus set a precedent (just prior to the purchase of "Russian America" via Alaska) for the appropriation of noncontiguous territories in the Pacific. Secretary of State William Seward manifested sovereign designs on Hawai'i in a letter to General William McCook, U.S. minister resident in Hawai'i, as early as 1867. "It is proper that you should know for your own information," Seward wrote, "that a lawful and peaceful annexation of the islands to the United States with the consent of the people of the Sandwich Islands, is deemed desirable by this government; and that if the policy of annexation should really conflict with the policy of reciprocity, annexation is in every case preferred."[54] In 1887, with a renewed reciprocity treaty, rights to Pearl Harbor were conceded as an exclusive coaling station and repair base providing a geophysical hegemony over the Northern Pacific that only Japan would challenge in the next century.[55] Annexation had been the preferred policy since the reign of King Kamehameha III, until reciprocity was no longer proving to be in commercial self-interest. But Seward's imperial vision of an American Pacific did not fully come about until 1898, in the context of the Spanish-American War and the extension of the Open Door policy, routing trade back and forth across the Pacific to Asia.

It remains important for Americans to know something about the "island paradise" of Hawai'i as Pacific location and culture; this place played a key economic, military, and maritime role in the production of an *American* Pacific that came into shape in the mid–nineteenth century with the linkage to Oregon and California. This fact of imperial outreach and the Asia peril would lead to the overthrow of the Hawaiian monarchy by the "missionary party" in 1893 and ratification of territorial status in 1898, after the Navy's "Asian Squadron" sank Spain's Pacific fleet in Manila

54. Seward is quoted in Meiric K. Dutton, ed., *A Letter from King Kamehameha V to the Bishop of Honolulu* (Honolulu: Loomis House Press, 1952), n.p.
55. Dudden, *The American Pacific*, 64.

Bay. Recognized for a century in international treaties and diplomatic exchanges between Europe and countries of Asia and the Pacific, the nation of these Native Hawaiians may now have the strongest claim to sovereignty of any indigenous group in the United States.[56] No longer just a missionary or sugar oligarchy, Hawai'i had moved, by the inexorable dynamics of Western geopolitical logic, from a condition of "independent sovereignty" to a position Queen Lili'uokalani, the last Hawaiian monarch, could lament in the 1880s had become "a mere dependency, either openly or under sufficient disguise, on the government of the United States."[57]

Herman Melville spent only four years in the watery domains of the South Pacific in the Marquesas and Hawai'i. But he was one of the first Americans to express a vision of how the international labors of the whaling industry, in a loose *extraterritorial* sway, were taking dominion over the northern reaches of the South Pacific, especially through the converting, industrializing, and managing of Hawai'i to prevail against British and French interests. (Britain annexed New Zealand in 1840, and France the Marquesas, Tahiti, and Moorea in 1842, as the Monroe Doctrine was invoked to warn Britain and France against annexing the Hawaiian islands.) Through master-narrative surveys of oceanic space in *Typee, Omoo, White Jacket*, and *Moby-Dick*, Melville's dream of islands, in Gavan Daws's phrase, "took literary possession" of the South Pacific.[58]

56. Michael Kioni Dudley and Keoni Kealoha Agard, *A Call for Hawaiian Sovereignty* (Honolulu: Na Kāne O Ka Malo Press, 1990): Charles F. Wilkinson, attorney for the Native American Rights Fund, "pointed out that Native Hawaiians have the strongest claim to sovereignty of any indigenous group in the United States because during the century before 1893, Hawai'i was recognized by the world as a sovereign nation. . . . France and England *and the United States* had internationally recognized treaties with Hawai'i which guaranteed its independence as a sovereign nation" (121).

57. Ibid., xix; Queen Lydia Lili'uokalani, *Hawai'i's Story by Hawai'i's Queen* (1898; Rutland, VT: Tuttle, 1964), 38. This last Hawaiian queen was also a fine poet and songwriter, whose works still haunt the U.S. imagination, if studied in the pathos of their modern context.

58. Daws, *A Dream of Islands*, 117. In the heady and business-oriented terms of A. Grove Day, the central canon-making scholar of the Euro-American presence as a literary archive establishing the White Pacific as such, from Melville and Pierre Lotti down to Charles Bernard Nordhoff, James Norman Hall, and Steven Goldsberry, "Melville was the first American of genius to make literary capital of the South Seas." See *Mad about Islands: Novelists of a Vanished Pacific* (Honolulu: Mutual Publishing, 1987), 59.

As a canonical work refiguring national narratives of appropriation and expansion, *Moby-Dick* expressed U.S. methods and interests in this region as these ranged from the capitalist rationality of Starbuck to the blindly transcendental hermeneutics of Ahab, whose white rhetoric churned the white whale into a symbol of that which opposes the U.S. will on this watery frontier and which it was worth dominating in waters, we should recall, between Japan and Hawai'i. For Ahab, if less so for Ishmael in his "Pacific becoming," this South Pacific was made to speak the wonders and horrors of American enterprise in its imperial outreach. "The uncounted isles of all Polynesia confess the same truth," Melville wrote in *Moby-Dick*, "and do commercial homage to the whale-ship, that cleared the way to the missionary and the merchant, and in many cases carried the primitive missionaries to their first destinations."[59] This remains a cautionary insight into national purpose and method, as economy precedes and installs the ideology of "freedom," even now in post-Mao China or in the vast commercial reaches of transnational cyberspace.[60]

The whaling industry would be just about over by 1855, to be replaced by sugar plantations and copra economies in the South Pacific and superseded in the world economy by the use of petroleum.[61] But the U.S. will to enterprise as a sublimated vision of extraterritorial conquest extended across the Pacific, Melville saw through the vision of Ishmael, would outlast Ahab and his demonized (if not indigenized) whale: ocean viewed not just as an extension of the western prairie frontier, but as implicating "the Pacific as sweatshop" and "whale ship as [global] factory." Melville was uncanny in his attempt to survey, enlist, and map powerful Asian interests in this new, interlinked Pacific. Though China, Korea, and Japan had tried to resist, bypass, or ignore the extraterritorial parceling of space by Western nations, Melville urged that these whaling ships of Nantucket would foreshadow and lead to the black ships of Commodore Perry, as these were unlocking Japan from global isolation in 1853. "If that double-bolted land, Japan, is ever to become hospitable," the novelist continued with his

---

59. Melville, *Moby-Dick*, 100.
60. I keep coming back to Melville in this study of "the American Pacific," if only to exorcise his imperial claims, if only all the better to affiliate myself with the energies and risks of what Deleuze called his "becoming native" and "becoming Pacific" via Ishmael's tactics and voice.
61. See Douglas L. Oliver, "Whalers, Traders, and Missionaries: 1780–1850," in *The Pacific Islands* (Garden City, NY: Doubleday, 1961), 97–116.

Butterfly-like fantasy, "it is the whale-ship alone to whom the credit will be due; for already she is on the threshold."[62] As the whaling industry shifted grounds from New Zealand to waters off Japan in the 1840s, Melville was there to survey, embody, and yet resist the will to global power in the transnational reaches of the American Pacific.

As canonical spectacle of destructive powers enacted in the Pacific, *Moby-Dick* conducted global politics, opening, traversing, and interlocking disparate regions and fresh markets into a coherent space of American fantasy and design, even as it linked with minor languages and other symbol systems through Pacific islanders and Singapore laborers. The whaling ships of Massachusetts here played John the Baptist in the watery domain to Asian-Pacific "Indians" and thus foreshadowed the coming of industry and Christian symbolism (blessing the wealth of nations) to redeem the local, pagan, minor Pacific from itself. Melville worried that Americans (such as David Reynolds) would awaken countries such as Japan and Korea, if not the "guano islands" of seagull excrement, from their precapitalist and predemocratic slumbers in Asia.[63] By the Guano Law of 1856, tellingly enough, the United States took strategic possession of numerous islands beyond Hawai'i for use in fertilizer materials and weaponry, founding a vision of U.S. tourist paradise on the material infrastructure of bird shit, imperial politics, dynamite, conversion, and war.

That Meiji Japan would assert a rival imperial force in the Asia/Pacific against falling into another extraterritorial market for the West—annexing Formosa, Korea, and parts of China with preemptive strikes—would lead to conflict and war across the twentieth century.[64] This geopolitical battle for regional hegemony would lead, with World War II, to the total militarization of the Pacific, in ways that have deformed these intricate but resource-poor cultures of Truk, Kwajelein, and Palau to the southwest of Pearl Harbor. By 1947, James Michener could write a book called *Tales of the South Pacific* that, subordinating (via caricature and romantic musing) these local interests, voices, and native mythologies, used islands in Micro-

---

62. Melville, *Moby-Dick*, 100.
63. Ibid., 108.
64. On Meiji Japan's attempt to articulate counterhegemony within the modernizing Asia-Pacific region, see Miyoshi, *As We Saw Them*. On the contradictions confronting Japan as "an Asian power ascending to dominance [in the Pacific] within a structure not of its own making," see Dirlik, "The Asian-Pacific Idea," 73–79.

nesia and Melanesia as mere backdrops of love and pain for American "men and women caught up in the drama of a big war"—the basis for the 1958 Broadway musical *South Pacific,* where *papalagi* war and loves projected from Broadway subsume the Toganese (actually Tonkinese) native interests and turn the locals (such as Bloody Mary, as we shall see in chapter 5) into prostitutes of Asian/Pacific culture and self.[65]

At an affirmative level of pragmatic energy, however, *Moby-Dick* comprised an imperial agon of space and helped to expand the reaches of the continental sublime into an oceanic encounter with power. Better than *Typee,* as that romance is infected with half-baked European primitivism, *Moby-Dick* represented Melville's self-divided national quest (through Ahab/Ishmael), in Deleuze's utopic sense of tracing a kind of westward flight, as a "whale-becoming which is not one of [Western subject/object] imitation," as an erratic, self-dispossessing encounter with the Pacific Ocean peoples and the ocean itself whereby European "binary machines" of mapping might break down in mutual cannibalization.[66] As if to terrify Japan with a spectacle of maritime ambition in the Pacific, Captain Ahab's own *Pequod* is destroyed by that specter of the national sublime—Moby-Dick as sublime commodity—sailing southeastward off "the far coast of Japan" only two years before this imperial kingdom would be opened to the world capitalist market. If the English-reading Japanese were not impressed by Melville's spectacle of Pacific might and his transcendentalized antagonists in Ahab/Ishmael, they would be, as Emerson argued, by such technological spectacles as the train and the telegraph, which Commodore Perry brought in miniature. This tactic worked well for an island culture and nation-state like Japan less impressed by geographical bulk than by the miniaturization of sublime infinitude and creations of sublime interiority.[67] Through the imagination of Pacific space in *Moby-Dick,* a specta-

65. James A. Michener, *Tales of the South Pacific* (New York: Fawcett, 1947). On the South Pacific as space of white fantasy, see Glenn K. S. Man, "Hollywood and the South Pacific," *East-West Film Journal* 5 (1991): 16–29, and Robert C. Schmitt, *Hawai'i in the Movies, 1898–1959* (Honolulu: Hawaiian Historical Society, 1988).

66. Gilles Deleuze and Claire Parnet, "On the Superiority of Anglo-American Literature," in *Dialogues,* trans. Hugh Tomlinson and Barbara Habberjam (New York: Columbia University Press, 1987), 36–44.

67. See O-Young Lee, *Smaller Is Better: Japan's Mastery of the Miniature,* trans. Robert N. Huey (Tokyo: Kodansha, 1982): "Our thesis, then, is that one aspect of the Japanese mind is an imaginative power that seeks to make things smaller," from bonsai trees and

cle of extraterritorial power had been staged to inspire international recognition and enlist national belief, just as the uss *Boston* would later be stationed in Honolulu Harbor in 1893 to manage, by a quiet display of military power, the bloodless overthrow of the Hawaiian constitutional monarchy by American businessmen.

In 1881, Emperor Mutsuhito of Meiji Japan would turn down King Kalākaua's offer of a dynastic marriage with Hawaiian royalty that would have, in effect, turned the "small nation" of Hawai'i into a Japanese colony or, as it had been toward England, a protectorate. We can sympathize with King Kalākaua's will to alter the imperial balance of power in the Asia-Pacific region, as well as his later attempt to unite island nations of Polynesia into a confederacy of Pacific power. This clever poet-king tried to shape the Pacific away from American and toward Native Hawaiian and Asian ends, but was doomed and defeated in the process. His fate can be seen through the jaundiced eyes of his American Hawaiian "white subject" and commissioner of immigration, William N. Armstrong. Circumnavigating the globe with the king in search of labor for Hawaiian sugar plantations, Armstrong remarks, "In the curious recesses of his Polynesian brain, the King had contrived a scheme of matrimonial alliance between the thrones of Japan and Hawai'i. He had a vague fear that the United States might in the near future absorb his kingdom. . . . Had the scheme been accepted by the Emperor, it would have tended to make Hawai'i a Japanese colony; a movement distasteful to all of the Great Powers."[68]

These imperial, uneven negotiations of Pacific space by Western powers

---

radios to the Sony Walkman and microelectronics (24). The "Japanese sublime," as Kojin Karatani once described it to me in conversation, seeks to miniaturize infinitude in a small space rather than dominate via spatial and territorial extension (as in the nineteenth-century landscapes of "the American sublime"). Perry prepared for his naval mission by reading some forty books on Japan available in New York and London (Miyoshi, *As We Saw Them*, 13) and brought miniaturized versions of modern American technologies (such as the railroad) to impress Japan with displays of the sublime. See David E. Nye, *American Technological Sublime* (Cambridge, MA: MIT Press, 1994), on the long-abiding idealization of such icons and forces as a national and global prerogative. See Dudden, *American Pacific*, 17–19 and chap. 6, as he works out Japan's uneven relationship since 1853 to " 'the Pacific Rim,' and even 'the American Pacific' with its intrinsically nationalistic bias" and entanglement in counterimperialist politics (262).
68. William N. Armstrong, *Around the World with a King* (1903; Rutland, VT: Tuttle, 1977), 62–63.

helped to open and interlock Japan and the Asia / Pacific to what Armstrong called (and promoted as) "the sphere of American influence over Hawai'i" in Washington.[69] The local Pacific could not, in this imperial instance, by any means resist the competing interests of such global powers as England, the United States, and Japan. The "hermit nation" of Korea would also have to initiate its own Open Door policies, at the urging of the U.S. Navy and Meiji Japan, during this era when imperial politics deformed the Asia / Pacific; postcolonial longings were a project for the future, as another Asia / Pacific space, Taiwan, got itself entangled in the imperial rivalry between Japan and China and the racial phobias of Australia.[70]

From 1820 if not earlier in its entangled contacts with nation-states, Hawai'i was fated to be troped into an American "crossroads of the Pacific." The territory was seen at times as helpless, given Armstrong's social Darwinist argument, "before the manifest destiny of America" reaching out, at century's end, to link North America to the markets of Asia. By geographical situation as much as through force, American commercial interests and a missionary oligarchy emanating from New England had turned the small Polynesian kingdom of the Kamehamehas into exactly what Armstrong gloated it had become in his era: "the crossways of the Pacific commerce."[71] Hawai'i emerged as crossroads over the Pacific to "the vast domains of Asia," as well as source of counterwisdom and contemporary conscience. Conjured into a paradise, pleasure periphery, and profit zone in the Pacific, Hawai'i proved object and victim of the Euro-American imagination, as literature and aesthetic "imagery was a compo-

69. Ibid., 62.

70. See Dudden, *American Pacific*, 140, on USN Commodore Robert Wilson Shufeldt's gunboat diplomacy in the "hermit kingdom" of Korea and the consequent Korean-American peace treaty. On Taiwan's entanglement in the imperial policies of Japan and the anti-Asia racial politics of reaction in Australia and the United States from 1895 onwards, see Kuan-Hsing Chen, introduction to *Trajectories: Inter-Asia Cultural Studies* (London: Routledge, 1998), 38–19, and Henry P. Frei, *Japan's Southward Advance and Australia: From the Sixteenth Century to World War II* (Honolulu: University of Hawai'i Press, 1991).

71. Armstrong, *Around the World*, 190. "Although it [the overthrow of the Hawaiian monarchy in 1893] was aggressive and made acutely so by the geographical situation of the islands at the crossways of the Pacific commerce, it was peaceful and bloodless; for of all weak races which have come in contact in any land whatsoever with the stronger races, the Hawaiians have suffered the least from injustice and physical dominance" (283).

nent of the decision-making of those Europeans who would enter the Pacific in their thousands and eventually dominate it."[72]

This vision of outside domination by imperial powers has to be re-imagined, historicized, and undone at places such as Bamboo Ridge in Hawai'i, at sites of cultural production such as Taipei and Suva, and at other contact zones of "Asian/Pacific" mixture and contention. Despite the preexisting cartography of imperial power and colonial nationhood, the "American Pacific" may now be located otherwise and elsewhere. It may well exist along lines of flight and the making of wings and diaspora, as well as in acts of possession and rooting down, those uneasy feats of statehood, cultural claiming, and prior settlement.

72. Bernard Smith, *Imagining the Pacific: In the Wake of the Cook Voyages* (New Haven: Yale University Press, 1992), 191. Smith's chapters 7 and 8 on "Constructing 'Pacific' People" are less inscribed with British imperial aesthetics, as he (having been influenced by the skepticism of Said's *Orientalism*) tries to distance "orientalist" conventions of the British imagination enforced and circulated by Cook's voyages. Smith remarks of Sir Joshua Reynolds's painting of *Omai* (1775), "Orientalist imagery was powerful enough to supervene even when an artist had a Tahitian [Omai, brought back to England on Cook's second voyage] in the flesh before him" (175). On the Euro-American iconography of the Pacific as well as Nativist recuperation and reactions then and now, see Nicholas Thomas, *In Oceania: Visions, Artifacts, Histories* (Durham, NC: Duke University Press, 1997), esp. chap. 1, "Partial Texts: Representation, Colonialism, and Agency in Pacific History." On gender dynamics of the colonial era that fetishized Pacific places and peoples as exotic and erotic objects to be possessed, romantically and politically, see Lenore Manderson and Margaret Jolly, eds., *Sites of Desire, Economies of Pleasure: Sexualities in Asia and the Pacific* (Chicago: University of Chicago Press, 1997); on Asia and inter-Asia as sites of internal colonization and imperial dynamics that complicate and interlock with those of the putative West, see Tani E. Barlow, ed., *Formations of Colonial Modernity in East Asia* (Durham, NC: Duke University Press, 1997).

CHAPTER 3

Megatrends and Micropolitics in the American Pacific:
Tracing Some "Local Motions" from Mark Twain to
Bamboo Ridge

Over Influenced
> —T-shirt slogan of Manu, critic of "the Pacific Way," in Epeli Hau'ofa, *Tales of*
> *the Tikongs*

American literature is an ocean.
> —Ishmael Reed, "The Ocean of American Literature"

BUILDING UP NEW ENGLAND, O'AHU

If the future of our country "lies in the Pacific," as Caspar Weinberger grandly claimed in the Reagan era as he outlined U.S. foreign policy by means of the trickle-up dynamic of transnationalization as a win-win ("voodoo") dynamic of free enterprise rippling around the Pacific Rim, its *past* is surely embedded there: uncanny ingredients such as our entanglement in imperial politics from the Marquesas Islands to the Philippines; indoctrination of the "savage" and "oriental" others into an Enlightenment ethos of Western-scaled modernization; the commercial and militarized extension westward of Manifest Destiny assumptions and policies to the fishing waters around Pearl Harbor; a vision of political grandeur as materialized in extraterritorial assimilation of indigenous peoples and alternative cultures; in short, the creation of Asian/Pacific *Calibans,* in such sites as Hawai'i and the Philippines, acculturated to a sense of their own inferiority to the mores, cultural symbols, and racial myths of New England culture.[1]

1. U.S. extraterritorial policies "predicated on commercial, rather than territorial control of other cultures and people," as readers of *Typee* realize, began sloppily in the pre-

"Patiently, and somewhat rigorously, no doubt, they [the New England missionaries] sought from the beginning to make New England men and women of these Hawaiians," Charles Nordhoff shrewdly observed of Honolulu residents in 1874, "and what is wonderful is that, to a large extent they have succeeded."[2]

By no means isolated, U.S. literary culture does play some part in producing and disseminating the national imaginary and converting local subjects, out in the remote and noncontiguous Pacific, to its set of foundational premises and cultural-political beliefs. Throughout the nineteenth century, *Americanization* of Hawaiian subjects was everywhere underway, from commercial contact, missionary settlement, and the installation of the plantation system. By 1864, U.S. President Lincoln could boast, in a letter to Elisha Allen, of this so-called *palapala* project (missionary education of Native Hawaiians through reading and writing, a word that has come to mean "literature" in Hawai'i): "Its people are free, and its laws, language, and religion are largely the fruit of our own teaching and example."[3] Furthermore, as Hawai'i came to be more fully linked and acculturated to the modern capitalist world system, it became a site not just of missionary conversion and plantation labor, but of tourist fascination and romantic endearment: "The tourists had all read Somerset Maugham, as preparation for their trip to the [Hawaiian] tropics, and went in for white linen suits and dresses," as James Jones was to remark in setting the scene for postwar

----

French Marquesas: Captain Joseph Ingraham arrived from Boston in 1791 and attempted, just after the formal end of the Revolutionary War, to annex them and did manage to rename them Washington Island and Federal Island; Captain David Porter later attempted, by force and imperial scheming, to annex the Marquesas in his efforts to interrupt British shipping in the Pacific during the War of 1812. See John Carlos Rowe, "Melville's *Typee*: U.S. Imperialism at Home and Abroad," in *National Identities and Post-Americanist Narratives*, ed. Donald E. Pease (Durham, NC: Duke University Press, 1994), 255–78; and T. Walter Herbert, *Marquesan Encounters: Melville and the Meaning of Civilization* (Cambridge, MA: Harvard University Press, 1980).

2. See Malcolm McIntosh, *Arms across the Pacific: Security and Trade Issues across the Pacific* (London: Pinter, 1987), 5, for one of the final cold war mappings of the entire Pacific as a binary US/USSR space. Nordhoff's comment on Hawaiians is from *Northern California, Oregon and the Sandwich Islands* (New York: Harper and Brothers, 1874), and is excerpted in W. Storrs Lee, ed., *Hawaii: A Literary Chronicle* (New York: Funk and Wagnalls, 1967), 293.

3. Quoted in Ralph Kuykendall and A. Grove Day, *Hawaii: A History, from Polynesian Kingdom to American Statehood* (Englewood Cliffs, NJ: Prentice-Hall, 1976), 193.

white romance on the beaches and in the bars of Oʻahu in *From Here to Eternity* (1951). "But you did not mind, not after a few drinks."[4]

When the "Kanaka" sailors so admired by Richard Henry Dana in *Two Years before the Mast* referred to the entire mainland United States as Boston, they merely had acknowledged the offshore domination of New England culture over the geography and polity of their own native space. These same Hawaiians were already toiling (as seen by Dana) in the leather works at San Diego. The better to make their way within a global political economy of wealthy nations that was transforming their life-world at Lahaina into something like a small Pacific Provincetown, and themselves into modern Hawaiians on the road to modern conversion and willy-nilly Americanization—like the pioneering orphan and first convert, Henry (Obookiah) ʻŌpukahaʻia, studying theology at Yale College in 1816, or, later, Akaiko Akana at the Hartford Theological Seminary before his return to preside over the influential Kawaiahao Church as the first Hawaiian pastor in 1918. Dana quotes a Hawaiian sailor he admires in San Diego defending, in mixtures of English and Hawaiian, his culture's reciprocal humanity against those cannibal fantasies from the West: "New Zealand Kanaka eat white man;—Sandwich Island Kanaka,—no. Sandwich Island Kanaka ua like pu na haole—all 'e same a' you."[5]

This vision of the "American Pacific" was effectively secured through the annexation of Hawaiʻi in 1898, those delicious Sandwich Islands discovered by Captain Cook and his team of natural historians, painters, scientists, and sex-crazed sailors. After a tourist survey of Pacific and Asian geopolitics with Henry Adams in Samoa, Hawaiʻi, and Tahiti concluded in 1901, American painter John LaFarge recorded the Adams family sentiment for empire: "The Pacific is our [that is, American] natural property. Our great coast borders it for a quarter of the world. We must either give up Hawaiʻi, which will inevitably then go over to England, or take it willingly, if we need to keep the passage open to eastern Asia, the future

---

4. James Jones, *From Here to Eternity* (1951; New York: Avon, 1975), 673.

5. Richard Henry Dana Jr., *Two Years before the Mast, and Twenty-Four Years After* (1840; Danbury, CT: Grolier, 1980), 144–45: "Boston (as they [Hawaiian sailors] call the United States." Reverend Akaiko Akana's *The Sinews for Racial Development* (1918) argued for renewed "race-consciousness" among Hawaiians as synthesized within a set of Christian workaday and American domestic values; it was reprinted as *Light upon the Mist: A Reflection of Wisdom for the Future Generations of Native Hawaiians*, ed. Eleanora M. DeFries (Kailua-Kona, HI: Mahina Productions, 1992).

battleground of commerce."[6] The Adams family vision of imperial succession proved prophetic on both counts: take Hawai'i the American "missionary-sugar oligarchy" did, in land contracts of Anglo-Saxon redemption (and territorial annexation) that sublimated into nonconquest so many acts of liberal appropriation. Slowly, this postindigenous Asia/Pacific became a region of global commerce and movement, as America's main corridor to Japan and China.

The Pacific peoples, Henry Adams suggested in letters and policy musings, nonetheless were recognizably "oriental," that is, childlike, bodily, mindless, savage-like, and as yet incapable of self-rule in the grand metaphysics of empire that extended from the Puritan mind and Federalist policies (such as the Monroe Doctrine invoked in Hawai'i in 1842) to the multiple waters of the Pacific. For Adams, caught up in his own private and national ironies of empire, Polynesia represented some kind of oceanic oblivion, a release of the Western ego from the modern ethos of labor, anxiety, and guilt: "to sleep forever in the trade-winds under the southern stars, wandering over the dark purple ocean, with its purple sense of solitude and the void."[7] But the Pacific, nonetheless, had to be absorbed into the American calculus of foreign policy in the imperial era, as the United States took into its quasicolonial possession strategic military and commercial sites of Hawai'i, Samoa, and the Philippine islands.

KING SUGAR HAS COME AND GONE
INTO TRANSNATIONAL TOURISM

With the discovery of gold in 1848 and completion of the transcontinental railroad in 1869, the state of California materialized into a center of capitalist accumulation and Pacific Rim presence. "Capitalist centralization"

6. John La Farge, *Reminiscences of the South Seas* (Garden City, NY: Doubleday, 1912), 153.
7. Henry Adams, *The Education of Henry Adams*, ed. Ernest Samuels (Boston: Houghton Mifflin, 1973), 316. On these post-"Puritan" materials, see Richard Drinnon, *Facing West: The Metaphysics of Indian-Hating and Empire Building* (New York: New American Library, 1980), 273, and chap. 18, "Outcast of the Islands: Henry Adams," on Asian-Pacific orientalism that expresses itself in attitudes such as that "the natives [of the Pacific islands], like all orientals, are children, and have the charms of childhood as well as the faults of the small boy" (249). For a materialized discussion of Adams as critic of American imperial ideology and market culture as globalized in the post–Civil War era, see Paul Bové, "Giving Thought to America: Intellect and *The Education of Henry Adams*," *Critical Inquiry* 23 (1996): 80–108.

continued in London, Paris, and New York City, to be sure, but geography was being restructured along sea routes of economic flux and cultural liquidity that link the space of Asia and the Pacific to global designs, many of which remained centered in Europe and the mainland USA. It was during this era of uneven geographical development and Manifest Destiny that the state of California began its "tilt to the global space economy of capitalism that would continue for the next century and a half."[8]

Crucial to this entry of California into the dynamism of this world system, as shaped along the Pacific Rim, was communication with (and representation of) Hawai'i as an in-between space transmitting the cheap labor and abundant resources of the Asian Pacific region to mainland America via the port cities of the West Coast. As mediating link to the markets of Canton and whaling waters off Japan, Hawai'i was within seventy years (from the arrival of the missionaries in 1820 to the downfall of the Hawaiian monarchy in 1893) appropriated to American interests by the twin strategies mandating *commercialization* along lines of enlightened development and, simultaneously, projecting an image of timeless *pastoralization*. The island spaces of O'ahu and Maui were linked to economic transformations of land and political identity into national appendages, yet at the same time preserved as pleasure peripheries of quasi-Edenic fantasy and recreation immune to capitalist destruction, remaining (in imagination) what Mark Twain mused were "the loveliest fleet of islands that lies anchored in any ocean."[9]

8. Edward Soja, *Postmodern Geographies: The Reassertion of Space in Critical Social Theory* (London: Verso, 1989), 190. Soja quotes a letter from Karl Marx to Friedrich Sorge in 1880 that expressed his fascination with the economic dynamism of California. " 'I should be very much pleased,' he wrote, 'if you could find me something good (meaty) on economic conditions in *California* . . . California is very important for me because nowhere else has the upheaval most shamelessly caused by capitalist centralization taken place with such speed.' "

9. Twain's comment, written to the Hawaiian Promotion Committee in a letter of thanks in 1908 and much used in tourist pamphlets and sites to this day (as at Volcano House on the Big Island), is discussed in Stephen H. Sumida, *And the View from the Shore: Literary Traditions of Hawai'i* (Seattle: University of Washington Press, 1991), 38–56. For the endurance of *contradictory* fantasies in the tourist industry, see J. D. Goss, "Placing the Market and Marketing Place: Tourist Advertising of the Hawaiian Islands, 1972–92," *Society and Space* 11 (1993): 663–88. Goss contends of Hawai'i Visitors Bureau materials sponsored by the State of Hawai'i: "The persistent themes of spatialization in these advertisements are perhaps unsurprisingly that of singularity and alter-

Edward Soja calls this (uneven) modernizing of local geography the process of peripheralization, meaning the differential distribution of power, interest, and capital across space and the domination of space by time; it was during this era that Hawai'i became central in the formation of an "American Pacific" linked to a Euro-American core.[10] As California is "centralized" in the transnational flow, Hawai'i is linked into plantation resource and tourist site in the same global dynamic.

Whatever Twain's later animadversions against U.S. imperialism in the Philippines in 1902 and his work in the Anti-Imperialist League in support of Emilio Aguinaldo, this powerful novelist had emerged (out of the remote West) to promote the linkage of Hawai'i to capitalist designs upon the Pacific three decades before this internationally recognized nation was overthrown by business interests in 1893 and annexed into an American territory in the organic act of 1900. This *de facto Americanization* of Hawai'i—as place of cultural identity and ethos of *malāma 'āina* (care for the sea and land)—into territory and state of democratic teleology is nicely summed up in the nation-building lyricism of two well-known Pacific scholars, Ralph Kuykendall and A. Grove Day, who boast (at the outset of their history of Hawai'i in 1948 as march of progress from "Polynesian kingdom to American statehood"), without irony or trace of native unrest, "The people of the Hawaiian Islands have passed, during the span of one hundred years, from the Stone Age into the Atomic Age."[11]

As cub reporter for the Sacramento *Union*, Twain crossed the eastern Pacific in 1866 on the *Ajax*, the first commercial steamship to transverse this space that had been awakened from Polynesian stability and linked to the world system and dynamics of Anglo-Saxon enterprise by the fateful

---

ity: the texts seek systematically to differentiate Hawai'i from other competing destinations and constitute Hawai'i in radical opposition to the mainland United States" (675).
10. Soja discusses this "social and spatial 'restructuring'" in "Watch This Space: An Interview with Edward Soja," working paper no. 9, Center for Twentieth Century Studies, University of Wisconsin–Milwaukee, 1990–1991, 6–10.
11. Ralph S. Kuykendall and A. Grove Day, preface to 1st ed., *Hawaii: A History, from Polynesian Kingdom to American Statehood* (Englewood Cliffs, NJ: Prentice-Hall, 1976), v. On Day's prolific, ambivalently racialized, and lifelong project to Americanize Hawai'i into a site of tourist consumption, literary fascination, and Pacific exoticism, see Paul Lyons, "Pacific Scholarship, Literary Criticism, and Touristic Desire: The Specter of A. Grove Day," *boundary 2* 24 (1997): 47–78.

voyages of Captain James Cook in 1778–1779 and Captain George Vancouver, who negotiated British protectorate status with King Kamehameha I from 1792 to 1794. Twain's twenty-five letters and retellings of his experience in *Roughing It* (1872) reveal that he had few qualms about promoting commerce between California and what he admitted was "the kingdom of Hawai'i." (By 1873, in a letter to the *New York Daily Tribune*, he would urge the outright annexation of the islands by the United States, something that Americans in Hawai'i had begun agitating for as early as the 1850s.)

Twain intuits that these new technologies of travel, shipping, and communication will reshape global space (in Lawson Inada's pungent phrase, "shrinking the Pacific") and allow the multifaced penetration of national interests into the Pacific and, thus, help fill the islands "full of Americans" and so many California capitalists placed into insider positions of regional domination.[12] In a letter from Honolulu to Sacramento on 19 March 1866, he argues for the compression of Pacific space-time by means of commercial shipping and in the name of (unequal) profit. "The main argument in favor of a line of fast steamers is this," he urges. "They would soon populate these islands with Americans, and loosen that French and English grip which is gradually closing around them, and which will result in a contest before many years as to which of the two shall seize and hold them."[13] As fledgling colonial power in the Pacific, America is playing third fiddle to France and Great Britain in the attempt to "seize and hold" such territories, Twain admits, but the infusion of California capital and commerce will soon offer a speedier, dematerialized means of expansionist conquest in which the American geopolitical positioning on the Pacific Rim will play a key role: "But if California can send capitalists down here in seven or eight days time and take them back in nine or ten [against trade winds], she can fill these islands full of Americans and regain her lost foothold.

12. Lawson Fusao Inada, "Shrinking the Pacific," *boundary 2* 21 (1994): 57–58. The Pacific is shrunk via feats of global imagination recalling diasporic migration patterns: "(with Taipei/Honolulu//conveniently between)."

13. Mark Twain, letter from Honolulu, 19 March 1866, in *Mark Twain's Letters from Hawaii*, ed. A. Grove Day (Honolulu: University of Hawai'i Press, 1966), 12. There may be better texts of Twain's letters, but Day's still has wide circulation in contemporary Hawai'i as one of the basic books tourists read, with Michener's *Hawaii*, to comprehend the American presence in Hawai'i and Hawaiians themselves.

Hawai'i is too far away now, though, when it takes a man twenty days to come here and twenty-five or thirty to get back in a sailing vessel."[14]

Linked to Asia and the Pacific via the connection to California markets, Hawai'i may no longer be a Boston-dominated game of cultural and economic capital.[15] No wonder that, as Twain says, "to the natives all whites are haoles—how-ries—that is, strangers, or, more properly, foreigners," whereas "to the white residents all white newcomers are 'Californians,'" that is, incoming American capitalists from the Pacific Rim.[16]

No wonder that, still to this day, *haoles* are marked by Hawaiians as white "outsiders" in this Asian/Pacific space, even as newer patterns of nonwhite capitalist flow from Tokyo and Hong Kong continue to shuffle up the region. Terese Svoboda captures the alien posture of amnesiac tourists "here to buy the beaches / for the natives" while nervously staring at themselves in the waters off Waikīkī Beach in contemporary Hawai'i:

> . . . you're not
> the devil, you're "howlee"
> as a full moon that rises apart
> from the condos must be howled at.[17]

Twain would later take a deeper interest in racial and cultural conflicts of indigenous citizens such as the hapa-Hawaiian Bill Ragsdale who died of leprosy, and he later attempted a Hawaiian novel to deal with historical ambiguities of "howlee" domination. Still, as Twain listened to the local culture in 1866, he heard only a subliterate gibberish immune to proper English understanding. "All were chattering in the catchy, chopped-up Kanaka language," he concedes, "but what they were chattering about will always remain a mystery to me."[18] The islanders' mixture of Hawaiian English into what linguists call Hapa Haole pidgin was not his concern: social domination via the spread of culture, at that point, was.[19]

14. Ibid.

15. On lingering patterns of cultural and economic dependency, see Noel J. Kent, *Hawai'i: Islands under the Influence* (New York: Monthly Review Press, 1983), and Paul F. Hooper, *Elusive Destiny: The Internationalist Movement in Modern Hawaii* (Honolulu: University of Hawai'i Press, 1980), e.g., chap. 4, "Our New Geneva."

16. Twain, letter of July 1866, *Letters from Hawaii*, 202–3.

17. Terese Svoboda, "The Little Grass Shack," *boundary 2* 21 (1994): 187–88.

18. Twain, *Letters from Hawaii*, 27.

19. On "makeshift English" compounded with Hawaiian words called *hapa haole* (half

With less ambiguity than Melville had evinced in *Typee*, Twain urges the supplanting of one feudal class system by another, that of industrial capitalism. Taking Native Hawaiians by Christian indoctrination out of their own "savage times" and "the customs of a barbarous age" into the democratic ethos of economic modernity, "The missionaries have clothed them [the native Kanakas, or Hawaiians], educated them, broken up the tyrannous authority of their chiefs, and given them freedom and the right to enjoy whatever the labor of their hands and brains produces, with equal laws for all and punishment for all alike who transgress them."[20] These "Kanakas," as he labels them into commoners, were not Pacific Indians nor ill-fitting contract laborers but *kanaka maoli*, "the true or real people" of the land he knows so little about but makes so much of in a four-month stay as, later, in the closing fifteen chapters of *Roughing It* in 1872.[21]

Although Twain finds the beaches of Diamond Head littered in 1866 with sun-bleached bones of dead Hawaiians, killed not by warriors (as he first guesses) but by European microbes and "epidemics" (as he later suggests "is the most reasonable conjecture," based on his proto-missionary source, the *History of the Hawaiian or Sandwich Islands* by James J. Jarvis, published in Boston in 1844) of venereal disease, tuberculosis, and typhoid fever (he nowhere mentions leprosy), he explains that the 60,000 Hawaiians he finds living (their number shrunk in some seventy years from something like 800,000 or, at a bare minimum, 400,000) will find an equal right to property and bodily protection under European law.[22] When the Hawaiians did not die of European microbes, Twain suggested, their culture would die from Christianization and the march of political

---

white) that formed the substratum of Hawaiian Creole English as it later evolved on the plantations, see John E. Reinecke, *Language and Dialect in Hawaii* (Honolulu: University of Hawai'i Press, 1969), 34–35, and Albert J. Schutz, *The Voices of Eden: A History of Hawaiian Language Studies* (Honolulu: University of Hawai'i Press, 1994), on "pidgin Hawaiian" (47–49) as postcontact language of discussion between Hawaiians and peoples from England, Asia, and other parts of the world impacting on Hawai'i's main language.

20. Twain, *Letters from Hawaii*, 54, 169.

21. In the words of the Hawaiian activist Dr. Kekuni Blaisdell, "The name for themselves that they gave to the first foreigners who asked was *not* 'Indians,' as Captain Cook called our ancestors in 1778, but *kanaka maoli* . . . 'true or real person.' " See " 'Hawaiian' vs. 'Kanaka Maoli' as Metaphors," *Hawai'i Review* 13 (1989): 77.

22. Twain, *Letters from Hawaii*, 61–62.

economy anyway, and he himself, at this point, endorsed this process of cultural displacement.

The discourse of international exchange remained, on some idealized level of imagining at least, symmetrical, centered in shared trade, founded on a balance of shared power and mutual wealth. From the time of Adam Smith, this expresses global capitalism's benign understanding of itself as an enlightened project of world development and democratization via the free market system: an eternal "reciprocity" treaty.[23] Examining the sugar plantations in Hawai'i in 1866 as a profitable means to link the cheap labor of the Pacific and Asia to the commerce of California and mainland America, Twain was prescient in his orientalist musings. "People are always hatching fine schemes for inducing Eastern capital [that is, in this context, the capital of the northeastern USA] to the Pacific Coast," Twain conjectures, but the new source of global capital is not in Europe but spread across Asia: "Yonder in China are the capitalists you want—and under your own soil [in the gold mines] is a bank that will not dishonor their checks."[24]

Twain grows giddy at the prospect of Chinese coolies pouring cheap labor, and surplus value, into Hawai'i and California, as the profits will soar and circulate from Honolulu to San Francisco and New York: "The mine purchased for a song by Eastern capital would pour its stream of wealth past your door and empty it in New York" to the expanding benefit of venturing American "capitalists if coolie labor were adopted."[25] Twain uses the medium of print capitalism, as did missionary New England with its first printing press, to disseminate a vision of the American nation-state as a hybrid community of laboring free agents in which the Pacific region would play an expanding part as source and oceanic medium for a "vast Oriental wealth" flowing from China to Sacramento, San Francisco, New York, and Boston (274).

23. See Mary Louise Pratt, *Imperial Eyes: Travel Writing and Transculturation* (London: Routledge, 1992), 84, and, more generally, on modes of "anticonquest" in the era of scientific travel and scientific travel writing after Cook's Pacific voyages set the stage for inland exploration of Africa and South America. Also see Edward W. Said, *Culture and Imperialism* (New York: Knopf, 1993), on the interlocking discourses of "empire, geography, and culture" and the twentieth-century shift from British to American ascendancy.
24. Twain, *Letters from Hawaii*, 272.
25. Twain, *Letters from Hawaii*, 272, letter to Sacramento *Union*, 10 September 1866, predicting, in Day's words, "the fabulous future of California and the Pacific" (xii).

According to Twain's managerial scenario of manifest destiny and the international division of labor, the "savage times" and still primitive space of Hawai'i would be annexed to fit the international design as guided under the sign of Anglo-Saxon management and redemption; the region is enlisted not as a site of cultural interest or Edenic fantasy, as Twain does with so much tourist charm elsewhere, but to link the Far East of China and the eastern coast of America to the flow of global capital and national profit, with little idealization hazing over the racism of this exchange. "Asia," in this discourse operative across Twain's journalism for the Sacramento *Union* and available to sugar plantation owners of Hawai'i and the textile mill and railroad owners of California, emerges as the source of a golden secret, outright capitalist wealth shorn of any cultural mystique or religious fascination: "The secret is in their cheap Chinese labor" (273).

Boasting for the shift from an economy of whaling to one of sugar in the islands (87) and urging that "this country is the king of the sugar world, as far as astonishing productiveness is concerned" (257), Twain argues for the promotion of Hawaiian trade: "It is of the utmost importance to the United States that her trade with these islands should be carefully fostered and augmented" (20). Why such a strategic interest? The next sentence puts Twain's political-economic cards right on the Northern Pacific table: "Because—it pays. There can be no better reason than that."[26] With space shrunk and value circulating across the waterways into a universal norm, the $400,000 in trade revenues Hawai'i generated to the United States could be multiplied exponentially via the speed of expanded commerce.

As he surveys the twenty-nine wealth-generating sugar plantations of Maui, Hawai'i, and O'ahu and compares them favorably to the slave-driven sugar economy of Louisiana, Twain notes that this Pacific island economy is founded not only in rich soil but in the surplus value of abundant labor, with an aggregate sugar yield of twenty-seven million pounds since 1852: "The principal labor used on the plantations is that of Kanaka men and

26. Ibid. "It is a matter of the utmost importance to the United States that her trade with these islands should be carefully fostered and augmented. Because—it pays." Elsewhere, though he basically supports the Americanization dynamic of Hawai'i in what he portrays as a miniature pseudo–British Empire, Twain pokes fun at the missionary project in Hawai'i: "The missionaries braved a thousand privations to come and make them [the Hawaiians] miserable by telling them how beautiful and how blissful a place heaven is, and how nearly impossible it is to get there" (53).

women—six dollars to eight dollars a month and find them, or eight to ten dollars and let them find themselves," reads the contract (270). As Twain has been documenting, the Hawaiian culture ("the Kanaka race") is dying out, and with it the Hawaiians themselves. Hard labor is here an ally to the Protestant ethic of capitalist domination: "The sugar product is rapidly augmenting each year, and day by day the Kanaka race is passing away" (270). The solution to this death of native labor is not social welfare but the importation of an even more abundant source of cheap labor and surplus value, as "the Government sends to China for coolies and farms them out to the planters at $5 a month each for five years."[27]

These Asian laborers are, to Twain's eyes, "peaceable, obedient men and women," "steady, industrious workers when properly watched" by the Christian management (271). Looking past the dying Pacific culture of the Hawaiians and toward labor ready to be extracted from Asia, Twain grows ecstatic at the prospect, as he confides to his Sacramento readers, "You will have coolie labor in California some day. It is already forcing its superior claim upon the attention of your great mining, manufacturing, and public improvement corporations. You will not always go on paying $80 and $100 a month for labor which you can hire for $5" (271). In this new international division of labor, each Chinese American coolie represents $95 a month of surplus value to the globally canny American, who, like the Connecticut Yankee in feudal England, can manage the Asian/Pacific interchange to his own profit as these Asians labor at a "drudgery which neither intelligence nor education are required to fit a man for—drudgery which all white men abhor and are glad to escape from" (272).

Obviously, browns, blacks, and yellows are fitted in this hierarchical racial scheme of Asian-Pacific management/labor for the *labor* part of the international division of space and time. The secret to Twain's vision of a passage to the fabled India and Asia of Columbus is, as Americans are finding out at the Mission Woolen Mill Company in California and on the Pacific Railroad Company, "cheap Chinese labor," "the cheapest, the best, and most quiet, peaceable and faithful labor" these American capitalists,

---

27. Ibid. Twain's capitalization of Hawai'i into "Pacific market" extends back to producing cultural capital for himself, as this passage from *Roughing It* (1872; Berkeley: University of California Press, 1972) makes clear: on his return to California from Hawai'i, Twain remarks, "I launched out as a lecturer now, with great boldness. I had the field all to myself, for public lectures were almost an unknown commodity in the Pacific market" (496).

in California as in the emerging sugar kingdom of Hawai'i, have ever found (273).

Contemplating the influx of cheap Chinese labor into Hawai'i and California, as well as the flow of wealth across the continental USA, Twain soon sounds like a latter-day Columbus who has stumbled on the "true Northwest Passage" to India, Japan, and Cathay as fabled source of wealth linking the "bursting coffers" of the Old World (Asia and Europe) to the triumph and glory of the New World (America) as mediator and liberator of global space: "To America it has been vouchsafed to materialize the vision, and realize the dream of centuries, of the enthusiasts of the Old World. We have found the true Northwest Passage—we have found the true and only direct route to the bursting coffers of 'Ormus and of Ind'—to the enchanted land whose mere drippings, in the ages that are gone, enriched and aggrandized ancient Venice, first, then Portugal, Holland, and in our own time, England—and each in succession they longed and sought for the fountainhead of this vast Oriental wealth, and sought in vain. The path was hidden to them, but we have found it over the waves of the Pacific, and American enterprise will penetrate to the heart and center of its hoarded treasures, its imperial affluence" (274). Twain's rhetoric soars into idealized sublimation of the Orient "over the waves of the Pacific," but this rhetoric of an imperial sublime is founded on the explicit repression of one source: the exploitation of Chinese coolie labor, what he takes to be the surplus value of racially inferior and culturally irrelevant Hawaiians and Asians who can provide the base of "this vast Oriental wealth."

Because it is located along the Pacific Rim and connected to the financial metropolis of New York, the state of California, Twain urges, should move to extract and control this abundant source of Asian-Pacific wealth: "California has got the world where it must pay tribute to her. She is about to be appointed to preside over almost the exclusive trade of 450,000,000 people—the almost exclusive trade of the most opulent land on earth" (274). Twain's orientalist fantasy of having discovered some "Aladdin's lamp" of cheap labor belies the fact that, just as a form of American slavery of blacks is being abolished through the Civil War, he is urging in 1866 upon Asians (as upon Hawaiians) the adoption of a new Asian-Pacific form of slavery and exploitation via contract labor. Race-based Exclusion Acts of 1882, 1924, and 1934 would soon put an end to this free flow of nonwhite labor from Asia. Twain seems not "to have wandered away from" his "original subject" (that is, building up sugar plantations in Hawai'i) so much as moved toward his "new subject," the territorial management and representational control, both symbolic and economic, of the Asia Pacific as space of American Manifest Destiny (275). The "westward" course of Europeans has found another climate to sublimate and absorb: the Asia-Pacific as a space of exotic culture and economic resources.

It did not take long, in the course of the world system, until this Pacific region came to be christened, after U.S. cultural agents such as General MacArthur, David Reynolds, and Paul Theroux, as "the American Lake." As in Whitman's "Passage to India" (if not Emerson's vision of the Over-Soul), the Pacific is seen as founded in some primordial Asia, calling America back to its original prosperity, and Twain's journalism circulated as literary advertisement for such expansionist progress across the Asia / Pacific.

Twain was not alone in this production of Pacific places into space for purposes of increasing national and global capital; as early as 1848, American policymaker Aaron H. Palmer had advocated the development of steam transportation in the Pacific and the establishment of San Francisco as the center of American trade with China.[28] In 1857, Henry M. Whitney's *Pacific Commercial Advertiser* of Honolulu would assess the future of Native Hawaiians in the following calculus of transpacific benefits: "Though inferior in every respect to their European or American brethren, they are not to be wholly despised. . . . They are destined to be laborers in developing the capital of the country. . . . In proportion as they come in contact with foreigners, and acquire correct habits . . . in that proportion do they rise in our estimation."[29] Later, William N. Armstrong, King Kalākaua's commissioner of immigration, on his trip to Asia in 1881 to import sugar laborers for Hawai'i plantations, declared that the king's "white subjects," unabashedly American in behavior and interests, already "held the brains

---

28. Ronald Takaki, *Strangers from a Different Shore: A History of Asian Americans* (New York: Penguin, 1989), 22. On antiimmigration acts targeting peoples from Asia as these impacted reactively white labor movements in U.S. Pacific Rim sites such as California, see Lisa Lowe, *Immigrant Acts: On Asian American Cultural Politics* (Durham, NC: Duke University Press, 1996), esp. chap. 1, "Immigration, Citizenship, Racialization: Asian American Critique."

29. Quoted in Helen Geracimos Chapin, "Newspapers of Hawai'i 1834 to 1903: From *He Leona* to the Pacific Cable," *The Hawaiian Journal of History* 18 (1984): 56.

and most of the property of the nation."[30] They need only take over the kingdom from the natives, which they did, to the horror and legal objections of President Grover Cleveland and the Blount Commission in 1893.

In 1903, after annexation, when the Pacific cable connected the island territory to the mainland, these white subjects, now more securely in control of what they had long derided as the "Empire of the Calabash," telegraphed the following message to President Theodore Roosevelt, fixing the progress of Hawai'i on the path to full statehood in 1959: "We all believe that the removal of the disadvantage of isolation will prove a strong factor in the building of a patriotic and progressive American Commonwealth in these islands."[31] Further, through making Hawai'i into a territorial possession and confederated state, the American Pacific was integrated into a region of commercial, political, and military domination. Hawai'i, through so many acts of economic and political goodwill, had become, in effect, occupied by that "foreign, colonial country called the United States of America," as Haunani-Kay Trask argues the case for renewed sovereignty in "Kūpa'a 'Āina [Hold fast to the land]: Native Hawaiian Nationalism in Hawai'i."[32] She expresses well the counterhistory and rewriting of the American Pacific as a site not of mutual benefit but of native ravishment and local appropriation shaped into being by the combined forces of missionary culture, plantation labor, and the tourist industry.

FROM MEGATRENDS TO MICROPOLITICS: TRACKING SOME "LOCAL MOTIONS"

The Pacific remains a multiple region, to be sure, defying Western categorization or easy framing into any national trajectory. Still, having sketched in this prehistory of the "local literature" movement as it emerged against

30. William N. Armstrong, *Around the World with a King* (1903; Rutland, VT: Charles E. Tuttle, 1977), 1.
31. Quoted in Chapin, "Newspapers of Hawai'i," 77. For a "thick" understanding of the Hawaiian nationalism movement as it battled with the English-language newspapers that enforced American political and commercial hegemony, see Chapin, *Shaping History: The Role of Newspapers in Hawai'i* (Honolulu: University of Hawai'i Press, 1996), part 3, "Nationalists versus the Oligarchy: An Uneven Battle, 1887–1899."
32. Haunani-Kay Trask, "Kūpa'a 'Āina: Native Hawaiian Nationalism in Hawai'i," in *Politics and Public Policy in Hawai'i*, ed. Zachary A. Smith and Richard C. Pratt (Albany: State University of New York Press, 1992), 244.

and within an "American Pacific," I want to oppose *megatrend* constructions of the Pacific against *micropolitical* formations of "local culture" in
the Pacific, especially as this sensibility for place has developed into an
affirmation of regional identity based loosely around the Asian/Pacific
journal and press Bamboo Ridge. As in prior chapters, Bamboo Ridge will
signify not merely the Honolulu journal and press by that name (see
chapter 4), but the cultural dynamic, within the Asia-Pacific, to reclaim
place and locality as basis of subnational identity.

Enamored with the culture of settlers from the metropolitan United
States, the University of Hawai'i needed to reorient toward the Pacific, as
the Hawaiian poet Dana Naone contended in the first issue of *Hawai'i
Review:* "What the University of Hawai'i needs to do now [to promote
Hawaiian sensibility] is turn around and face the mountains of Mānoa.
When we are aware of the mountains in our lives again, we will know what
to do."[33] "To turn around and face the mountains of Mānoa" means to deal
with the dynamics of Hawai'i's multicultural and indigenous reassertion,
but also to contend against a national heritage of arrogance toward the fate
of the Hawaiian people and their race and culture as Ka Lāhui Hawai'i (the
Hawaiian nation).

Dereifying Hawai'i as *South Pacific* fantasy material into "American Pacific" history is meant to estrange the entire colonial heritage. Analyzing
what Albert Wendt called "the newest literature in the world" (meaning
"the written literature of the Pacific"),[34] as we have observed, the Indo-
Fijian author Subramani breaks Pacific literature and its postcolonial
emergences into six cultural-political regions: Papua New Guinea, French
Pacific, American Pacific, Spanish Pacific, Australia–New Zealand, and
the English-speaking British Commonwealth countries centered around

33. Dana Naone, "Editorial Note," *Hawai'i Review* 1 (1973): 2. Arriving in Hawai'i fresh
from UC Berkeley in 1976, I was told by a member of the English Department at the
University of Hawai'i at Mānoa in 1980 that my publication on Milton Murayama was
"slumming" and would do my career little good as the goal was "to publish nationally"
and the local was minor and irrelevant. The English Department's mind-set toward
local culture at that point—with some few exceptions—was a continental, Pacific Rim,
and Stanford- and Harvard-leaning operation, in the "white knight press" tradition of
A. Grove Day, Carl Stroven, and James A. Michener. For a discussion on teaching and
canonizing "Pacific literature," see Rob Wilson, "A. Grove Day: A Critical Appreciation,"
Honolulu Advertiser, 3 April 1994, B1–4.
34. Vilsoni Hereniko, "An Interview with Albert Wendt," *Mānoa* 5 (summer 1993): 56.

Fiji.[35] This classification, which I have earlier invoked, is based not on ethnic grouping or national boundaries, nor on large-scale racial categories such as Melanesian, but on the lingering effects of colonial orientation within what Wendt proposed, in 1976, constituted "the literature [in English] of the New Oceania."[36]

Western-generated maps have consequences: shaping cultural flows, knowledge exchanges, and flows of labor and emigration. "American Pacific" is meant to imply just one *postcolonial* region that (like other sites of contention in the contemporary Pacific, from Guam to Chuuk) remains, in Subramani's phrase, "oriented towards the power that colonized it" and includes the former U.S. Trust Territory of the Pacific Islands (the Republic of the Marshall Islands, the Republic of Belau, the Federated States of Micronesia, the Commonwealth of the Northern Marianas), Guam, and American Samoa.[37] Given this United Nations frame around the networks and movements across Oceania, I am more likely to encounter a student from Guam, Belau, or American Samoa at the University of Hawaiʻi at Mānoa then one from French Tahiti or Maori New Zealand, even though the links to Fiji and the University of the South Pacific have proved strong in Hawaiʻi as a conjunction of cultural emergences through such authors as Wendt, Russell Soaba, Puanani Burgess, Richard Hamasaki (alias Redflea), Subramani, Nora Brash, Epi Enari, and Vilsoni Hereniko.

35. Subramani, *South Pacific Literature: From Myth to Fabulation* (Suva, Fiji: University of the South Pacific Press, 1986), ix–xii. Also see his collection of Indo-Fijian fiction, *The Fantasy Eaters* (Washington, DC: Three Continents Press, 1988).

36. Albert Wendt, "Towards a New Oceania," in *A Pacific Islands Collection*, ed. Richard Hamasaki and Wayne Westlake (Honolulu: Seaweeds and Constructions, 1984), 71–85: "This artistic renaissance [in the Pacific] is enriching our cultures further, reinforcing our identities/self-respect and pride, and taking us through a genuine decolonization; it is also acting as a unifying force in our region. In their individual journeys into the Void, these artists, through their work, are explaining us to ourselves, and creating a new Oceania" (85).

37. Subramani, *South Pacific Literature*, 11. Also see the lyrical polemics of Pio Manoa, "Singing in Their Genealogical Trees," *Mana Review* 1 (1976): 61–69, for a counter-memory to settler colonization: "Our poets will sing in their genealogical trees because their several [group] identities are at stake" (69). Also see Vicente M. Diaz, "Simply Chamorro: Telling Tales of Demise and Survival in Guam," *The Contemporary Pacific* 6 (1994): 29–58, and Theophil Reuney's remarkable (animistic) remapping and renaming of the Pacific space from within the indigenous lore and ecological wisdom of Chuukese culture, "The Pulling of Olap's Canoe," *boundary 2* 21 (1994): 254–58.

By "American Pacific," I do not intend to imply *the entire Pacific* troped as a geopolitical unity that, since the end of World War II when global hegemony passed to the United States, has been dominated by this super-power and its vision of extraterritorial enterprise. ("Sit back, relax, enjoy your flight over the Pacific pond," I once heard a United 747 pilot comfort passengers on a night fight from Honolulu to San Francisco.) Though this "American Pacific" began to solidify during imperialist struggles for Samoa and Hawai'i between 1873 and 1900, this categorization assumed sway only after World War II, when the United States had defeated Japan and took control, via "strategic trust," over Micronesia and territories of strategic interest. Arthur Power Dudden has written a history called *The American Pacific: From the Old China Trade to the Present* organized around this assumption of postwar liberal hegemony; Gerald Segal has challenged such a view of interdependency by showing a Pacific community that, split by culture, ideology, and distance, is increasingly "moving to multipolarity."[38] To some extent, it is the projection of this "American Pacific" liberalism that is being challenged, shaken, and dispersed by the Asian/Pacific axis that animates the shaping of contemporary "Pacific" discourse. My analysis aims to estrange and distance this "American Pacific."

Hawai'i can be constructed as a place on the Pacific Rim (within the sphere of American designs upon the Asia/Pacific region as a historical formation) but not entirely of it. This marginality remains so for many reasons, ranging from location as pleasure periphery to pressures of internal diversity. It is, after all, an island culture tied to Pacific and Asian origins and flows. Despite pretensions to being the Geneva-like center of Pacific Rim planning and global finance, hidden within Hawai'i is not only Bamboo Ridge but another nation, the nation of Ka Lāhui Hawai'i, though "the term *nation-state* tends to perpetuate the obscuring of this fundamen-

---

38. Arthur Power Dudden, *The American Pacific* (New York: Oxford University Press, 1992), 262. In *Rethinking the Pacific* (London: Oxford University Press, 1990), Gerald Segal summarizes the "American Pacific" as it solidified across the nineteenth and twentieth centuries: "The largest of the white-settler states of the Pacific, the United States, had begun to create its own empire. With its growing Pacific population and an equally expanding naval presence in the Pacific, the United States, like the Europeans before it, was beginning to think and act 'Pacific.' Unlike all the 'European' powers except Russia, the United States was a Pacific power with home territory lapped by Pacific waters. Like Russia, the United States was a rival empire likely to stay in the Pacific" (271).

tal fact."[39] ("I am calling from the United States, *not* Hawai'i," as a caller to a c-SPAN television talk show put it in 1997, protesting the spread of Asian moneys into the American polity from such racially weird and mixed places of oriental suspicion as Hawai'i or, worse yet, Taiwan.)

As the "Pacific Rises" and "Pacific Century" discourse proposes "the economic congealing of the Asia/Pacific region" into the imagined community of the Pacific 2000 (excluding Oceania for the most part) as a liberal market coprosperity sphere,[40] this is a language driven by megatrends and megabucks. As the global culture marches into the coprosperity sphere toward "the Pacific Century," this discourse crystallizes around yen power and the enchanted dynamism of postmodern Japan and the Four Dragons. Not so much threatening as confirming the teleological premises of world capitalism in its latest phase of boundary-bashing outreach across the last ocean—"Water," in Chris Connery's formulation, "is capital's element"[41]—this Pacific assumes, at core, a Chinese flow of capital and labor from Hong Kong to Vancouver and Canton to Seattle, the flux of Koreans and Vietnamese into mixtures of Los Angeles, and above all the promise (and threat) of "the Rising Sun."

As discussed in chapter 1, "Pacific Rim" discourse would serve to sublimate structures of dependency in an offshore transnational division of labor:[42] this Oceania is calibrated in the flow of iron ore from mines in

39. Edward H. Spicer, "The Nations of a State," *boundary 2* 19 (1992): 31. Attempts to develop Hawai'i into a Pacific Rim center of international finance and strategic vision are discussed in Paul F. Hooper, *Elusive Destiny: The Internationalist Movement in Modern Hawai'i* (Honolulu: University of Hawai'i Press, 1980), and, more critically in terms of a dependency model, in Kent, *Hawai'i: Islands under the Influence*, chap. 7, "The Pacific Rim Strategy."

40. Robert B. Oxnam, "Asia/Pacific Challenges," *Foreign Affairs* 72 (1993): 60. As discussed in chapter 1, the Pacific Rim bespeaks some dream of interconnection and cosmic closure whose telos implies something post-Fordist, innovative, and cybernetic, such as "Cyborgs across the Asia-Pacific!" This New Pacific would evoke a transnational space of zaibatsu miracles and Confucian cyborgs.

41. On the Pacific Rim myths of space and oceanic dynamism, see Christopher Connery, "Pacific Rim Discourse: The Global Imaginary in the Late Cold War Years," in *Asia/Pacific as Space of Cultural Production*, special issue of *boundary 2*, ed. Rob Wilson and Arif Dirlik, 21 (1994): 30–56.

42. See Ravi Palat, "Introduction: The Making and Unmaking of Pacific-Asia," in *Pacific-Asia and the Future of the World-System*, ed. Ravi Palat (Westport, CT: Greenwood, 1993), 3–20.

Australia to car factories in Nissan Zama, in the flow of high-tech sneaker designs from the Pacific Northwest to factories in Mainland China. The spread of this Pacific Rimspeak, as Bruce Cumings disenchants the hyperbole, emerges from within the American unconscious of Pacific tropes.[43] In the latest postmodern version of transnational cyberspace, *Homo Pacificus* will negotiate transpacific infinitude with Apple microcomputer and Sony Walkman interfaced, retracing the voyages of Balboa and Magellan to reclaim possession of El Mar Pacificó. (Imploded, this may be the tacit quest-romance of North American cyberpunk as cowboy capitalism goes virtual technology across the Asia/Pacific.)

If this "New Pacific" rises around an Asian/Pacific cyborg capable of Buddha nature yet turning out a Mazda Miata bound for Fashion Island in Southern California, this Cyborg Pacific also assumes the surveillance of CINCPAC (Commander-in-Chief, U.S. Pacific Command) holding at bay the threat of local crisis from North Korea to Easter Island, from Subic Bay to Nome. Given the battle of transnational and postcolonial dialectics, cold war rationales such as this are fast dissolving into something more porous in its makeup, such as "Asia/Pacific." Perhaps, by now, "the luster is off the American model" of economic mastery, as Michael Oksenberg admitted in his state-of-the-Pacific address to the East-West Center (28 October 1992), mapping what he called "Megatrends across the Asia/Pacific." This New Pacific remains a Pacific Rim fantasy, nonetheless, in which whole cultures and their complex politics of postcolonial identity count for almost nothing. If Oksenberg's vision invoked the power of Japan and Korea, the collapse of Russia as military threat, the rise of the "New China" and its rearmament, the instability of Pakistan, satellite-powered Turkey and massive Asia, his talk was typical Rimspeak, in that it contained *no* mention of any culture, place, or movement within the entire Pacific. Not even the simplest allusion to Hawai'i, where this president of the East-West Center lived and his discourse was located (until he was fired).

"Asia/Pacific" presumes a community of social scientists and policy planners who claim the right to know the dynamics and thinking of the Pacific Rim.[44] For the most part, it is an Asia/Pacific that, as representa-

43. Bruce Cumings, "The Political Economy of the Pacific Rim," in *Pacific-Asia and the Future of the World-System*, ed. Ravi Palat (Westport, CT: Greenwood, 1993), 22.
44. Peter Gourevitch, "The Pacific Rim: Current Debates," *Annals of the American Academy of Political and Social Science* 505 (1989): 9.

tional excludes not only Pacific Basin countries but "peasant Asia" as well.[45] As in APEC formations (see chapter 1), it worries about the promise/threat to the hegemony of the U.S. presence in the Pacific. But these Rim-driven cartographers make cognitive maps that still leave Pacific islands off contemporary charts, as Epeli Hau'ofa observes in *Tales of the Tikongs*, "because they can't be bothered looking for a dot sufficiently small to represent it faithfully and at the same time big enough to be seen without the aid of a microscope."[46]

Cultural politics may be off the map of megatrend planners who would make "Pacific" mean what the free market wants it to mean: *a decommunized coprosperity sphere* watched over by machines of loving grace, such as Patriot missiles and nuclear submarines. For example, the great China watcher, Michael Oksenberg, tried to turn back the clock across the Pacific and reorganize the East-West Center into a post–cold war think tank wherein cultural laborers will work hand in glove with U.S. Pacific command officers, and he was riding a megatrend here.[47] *Megatrends 2000* excludes Hawai'i or any interior Pacific place in its tech-driven mapping of "The Rise of the Pacific Rim."[48] Robert B. Oxnam continues the forgetting of these local narratives when he maps "Asia/Pacific Challenges" (for *Foreign Affairs* in its "America and the World 1992/1993" issue) and finds no polity across Oceania worth mentioning as promise or threat to U.S. geopolitical interests in "foreign affairs."[49]

45. Palat, "Introduction," 4.

46. Epeli Hau'ofa, "Blessed Are the Meek," in *Tales of the Tikongs* (Auckland: Penguin, 1983), 68.

47. For a journalistic discussion, see John B. White, "The Ox, the Hawks and the Moles," *Honolulu Weekly* 3 (3 February 1993): 4–7, and William Kresnak, "Oksenberg Dismisses Fears of Spy Training, Scaled-Back EWC Role," *Honolulu Star-Bulletin*, 21 February 1993, A3–A5. These cold war rationales are falling apart as the East-West Center has been defunded and downsized by federal and state budget cuts in 1995–1997.

48. John Naisbitt and Patricia Aburdene, *Megatrends 2000: Ten New Directions for the 1990s* (New York: Avon, 1990), chap. 6, "The Rise of the Pacific Rim." A historical geography of the Asia/Pacific that excludes island cultures and critically focuses on the Tokyo to Singapore axis is provided by David Drakakis-Smith in *Pacific-Asia* (London: Routledge, 1992), who explains Pacific discourse in these terms: "Terms such as 'Near' and 'Far' East are thus anachronisms since they described geographical location with regard to the European colonial powers. We are about to enter the Pacific century and this part of Asia has renamed itself in preparation" (3).

49. Oxnam, "Asia/Pacific Challenges," 58–73.

Simon Winchester portrays the *Pacific Rising* as a big, tech-driven "new world culture," but he can only figure Hawaiian culture, at the tag end of his vision emanating from Hong Kong, as the all-but-extinct oʻo bird on Kauaʻi, whose feathers were once plucked to form the capes of King Kamehameha.[50] Emptied of native claims, shorn of continuity, Hawaiian culture is figured, at best for Winchester, as some haole hippies washed up from the 1960s into taro valleys on Kauaʻi and trying to relive "mystic associations with long-vanished Hawaiian cultures, with men and women whose ghosts still drifted around their ruined *haeus* [sic] and tumble-down villages, and gave out the alluring siren call of . . . Polynesia!"[51]

No siren calls for native sovereignty can be heard in this New Pacific, as ratified by Winchester, the Asia-Pacific editor of *Condé Nast Traveler*. This tiny black oʻo bird "was once a symbol—known as far away as the University of Oxford"—of Hawaiian culture, "which now, like so much of the essence of Hawaiʻi itself, has almost vanished clear away," Winchester claims.[52] From the gaze of the Pacific Rim, Hawaiʻi is a native-emptied wilderness lingering in the ocean for TNC tourist rejuvenation, a quaint time warp or late-Darwinian metaphor for primitive preservation.

"See Naples and die," wrote Jack London for *Cosmopolitan* in 1916, but "*See Hawaii and live,*"[53] especially if you are one of London's tourist-set benefactors of what he calls the U.S. "globe-trotters" pursuing sensations of intense life as white royalty in Duke Kahanamoku's surf off Waikīkī Beach.[54] One hundred years after its American takeover, the culture of

50. Simon Winchester, *Pacific Rising: The Emergence of a New World Culture* (New York: Prentice Hall, 1991), 374.

51. Ibid., 371.

52. Ibid., 374.

53. Jack London, "My Hawaiian Aloha," published in three parts in *Cosmopolitan Magazine* in September, October, and November 1916; reprinted in King Hendricks and Irving Shepard, eds., *Jack London Reports: War Correspondence, Sports Articles and Miscellaneous Writings* (Garden City, NY: Doubleday, 1970), 393. As London observes, "The white man is the born looter. And just as the North American Indian was looted of his continent, so was the Hawaiian looted by the white men of his islands. . . . And let this particular *haole* who writes these lines here and now subscribe his joy and gladness in the Hawaiian loot" (382–83). See Dennis Kawaharada and Rob Wilson, "Rejecting Jack London," *Honolulu Advertiser*, 18 April 1993, B3, for letters to the editor opposing a statue of London in Waikīkī.

54. Jack London, "A Royal Sport: Surfing at Waikiki," in *Stories of Hawaii by Jack London,*

Hawaiians has seemingly become for such travel writers (claiming insider knowledge) a mummified bird displaced from use-value by "the unchanging Coppertone-and-Coors rituals of the perpetual summertime of this mid-Pacific American possession."[55] (The IMAX Waikīkī focuses a similar narrative about an endangered flower on the cliffs of Kaua'i, which a scientist is doing his heroic best to preserve.) The Pacific has been turned into wilderness shorn of natives, their history, or ties to place.

There is little Pacific content in any Pacific Rim vision, in short, as this discourse of export-driven coprosperity and global integration into the world system spreads and "[searches] out its incipient material base, targeted toward exporters with Asian markets or importers of Asian products."[56] At best, Pacific islander culture lingers on as something exotic and different to be marketed, simulated, and consumed—as "ex-primitive" delight.[57] In time, given image culture,[58] the Polynesian Cultural Center will displace Disneyland as the vanguard of Pacific simulacra and its consumption of local history, with its staging of Polynesian cultural totality by Mormon exchange students at BYU Hawai'i: "Experience all the cultures of Polynesia! All in one place!" as the sign says. It is not unusual, on a clear day in O'ahu, to see Tahitian dancers posing as Hawaiian hula girls giving the *shaka* sign and saying "Howz it" to a busload of Korean tourists dressed in gaudy aloha shirts with Nikons mimicking the global-consumption style of their Pacific Rim rivals, the Japanese.

This Rimspeak integration of the Asian/Pacific peoples into material presence and the modernization dynamic of capitalist prosperity is a post–cold war American invention; as Bruce Cumings and Christopher Connery have made tirelessly clear, " 'Rim' is an American construct, an inven-

---

ed. A. Grove Day (Honolulu: Mutual, 1990), 269. For portraits of Melanesians as "niggers," see Jack London, *South Sea Tales*, ed. A. Grove Day (Honolulu: Mutual, 1985), e.g., "The Inevitable White Man."

55. Winchester, *Pacific Rising*, 374.

56. Cumings, "The Political Economy of the Pacific Rim," 21.

57. See Dean MacCannell, "Cannibalism Today," in *Empty Meeting Grounds: The Tourist Papers* (London: Routledge, 1992), 17–73, on "cannibal-capitalism" simulating and consuming "ex-primitive" cultures of the Pacific.

58. See Mitsuhiro Yoshimoto, "Real Virtuality," in *Global/Local: Cultural Production in the Transnational Imaginary*, ed. Rob Wilson and Wimal Dissanayake (Durham, NC: Duke University Press, 1996), 107–18.

tion just like the steam engine, incorporating the region's peoples 'into a new inventory of the world.' "[59] At core, Pacific Rim discourse remains a *post–cold war construct* of American invention in that it posits a new vision and promises a global forgetting, dependent on a hoped-for amnesia in which communist phobias across Asia might be elided and the war in Vietnam would end up, like the Korean war, a forgotten one.[60] If Hiroshima and Nagasaki connoted American hegemony over the Asian-Pacific, this new Pacific calls out for another mythology: a "psychogeography of Capital" shaken and dispersed from American control that "Pacific Rim" imaginings (in state-funded institutions in California), rose, from 1975 to 1990, to help provide.[61]

Seen only as dry and small land and thus as outside the ever-flowing Asian/Pacific loop, these resource-poor Pacific islands count little in any megatrend calculus of the Pacific. Epeli Hauʻofa has countered such arrogant mappings with his own myth-charged portrayal of primordial yet postmodern "Oceania" as an interconnected, immense, and dispersed "Sea of Islands."[62] This big "Oceania" as mythic space for such Tongan and Samoan ex-settlers in Auckland and Oakland overrides fixed national borders and colonial divisions (such as Polynesia from Melanesia) and has generated its own diasporic networks of symbol making, small-scale trade, and cultural exchange. This ever-changing Oceania extends its grand reach into space and earth and the Pacific, from Auckland to Los Angeles and Tahiti to Hawaiʻi. Pacific places need not be discounted as so many scattered, tiny islands incapable of becoming a transnational space like, say, the city-state of Singapore.

When the "Pacific Basin" figures into these social science mappings, it is only as a tourist paradise or as ecological waste, compensating for the excesses of a global system driven by territorial extension battering down Chinese walls and Puna rain forests with new waves of Nike sneakers and

59. Cumings, "The Political Economy of the Pacific Rim," 23.
60. Ibid., 24.
61. Connery, "Pacific Rim Discourse," 30–56.
62. Epeli Hauʻofa, "Our Sea of Islands," lecture, Department of Sociology, University of the South Pacific, Suva, Fiji, to the East-West Center of the University of Hawaiʻi, March 1993. This essay appears with a range of Pacific-based responses to Hauʻofa's "big vision" in *A New Oceania: Rediscovering Our Sea of Islands*, ed. Eric Waddell, Vijay Naid, and Epeli Hauʻofa (Suva, Fiji: University of the South Pacific Press, 1993).

Seattle grunge. The "Pacific Basin" trope itself badly prefigures this space as a vessel waiting to be filled or emptied, a remote vacancy calling out to be utilized and inscribed. Once the inner Pacific gets represented in such terms, as Paul Sharrad outlines, it becomes easier "to engage in whaling, sea-bed mining, and drift-net fishing on one hand and dumping toxic wastes and urban rubbish on the other."[63] Countering this delusion of emptiness, the mythopoetic fictions of Albert Wendt, Patricia Grace, Epeli Hau'ofa, and others would now resettle and reclaim this *Pacific void* with indigenous myths of Maui and postcolonial laments, such as "Over Influenced!" Sharrad tracks an emerging Pacific community that is convinced that "Oceania" is not just space but a place, "not a blank on a map to be traversed or filled in, but a series of habitations."[64] Linked to these broader dynamics, sites of multicultural invention such as Bamboo Ridge trace the impure and minor languages of such a habitation in the Asia/Pacific.

Another vision of the Pacific, one more decentered from the prior Euro-American axis, presents the challenge of alternative visions and trajectories, disparate polities dispersed along the global/local interface of postcolonial cultures. To speak of this Asia/Pacific as *postcolonial* is problematic given the evidences of neocolonial practices in independent or self-governing nations, as Vilsoni Hereniko has claimed. This Rotuman playwright and cultural activist goes so far as to remind Pacific Rim planners that, "In the French colonies, New Zealand, and Hawai'i, where indigenous peoples are still struggling for sovereignty in their own land, the term [postcolonial] is meaningless."[65]

"Honolulu may be the most successful multiracial culture in the world," remarks Paul Theroux in *The Happy Isles of Oceania*.[66] If full of happy faces

63. Paul Sharrad, "Imagining the Pacific," *Meanjin* 49 (1990): 599.

64. Ibid., 605.

65. Vilsoni Hereniko, "Representations of Cultural Identities," in *Inside Out: Literature, Cultural Politics and Identity in the New Pacific,* ed. Vilsoni Hereniko and Rob Wilson (Boulder, CO: Rowman and Littlefield, 1999), and Hereniko's carnivalesque study of Pacific comedic genres, *Woven Gods: Female Clowns and Power in Rotuma* (Honolulu: University of Hawai'i Press, 1995). Also see his critical play on the complications of politics and cultural identity in Fiji, "The Monster (A Fantasy)," in *The Arts and Politics in Oceania,* ed. Karen Nero, published as a special issue of *Pacific Studies* 15 (1992).

66. Paul Theroux, *The Happy Isles of Oceania: Paddling the Pacific* (New York: Putnam, 1992), 477: "Honolulu may be the most successful multiracial culture in the world. At

in the hills around Kahala Mall, Hawai'i still represents the threat of spatial, racial, and linguistic mixture as well: a local Asia/Pacific undoing of national homogeneity. In techno-euphoric versions of Rimspeak, the Pacific Ocean simply dissolves into cyberspace as an element of capitalist time, merging Pacific space into time and both into the quest-romance of late-imperial profit. Adhering to the local at Bamboo Ridge, to the contrary, posits another way of imagining the relationship of region, nation, and globe in which difference is not subsumed nor made static but circulated and affirmed.

"Crossroads of the Pacific" and mongrel "contact zone" of autoethnography and pidgin language fusion where Asian and Pacific cultures go on colliding with Euro-American interests in a once sovereign land, Hawai'i remains a strange place to live: even Hawai'i Kai, a shopping-mall-laden suburb developed on Bishop Estate land in the first year of statehood (1959) by California industrialist Henry Kaiser, still has *mana*. Just windward of Hanauma Bay, where Elvis Presley played a brazen local tour guide crooning courting tunes in a grass shack with some Hawaiian beach boys in *Blue Hawaii*, sits Bamboo Ridge, the fishing hole that gave the journal committed to nurturing "local literature" its name and founding mythology of "fishing for gods [poems] off Bamboo Ridge" since local culture asserted claims to place-bound identity in the late 1970s. Bamboo Ridge is a site at the foot of Koko Head lava cliffs where local-Japanese fishermen would exchange fish for the use of donkeys from a Portuguese pig farmer back in the 1930s in a kind of barter ecology and network of reciprocity linked back, as well, to a Hawaiian sense of *mālama 'āina* (care for the sea and land). A "multitude of [bamboo] fishing poles" can still be seen on a good day and a distinctive slide-bait method of ocean casting is used, but, as Tony Lee laments in a short story about these local memories and mores, "nowadays not like before."[67]

As will be more fully explored in the next chapter, Bamboo Ridge—as

---

least, I have not seen another to rival it," he concludes after some strained racial encounters with "xenophobic islanders" (355) in the Pacific, especially Samoa.

67. Tony Lee, "Nowadays Not Like Before," in *The Best of Bamboo Ridge*, ed. Eric Chock and Darrell H. Y. Lum (Honolulu: Bamboo Ridge Press, 1986), 167–74. On the quasi-Japanese mythology of the Bamboo Ridge site, see John Clark, *The Beaches of Oahu* (Honolulu: University of Hawai'i Press, 1978), 28.

place and symbol—sits in the middle of "one of the most heated real estate markets in the world" on a Pacific island where, since the days of King Kamehameha I (who first unified the islands), any governing group has drawn its power and structure from the land.[68] If succumbing at times to hazy nostalgia or the simple tactics of ethnic identity, the local literature movement in Hawai'i seeks to assert its distinctive language and place-bound commitments against the sway of technologies of representation and the ideology of the unified nation-state for whom even "Asian-Pacific Americans" are prime candidates for cultural assimilation. As discussed in chapter 4, Bamboo Ridge signifies the affirmation of a place-bound localism that emerged in the late 1970s in Hawai'i to counter, in effect, any Pacific Rim discourse urging global integration and transnational interface that was simultaneously being conducted along routes of Asian-Pacific exchange. Articulated against the sway of liberal megatrends, a politics of regional affirmation and cultural identity continues to emerge in Hawai'i. The local ground has materialized into alternative visions and claims on "the American Pacific."

The catchall label "Pacific" can serve, in this construct, despite its implications of race and class differences, as an empty signifier to put together with "Asian" in order to amass some political bulk ("this nation's fastest growing racial group") as a demographic nation-state entity.[69] I refer here to the coalition-building strategies of LEAP, Leadership Education for Asian Pacific (Americans); this minority project came under attack

68. George Cooper and Gavan Daws, *Land and Power in Hawai'i: The Democratic Years* (Honolulu: University of Hawai'i Press, 1990), 10. Hawaiians voyaging from the Marquesas Islands have settled in this region around Kuli'ou'ou and Waimanalo (with its "rich alluvial lands, permanent stream flow, and extensive reefs with abundant fish and shellfish") from around A.D. 300. See Patrick K. Kirch and Marshall Sahlins, *Anahulu: The Anthropology of History in the Kingdom of Hawai'i*, vol. 2, *The Archaeology of History* (Chicago: University of Chicago Press, 1992), 13, who claim that the Hawaiian culture and ecology were threatened not only by white colonialism but also by "a radical shift in the chiefly pattern of exactation, as the chiefs [after Kamehameha I] struggled to maintain their political economy of grandeur in the face of mounting debts and external pressures to pay up" (167).
69. See the essays collected in *The State of Asian Pacific America: Policy Issues to the Year 2020* (Los Angeles: LEAP Public Policy Institute and the UCLA Asian American Studies Center, 1993) to characterize "Asian Pacific Americans" as "this nation's fastest growing racial group."

during a recent conference in Honolulu, where the language of Hawaiian sovereignty voiced claims, supported by local participants, for an alternative Pacific "nation within a nation" that would reject liberal illusions of U.S. nation-state integration.[70]

At one extreme, Hawaiian writers have become increasingly committed to the achievement of native sovereignty on a strong "nation within a nation" model, and would resist assimilation to any localism that is premised in liberal assumptions of American acculturation: to claiming space, say, in the *Heath Anthology of American Literature*. (Bamboo Ridge, in such a view, may be another American fishing hole in a decimated native ecology.) Part-Hawaiian writers such as Joseph Balaz, Dana Naone Hall, and Michael McPherson have moved away from writing bland, dislocated poems that could be set Anywhere USA to express a grounding in and articulation of the local/Hawaiian amalgamation of traditions.

In McPherson's uncanny poem of place "The Waking Stone," the personal ʻaumakua of the Hawaiians, a shark god propitiated as family protector, is driven wild by the toxic wastes of a golf course, but the Hawaiian god, like an uncanny, still returns at night to haunt the skies and repossess ocean and ground (as David Malo explained Native Hawaiian religious sensibility, "The number of the gods who were supposed to preside over one place or another was countless").[71]

> The sharks here cannot be trusted.
> Poisons in their meat make them crazy,
> they feel no bond of loyalty or kinship
> nor any longer honor the ancient ways.
> Living seas near shore are stained
> with runoff from the burning fields,
> effluents open like brown dark flowers

70. See Haunani-Kay Trask, "*Kūpaʻa ʻĀina:* Native Hawaiian Nationalism in Hawaiʻi," *Politics and Public Policy in Hawaiʻi,* 244–50.
71. "The Waking Stone," *Chaminade Literary Review* 14 (1995): 17. David Malo's comment is from *Hawaiian Antiquities (Moolelo Hawaiʻi),* trans. Nathaniel B. Emerson (Honolulu: Bishop Museum Press, 1951), 83. Even more so than Kamakau or Malo, John Papa Ii, in *Fragments of Hawaiian History,* trans. Mary Kawena Pukui (Honolulu: Bishop Museum Press, 1959), propagates a post-Christian Hawaiian sensibility polarized along dark/light Enlightenment binary lines: "So it was that true light came from foreign lands, the United States and Europe. And here it is, burning brightly with us" (106).

and coax the gray swimmers to frenzy.
Spirit warriors are returning to land,
they stand and cast a spectral gaze
over plains now littered with debris.
On the seventh green of a golf course
an old one rises from under the cup
and scatters caddies like reef fish,
a trail of balls and putters and bags.

"Spectral" beliefs in Hawaiian gods and spirits of place are not anomalous to McPherson, but are shared by many residents on the Big Island of his birth and have even helped to mobilize resistance against transnational golf resorts and geothermal plants built on once sacred lands, volcanic sites, and once sacred shark-infested waters.

The 1993 "sovereignty issue" of *Hawai'i Review* commemorating—and, by diverse voices and genres, contesting—the disposal of queen Lili'uokalani by the missionary-sugar oligarchy in 1893, ends with Mark Rutter's caustic little poem, "Tory Wig." It is a haiku to the Euro-American will to possession across a native-emptied Pacific, for purposes of monumentality:

Churchill statue:
the firm, determined chin,
the guano toupee.[72]

The *guano toupee* may be a souvenir to the American presence as it took possession of the Pacific. In 1856, Congress enacted the so-called Guano Law that empowered the U.S. president to take over bird shit–rich islands in the Northern Pacific and absorb them as "appertaining to the United States" with its interests in fertilizers and high explosives during the Civil War.[73] One of these guano-rich islands was Johnston atoll, called Kalama Island by Hawaiians, which is being used as a nuclear weapons incineration site by the USA, dumping ground for a kind of cold war bird shit.

To solidify the Pacific into a terrain of American frontier interest, the discourse of Manifest Destiny had to be extended westward across the waters. By means of this east-to-west continental rhetoric, as Richard Drinnon argues in *Facing West*, American Adams such as William Seward, Henry Adams, Jack London, and Secretary of State John Hay could "be-

72. Mark Rutter, "Tory Wig," *Hawai'i Review* 16 (1993): 124.
73. Dudden, *The American Pacific,* 65.

lieve the Pacific an empty space, the watery extension of the once-virgin continent, with the isles of the uttermost seas uninhabited, save for child-like counterparts of the once merciless savages."[74] The dynamics of continental possession, by which indigenous claims might be eradicated into the higher light and air of a Bierstadt painting, were extended into watery domains, even as a near feudal system of plantation labor took possession over the taro fields of the Hawaiian islands. This national possession was founded, in effect, on an oceanic gaze across Pacific island bird shit and what Henry Adams called those "wretched lava-heaps" of island cultures.

Churchill's gaze across the American Pacific as pacified space could have been captured, in Hawai'i, as the gaze across the sugar plantations and ocean liners of Sanford B. Dole (the first white president of the Hawaiian Republic after American annexation), or perhaps that of President James Monroe gazing over the azure sea routes toward Tokyo, Manila, and Canton.[75] The Monroe Doctrine was effectively invoked by the United States as early as 1842 to deter France and Great Britain from annexing the Hawaiian islands—before the United States could do so in 1898. By 1949, battles at Pearl Harbor and Hiroshima had deformed the indigenous Pacific: "eye of the earth; and what it watches is not our wars," as Robinson Jeffers wrote in "The Eye" in 1941.[76] General Douglas MacArthur could look out over the Pacific as an "Anglo-Saxon lake" at the end of World War II and see the western coast of the USA not in California but off East Asia: "The strategic boundaries of the United States are no longer along the Western shore of North and South America; they lie along the Eastern coast of the Asian continent," he claimed in 1948.[77]

In an essay on "Pu'uloa and the Overthrow," in the "sovereignty issue"

74. Drinnon, *Facing West*, 250.

75. See Gerald Vizenor, "Manifest Manners: The Long Gaze of Columbus," *boundary 2* 19 (1992): 223–35, on the imperial gaze on Mesoamerican "Indians" passed down from Columbus to New World entrepreneurs such as Sanford Dole.

76. Robinson Jeffers, "The Eye," from *Be Angry at the Sun* (1948), in *Selected Poems of Robinson Jeffers* (New York: Vintage, 1965), 85.

77. Quoted in McIntosh, *Arms across the Pacific*, 37. In an address in Seattle in 1951, MacArthur further suggests American ties to the Pacific Rim—as some kind of expanded national border: "Our economic frontier now embraces the trade potentialities of Asia itself, for with the gradual rotation of the epicenter of world trade back to the Far East whence it started many centuries ago, the next thousand years will find the main problem the raising of the sub-normal standards of life of its more than a billion people" (quoted in Cumings, "Political Economy of the Pacific Rim," 36).

of *Hawai'i Review,* a Marine stationed at Pearl Harbor, Mehmed Ali, worries how his own presence extends back to the U.S. marines who disembarked from the USS *Boston* in 1893 to help, with spectacle of military force, in the overthrow of Queen Lili'uokalani. Invoking the Hawaiian name for their fish pond, Pu'uloa (Pearl Lake)—Ali wanted, in fact, to italicize the English place-names as the exotic ones—and cultivating the old fishing ways of the Hawaiians for whom fishing was a kind of prayer, Ali rejects his role of "armed occupier of Pu'uloa" and decides that the best thing he can do to serve the cause of Hawaiian sovereignty is to leave Hawai'i when his tour as U.S. Marine corporal ends.[78] In an essay aligning a non-Hawaiian to the preservation (and politicization) of Hawaiian beliefs, Joseph Chang shows in "Pele in a Christian Court" that native claims against the True/Geothermal Project in the Puna rain forest are doomed to defeat in an American court for whom nature is already changed into commodity and for whom Pele worship at Puna can only be validated, not by native animism, but by truth-claims of Western archaeology proving unbroken continuity of such practice.[79]

To pressure these "local motions" as subnational force, I would like here to sketch in some key events and themes of the ongoing "local literature" movement happening in Hawai'i, and flesh this out more fully in the next chapters. The time and place of origin can be linked to three events: first, the Talk Story conferences held in Honolulu and on the Big Island in 1978 and 1979. This multiethnic forum served as a catalyst to theorize and fill in the lack of literature written by and for locals; the false history and fake images of Hawai'i had to be countered by a different set of narratives and images to evoke what John Dominis Holt called "the unexpurgated Hawai'i."[80] If only tacitly, this movement was tied to the *decolonization* of the Pacific as an undoing of exotic/erotic constructions by outsiders. As Subramani described this process at the 1979 InterChange conference held in Honolulu, a Symposium on Regionalism, Internationalism, and Ethnicity in Literature, "There are very sociological reasons for the [belated] emergence of the writer in the South Pacific. And the kind of ques-

78. Mehmed Ali, "Pu'uloa and the Overthrow," *Hawai'i Review* 16 (1993): 34–35.

79. Joseph Chang, "Pele in a Christian Court," *Hawai'i Review* 16 (1993): 42–45.

80. John Dominis Holt, response to O. A. Bushnell, "The Plight of the Regional Writer," in *InterChange: A Symposium on Regionalism, Internationalism, and Ethnicity in Literature,* ed. Linda Spalding and Frank Stewart (Honolulu: InterArts Hawai'i, 1980), 67.

tioning being asked in Hawai'i at the moment, about the non-emergence of a literature, is the sort of question we were asking about a decade ago in the South Pacific."[81]

A second key event is the development of Bamboo Ridge journal and press in 1978 as a forum for local commitments in literary expression, as I have suggested. Without slighting outlets such as Richard Hamasaki's Pan-Pacific *Seaweeds and Constructions* or Joe Puna Balaz's expressly Hawaiian journal *Ramrod* or Susan Schultz's language-experiment-based *Tinfish* journal, this means of production has been crucial. Under the editorship of Chinese American poet Eric Chock and fiction writer Darrell Lum, and drawing on a racially diverse coalition of writers who met regularly, Bamboo Ridge started up a key outlet for a literature grounded in local scenery and language. It was pluralist, but mostly expressive of Asian-Pacific American concerns, which has led to tensions both for Hawaiians and for local haoles who feel the journal is not expressive enough of their own views.

Third, in 1975, Milton Murayama's self-published novel *All I Asking for Is My Body* portrayed plantation life on Maui in its full historical struggle; Murayama showed, with a crafty use of pidgin English and Japanese/ standard English and Japanese, the struggles of the Oyama family and their Japanese values as transformed and "Americanized" in Hawai'i. With expressive use of pidgin, its rooted portrayal of Japanese values as these altered and endured in the American context, its loving yet scathing portrayal of the plantation community on Maui during the 1930s, its unflinching analysis of the trauma Pearl Harbor represented to local Japanese, and, above all, its characterization of the Oyama family in all the trials of labor and assimilation, this novel can be said to have inaugurated a new era in the literature of postcolonial Hawai'i.[82]

81. Subramani, response to Albert Wendt, "The Return Home," in *InterChange: A Symposium on Regionalism, Internationalism, and Ethnicity in Literature*, ed. Linda Spalding and Frank Stewart (Honolulu: InterArts Hawai'i, 1980), 73.
82. See Milton Murayama, *All I Asking for Is My Body* (Honolulu: University of Hawai'i Press, 1988), as well as his long-awaited novels on the Oyama family saga, *Five Years on a Rock* (Honolulu: University of Hawai'i Press, 1994) and *Plantation Boy* (Honolulu: University of Hawai'i Press, 1998) on the Japanese diaspora of labor and cultural mores to plantation Hawai'i as it Americanized under the rise of the Democratic Party and the union-based movements for a decent middle-class life.

After Murayama's work and the Hawaiian-based fiction of John Dominis Holt, "local literature" no longer implied a stigma of regional irrelevance but provided a slogan of multicultural proliferation that, continuing on in the 1980s and 1990s, has made the ethnic heritage and linguistic diversity of Hawai'i into the medium of a distinctive literature.[83] Second-, third-, and fourth-generation authors such as Juliet Kono, Rodney Morales, Zack Linmark, Barry Masuda, Diane Kahanu, Gary Pak, Nora Cobb, and Lois-Ann Yamanaka can now build on and extend this work. The 1980s saw expanding diversity, conflict, and especially the literature of Hawaiians writing in English and using mixed or some Hawaiian English as well as Hawaiian Creole English (pidgin). *Sister Stew,* published by Bamboo Ridge Press in 1991, added a fuller range of Asian/Pacific American perspectives of women, as in the dismembered body rage of Lois-Ann Yamanaka's "Parts," a poem that disrupted local decorums of reticence about the body, family, and place.[84] (Yamanaka continues to feel the heat of the local community, with its race and class divides, come down on her nationally successful work.)

According to Dana Naone Hall's *Mālama: Land and Water,* Hawaiian identity is not just biologically determined, but can be better based on "a distinctly Hawaiian relationship to the life of the place."[85] (Naone's defini-

---

83. See Sumida, *And the View from the Shore,* chap. 4, "Hawai'i's Complex Idyll: *All I Asking for Is My Body* and *Waimea Summer.*"

84. Cathy Song and Juliet Kono Lee, eds., *Sister Stew: Fiction and Poetry by Women* (Honolulu: Bamboo Ridge Press, 1991). In 1997 and 1998, as mentioned in my preface, Yamanaka's desublimated literary works came under strong attack from other ethnic groups in Hawai'i, especially Filipinos, who found her portrayals of their at-risk groups stereotypical, racially abjecting, and degrading. See Candace Fujikane and Michelle Skinner, "Two Perspectives on *Blu's Hanging,*" *Honolulu Advertiser,* 5 July 1998, B1–4, as well as Fujikane's much more ambivalently phrased reading in "Reimagining Development and the Local in Lois-Ann Yamanaka's *Saturday Night at the Pahala Theater,*" in *Women in Hawai'i: Sites, Identities, and Voices,* special issue of *Social Process in Hawai'i,* ed. Joyce Chinen, Kathleen O. Kane, and Ida M. Yoshinaga (1997). The Association of Asian American Scholars meeting in Honolulu in July 1998 came into a massive heated debate over the awarding of literary awards to Yamanaka's two most recent works: see the forthcoming special issue of *Amerasia,* ed. Jonathan Okamura and Candace Fujikane, on the Yamanaka controversy and race relations in Hawai'i.

85. Dana Naone Hall, ed., *Mālama: Hawaiian Land and Water* (Honolulu: Bamboo Ridge Press, 1985), 7.

tion is in keeping with the way Pacific ethnographers claim that identity has traditionally been constituted throughout Oceania, not by blood and substance but by cultural predisposition and geographic location.) This open-ended definition fits the hybrid one articulated in Holt's ground-breaking turn in 1964 back to hapa-Hawaiian "ethnic consciousness" and aboriginal grounds of blood, place, and artistry in his self-published essay, "On Being Hawaiian": "We are inescapably heirs to this welter of tradition, whether we like it or not."[86] Given the Fanon-like binaries of Haunani-Kay Trask, any open-ended definition of "Hawaiian at heart" such as Bamboo Ridge's pluralist and culturally hybrid definition of "local" Hawaiian raises trouble. Trask contends that, given the struggle for native sovereignty and unresolved land claims, as well as the two hundred years of cultural deni-gration in Hawai'i where mainland norms governed, " 'Local' does not translate into 'indigenous.' "[87] As the Pacific gets further decolonized and the nation of Ka Lāhui Hawai'i is shaped along self-determined lines, this "Hawaiian" literature will have to cut its own space and define its own rela-tionship to place and history rather than be assimilated into any American multicultural project such as Bamboo Ridge can, at times, appear to be.

Related to Bamboo Ridge's brand of a "distinct sensitivity to ethnicity" is the lurking fear of "becoming haolified": that is, the threat of homoge-nizing into whitewashed American and thus repressing Asian/Pacific or Hawaiian parts of cultural-political identity. Rodney Morales's exploration of hapa-haole identity in "Daybreak over Haleakalā" or Holt's novel of Big Island ranching life *Waimea Summer* are exemplary explorations of this

86. John Dominis Holt, *On Being Hawaiian* (Honolulu: Topgallant, 1964), 18. In con-texts of the Hawaiian Homerule movement and the U.S. civil rights struggle, Holt asserts, "Our young people look now with fervor to the possibility of becoming once again Polynesian Hawaiians in spirit. . . . We are links to the ancients: connected by inheritance to their mana, their wisdom, their superb appreciation of what it is to be human" (9).

87. Haunani-Kay Trask, "Indigenous Writers and the Colonial Situation," in *Publishing in the Pacific Islands*, ed. Jim Richstad and Miles M. Jackson (Honolulu: Graduate School of Library Studies at the University of Hawai'i, 1984), 80: "While the subject matter may be 'local' here, the trend-setting is mainland American, especially the west and east coasts. The Pacific community, including the Native Hawaiian community, is absent as a subject and a style. 'Local' does not translate into 'indigenous.' " This is a prescient comment concerning the future direction of local literature in the 1990s, in the work of Trask, Balaz, and many others not Hawaiian by blood.

Hawaiian cultural schizophrenia. A poem such as Puanani Burgess's "Choosing My Name" suggests that Hawaiian identity is not so much given as *reclaimed* in a process of burrowing beneath cultural layers of pre-given American names such as Christabelle and Japanese ethnic names such as Yoshie to discover connections of self to place in the "piko name."

> Puanani is my chosen name,
>> my piko name connecting me to the ʻāina
>> and the kai and the poʻe kahiko—
>> my blessing; my burden;
>> my amulet; my spear.[88]

Finally, there has been the deeply rooted growth of Hawaiian consciousness poems in *Mālama* (1985) and *Hoʻi Hoʻi Hou* (1984), which show a commitment to land and Hawaiian attitudes toward land/culture, a complex of values called *aloha ʻāina* or *mālama ʻāina* and a sense of *ʻohana* (extended family); the demilitarization of Kahoʻolawe Island, accomplished in 1990 after some fifty years of U.S. bombing; native pastoral ethos; the rise of culture-based tactics linked to indigenous cultures in South Pacific and Native American struggles; the circulation of double language poems, or ones written wholly in the Hawaiian language; the use of musical and dance traditions linked to *mele* (chants and songs) more than to the transmission of Euro-American literary traditions; the use of "aboriginality" as countervision. This has resulted in the formation of the first distinctly Hawaiian literary and cultural journal in Hawaiʻi, *ʻŌiwi: A Native Hawaiian Journal,* which appeared in December 1998 under the informed and scholarly editorship of Darlaine Mahealani Dudoit and Kuʻualoha Meyer Hoʻomanawanui and is a fine piece of collective, mixed language, and multiple-voiced work.

In such works of rooting down and in-mixing Hawaiian culture, the

---

88. Rodney Morales, *The Speed of Darkness* (Honolulu: Bamboo Ridge Press, 1988), 86–105. John Dominis Holt, *Waimea Summer: A Novel* (Honolulu: Topgallant, 1976), ends with its narrator, Mark Hull, embracing a vision of his royal Hawaiian lineage despite being hapa-haole in blood and lifestyle (192–93), after he had earlier dreamed he was one of Cook's British midshipmen being attacked by the young Kamehameha (47). Burgess's poem is anthologized in Joseph P. Balaz, ed., *Hoʻomānoa* (Honolulu: Ku Paʻa Press, 1989), 40. See chapter 6 below, for more on these indigenous dynamics in Holt and others.

Pacific is affirmed and re-created as space and ground of cultural production—along lines of flight from national hegemony and imperial common sense to regional contestation—in roots and wings, prayers, poems, polemics, and songs of Asian/Pacific location. The "South Pacific," as we shall further see in the next chapters, cannot be located as and where it was in the cold war past of such writers as Twain and Michener, as a silenced part of the U.S. white settler imaginary and its own grand will to democratic-commercial sublimation into itself.

Blue Hawai'i:

Bamboo Ridge as "Critical Regionalism"

Well, it did not feel good to be a writer in a place that is not a writing culture, where written literature is only a few hundred years old. The literary community in Hawai'i argues over who owns the myths and stories, whether the local language and writings should be exported to the Mainland, whether or not so-and-so is authentic, is Hawaiian. . . . I felt the kapu—these are not your stories to write; these myths are not your myths; the Hawaiians are not your people. You are haole. You are katonk.

      —Maxine Hong Kingston, preface to *Hawai'i One Summer*[1]

When they picture the beaches, the ocean, the weather, the green-ness, people ask worriedly, "Can you work in Hawai'i?" as if tropical decadence affects a writer's brain like a ripe papaya. When I first arrived here [from California in 1967], I kept thinking about Odysseus in the Land of the Lotus-Eaters and how he had to leave—Lotusland a temporary, deceptive and dangerous

1. Kingston (along with her actor husband, Earl Kingston, who worked in local Mānoa theater and, like many struggling locals in drama, did bit parts on *Hawaii Five-O*) was an important and caring member of the "local writing community" from 1967 to 1984, leaving after *Woman Warrior* propelled her into global status to teach at the University of California at Berkeley. She humorously captures some of the cultural and racial tensions, as well as the so-called apolitical and cultural differences from mainland Asian American writers of that time, such as Frank Chin and others, in an essay written for the *Los Angeles Times* on the 1978 Talk Story conference and included in her latest book as "Talk Story: A Writer's Conference," in *Hawai'i One Summer* (Honolulu: University of Hawai'i Press, 1998), 47–51.

place. I have since learned, of course, that hardly anybody eats lotuses here. We work.

—Maxine Hong Kingston, foreword to *Talk Story: An Anthology of Hawai'i's Local Writers*[2]

THE SENSES OF *DISPLACEMENT*

When I look around the "Lotusland" island space of O'ahu where I have worked daily at the University of Hawai'i at Mānoa since 1976, toward lush green Mānoa Valley or the expanding commercial sprawl of Ala Moana and Waikele supermall, or the venerated military operation that is Pearl Harbor, I no longer can think "east" and "west" as geographical orientations. I have learned to posit *mauka* ("inland toward the mountain") and *makai* ("toward the sea") as bioregional orientations, though the interactions of East and West, Pacific and Atlantic, local and international, in cultural and economic senses, are so commingled and mobile that ocean-front Waikīkī Beach (where I lived for several years in the Island Colony on so-called Seaside Avenue) looks like a confusion of the Ginza malls of Tokyo with the sun-lotioned streets of Miami Beach.

Wing Tek Lum, Chinese American poet of *Bamboo Ridge* affiliation who lives and works as CPA cum poet in his birthplace, Honolulu, has confronted this problem of geopolitical dislocation and displacement while trying to figure his own place, growing up in multiethnic Hawai'i, on the map of world history and within the glitzy hybridity of postcolonial change in the Pacific:

2. This very differently inflected portrait of the "local writing" scene in Hawai'i, imaged expressly from an insiderized "we writers work hard here" kind of situated voice, is in Kingston's insightful and counter-Tennysonian foreword to *Talk Story: An Anthology of Hawaii's Local Writers*, ed. Eric Chock, Darrell H. Y. Lum, Gail Miyasaki, Dave Robb, Frank Stewart, and Kathy Uchida (Honolulu: Petronium Press/Talk Story, Inc., 1978). (Petronium Press was a small and elegant poetry press run by Frank Stewart, who early on was a supporter of the "local literature" emergence and later branched into more international, regional, and U.S. nation-based work as founding editor, with Robby Shepard, of *Mānoa* journal.) The original Kingston piece was published in the *Los Angeles Times*, 4 June 1978, under the insulting heading (with icon of a Sumo pen-warrior wrapped in U.S. and Japanese national flags), "Talk Story: No Writer Is an Island—Except in Hawai'i," A3.

O
East is East
and
West is West.

but
I never did
understand
why
in Geography class
the East was west
and
the West was east
and that no
one ever
cared
about the difference.[3]

Here bespeaking a micropolitics of local perception, Lum's poem de-familiarizes (for readers of an early "East/West issue" of *Hawai'i Review* I helped to edit and compile) the fact that the global project in Anglo-Saxon redemption and colonial "metageography" has been utterly disturbed in the Pacific. Where are "East" and "West" given the rise of an Asian/Pacific region wherein European orientations of "the Orient" and "the Far East" into exotic unity are riddled with uneven development if not dissolved into the murky horizon of the ocean?[4] In terms of the world system, how can

3. Wing Tek Lum, "East/West Poem," *Hawai'i Review* 10 (spring/fall 1980): 140. Lum's commitment to forging a Chinese American identity in a language of regional location occurs more fully in his first collection of poems, *Expounding the Doubtful Points* (Honolulu: Bamboo Ridge Press, 1987). For related concerns in writing local China culture, see Eric Chock and Darrell H. Y. Lum, eds., *Paké: Writings by Chinese in Hawai'i* (Honolulu: Bamboo Ridge Press, 1989).

4. On Pacific Rim constructions of "the Pacific" as a commercial and geographical region, "Basin" and "Rim," as well as the way this largely occidental invention obfuscated the Asian and Pacific content and motions of this same region, see Arif Dirlik, "The Asia-Pacific Idea: Reality and Representation in the Invention of a Regional Structure," *Journal of World History* 3 (1992). Japan's hegemonic aspirations in the Asia-Pacific region since the early 1970s, culturally and economically, cannot be gainsaid;

one map the unstable relationship of global core (center) and local margin (periphery), when ex-colonial "global cities" such as Tokyo, Sydney, Hong Kong, Los Angeles, and Vancouver (if not New York City) can override Honolulu (in the Pacific Basin as such) with claims to be the metropolitan "center" of this sprawling and cybernetic "Asia-Pacific" region?[5]

As these Euro-American–centered tactics of metropolitan centrality get estranged and a more "postcolonial" politics of ethnic/indigenous identity goes on emerging in varied languages of minority resistance, a stance of "local" implication yet "global" and U.S. national import has managed to worry and "care about" theorizing/imagining this fate of Pacific island regional *difference*. Even now the so-called Pacific Basin serves as testing ground and crossover site for currencies, weapons, and standardized products (not the least simulacrous of which are the atomic weapons tested by France in the oceans of the South Pacific) from the Atlantic, cybernetic Asia, and the New Pacific of primordial and diasporic "Oceania" of wayfaring islanders. Lum's questioning of his cultural identity as a "Chinese-Pacific-American" poet in Hawaiʻi demands (as I have been claiming in this study) a more concrete and cultural-specific sense of where self and community are situated in the "Asian and Pacific Rim" as space of cultural production/difference/resistance; not only in relation to the much dreaded and emulated "Mainland" of Los Angeles or New York City, where ethnic literature is now in, but in relation to those high-finance (yen/dollar) interactions of Tokyo, Hong Kong, Toronto, Sydney, and Kuwait.

Geopolitical *dislocation* remains a plight of local identity, audience, and community for writers in Hawaiʻi as they still in the 1990s try to figure forth, in literature as in other cultural-political genres, their (unrepresented or underrepresented) place, literally, on or off the global map, as well as their token exclusion/token inclusion within multicultural canons of national representation as liberal pluralism, such as the reform-minded *Heath Anthology of American Literature* (1990).[6] Some 2,397 miles west of

---

Honolulu's Kahala neighborhood, for example, has seen the influx (and outflight) of Japanese investment, as has Waikīkī Beach.

5. For a telling and situated portrait of this global/local and postcolonial plight, see Pamela Sachi Kido, "Local Identity in a (Trans)Nationalist Hawaiian Space," in *The Office for Women's Research Student Working Paper Series: Women in Hawaiʻi, Asia and the Pacific,* ed. Judy Rohrer (Honolulu: University of Hawaiʻi at Mānoa, 1995), 22–24.

6. Heath's canonization of Hawaiian writers occurs in the Asian American guise of a Los Angeles/UC Irvine poet, Garrett Hongo, as well as through the work of Cathy Song,

San Francisco and Los Angeles, "place" and place-based imagining in Hawai'i (as well as the related particularities of language, history, and value) remains an enchanted ground and enigma of the imagination for such "local authors."

For Hawai'i has become a state whose noncontiguous location off the continental mainland cannot gainsay the fact that it abides within the U.S. historical project of Manifest Destiny as a space that was used as military, tourist, and commercial outpost substantiating our imperial outreach in the Asian/Pacific region. As discussed earlier, the nation of Hawai'i was annexed in 1898, five years after Queen Lili'uokalani was deposed by white American business/military interests in an act of republican will to state power, print capitalism, and land-base control; it remains the key Pacific site of the battle for supremacy that was initiated or aggravated at Pearl Harbor by rival powers (Western and Asian) for Pacific regional hegemony.[7]

So-called haolification through the white mythology of American English and its attendant dilemmas of self-division (cultural schizophrenia) registers an identity theme energizing the often pidgin-based literature of contemporary Hawai'i. The geopolitics of Hawai'i's relationship to "the

---

a poet from rural O'ahu who after a decade has returned from Wellesley and Denver to live in the state. Ethnically inflected in theme and imagery, both of these much anthologized writers have much to admire in their work. Although both have appeared in *Bamboo Ridge*, their poetry is not tied to any "local literature" discourse as such but to forms, rhetorical protocols, tones, and terms of logocentric imagery that can be identified with "workshop" poetry. Responding to a symposium question in "For Whom Does the Poet Write?", *Mānoa: A Pacific Journal of International Writing* 3 (1991), Song reveals the basic nature of this commitment: "Let's face it—you write for that cold girl in graduate school, the one in the Advanced Writing Workshop, you know the one who could rattle off Yeats and Hopkins at the drop of a hat, who smoldered poems with allegorical themes on Desire, Love, Jealousy, and Hate, who dismissed every poem you ever brought to class. . . . You write with the hope that she'll read your gorgeous poems in *APR* and *The New Yorker*" (108). Song's anthology, *Sister Stew: Fiction and Poetry by Women* (Honolulu: Bamboo Ridge Press, 1991), coedited with Juliet S. Kono, shows a stronger turn toward nurturing place-bound commitments and off-voices.

7. For a counterhistory of the state from a Hawaiian point of view advocating the recovery of political and cultural sovereignty, see Haunani-Kay Trask, "Hawai'i: Colonization and Decolonization," in *Class and Culture in the South Pacific*, ed. Anthony Hooper, Steve Britton, Ron Crocombe, Judith Hunstman, and Cluny Macpherson (Suva, Fiji: University of the South Pacific, 1987), 154–75. For works in Hawaiian cultural poetics written in English and/or Hawaiian mixtures, see Joseph P. Balaz, ed., *Ho'omānoa: An Anthology of Hawaiian Literature* (Honolulu: Ku Pa'a, Inc., 1989).

Mainland" USA is aptly diagnosed in a poem by Joseph Puna Balaz from the recent Aloha ʻĀina Concert film, "Da Mainland to Me." Balaz uses a stubbornly Hawaiian Creole English that embodies the very linguistic *marginality* of being identified as outside, minor, other, different, exotic, distant, unreal to a place of cultural domination (in this context, to the mainstream pop culture of Northern California):

> *Eh, howzit brah,*
> *I heard you goin mainland, eh?*
>   No, I goin to the continent.
> *Wat? I taught you goin San Jose*
> *for visit your bradda?*
>   Dats right.
> *Den you goin mainland brah!*
>   No, I goin to da continent.
> *What you mean continent brah?!*
> *Dah mainland is dah mainland,*
> *dats where you goin, eh?!*
>   Eh, like I told you,
>   dats da continent—
>   Hawaiʻi
>   is da mainland to me.[8]

As Balaz reconfigures Hawaiian island space-time in this poem, what is the *mainland* of power, work, community, and family, as providing some shared ground where language and culture fit in: Hawaiʻi or California, "the mainland" or "the island" of a (globalized, transnational, intertextual) workaday existence?

Balaz's pidgin retort to his unquestioning friend is staunch, terse, *local* in some committed sense that speaks as grounded in the body, language,

---

8. Joseph P. Balaz, "Da Mainland to Me," *Chaminade Literary Review* 2 (1989): 109. Urging flights of "minor literature" and *nomadic* counterlanguages of political minorities, Deleuze and Guattari would urge authors such as those at Bamboo Ridge "to make use of the polylingualism of one's own language, to make a minor or intensive use of it, to oppose the oppressed quality of this language to its oppressive quality, to find points of nonculture or underdevelopment, linguistic Third World zones by which a language can escape" urban standards and genteel oppressions. See Gilles Deleuze and Félix Guattari, *Kafka: Toward a Minor Literature,* trans. Dana Polan (Minneapolis: University of Minnesota Press, 1986), 26–27.

and power of place-based identity: *Hawai'i is da mainland to me* becomes a kind of slogan of regional resistance. Written in a minority diction, though, Balaz's pidgin poem of place was not published, then or now, in *The New Yorker* or the *American Poetry Review* (with more "workshop"-oriented poets, such as Garrett Hongo and Cathy Song, for example, who are widely used these days by Norton and Heath anthologies to represent—in a token and palatable form of ethnic formality and local color—the various literatures of Hawai'i).[9] Instead, Balaz was (and still is) published in one of the staunchly local journals that (as in his own work as editor and anthologist of Hawaiian literature) has helped to promote and nurture such a "local" aesthetic. Given the fomenting Talk Story conferences of 1978 on O'ahu and 1979 on the Big Island, and the large-scale Hawaiian literary renaissance and cultural nationalist struggles of the 1970s and 1980s, this literature has flourished and emerged, belatedly, in keeping with larger decolonizing trends across what Subramani and I have called, polemically and ironically, the "American Pacific."[10]

Since achieving American statehood in 1959 has aggravated the impact of technological modernity and installed a large-scale and globalized tourist-driven economy of high-rises, urban sprawl, and cash nexus on the Hawaiian islands, "Hawai'i" has become a place/sign up for grabs within the literary and filmic capitals: something Hollywood (or agents such as Tom Selleck, Al Masini, and David Hasselhoff) could inject as azure backdrop of local color for a detective or beach-blanket drama to work; use as an exotic landscape cavorting its Royal Hawaiian Hotel trope of "she's our beloved pink-lady of Waikīkī"; could evoke as erotic site of vacation bliss

9. Charles Bernstein has rightly mocked the "packaged tours" of "local color," ethnic locales, and marginal communities that "official verse culture" in the United States will tolerate as part of its house multicultural anthologies: "To be sure, signature styles of cultural differences can be admitted into the official culture of diversity if they are essentialized, that is, if these styles can be made to symbolically represent the group being tokenized or assimilated." See "State of the Art," in *A Poetics* (Cambridge, MA: Harvard University Press, 1992), 6–7. Experimentation in pidgin would be anathema to this verse formalism and conviction of pastoral care for the self and language.

10. For an early manifestation of a "local culture" movement in Hawai'i, see Eric Chock, Darrell Lum, Gail Miyasaki, Dave Robb, Frank Stewart, and Kathy Uchida, eds., *Talk Story: An Anthology of Hawai'i's Local Writers* (Honolulu: Petronium Press/Talk Story, Inc., 1978). On "American Pacific" considered as one area in an ever decolonizing, multicentered Pacific region, see Subramani, *South Pacific Literature: From Myth to Fabulation* (Suva, Fiji: University of the South Pacific, 1985).

and savage excess that airline companies such as United refuse to let die; or disseminate around the globe as an ad-poem to sell punch, sun lotion, and condominiums. Even a compelling local-set movie such as *Diamond Head* (1962) had nothing to do with Diamond Head as such, but simply used this tourist icon of an extant volcano on Oʻahu to evoke (on Kauaʻi!) the strangeness of a racially mixed-up place moving by raw state politics from plantation system and ex-colonial territory to settler state.

In short, Hawaiʻi functions as a fantasyscape or what Maxine Hong Kingston termed the "Lotusland" of Asian/Pacific ethnicity that Westerners reimagine into an island of bliss and exotic mores, full of surfer-girl lyrics, sexual escapades, and guru-initiation movies such as *North Shore, Paradise, Hawaiian Style,* and *Joe versus the Volcano*. Against Native Hawaiian opposition, Diamond Head has already become the site of the first state film studio, the brand-new $10 million sound stage Hawaiʻi Film Studio, to stimulate icons of commercial and popular representations, as Hawaiʻi shifts from an agricultural to an all-out tourist image mode of becoming Miss Universe (see preface). Writing in the local papers from diverse walks of life and subject positions of ethnicity and class, people cheer when Hawaiian culture gets repackaged and renarrated through the plights of a white nuclear American family exiled from the streets of New Haven to confront the quaint customs of a Big Island "paradise" on Steven Bochco's family drama *Byrds of Paradise* (1994), which uses the premise of *Northern Exposure* gone Pacific. They beckon to *Baywatch* and the Miss Universe shows to come and work Hawaiʻi over into a marketable image as a resort-haven heaven full of beefcake, beaches, primitive ways, aboriginal remainders, and hot babes. Only a Southern California could envy such a trope of faraway bliss.[11]

Within mainland genres, however, "Hawaiʻi" gets commonly projected as some "South Pacific" ethnoscape of erotic/exotic vacation bliss (see United Airlines ads and my next chapter) and fantasized as ahistorical Eden of sexual excess that can satisfy (if only at a symbolic-fantasy level) longings for a precapitalist *paradise* ("Hawaiian-style") of bodily fulfillment and tribal community on the one hand and release from traumas of

11. Well, the islands of Hawaiʻi do still contain the "very best" beaches in the United States, if not the world, as even Florida-based researchers into coastal geology and resort tourism admit. See "Maui Beach Named Nation's Very Best," *Honolulu Advertiser,* 28 May 1999, A1. *Maui No ka ʻoi* ("Maui indeed is the best"), as we commonly say here.

overwork in Tokyo (or underemployment in Boston) on the other. Whatever its troubled U.S. history of colonization and conversion cum plantation settlement, Hawai'i nowadays flips over into the stereotypical moviescape I will trope in this chapter as the Elvis-dreamy image of "Blue Hawaii": a garden of the South Pacific as filmed in these azure islands, but scripted and produced (conceptualized, narrated, and banked on) for that native son *kama'āina*, Elvis Presley, to play a crooning tour guide "local," back from the U.S. Army, with lots of strings and mockery from the metropolis attached.[12] Even now the Pacific goes on being exoticized, imagined, and circulated from these indigenously troubled and racially conflicted islands, but fantasized by such images and packaged narrative tours to serve the interests (cultural genres) of Hollywood, Tokyo, Melbourne, and New York.

Simplistic reduction of Asian-Pacific cultural difference/history into a lush seascape set apart from the migratory patterns and struggles of social formation needs to be interrogated and challenged by postmodern local writers-subjects for whom Hawai'i is more than a quirky postcard from hula land or chunk of exoticism/orientalism rife with lazy Kimos, Japanese Yakuza, sexpot Suzy Wongs, or Maugham-like opium smokers in white bucks and drenched in "yellow light" on Hotel Street. Drive in along Pearl Harbor and the Nimitz Freeway to H-1 from the Honolulu International Airport, with its all-beckoning neon "Aloha" sign glowing around the clock and your senses will soon confide and realize an alternative message: O'ahu and the Outer Islands are far from the simple-minded pastoral "savage paradise" you had been promised as packaged from the snowy streets or toxic sunsets of afar. You don't need Bumpy Kanahele or the Hawaiian beach squatters at Waimanalo to tell you that O'ahu is not just some suburb of California or Maui, not just another site of Sierra Club rejuvenation sessions out there in what D. H. Lawrence once emptied of all native representation as "the void Pacific."[13]

12. For a critique of the Micheneresque U.S. Pacific as ongoing site of erotic subjection and an undertheorized militarized absorption, see Carolyn O'Dwyer, "Perspectives on Paradise: Points of Surveillance/Visions of Desire in the South Pacific," which forms part of her doctoral dissertation being written in Australia; also see her informative critical essay, "American Identity across the Pacific," *Antithesis* 7 (1995): 123–37.

13. In Leonard Michaels, David Reid, and Raquel Scherr, eds., *West of the West: Imagining California* (Berkeley: North Point Press, 1989), D. H. Lawrence argues for the *westward* march of culture across continental frontiers: "California is a queer place—in a way, it

NEGOTIATING THE U.S. GLOBAL/LOCAL CONDITION

A cultural politics of place-bound identity expressing these symbols/ acts/tactics of local resistance to metropolitan centers of culture has accelerated into expressing the decentered geopolitics of *dislocation* and *displacement*. "All that was local becomes increasingly globalized, all that is global becomes increasingly localized," as Edward Soja claims of urban transformations now taking place to globally restructure the Pacific Rim.[14] This push-and-pull aspect of contemporary postmodernity—argued for in diverse cultural studies sites such as the formulation of the creolized recuperation of the Anglophonic novel undertaken in "english" margins of the dismantled British commonwealth in *The Empire Writes Back;* Kenzaburo Oe's postwar commitment to the regional periphery of a residually imperial and centrist Japan; the literature of "the Pacific Way" as comprising some multiplex region of postcolonial solidarity and resistance; as well as Kenneth Frampton's uncanny, tactile, and architectural advocacy of "a place-conscious poetic" of rearguard resistance to mainstream technocratic culture—assumes that such peripheral cultures are threatened, on

has turned its back on the world, and looks into the void Pacific" (xi). *West of the West* is a feast of ideological imagining, starting with Theodore Roosevelt's closed-frontier lament for "the true west," "When I am in California, I am not in the west. I am west of the west" (xi), and ending with Christopher Isherwood's posthistorical glimpse of Edenic banishment into shopping mall sprawl, cinematic simulation, and freeway norm: "California is a tragic land—like Palestine, like every promised land" (309). It never occurs to born-again Californians that there might be an American geography west of their own Edenic dreaming, except to appropriate as a suburb or a mimic footnote, like Maui out glimmering in "the void Pacific." As Shiva Naipaul puts this hegemonic Pacific Rim assumption, "What California is doing today, the rest of the United States will be doing tomorrow" (277). The Hawaiian local is posited exactly against such regional arrogance and APEC-like vanguard assumptions to dominate the periphery and the interior Pacific. See Eric Chock's elegy for the Hawaiian activist George Helm, "Poem for George Helm: Aloha Week 1980," in *Last Days Here* (Honolulu: Bamboo Ridge Press, 1990), 52–54.

14. Edward Soja, "It All Comes Together in Los Angeles," in *Postmodern Geographies: The Reassertion of Space in Critical Social Theory* (London: Verso, 1989), 217. In a claim I would pluralize, Soja argues that this postmodernized Los Angeles has become "the financial hub of the Western USA and (with Tokyo) the 'capital of capital' in the Pacific Rim" (192) and, later, that "securing the Pacific rim has been the manifest destiny of Los Angeles" (225) from the USA's financial and military perspective. (On such attitudes, see n. 7 above.)

several fronts, from ongoing pressures of global commodification and the push toward shopping mall unity.[15]

Given technologies of globalized production and a virtually neo–cold war militarization of the Pacific, while these "local" cultures work "to qualify the received consumerist civilization through a consciously cultivated 'culture of place,'" as Frampton urges at the global/local interface in Great Britain, whole neighborhoods or cities may turn placeless, change, thin out, or dissolve without trace of nostalgia, as outside languages and image technologies flow into and inhabit the inside, deregulated industry turns predatory and mobile and flights of offshore world capital flow into, and out of, localities with the fury of those cyberpunk cowboys in *Neuromancer, Barbarians at the Gate, Mad Max,* and *Blade Runner.*[16] (Los Angeles at times seems a worst-case scenario of this.)

If the "the local" encounters "the global" via transnational reconfigurations of region, language, identity, and place, this dynamic of fluid capital often molests and absorbs the local with effects of cultural and economic uprooting. Such an effect has been called a "poetics of disgust" and often entails a sensibility rooted in bewilderment, mimicry of the metropolitan or imperial center, creolized pastiche, tactical resistance, and an unequal distribution of information, profit, and pain.[17] Drinking a glass of Meadow

15. How "'standard' British English" gets infiltrated with creolized pidgin "english" and how "concerns with place and displacement" mark postcolonial genres is outlined in Bill Ashcroft, Gareth Griffiths, and Helen Tiffin, *The Empire Writes Back: Theory and Practice in Post-Colonial Literatures* (London: Routledge, 1989), 8–77. Oe's poetic of Japanese-folk marginality is articulated in Kenzaburo Oe, "The Center and the Periphery," in *Writers in East-West Encounter: New Cultural Bearings,* ed. Guy Amirthanayagam (London: Macmillan, 1982), 46–50, and Masao Miyoshi, *Off Center: Power and Culture Relations between Japan and the United States* (Cambridge, MA: Harvard University Press, 1991), 238–41. The "Pacific Way" is traced in Ron Crocombe, *The Pacific Way: An Emerging Identity* (Suva, Fiji: Lotu Pasifika Productions, 1976), and Subramani, *South Pacific Literature: From Myth to Fabulation.* Frampton's place-bound position within "postmodernity" is outlined in "Towards a Critical Regionalism: Six Points for an Architecture of Resistance," in *The Anti-Aesthetic,* ed. Hal Foster (Port Townsend, WA: Bay Press, 1983), 16–30.

16. See Kenneth Frampton, "Place-Form and Cultural Identity," in *Design after Modernism: Beyond the Object,* ed. John Thackara (London: Thames and Hudson, 1988), 51–66.

17. On this late-capitalist dismantling of locals and locales, see Sianne Ngai, "A Poetics of Disgust," in *Disgust and Overdetermination,* special issue of *Open Letter* 10 (1998), edited by Jeff Dirksen in Toronto. For some innovative takes on local deformations in

Gold milk or eating one of the Dole pineapples in Hawai'i, for example, you consume the synthetic by-product of a Green Revolution with untoward local consequences. As Darrell H. Y. Lum's image of this EDB syndrome trenchantly suggests, "the local" may not be all that natural and threatened as such, may be toxic to your very survival as a local: "Of course, there are the nature themes which, according to some visiting writers, appear too much and too often in local literature. But why shouldn't we [Hawaiian authors] write about nature when locals know that the EDB (ethylene dimethylbromide, more simply, ant poison) sprayed on the pineapples shows up in the drinking water years after they stop using the insecticide. This isn't standing-in-awe-of or ain't-it-beautiful nature writing that we're talking about."[18]

Given the big restructuring of the Pacific Region from APEC to Papua New Guinea at the global/local interface, by 1994 in Hawai'i, Dole pineapples had (seemingly) gone the way of postmodernity and become simulacra of the dying agricultural market in Hawai'i that is phasing out the entire island of Lāna'i, as I write, into a totally planned and manipulated space of golf courses and tourist resorts, again to the chagrin (and impotence) of local workers who have labored, often for three or four generations, in such local pineapple fields, and now are asked to service these new hotels with a Big Aloha smile. But remember, as well, Wing Tek Lum urges in a poem called "Local Sensibilities," this pineapple is another object that is not just tourist icon but has been invested with local labor and memory: "When I see a pineapple, / I do not think of exotic fruit sliced in rings / to be served with ham, / more the summer jobs at the cannery / driving a forklift or packing wedges on the line."[19]

The result of this big APEC-like drive to regional economic integration may be the banal transformation of the Native Hawaiian landscape of

Hawai'i, see Bill Luoma, "KPOI 97.5 The Rock You Live On," in *Works and Days* (West Stockbridge, MA: Hard Press/The Figures, 1998), 103–9; Juliana Spahr's exploratory attempt to merge the two postmodernities of deracinated, language-based experimentation with situated and embodied location in *Spiderwasp, or Literary Criticism* (New York: Spectacular Books, 1998); as well as Susan Schultz's ongoing work as innovative editor of *Tinfish* to make the postmodern and the postcolonial poetics of the Pacific and Asia region interact across subject positions and sites.

18. On the place- and language-bound ethos of "local writing" in Hawai'i, see Darrell H. Y. Lum, "Hawai'i's Literature and Lunch," *East Wind* (spring/summer 1986): 32–33.

19. Wing Tek Lum, *Expounding the Doubtful Points*, 67.

O'ahu into an advanced tourist mode of shopping mall redemption, as we go on searching for sacred jewelry at Riches, Kahala Mall. At the Polynesian Cultural Center on O'ahu, "Polynesian" culture ("See Polynesian Culture! All in one place!" goes the motto) is performed as one big ex-primitive spectacle for transnational tourist consumption, as Andrew Ross has shown and I will discuss more fully in the next chapter. Expanded and intensified in the transnational imaginary of global tourism, this will generate a neospace in "the American Pacific" fit for the well-off of the First World such as visitors from Japan, the United States, and Europe to vacation in, stylize, pacify, simulate, parody, desacralize, and consume.

Any version of the *local* or *regional*, as I have been urging in this study, will thus have to be spread on some cognitive map of *global postmodernity* that Fredric Jameson, David Harvey, Arif Dirlik, Meaghan Morris, Stuart Hall, Edward Soja, and other post-Fordist cultural geographers and critical theorists have conceptualized as that "world space of multinational capital" in which the material/tropological production of Asian-Pacific culture, in Los Angeles or Vancouver as in Honolulu, now takes place. Describing the by-now-lost $15 billion that circulated in the seventy countries from Panama to Luxembourg, Hong Kong, and the Cayman Islands, where the Bank of Credit and Commerce International (BCCI) was, as it were, located, a U.S. investigator puts the matter of this postmodern dislocation succinctly: "[BCCI capital] was located everywhere but regulated nowhere," which recalls the medieval sense (still presumed by Emerson and William James) of an omnipotent godhead whose "center [of power] was everywhere and whose circumference was located nowhere."[20] Transnational capital is not some U.S. market god, to be sure, nor is "the local" or indigenous struggle over in the Contemporary Pacific.

At a micropolitical level of cultural production, to be sure, local places and/or minor languages can still disturb and fragment prior configurations of imperial domination; spatial and temporal coordinates of this new heteroglossic condition of global/local interaction have to be imagined and brought to public consciousness. Local culture as such "demands a priority of attention" as one site where such cognitive mapping, adjustment, and

20. On global postmodernity, see Fredric Jameson, *Postmodernism, or, The Cultural Logic of Late Capitalism* (Durham, NC: Duke University Press, 1990). On BCCI, I quote from Robert Jackson, "BCCI's Shadowy Web Aided Noriega in 'Shell Game,'" *Honolulu Advertiser*, 12 August 1991, D2. Also see *The Postmodernism Debate in Latin America*, special issue of *boundary 2*, ed. John Beverley and José Oviedo, 20 (fall 1993).

counterhegemonic resistance can and will take place.[21] Given these computerized transformations of region, community, and place, questions of
where to locate these emerging modes of postcolonial cultural production
and amplify strategies of "local literatures" within this globalizing economy of market instantaneity and environmental molestation can no longer
be phrased as questions of Who am I? or Where is my origin? but something like Where are we? or Where are we going? as a community with a
disintegrating ethos of the tactile, natural, vernacular, and near.

Because local culture as such occurs within a boundary-bashing world
system that goes on dismantling places and nation-states into transnational fusion and, more specifically, misrepresents whole regions of cultural and political-economic difference (such as that area that Japan and
the USA have managed as "the Asia and Pacific Rim"), contemporary
questions of "the local" or "regional" will need (increasingly within postmodern high-financial capitalism) to be articulated in conjunction with
thinking through these configurations of "the global" if any community of
regional resistance is to have staying power. Aligned with cultural-political
emergences, postmodern critical theory can play some affiliated role in
preserving and up-building the local Pacific as space of cultural production
and indigenous survival.

Rejecting more fixed assumptions of cultural purity, "self-orientalizing"
binary logics, or racial priority, cultural production in "the Pacific Way" has
emerged since the early 1970s to invent some hybrid culture of resistance
grounded in place, language, and the will to collective decolonization.
Albert Wendt, the uncanny and tricksterlike Samoan German novelist,
argues from this Pan-Pacific perspective, and advocates the use of postcolonial English, remade and creolized, as a language capable of regional
linkage and historical solidarity among the Oceanic cultures of twelve
hundred indigenous languages, English, French, Hindi, and Spanish, as

---

21. Arif Dirlik, "Culturalism as Hegemonic Ideology and Liberating Practice," *Cultural
Critique* 6 (1987): 13–19. On the recovery and recoding of "Hawaiian" attitudes toward
place and ocean as ground of cultural identity and spiritual praxis, see George Huʻeu
Sanford Kanahele, *Kū Kanaka: Stand Tall, A Search for Hawaiian Values* (Honolulu:
University of Hawaiʻi Press, 1986), chap. 7, "A Sense of Place"; Herb Kawainui Kane,
"The Seekers," *Mānoa* 5 (1993): 15–23, on the Polynesian diaspora across the Pacific
Ocean; and Richard Hamasaki, "Mountains in the Sea: Emerging Literatures of Ha-
waiʻi," in *Readings in Pacific Literature,* ed. Paul Sharrad (Wollongong, Australia: Univer-
sity of Wollongong Press, 1994).

well as various forms of pidgin: "Our quest should not be for a revival of our past cultures, but for the creation of new cultures, which are free of the taint of colonialism and based firmly on our own past." Wendt has theorized and evoked, as well as anthologized, this collective process as the ongoing, multisited work of inventing a new tattoolike postcolonial culture of "a new Oceania."[22]

This prophetic vision of "Oceania" rooted in the past (as in Epeli Hau'ofa's recent vision of Pacific grandeur based on diasporic networks linking Auckland to Tonga, Honolulu, and Los Angeles) remains a complex, contradictory, and multicentered space of production. As Indo-Fijian novelist and literary critic Subramani has argued of these staggeringly complex cultures of the Pacific, "Each of the regions is oriented towards the power that colonized it: Papua New Guinea, after independence, is still linked to Australia; the French territories are connected to France; the American territories gravitate towards the United States; Easter Island is totally dependent on Chile," whereas the Polynesian and Melanesian regions such as Fiji and Tonga that had been grouped together during the British colonial era still look to London.[23] As an "American Pacific" case in point, I situate Hawai'i as exactly such a region of cultural imagining and site of critical resistance that must be elaborated, in the region of the Asia/Pacific Rim, within a global context of image manipulation that we might want to call, after the dismantling of the Berlin Wall, the ratification of START, and wars in the Persian Gulf and Yugoslavia, "the New World Disorder."

Drawing on my own involvement as a writer and critic of the local literature scene for over twenty years, since moving here from western Connecticut and Berkeley, California, in 1976, I will focus on the struggle to mime and express an "authentically local" culture of Hawai'i as positing one such discourse of what can be called "critical regionalism." My goal here is not to invent a "local nation" as such, but to articulate the regionally and ethnically inflected literature that has materialized in Hawai'i since 1975 as some protopolitical ground, however fragile, for cultural resis-

22. See Albert Wendt, "Towards a New Oceania," in *Writers in East-West Encounter: New Cultural Bearings*, ed. Guy Amirthanayagam (London: Macmillan, 1982), 202–15, and "Novelists and Historians and the Art of Remembering," in *Class and Culture in the South Pacific*, ed. Anthony Hooper, Steve Britton, Ron Crocombe, Judith Huntsman, and Cluny Macpherson (Suva, Fiji: University of the South Pacific, 1987), 78–91; and Epeli Hau'ofa, "Our Sea of Islands," *The Contemporary Pacific* 6 (1994): 147–61.
23. Subramani, *South Pacific Literature*, x.

tance, projected subnational community, and the *coalitional recovery* of counterhistory and multivoiced critique (by the local) to Euro-American domination. The literature of Bamboo Ridge, in this reading, is written within yet against the prior cultural formations and national assumptions of the American Pacific canon, as dominated (still?) by white male authors such as Jack London, Paul Theroux, A. Grove Day, and the Mr. Biggie of the white Pacific mythology, James Michener. Here reconstructed into the multicultural Asian/Pacific dynamics of "local literature," Hawai'i goes on emerging as an alternative space and expressive locality of counter-hegemonic discourse. A strategic localism is still growing that aims at resisting, contesting, and constructing, by means of community struggle, willed theory, and individual imagination, iconic threats of external domination and/or internal sublimation.

At the outset, I will foreground certain qualities, attitudes, tactics, and aspirations that would constitute this culture of the "authentically local." I then focus on two literary institutions in contemporary Hawai'i that have been crucial to the formation of a distinctly Hawaiian literature marked by these voices and tones of regional resistance. *Bamboo Ridge* is a mostly Asian American local journal formed in 1978 (in conjunction with the Talk Story conferences in Honolulu and on the Big Island organized by Stephen Sumida, Marie Hara, Arnold Hiura, et al.) that has served as the main outlet for the publishing and support of "literary regionalism" as voiced and promoted in the islands. I also touch on the collective social work of the Hawai'i Literary Arts Council (HLAC), a statewide and town-gown coalition of writers based in Honolulu that, since its formation in 1974, has challenged, stimulated, at times even opposed this local regionalism with outside influxes of national and international pluralism.

WHAT IS "AUTHENTICALLY LOCAL" ANYWAY?

One of the buzzwords in American education and literature today is "multi-cultural." But Bamboo Ridge has been multi-cultural from the beginning [1978]. We didn't follow any Mainland trends. In this case, they chased after us.
     —Darrell Lum[24]

24. Quoted in Ronn Ronck, "Write On," *Honolulu Advertiser*, 24 October 1991, B2, on Lum's winning the 1991 Elliot Cades Award for Hawaiian Literature with Juliet Kono Lee.

One of the crucial—if still undertheorized—thematics of "local literature" cultural production that has emerged in Hawai'i since the Talk Story conference started shaking up the by-products, voices, and forms of local literature and history, especially as this literary scene has been clustered around literary journals such as *Bamboo Ridge, Ramrod, Seaweeds and Constructions,* and other cultural journals of local commitment such as *Hawai'i Review* and the *Chaminade Literary Review,* has been the claim that "local literature" can *somehow* be recognized as such, by language, style, and cultural attitude, as "authentically local." All well and good—as strategic assertion of some enduring cultural *difference.* But what, exactly, is this complex of qualities and language codes or poetic decorums that would be embraced and circulated as "authentically local"?

In a colorful polemic urging forms of ethnic and cultural "authenticity" titled "Local Literature and Lunch," Darrell Lum brought some honest clarity to this problem of defining the "authentically local" when he contended that "a number of Hawai'i writers choose to describe themselves as local writers of 'local literature' (as opposed to 'Asian American' literature, largely a mainland term, or 'Hawaiian' literature, which the locals know means native Hawaiian literature."[25] By theory, as well as his own literary practice in pidgin-based works of compassionate originality such as *Sun* and *Oranges Are Lucky,* novelist and playwright Lum along with authors of diverse cultural-political commitment such as Eric Chock, Joseph Puna Balaz, Dana Naone Hall, Lee Tonouchi, Marie Hara, Rodney Morales, Michael McPherson, Juliet Kono Lee, and an array of others have gone on to align their writings with this would-be, mainland-resistant category we at times differentiate and commend as *authentically local.*

Invocations of U.S. free market pluralism can be an easy cure to soothing the tensions and contradictions that animate the "authentically local." It can be another way, finally, of absorbing and containing (by American liberal pluralism) the stronger ("decolonizing Pacific") drive to Hawaiian sovereignty, land rights, native religion, and cultural recovery now taking place by those who do not identify themselves as hyphenated ethnic Americans but as indigenous "Native Hawaiians."[26] Lum's trou-

---

25. Darrell Lum, "Local Literature and Lunch," in *The Best of Bamboo Ridge,* ed. Eric Chock and Darrell H. Y. Lum (Honolulu: Bamboo Ridge Press, 1986), 3.
26. See Richard Hamasaki, "Singing in Their Genealogical Trees" (Master's thesis, Pacific Studies Department, University of Hawai'i, 1990), for a "Hawaiian" take on local

bled, wary, weary, three-category separation of "the local" from *both* "Asian American" and "Hawaiian" literatures suggests the racial difficulties and cultural-poetic dangers any exclusionary or *fractal* definition of "the local" would now confront (as in the critiques of Lois-Ann Yamanaka, which posit her as hostile to the social/literary emergence of subjected social groups such as the Filipinos and the Hawaiians) when articulating racial, linguistic, and historical dynamics and the fluid borders of the multi-cultural literature scene now emerging in Hawai'i.

Even if we could identify a complex of styles and attitudes, rooted in a tactile and loving sensibility for place or an enduring taste for pidgin English (as in the *Hybolics* journal started up in 1999 by Lee Tonouchi, a guerrilla-warrior poet of the "Pidgin English major") that is supposedly *different* from mainland Asian American writing, for example, what would "local" mean anymore in an era of transnational finance and global hybridity? What is "local" when a colorful and funky Hawaiian surf shop calling itself Local Motion can be bought out lock, stock, and stylistic barrel by a clothing conglomerate from Japan, who actually treats the local workers pretty well? (MTV's *Real Life* series of 1999 is moving from the Starbucks of Seattle to the Local Motion coffee shop in Waikīkī Beach to give a "twentysomething" view of Hawai'i's real world.) In other words, what kind of purchase would "the authentically local" aesthetic slogan imply toward articulating/*resisting* larger, more hegemonic forces in a shopping mall world? (Ironically, Lum used this very Local Motion shop in 1986 to represent a creative aspect of the local culture movement in his own essay, "Local Literature and Lunch," making the local culture consumable-as-sign by locals and tourists alike.)[27]

---

literature as emerging from a Pan-Pacific territory of cultural-political struggle, linguistic injustice, decolonization, and the quest for sovereignty. Tracking the movement from "non-regional and non-Hawaiian themes towards a more explicit Hawaiian consciousness" (3) in poets of Polynesian origin, Hamasaki urges that the "emergence of contemporary Hawaiian writers coincides with the emergence of Pacific island writers" in places such as Papua New Guinea and Fiji (22). Also see the anthologies of Hawaiian literature, ecology, and history edited by Rodney Morales, *Ho'i Ho'i Hou, a Tribute to George Helm and Kimo Mitchell* (1984) and Dana Naone Hall, *Mālama: Hawaiian Land and Water* (1985), both published by Bamboo Ridge Press in Honolulu.

27. As Darrell Lum oddly argued the case for local difference in "Local Literature and Lunch," "There's an island surf shop called Local Motion where you can buy T-shirts that say 'Locals Only.' Anyone can shop there, even tourists. And locals and tourists

Theorizing local identity and "Asian Pacific American" selfhood in "Waiting for the Big Fish: Research in the Asian American Literature of Hawai'i," his early and helpful foray into historicizing local literature in *The Best of Bamboo Ridge,* Stephen H. Sumida began to challenge more tired colonial commonplaces (as in A. Grove Day) that Hawai'i had produced no distinctive literature of its own with a crucial counterargument contending that an "authentically local, Hawai'i literature began unmistakably to sound its voice in the postwar years."[28] As one of the moving-and-shaking professional organizers in the Talk Story scene circa 1978–1981, Sumida fully knew the impetus driving this local culture of Hawai'i, as it emerged and sought to counter the more fake-paradise and erotic primitivism images circulating in the U.S. mass media genres and mainland literature. The genre of *Blue Hawaii* as seen, say, from a whiskey-hazed 747 window or the hegemonic view from a Hollywood Porsche. Sumida, Lum, Chock, Marie Hara, and others wanted to seize the local narrative apparatus, as it were, to recall, represent, and begin to circulate more place- and ethnicity-rooted images and "talk story" of a Hawai'i they could recognize as their first cultural home. Journals, presses, and coalitions soon emerged in the 1980s to fill in the literary gap, whereas prior to this time such outlets did not, broadly speaking, exist. Theory and cultural criticism tagged along, as here, rather than led in trying to articulate what needed to be (poetically/politically) done.

Working as an instructor in English and American studies at the University of Hawai'i at Mānoa in the 1970s, Sumida had been stung by a remark made by James Michener while putting *A Hawaii Reader* anthology to market (with A. Grove Day) during the first year of statehood (1959), the same year that Michener's huge *Hawaii* propagated his pseudohistory of Hawai'i as seen from the point of view of U.S. missionary settlers. Michener had urged that those mixed Hawaiian citizens, "Oriental in ancestry," "having arrived in the islands as laboring peasants . . . did not produce a literature of their own."[29] The grand orientalism of such self-

---

alike buy 'Locals Only' shirts because they're brightly colored, full of geometric New Wave designs, and they say 'Hawai'i' right there in front" (3).

28. Stephen H. Sumida, "Waiting for the Big Fish: Recent Research in the Asian American Literature of Hawai'i," in *The Best of Bamboo Ridge,* ed. Eric Chock and Darrell H. Y. Lum (Honolulu: Bamboo Ridge Press, 1986), 312.

29. Michener's rather infamous comment from 1959 is quoted in ibid., 304.

blinding liberal attitudes (Michener was a great fan and collector of traditional Japanese art, to be sure) helped to create a false U.S. canon and contributed to a dominant set of misrepresentations and clichés of Hawai'i as propagated by mainland writers such as Twain, London, Taggard, and May Sarton, and Europeans Stevenson and Maugham, "shanghaied in Honolulu," as it were, or poets such as Rupert Brooke who amazingly wrote of Waikīkī in 1913 that "Somewhere an ukulele thrills and cries / And stabs with pain the night's brown savagery."[30]

Arguing for a more grounded countermemory to the white canon of Michener, Magnum P.I., Elvis, Muffy Hanneman, Jocelyn Fujii, Theroux, and the crew who work in the Hawai'i Visitors Bureau tourist industry of pastoral-paradise bliss, so as to recall how "night's brown savagery" threatens the Royal Hawaiian Hotel with racial and cultural otherness, Sumida, in *And the View from the Shore: Literary Traditions of Hawai'i*, has gone on to flesh out some of the cultural genres, themes, tones, language tactics, authors, and works that constitute the multicultural literature of what I have been calling the "authentically local."[31] Drawing on extraliterary genres such as newspaper writing, mele songs, hula chants, histories, and the work of stand-up comedians, as well as critically reading important narrative examples of the "local literature" tradition such as Murayama's *All I Asking for Is My Body* (1975), Holt's *Waimea Summer* (1976), and O. A. Bushnell's *The Return of Lono* (1956), Sumida has articulated some of the textual/ideological and ethnic multicultural ingredients of what it means for the postmodern literature of Hawai'i to become, or remain (against all odds), "authentically local."

For Sumida, "local" signifies not so much a racial or even a geographical criterion as a commitment (*ethos*) to articulating some shared *ground* (Hawai'i as generating a "sense of place") and conviction of *history* (one

---

30. Rupert Brooke, "Waikiki," in *A Hawaiian Reader*, ed. A. Grove Day and Carl Stroven (Honolulu: Mutual, 1984), 217. I write more fully on this problematic—the Michener/ Day white canon of the U.S. "South Pacific" as a babbling and crass Bloody Mary—in chapter 5.

31. Stephen H. Sumida, *And the View from the Shore: Literary Traditions of Hawai'i* (Seattle: University of Washington Press, 1991). Subsequent references to this important study occur parenthetically. Teaching local literature over the years in Hawai'i, Taiwan, and California, in courses of Pacific cultural poetics such as "Imagining Hawai'i" and "De-Orientalizing the American Pacific," I keep coming back to this Sumida study, pro and con, and fully recognize the scope of its insights.

that recalls plantation history as well as forces of colonial appropriation) as well as embodiment in some "authentic" *language* or image ("local style"). As Sumida once urged on the brilliant local poet/critic and journalist Tino Ramirez while recalling his pastoral roots in the Sumida family's Aiea watercress farm on Bishop Estate land, local presupposes a commitment to *cultivate* the agricultural/cultural ground of Hawai'i in both material and cultural senses: "You have to take care of the land because it supports you. If you don't, the island turns into a dump for imported resources and there's no life. Culture is the same: The word implies planting, tending and nurturing."[32]

And the View from the Shore is, in Sumida's own words, "intended as a catalyst" to help cultivate, preserve, and transmit this local culture of the "Asian Pacific," and it is certainly—if unevenly—that. As the first U.S. scholarly narrative to attempt to describe, in sweeping summary for both local and mainland American studies and Asian American studies consumption, the "literary traditions of Hawai'i" as a distinctive set of genres (primarily what he distinguishes as the "complex idyll" versus the more "heroic"), language styles (which express vernacular values rooted in pidgin English, though not exclusively so), and cultural attitudes (largely for him a mixed-custom ethos of extended family, community, and abiding commitment to local ecology as well as *mālama 'āina*, for example), Sumida's pioneering book is bound to provoke critiques, counternarratives, and critical perspectives from the Pacific shore that would challenge some aspects of his groundbreaking summation. Whatever reservations have emerged, writers and scholars immersed in the local Hawaiian literary scene, myself included, have much to be grateful for in his generous-hearted, brave, and category-defining study.

Admitting my respect for Sumida's American Pacific study, I do find much to contend with in his overall analysis and critical narrative, not the least of which is its *sublation* (canonical absorption) of an indigenously Hawaiian perspective into that of a dominantly Asian American one; its brand of liberal American pastoralism linking child and laboring peasant of the formative plantation-era culture to a sense of place; as well as, above

---

32. Quoted in Tino Ramirez, *Honolulu Star-Bulletin,* 13 April 1991. In a review of Sumida's critical study in *Hawai'i Review* 17 (1993): 9–10, Pamela Sachi Kido ends with this moral: "One would hope that someday self-styled 'expatriates' like Sumida writing from distant shores (namely, the Great Lakes) will return to Hawai'i to enrich the local communities of which they so fondly speak."

all, its very recognizably Euro-American urge to categorize if not to compel literature from the "pastoral" to the "heroic" as dominant modes of local-cultural production. Virgil and Milton may have moved from youthful pastoral to more heroic epic modes of representation in *The Aeneid* and *Paradise Lost*, establishing the *canonical pattern of the Western imagination*, but why should Hawai'i's writers follow this very Eurocentric or canonical pattern so rooted in imperial ambition and the will to nation-building domination? Minor literature needs, in some ways, to remain minor and other and need not aspire to national criteria and forms, it seems to me.

Oddly enough, Sumida seems to second the Asian American and main-landish claim of Frank Chin that, in Sumida's words, Hawai'i's writers should go "beyond the established limits to take pidgin [English] from the pastoral [as in Lum's short stories] into the heroic [as in Bushnell's novels]" (103). Resisting any *teleological* use of generic categories, especially im-ported ones, why should Hawai'i's writers aspire to works of "the he-roic," that most Eurocentric, male-based, and even imperialist of forms as these literary prototypes come down "from da mainland" through Homer, Milton, and Whitman to these Polynesian shores? If Sumida's study started out as a view from the shore of Hawai'i to the mainland and depended on perspectives of marginalization, difference, and critique, *And the View from the Shore* has ended up, by disciplinary reversal and the type-assimilating if not all-engulfing pluralism of American studies, a view from the shore of the mainland to Hawai'i as comprising a recogniz-able literary territory after all. U.S. pastoralism, as literary ideology of the nature-loving self, still needs to be distanced and critiqued, because ("sim-ple" or "complex," "hard" or "soft") such U.S. pastoralism remains, I would claim, the dominant and market-mystifying ideology of liberal Americanists, such as Sumida's ancient mentor at Amherst, Leo Marx, who indeed hovers over the central terms and American literary mythol-ogy of this study.[33]

---

33. Simple or complex, *pastoral* too easily becomes a literary way of ignoring or contain-ing the historical fate of how fully nuclearized, ecologically threatened, and commodi-fied Hawai'i and "the American Pacific" already are; we expect this from *New Yorker* poets writing landscape poems set in Hawai'i, or racially obtuse movies such as *North Shore*, but not from "authentically local" poets and critics of *Bamboo Ridge*. A study of "pastoral" that trenchantly sets this literary mode (transformed by Americans from Great Britain) within the class dynamics of labor, social community, and injustices of global capitalism is offered by Raymond Williams, *The Country and the City* (New York:

Reemerging in the back-to-nature movement of the 1960s, American pastoralism recycled a set of utopic conventions that allowed nature to exist as retreat from hegemonic forces of technology and industry. Such pastoralism assumes a green space of transcendence wherein (European) art and (American) nature can come into harmony and cultivation as an "earthly garden" or recuperated Eden (as at Walden Pond in 1854, for example). Such was and may still be the dominant myth—or so-called myth at first sight—of the American studies "field imaginary," beholden as it still somewhat is to the nineteenth-century ecological romanticism of Thoreau and Muir.[34] It proves cumbersome to see Sumida read the literature of Hawai'i through these Euro-American categories of pastoral/heroic, and he even posits the oddly aboriginal notion that the pastoral genre had seemingly sprung forth from Hawaiian volcanoes and indigenous chants, that is, that there was some primordial "Polynesian pastoral" here before the ships arrived from England, America, and France. "These concepts [of pastoral and heroic] were ready-made well before the arrival of James Cook's expedition in 1778," Sumida claims (4), so that non-Western native mythologies and Eurocentric haole forms of "literature" (itself a value-laden category) conspired and cheerfully fused to produce the (pastoral) illusion and (heroic) adventure conjuring a narrative turning "Hawai'i into paradise."[35]

Not until Sumida gets around to critiquing Twain's abandoned and

Oxford University Press, 1973). Also see Lawrence Buell, "American Pastoral Ideology Reappraised," *American Literary History* 1 (1989): 1–29, for a critical perspective on the ambiguous politics of pastoralism as American-liberal ideology.

34. Three "Americanist" works that are doing something quite different and new in mapping the field imaginary are Werner Sollors, ed., *Multilingual America: Transnationalism, Ethnicity, and the Languages of American Literature* (New York: New York University Press, 1998), with its "English plus" policies and canons; Lawrence Buell, *The Environmental Imagination: Thoreau, Nature Writing, and the Formation of American Culture* (Cambridge, MA: Harvard University Press, 1996), with its critique and vision of ecological nature; and José David Saldívar, *Border Matters: Remapping American Cultural Studies* (Berkeley: University of California Press, 1997), with its powerful hemispheric vision of transnational in-betweenness and Chicano emergences across nation-state borders and modes.

35. A more critical genealogy of Hawaiian Pacific/American pastoral is called for, one more critically situated within colonial dynamics of translation and exchange, as in the Pacific studies of mediated exchange and white-settler codes in Nicholas Thomas, *Colonialism's Culture: Anthropology, Travel, and Government* (Princeton: Princeton University Press, 1994).

racially tormented novel of Victorian Hawai'i, by way of having earlier exposed the Western primitivism and "noble savage" fantasies of Melville, Cooper, and James Jackson Jarves, does he begin to acknowledge and confront the troubled U.S. colonialist dynamics of such uneven cultural exchanges. Sumida argues that although Twain promoted a soft pastoral and touristlike image of Hawai'i as "the loveliest fleet of islands that lies anchored in any ocean," Twain had thought more darkly and historically in this contradictory novel, brooding over the antipastoral impact of disease, greed, legalized theft, racism, and industrial capitalism on the "island kingdom sitting in the path of America's Manifest Destiny" (39). As Twain intuited, and as discussed in chapter 3 here, this place of Diamond Head and Pearl Harbor has much to teach any American Adam innocent how deeply the United States has been grounded as agent in the history of colonial appropriation, outreach, and the cultural-political policing of its "South Pacific."

Sumida's final chapter, "Hawai'i's Local Literary Tradition," provides an ample survey of key themes and language tactics that emerged in the context of Talk Story and Bamboo Ridge in 1978–1982. Trying to acknowledge as well as come to terms with distinctive *Hawaiian* traditions running through, deepening as if by some cultural priority, and energizing the local, Sumida urges that "the Hawaiian culture was rich in chants, dance, poetry, history, legend, and countless other arts" (272), and goes on to draw this future-oriented moral from such authentically local/indigenous mixed cultural production: "It seems to me that in this [cultural production by Hawaiians] is a recognition—from a people's actual hard experience of living on islands—that the arts, too, are absolutely necessary for survival" (272). The local, so stated, is not so much a *residual regionality* (as it often seems in the American South), but functions as an *emergent tactic of place-bound identity;* this becomes a kind of Pacific localism capable of making claims on, decentering, and contesting—unsettling, so to speak—the national center and its canonical ways.

This movement toward recovering Hawai'i, seen and coded as a deeply indigenous territory of first possession and prior identity with the 'āina (land), is one that Native Hawaiians, in biological as well as geopolitical senses, refuse to let die as just another dead metaphor or semiotic dance by white men on English-speaking Bibles. Rather, this turn toward recovering indigenous customs and native language ('ōlelo) in the sovereignty movement sees the issue as a life-and-death imposition on Hawaiian culture as a valid way of life. As Haunani-Kay Trask claimed in a bracing, starkly clarifying talk she gave at the East-West Center in 1984, " 'Local' does not translate into 'indigenous' " because the Hawaiian writer is not so much concerned with literary ambition or with fitting the norms and codes of American multiculturalism as with voicing "a necessary struggle against extinction."[36]

BLUE HAWAII AND BAMBOO RIDGE

With the changing political context and the Hawaiian Sovereignty Movement of the 90s replacing the Hawaiian Renaissance, there has been a realignment of power and redefinition of terms. Instead of the old, colonial Local/Haole paradigm, present day Hawai'i politics also forms around other cultural groupings. Perhaps the main political perception is the Hawaiian/Other paradigm, in which Other includes all others.

—Eric Chock, "The Neocolonization of Bamboo Ridge: Repositioning Bamboo Ridge and Local Literature in the 1990s"[37]

Confronting this sense of cultural displacement and ongoing dangers of cooptation into the American nation-state and its "Aloha State as real estate" vision of place, it should come as no surprise that many Hawaiian writers, both indigenous and "local"-affiliated, remain spiritually *blue*: blue as a plantation worker before the war, blue as an oblivion-inducing tourist drink, blue despite abiding in an ethnological paradise of flowing mai tais and see-through clothes, blue as the Delta blues of Robert John-

36. Haunani-Kay Trask, "Indigenous Writers and the Colonial Situation," *Pacific Islands Communication Journal* 13 (1984): 78–79. For a probing critique of Trask's decolonizing vision and inverted master/slave dialectics of blood, identity, and land as one huge metaphor of primordial nationhood, see Christopher Connery, "Land, Sea, and Capitalism," which forms part of a larger forthcoming study on the transnational and local cultural politics of the Pacific Rim.

37. Talk given at the UH Mānoa English Department Colloquium Series, 2 May 1996, while Chock was distinguished visiting writer in the department; his essay was published in *Bamboo Ridge* 69 (1996): 19. This essay has provoked a lot of critiques on the home front, and it is hard to see, finally, whether Chock is admitting that Bamboo Ridge is part of the neocolonizing U.S. apparatus (as Hawaiians such as Trask and their local allies Dennis Kawaharada, Laura Lyons, and Richard Hamasaki say it has become), or, as his title all too ambiguously hints, Bamboo Ridge journal/press is itself being "neocolonized" by such revisionist views from within blood-based paradigms of identity and local culture. (It would take another book to unpack this bind.)

son despite the lure of surf, the call of body bliss, the Pacific way of ocean, earth, and sky. Given the multicultural diversity of Hawaiian society ranging from work-ethic Japanese to land-grabbing developers to the generous, live-and-let-live Samoans, say, or Koreans who seem (even displaced in America) to run on ginseng, Confucius, and moral methedrine, Hawai'i needs to be taken into American consideration as a region with a distinct history and multicultural diversity worthy of recognition.

Bamboo Ridge Press has managed successfully, if erratically at times, within two decades to serve these diverse local audiences, styles, and tastes since its Talk Story conference in 1978 created an enduring narrative/ poetic outlet. This journal of Hawai'i writers is based around an ethos and coalition of forces; it depends on a hardworking, canny, voluntary, and plural-spirited group of locals based around Eric Chock, Marie Hara, Wing Tek Lum, and Darrell Lum, whose goal is much the same since its founding in 1978: to promote the literary arts in the island, both by nurturing an intricate array of local talents, old and young, and by juxtaposing their work with better-known talents from the outside world such as William Stafford (or, at times, Garrett Hongo's touristic "Volcano") to challenge the writing that goes on here or to make larger, place-based claims on "America" considered as a cultural-political artifact. You can find a new post-America by fishing for literature at Bamboo Ridge.

Cultivating the growth and spread of "local writing" in the islands, Bamboo Ridge has given ground and place to help materialize, in distinct language, the spirit of "local writing" since its inception after the Talk Story conference. The magazine and press have functioned like the fishing place near the waters off Koko Head on O'ahu and the particular style of its slide-bait fishing it is named after: at once as a place of nourishment and as a place of *mana*, diverse voices (fishing poles) who go "searching for his/her god [poem] off Bamboo Ridge," as Tony Lee writes in his flashback story on the ways of old, "Nowadays Not Like Before."[38]

Bamboo Ridge Press remains a place/metaphor of spirit power and ecological poetics, *local* in some William Carlos Williams sense of loving the ground and body of place in full dirt-filled particularity. Bamboo Ridge is a place of daily love, work, and fishing for sustenance, hardly at all like the Hanauma Bay (not so far from the Bamboo Ridge fishing hole) that

---

38. Tony Lee, "Nowadays Not Like Before," in *The Best of Bamboo Ridge*, ed. Eric Chock and Darrell H. Y. Lum (Honolulu: Bamboo Ridge Press, 1986), 167–74.

served as the backdrop for that local tour guide, Elvis Presley, to croon
his own moonstruck love songs to while courting a moonstruck tourist-
wahine and his part-Hawaiian/Tahitian royal sweetheart in *Blue Hawaii*.

It needs to be recognized, given the plight of Hawaiian Creole English
as used for imaginative effects, as well as given the reign of commodity
forms within the literary/filmic marketplace where "poetry" often seems
too self-enclosed if not irrelevant, that nurturing "literary pluralism"—in
some radical sense allowing for mingled subjects, sublanguages, and plural cultures resisting master narratives of racial or technocratic unity—is
no small feat in our hodgepodge-quilt Hawai'i. This call to build up "literary pluralism" remains necessary in Hawai'i given the sway of mainstream (and mainland) marketing and genre categories over minority languages and (merely) regional literatures. Local literatures are for the most
part ignored or reprocessed, given the territorializing reach of American
empire, as it were, that can encode the ordinary lyric subject with liberal
arguments and terms, reification of transnational capital, its own brand of
add-one-more-ethnic-and-stir pluralism turning the USA into a gigantic
shopping mall of which O'ahu's Ala Moana or Newport Beach's Fashion
Island are sublime instances.

Scrappy outlets for Hawaiian writing like these have cultivated a literary
heteroglossia of mixed voices and local tongues that might otherwise be
starved out or go unrecognized in this state so far as it is (in a way, *luckily*)
from the bright-lights-and-big-city voices of New York and Hollywood.
Bamboo Ridge as main literary outlet of such localism and works of Asian
American heteroglossia since 1978 has nurtured not a "fantasy island"
literature of the islands, written by clever (I could even say unwittingly
imperialist) outsiders. A historically acute literature of Hawai'i, *local* in
this cutting sense means in touch with the traditions, forms, terms, the
body and ground of this much-imaged and much-contested place. *Local*, in
this contested sense, means the polyvocal enactment of critical regionalism, a strategy of resistance from postmodern architecture, to which my
argument will return.

Without journals like Joseph Puna Balaz's more Hawaiian and pidgin-
oriented *Ramrod* and *O'ahu Review*, Michael McPherson's *Hapa*, Pat Matsueda's *The Paper*, and Richard Hamasaki's Pacific-oriented and internationalist *Seaweeds and Constructions*, which has aligned local literary
production with decolonizing literatures of "the Pacific Way," local writers
would have been silenced or died off without writing. Not everybody can

make the superwoman-like leap from teaching English at Midpac and UH to the *Dick Cavett Show* through the worldwide distribution exposure of Random House, as Maxine Hong Kingston did.[39] Not everybody, that is, has Kingston's spiderlike patience and endurance, her touch of narrative genius and canny sense of Asian American market self-positioning—a woman warrior indeed who could even subvert the petunia elegies of *The New Yorker* with her tripmaster-monkey rapping out urban trauma like a Chinese American Whitman on acid.

The eccentric fate of Milton Murayama, self-published and belatedly recognized, seems much more likely for any willfully local writer, committed to terms and values of one place and off-voices. Such a writer is committed, that is, to the narrating and lyric documenting of a particularly troubled history of Japanese American plantation workers in wartime Hawai'i, many of whom confronted cold war exclusion on into the 1950s and statehood, as Sumida has exposed and as I have written about for the Hawai'i Writer's Conference on Murayama's multilanguaged novel of Japanese plantation life as a working-class pastoral.[40] Murayama's second novel, published by the University of Hawai'i Press in 1994, circulates as blessing and proof of artistic survival *in and through the local.*

As for Bamboo Ridge, well, Bamboo Ridge remains Bamboo Ridge as it enters the year 2000 and publishes works of local pidgin as well as mongrel theory, like my "Postmodern X: Honolulu Traces."[41] Spunky, vital,

39. For another, more caustic and innovative way of looking from the Asian American mainland at the production of Chinese American literature, see Frank Chin, *Bulletproof Buddhists and Other Essays* (Honolulu: University of Hawai'i Press, 1998). Chin remains, of course, one of Kingston's biggest opponents, seeing her as a kind of self-orientalizing American Mulan.

40. On plantation communities and ethnic determinations that marked the complex class warfare that dominated Hawaiian daily life from 1840 to 1960, see Ronald Takaki, *Pau Hana: Plantation Life and Labor in Hawai'i* (Honolulu: University of Hawai'i Press, 1983). On Murayama's plantation novel, in addition to the Sumida scholarship cited above, also see the heteroglossic analysis of dominant and minority voices in Rob Wilson, "The Language of Confinement and Liberation in Milton Murayama's *All I Asking for Is My Body,*" in *Writers of Hawai'i: A Focus on Our Literary Heritage,* ed. Eric Chock and Jody Manabe (Honolulu: Bamboo Ridge Press, 1981), 62–65, and Rob Wilson, "Review: *All I Asking for Is My Body,*" *Bamboo Ridge* 5 (1979–1980): 2–5.

41. Forthcoming in *Bamboo Ridge* 75 (1999); for a revised and expanded version of this poem/essay on the death and rebirth of the Honolulu local, see chapter 9.

ongoing, broad-hearted, ecological, political, spiritual, micropolitical, cosmic, poor, yet *blue: blue* in some sense that early Elvis of Sun Records could
figure out as heart-tone; blue as the poetry of lyric Memphis and his
gigantic-hearted mother; blue as the azure depths off Hanauma Bay; blue
as the uncapturable gratitude toward place; blue in the glut and glamour
of literary magazines like blue shave-ice or ice-shave. The *Best of Bamboo Ridge* anthology that came out in 1986 and has been widely used in
courses in Hawai'i and on the mainland (for example, at UC Santa Cruz,
where undergraduate Sarah Wilson was studying "Asian American literature" and reading about her father's gratitude to Italian American love in
"Anita Sky") is just one installment of a scrappy and multiple project in
voicing critical resistance and regional self-invention.[42]

"Hawai'i," as a distinct way of life and counterlanguage, is now and
again threatened by antipluralist forces of cultural homogenization. As
Juliet Kono Lee portrays through her mishmash son in "Yonsei," American pop culture threatens to abolish memory, override ethnic tradition,
and render place unrecognizable to those who once inhabited it. The
mother chides this fourth-generation son oblivious to Japanese American
traditions on the Big Island as he heads out to surf, "shouldering a radio, /
smouldering the speaker / into your ear":

> You live so far
> from what connects you.
> You have no recollection
> of old plantation towns,
> of rains that plummeted
> like the sheaves of cane,
> the song of flumes,
> the stink of rotting feet,
> the indignities of hard labor.
> Your blood runs free
> from the redness of soil.[43]

42. Rob Wilson, "Anita Sky," in *The Best of Bamboo Ridge*, ed. Eric Chock and Darrell
H. Y. Lum (Honolulu: Bamboo Ridge Press, 1986), 111.
43. Juliet S. Kono [Lee], "Yonsei," in *Hilo Rains* (Honolulu: Bamboo Ridge Press, 1988),
102–3.

Just putting koa-wood counters in McDonalds Waikīkī or Peggy Hopper sailboats on the McDonalds walls in the Hawaiʻi Kai Shopping Mall does not constitute a "local style" of critical-regional resistance in any credible sense. Nor does putting Suzy Wong dresses and white bucks on Hotel Street characters result in a distinctly "Hawaiian" literature, even if that convention-coded writer is/was "Hawaiian" and readers on the mainland, especially New York City, cannot tell or don't care to know the historically necessary *difference* as an act of critical/stylistic resistance. This postmodern strategy of "critical regionalism" would resist, through local styles and tones, the threat of technocratic modernization and Western "reason" to folk cultures and indigenous traditions or regional locales.

As Kenneth Frampton outlines, such an aesthetic rooted in "rearguard" poetics can and will be enunciated as a kind of counterhegemonic discourse to Western modernity in its globalizing modes of transnational installation. "Regionalism," as an entrenchment in local style and modes, need not be some postmodern code term for a neoromantic retreat from history into boyhood sentiment or those hazy Southern charms of pastoral submission. Given the rise and spread of global postmodernity, Frampton argues for deploying richer tactics of "local culture" to resist threats of homogenization and Western modernity; he assumes that counterlanguages and counterforms to the "logic" of high-tech and capital-intensive life forms can be self-consciously inflected as regional style without succumbing to decoration, fraud, or decadence.[44]

Two collections I would again commend as articulating such an aesthetic of "critical regionalism" are the pidgin-based stories of Darrell Lum in *Sun* (1980) and the hybrid lyrics of place-bound identity in Eric Chock's *Last Days Here* (1990). Both of these authors have served for over twenty years as founding and changing editors of Bamboo Ridge. Chock depicts the sway of local culture as a ground of commitment and critique to international capital in a localist poem called "Home Free," for example, where the sense of threat is imminent (as his book title, *Last Days Here*, suggests):

44. See Kenneth Frampton, "Towards a Critical Regionalism: Six Points for an Architecture of Resistance," in *The Anti-Aesthetic*, ed. Hal Foster (Port Townsend, WA: Bay Press, 1983). On the mobility, impurity, and fraudulent constructions of "the local" from a post–Bamboo Ridge perspective, see Barry Masuda, "The Divided Local: A Personal Foray into the Problematics of Local Literature in Hawaiʻi" (Honors thesis in English, UH Mānoa, 1994).

I am like my father
who never left Hawai'i,
working the dry docks at Pearl,
sending the ships back
to some foreign port
or out at sea.
He would rather go home after work
to the quiet place beside the stream.

. . . .

But now I stand beside
what used to be our stream:
the smell of grease or garbage reeks.
The influx of certain birds
limits the number of mangoes I can eat.
Even the TV, where he used to say,
"Come quick Mommy, we can go to Paris,
for free!"
is no longer clear enough
without a cable hook-up
so fenced in are we
with condominiums walking up from town,
into our valley.

Chock turns from showing images of local molestation to utter a future-oriented plea of community entrenchment, place-bound identity, and the will to dwell in Hawai'i in terms that, like fee-simple real estate, will remain "home free":

Now that I've grown up, and gone away,
I want to develop my own sense of green.
I want to be able
to cup my hands in a clear stream.
All I want
is to be home free.[45]

As critics such as Frank Chin, Richard Hamasaki, Dana Naone Hall, Keri Hulme, and Lawson Inada have urged, writers of ethnic origin and place-

45. Eric Chock, "Home Free," in *Last Days Here* (Honolulu: Bamboo Ridge Press, 1990), 74–75.

bound identifications (indigenous or otherwise) need *not* ride this hyphen of self-conflicted identity to mainstream marketings, self-positioning of "voice" forever centered in London and New York. The stylistic result could be the authenticity of voice that the career of Murayama embodies for us or the locally inflected poetry of Chock, who registers his stance of polylingual localism so far from the workshop spotlights of Wesleyan, Iowa, and Yale. The end result could just as well be oblivion, regional irrelevance, which means a form of administering national silence. Clinging to location and forging some place-bound community within the Local Pacific can be a way of revaluing, renarrating, and reimagining the local/margin not just as *space of deprivation* and colonial victimhood, but as *space of possibility* and cultural innovation.

THE LABORS OF HLAC

Founded on Oʻahu in 1974 with the express aim "to serve the literary arts in Hawaiʻi," the Hawaiʻi Literary Arts Council, with modest funding from the State Foundation on Culture and the Arts and usually with supplemental funding from the National Endowment for the Arts, in addition to arranging an incredibly diverse program of readings for Oʻahu and the outer islands, has maintained such formative programs as Poets in the Schools (again, under Eric Chock's leadership) and the useful Hawaiʻi Children's Literature Conference, and puts out a pluralistic magazine *Literary Arts Hawaiʻi* (now called *Kaimana*) under the care of editors such as Jill Widner and Pat Matsueda in the past and Tony Quagliano, Anthony Friedson, and Joseph Stanton in the present.

Writers brought to read in Hawaiʻi every month since 1974 have shown diversity and range: Margaret Atwood, Gary Snyder, Cathy Song, Albert Wendt, Arthur Sze, Ron Silliman, Victor Cruz, Milton Murayama, Charles Bernstein, Joseph Heller, Sylvia Watanabe, John Ashbery, Vili Hereniko, Bill Luoma, Michael Ondaatje, Michael Stephens, Ursule Molinaro, John Yau, Roy Miki, Jerome Rothenberg—just to name a few that remain vivid in my memory. Most of these writers came from the mainland; this, at times, provoked some local controversy and tension, as Steve Sumida has documented. Given such a cantankerous *inside* grounding in traditions (Bamboo Ridge et al.) and this *outside* influx of techniques and ongoing challenges (via HLAC et al.), is it any wonder that a new literature has emerged so fully in the 1980s? Audiences for such HLAC-sponsored literary readings over the years have ranged in size from full houses of around 150 at the Korean Studies Center and 1,200 at Church of the Crossroads (Gary Snyder), to those attended by three or four friends of the author and a flickering candle (Edith Shiffert of Kona, now of haiku-laden Japan). The glut of these myriad readings go on until the would-be local poet might flee back to the oceans of the North Shore to get his or her head together; or to the sanctuary of actual fishing off Bamboo Ridge; or to drink alone with the radio; or (like myself) to play Robocop basketball on Roy Sakuma Productions' court on Sunday instead of going to mass or staying home to become an NBA couch potato.

The Council still encourages and would build up resident writers in Hawai'i through awards such as the Hawai'i Award for Literature (which was given at the state capitol to Reuel Denney for 1988, for example) and the Elliot Cades awards (given to Juliet Kono Lee and Darrell H. Y. Lum in October 1991), two substantial awards to recognize "promising" and "middle-level" local writers at points in their careers when such honors can do their writerly souls and pockets maximal good. I call attention to this HLAC history if only to suggest, in Pacific local terms, that there is a link between literacy and literature. The cultivation of reading and writing skills not only by Bamboo Ridge and HLAC (not to mention the local-drama ferment around the plays of "Kumu Kahua") but by citizens needs to be encouraged "at both ends of the spectrum," as Frank Stewart of the University of Hawai'i at Mānoa Creative Writing Program noted. Young people in Hawai'i do need to encounter not only the basics of language but the most challenging and imaginative uses of their language. The result for Hawaiian-grown children will be that inward creativity, synthetic thinking, and leaps across boundaries that can come about in whatever field the student chooses to apply his or her talents.

I want to illustrate this work on the spirit-body of local literature and minority languages in Hawai'i with one more anecdote. In 1987, I participated in a reading to celebrate the appearance of *Bamboo Ridge 33*. Such potluck-like readings to celebrate *Bamboo Ridge, Hawai'i Review, Ramrod,* and *Chaminade Literary Review* are sponsored by HLAC, often giving small funds for writers to come from the outer islands. These community-building readings of local imagination and regional commitment, like those of Language Poets in Berkeley, have become necessary events for local writers to hear tones, themes, terms, moves, images, challenges from the Outside—"voices"!

After I had read a few poems of my own on love, nation, transcultural negotiation, and death into hybridity in Seoul, I sat down next to Jonathan Penner (then a visiting novelist at UH Mānoa from the University of Arizona) to hear other readers. I was struck by the usual diversity of voices and forms at any Bamboo Ridge event—the generational portraits of Mavis Hara, Diane Kahanu, and Wing Tek Lum; the growing-up-local narrative of Rodney Morales; the wry family images of Barbara Guerin; the aestheticized nature poems of Reuben Tam—but I was impressed, in particular, by a short story by Gary Pak, "The Valley of the Dead Air," about a stench on a plantation that not even the old kahunas can remove. Pak's story uses a range of pidgin voices to capture folk culture, as well as a more sophisticated narrative voice with political insights that recalled the materialist perspectives into social community of Latin American novelists.

As place-bound identity was given voice, many were struck by this energetic Korean American writer. I thought to my all-too-pedagogical soul, Wow, here are new writers who are building on the narrative traditions of people like Milton Murayama and Maxine Hong Kingston, but taking it further, in a new direction, writing about the state and its history in a way that still needs to be done. Hollywood, watch out—Hawai'i is so much more than the backdrop for a cops-and-robbers show with glitzy cars, Polynesian dolls, beach-bingo Republicans with Detroit Tigers caps whose ideal of American womanhood is, well, Nancy Reagan.

As I mused on this "local" story, Penner turned to me and asked, "Are your writers *all* this good here?" I wanted to say Yes, of course, because a conviction of *local pride* had stemmed from a kind of maternal-paternal delight in *generativity*, the sense that I and others such as Faye Kicknosway, Craig Howes, Joseph Chadwick, Cristina Bacchilega, Marie Hara, and Lorne Evans Hershinow (through teaching, through slave labor, and through nurturing vital outlets such as Bamboo Ridge and Joe Balaz's even more pidgin-based *Ramrod*; through participating in events such as reading groups and journal readings that are cosponsored by HLAC) had helped hand on literary traditions and tools that could serve to shape the future, in specific ways that neither I nor any jaded literary old-timer could foresee. (Gary Pak's stories were later gathered into an award-winning collection of Hawaiian magical realism, *Watcher of Waipuna*.)[46]

46. Gary Pak, *Watcher of Waipuna* (Honolulu: Bamboo Ridge Press, 1992). Also see Pak's latest novel of diasporic localism, which offers a transpacific vision of Korean

Although it may sound like some weird chemical you add to pluralize lily-white American milk, HLAC has proved to be something you can add to literacy/literature in Hawai'i as a catalyst of pluralism with benign effects. For this remains the work that HLAC does: it is a kind of work upon and within the creative spirit, and it does not go away, and no one can tell the result, it is so grounded and infinite. The Council builds up; the bottom line is, so to speak, that these benefits are as real and as lasting as hotels or high-tech bombs, as the work of writers as diverse as Gary Pak, Lois-Ann Yamanaka, Zack Linmark, Barry Masuda, Kathy Dee Banggo, and Milton Murayama can attest. A literature "mired into this locality" has surfaced to express the languages, cultures, and differences of Hawai'i as a distinct cultural region in the Pacific threatened (from within and without) by national oblivion and transnational molestation.

ACTING LOCALLY

As a place-bound heteroglossia, "local-color" regionalism in the United States has long worked to dissolve the hold of federal consensus into a plurality of competing claims and fractured representations. Since the 1860s, "local-color" regionalism has created a centrifugal force within the ideology of U.S. national unity that the Civil War helped to solidify, tenuously, into place. Claims of sectional diversity and recalcitrant particularity would have their say, both North and South, if not from Maine to California. And the first of such mainland rhetorics that emerged to signify national difference was the literature of "local color": in other words, a U.S. literary regionalism tied to cultural specificity of place, particular metaphors of geography, and markers of local language and local identity.[47] Locally inflected authors of place-saturated vernacular such as Sarah Orne Jewett, Harriet Beecher Stowe, Bret Harte, and Charles Chesnutt expressed the counternational values and customs tied to differentiated

---

revolutionary nationalism and class struggle as carried over to the plantations of Hawai'i, *A Ricepaper Airplane* (Honolulu: University of Hawai'i Press, 1998), as well as his ongoing critical work linking the local historical novel to forms of Hawaiian cultural nationalism.

47. On "decentralizing" tactics of region, race, and ethnicity as expressed in American "local-color" authors and movements, see Jules Chametzky, *Our Decentralized Literature: Cultural Mediations in Selected Jewish and Southern Writers* (Amherst: University of Massachusetts Press, 1986).

places and prior languages that mocked, challenged, and opposed the dominant forces of industrial, urban, and federal integration.[48] *Location* as place-bound identification was given a residual dimension as national oppositionality and critique, especially in the American South, where regionality continues to comprise a tormented ground of historical difference and subcultural affirmation in authors as diverse as Kate Chopin, William Faulkner, Eudora Welty, Bobby Ann Mason, and Larry Brown.

Languages of ethnic diversity emerged to voice the play/difference of alternative metaphors, folk customs, ethnic values, and religious beliefs as posited against homogenizing forces of Americanization. Absorption of regionality or indigenous identity into master narratives of national unity or standardization was challenged by counterhistories specifying the racial and religious torment imposed by the nation-building project. Regional identities were regrounded in ethnic emergence, and such literature remains trenchantly fragmented, fractal, mobile, multiple, constructed, and diverse.[49]

This local-based identity politics ("All politics are local," as Tip O'Neill once urged) has taken ever new twists within the postmodern USA: "The regionalism of our own times is a regionalism of race and gender," Philip Fisher has claimed, and, articulated as such, remains at times fixed, nonnegotiable, not subject to national absorption.[50] In other words, this ideologically consolidating scholar of American studies centrality would collapse the centrifugal claims of geography, ethnicity, race, and gender into recurring "regional" forces (either transitional or paradoxical, depending on the rhetoric) of national disintegration and political dissent. Though others can challenge Fisher's depoliticizing homogenization of historical diversity into discursive sameness if not de-eternalize the larger claim underwriting these contradictory forces of plural dissensus that "regional-

48. Jewett's "local color" Maine pastoralism is defended as a subfederal and antiindustrial critique in Louis A. Renza, *"A White Heron" and the Question of Minor Literature* (Madison: University of Wisconsin Press, 1984).

49. For another, more canonical look at American Pacific literature and its thematic struggles to overcome textual heritages of exoticism, primitivism, and orientalism carried into the Pacific, see Roger J. Bresnahan, "Islands in Our Minds: The Pacific Ocean in the American Literary Imagination," in *Reflections on Orientalism* (East Lansing: Asian Studies Center of Michigan State University, 1983), 3–13.

50. Philip Fisher, introduction to *The New American Studies: Essays from Representations* (Berkeley: University of California Press, 1991), xiii.

ism is always, in America, part of a civil war within representation," it does not make contemporary sense (from an indigenous/local Pacific point of view) to describe these forces for critical regionalisms as historically over.[51]

Given the sway of transnational capital and such decentered modes of spatial molestation across nation and region as APEC, GATT, and NAFTA, local Pacific regionalism can have enduring critical force within the national polity. Nor does it make sense to absorb local struggles into eternal paradoxes or structural episodes of the American polity. To do so can be ideologically disenabling except to those whom this federal, and commercial, American unity most benefits and for whom regionalism is already over. Claims of Native American regionality would argue otherwise. The claims of Hawaiian regionalism, as I have urged, have been tied to the ongoing struggles to voice an oppositional sovereignty, that of indigenous Hawaiians struggling to articulate and achieve nation-within-a-nation status in 1993, one hundred years after their territory was annexed and their legal claims effectively silenced. Even the *Wall Street Journal* has called attention to this national injustice, and the state of Hawai'i is moving inexorably toward the recognition of Hawaiian claims to legal, territorial, and cultural separation (as in the ratification of "Hawaiian immersion" programs in Pūnana Leo elementary school). Even the multicultural forces loosely banded around Bamboo Ridge continue to challenge the myths and unity of national hegemony within homegrown literature and place-bound lives.

To invoke that bumper-sticker refrain of regional pride/identity that registers rooted senses not yet coopted into a marketing strategy of local penetration by the *Harvard Business Review*, "Lucky you live Hawai'i." Why remain *local?* Local can be a rallying cry to get beyond some apolitical and white left-brain-generated *Blue Hawaii* invented and marketed in Hollywood and New York for global distribution. Local in this dynamic and nomadic political sense means *thinking globally*, that is transnationally, but *acting locally*, that is, by means of a canny regional coalition, as Darrell Lum's comment on the EDB sublime of "nature" recognizes as ground of Hawai'i's commitment to preserve the land.

Hawai'i is not *Blue Hawaii;* the site is not just some trope of an erotic/exotic South Pacific. It is not just a myth of primitive essence, nor a sexy backdrop for Tom Selleck or Jack Lord to lord it over some mixed-race

51. Ibid., xiv.

English-mangling locals. Hawai'i is not just real estate; not just the site of "gee-ain't-it-beautiful" postcards and plumeria-laden love lyrics.[52] As Diane Kahanu boasts, using her pidgin English as local tactic of deterritorialized struggle and means of resistance against domination from distant cities and foreign powers,

> Pidgin safe.
> Like Refuge, Pu'uhonua,
> from the City.[53]

"Local poems" lovingly—yet cuttingly (as in wilder new works by Justin Chin, Kathy Dee Banggo, Lois-Ann Yamanaka, Barry Masuda, and Zack Linmark that have come under criticism from various national and ethnic groups for their postlocal strangeness, not to mention the early crazed-pidgin poems of Michael McPherson such as "Auntie Kinau on the King Street Tram" from *Singing with the Owls*)—can begin to express these dynamics of place-based identity in a language/sensibility worth preserving through the social workings of literature, as through other spiritual-material means.[54]

52. On fantasies by Euro-American artists such as Gauguin, Stevenson, Twain, Wallace Stevens, Paul Theroux, and Marlon Brando that "make explicit the equation tropics/ecstasy/amorousness/native," see Abigail Solomon-Godeau's take on French colonial primitivism in "Going Native," *Art in America* 77 (July 1989): 119–28.
53. Diane Kahanu, "Ho. Just Cause I Speak Pidgin No Mean I Dumb," in *The Best of Bamboo Ridge*, ed. Eric Chock and Darrell H. Y. Lum (Honolulu: Bamboo Ridge Press, 1986), 43.
54. On the dynamics of Hawai'i's "local literature" within frameworks of global/local postmodernity, see Susan Schultz, "Towards a Haole Poetics," in *A Poetics of Criticism*, ed. Juliana Spahr et al. (Buffalo, NY: Leave Books, 1994); Barry Masuda's honors thesis on the constructed "local" (see n. 44 above); Candace Fujikane's 1996 doctoral thesis from the UC Berkeley English Department on "cultural nationalism" in Hawai'i; Paul Toguchi's studies on local Japanese working-class identity and the Hawaiian sovereignty struggle; and, in the lineage of John Dominis Holt's Ku Paa Press, see Dennis Kawaharada's archive of Hawaiian literary/natural attitudes, translations, and works, *Storied Landscapes: Hawaiian Literature and Place* (Honolulu: Kalamakū Press, 1999). For further discussion, see chapter 6 below.

CHAPTER 5

Bloody Mary Meets Lois-Ann Yamanaka:

Imagining Hawaiian Locality, from South Pacific
to Bamboo Ridge and Beyond

and if especially
those insistent mushrooming discourses
on life for all Pacific
spell genokamikaze through and through—
then I'll gather up this debris; up, once
all over again: for you, Island.
        —Russell Soaba, "Island: ways of immortal folk"

"*South Pacific* will run forever!" Walter Winchell once remarked of the smarmy cold war Rodgers and Hammerstein musical. But, from Suva to Papua New Guinea to the local site of Bamboo Ridge in Hawai'i, Pacific-based writers have challenged these James Michener–like U.S. national productions of Asian/Pacific and indigenous cultures with local constructions of place, sublanguages, and alternative grounds of identity. This chapter will counter the global machinery of cultural texts such as *South Pacific* and *Blue Hawaii* with interior constructions of the "Asia/Pacific" as place and identity and posit, at the core, the turn within Asian/Pacific literary culture in Hawai'i toward expressing and coalescing into some kind of *oppositional regionalism*. This Pacific regionalism, at its most powerful reimagining of place, nation, and language in Maori novels such as Keri Hulme's *Bone People* (1983) and Patricia Grace's *Potiki* (1986), as well as such signal works of Hawai'i's "local literature" as Milton Murayama's *All I Asking for Is My Body* (1975), John Dominis Holt's indigenous pastoral novel, *Waimea Summer* (1976), and trenchant poetry collections such as Michael McPherson's *Singing with The Owls* (1982), Eric Chock's *Last Days*

Here (1990), and Lois-Ann Yamanaka's *Saturday Night at the Pahala The-atre* (1993), would—implicitly or at times—fracture the white nation-state imagination in its tropological sway over the Pacific.[1]

Running through this chapter's discussion of the "local" Pacific will be four strands of thinking linked around related concerns of language, na-tion, and place: (1) the attempt to resist "symbolic domination"[2] by the norms, tropes, and genres of literary culture imported and imposed from the mainland or from Europe; (2) the poetic "recreolization"[3] of English as a connotative signifier of bonds to local culture and multiethnic commu-nity worth preserving for purposes of expression and sense of control (hence the building up of a polylingual literature of the local and minor); (3) the contradiction-ridden yet coalitional articulation of what Raymond Williams called the "bond to place" within a globalizing economy of trans-national circulation that would construct and produce the local/locality into a tourist icon and decenter formations of class-based resistance; and (4) given this globalizing transnational economy, the need for cultivating "bonds to place" as a means to building up what I have called critical regionalism within a postmodern culture of simulacra and sign flux.[4]

1. Keri Hulme, *The Bone People* (Auckland: Spiral/Hodder and Stoughton, 1983); Pa-tricia Grace, *Potiki* (Auckland: Penguin, 1986); Milton Murayama, *All I Asking for Is My Body* (San Francisco: Supa Press, 1975); John Dominis Holt, *Waimea Summer: A Novel* (Honolulu: Topgallant, 1976); Michael McPherson, *Singing with the Owls* (Honolulu: Petronium Press, 1982); Eric Chock, *Last Days Here* (Honolulu: Bamboo Ridge Press, 1990); and Lois-Ann Yamanaka, *Saturday Night at the Pahala Theatre* (Honolulu: Bam-boo Ridge Press, 1993).

2. On "symbolic domination" of culture achieved via distinctions of language, taste, and "cultural capital," see John B. Thompson, "Symbolic Violence: Language and Power in the Writings of Pierre Bourdieu," in his *Studies in the Theory of Ideology* (Berkeley: University of California Press, 1984), 48–61.

3. See Charlene J. Sato, "Linguistic Inequality in Hawai'i: The Post-Creole Dilemma," in *Language of Inequality,* ed. N. Wolfson and J. Manes (Berlin: Mouton, 1985), 255–72.

4. On "bonds to place" as ground of transnational resistance, see Raymond Williams, "Decentralism and the Politics of Place," in *Resources of Hope: Culture, Democracy, Socialism,* ed. Robin Glade (London: Verso, 1989): "But *place* has been shown to be a crucial element in the bonding process—more so perhaps for the working class than the capital-owning classes—by the explosion of the international economy and the destruc-tive effects of deindustrialization upon old communities. When capital has moved on, the importance of place is more clearly revealed" (242). Katharyne Mitchell has shown the disruptions of place-bound identity in Vancouver on the Northwest Pacific coast of Canada; see "Multiculturalism, Or the United Colors of Capitalism?" *Antipode* 23

For an American audience newly conscious of a global destiny, *South Pacific* conjured Pacific space into a settler's paradise of enchantment, racial harmony, and (to be sure) military necessity. This "musical play" opened in 1949 and ran for close to two thousand performances, won the Pulitzer prize that year for drama, and played across the United States to box office records as it went. Based on two racially tormented love stories from James A. Michener's Pulitzer prize-winning book, *Tales of the South Pacific* (1946), the play's fable of racial and cultural encounters reactivated by the Pacific war, as Patricia G. McGhee has observed, "was well known to audiences when it auditioned in Boston in 1946."[5]

Michener, a national-popular novelist who has given something like $13 million over twenty years to institutions such as the University of Iowa Writing Program and has seemingly written about every landscape under the sun, continues to receive ample royalties from *South Pacific*. Even as recently as 1994, the musical was being performed by the Army Community Theater at Fort Shafter in Honolulu. That the U.S. military needs to keep performing *South Pacific* as a fantasy of Pacific space imposed on Hawai'i and its Asian/Pacific characters is the cold war master narrative I want to expose and contest.

As a fable of cold war necessity, *South Pacific* absorbed the Pacific into its master narrative of militarization and technological development. This story may have ended in October 1990 when, among related events of postindustrial dismantlement and internal dissent, a presidential order ceased the bombing of Kaho'olawe island in Hawai'i. This special locus of what Davianna McGregor calls "spiritual and cultural identification" for the Hawaiian sovereignty struggle was demilitarized and reclaimed for indigenous usage after having been targeted since World War II as a bombing and gunnery range.[6]

Why associate *South Pacific* with the struggle for indigenous sover-

---

(1993): 263–94. In a related global/local study, see David Harvey, "From Space to Place and Back Again: Reflections on the Condition of Postmodernity," in *Mapping the Futures: Local Cultures, Global Change,* ed. Jon Bird et al. (London: Routledge, 1993), 3–28.
5. See Patricia O. McGhee, "*South Pacific* Revisited: Were We Carefully Taught or Reinforced?" *The Journal of Ethnic Studies* 15 (1988): 124.
6. Quoted in Jon Yoshishige, "U.S. Vote Brings Kahoolawe Home," *Honolulu Advertiser,* 11 November 1993, A1. For related decolonizing struggles, see David Robie, *Blood on Their Banner: Nationalist Struggles in the South Pacific* (Leichhardt, Australia: Pluto Press Australia, 1989).

eignty and place-bound identity that is occurring in contemporary Hawai'i? Although situated in the "Northern Pacific" and strategic to the American commercial presence across the Pacific Ocean since the sandalwood, fur, and whaling trade of the 1820s and the imperial rivalries with France and Great Britain in the 1840s, Hawai'i has long played "South Pacific" to the cultures and power of Northern capital, whether sugar money from California, Bibles and whaling ships from Boston, or the resort hotel interests from Indonesia and Japan. This is palpable in the sugar rhetoric of Mark Twain, who, as a journalist in 1866, urged that "if California can send capitalists down here in seven or eight days time and take them back in nine or ten [via commercial steamships], she can fill these islands full of Americans and regain her lost foothold" in the Pacific.[7] American sugar interests did so around the coaling station of Pearl Harbor, importing Asian labor and, in time, displacing native peoples and outlawing Hawaiian as a language of public instruction en route to annexation under the imperial presidency of William McKinley.[8]

Set on some unspecified generic colonial French Pacific island in World War II, the 1958 movie version of *South Pacific* "was filmed on Kaua'i, with scenes at the Berkmyre estate overlooking Hanalei Bay, Lumaha'i Bay, Ha'ena, Kalapaki Beach, and Barking Sands, plus one brief scene on O'ahu," and thus, even more so than the play, helped to evoke a white mythological fantasy of "one enchanted evening" in Paradise for an American mass-tourist audience soon to disembark from their planes onto the state of Hawai'i.[9] Via the pidgin-speaking and Asian/Pacific persona of Bloody Mary, American innocents (like Nurse Nellie) were offered a disfigured embodiment of those far-flung Asian/Pacific cultures willing (through people like her) to be absorbed, acculturated, and contained in their global economy of signs.[10] Hollywood (what some in Hawai'i like to

7. Mark Twain, *Letters from Hawaii*, ed. A. Grove Day (Honolulu: University of Hawai'i Press, 1975), 12.
8. See Michael Dougherty, *To Steal a Kingdom: Probing Hawaiian History* (Waimanalo, HI: Island Style Press, 1992), 165–79.
9. Robert C. Schmitt, *Hawai'i in the Movies, 1898–1959* (Honolulu: Hawaiian Historical Society, 1988), 73.
10. On gender dynamics of the U.S. colonial gaze on postwar Pacific subjects, see Margaret Jolly, "From Point Venus to Bali Ha'i: Eroticism and Exoticism in Representations of the Pacific," in *Sites of Desire, Economies of Pleasure: Sexualities in Asia and the*

call "Haolewood") operated with the Department of Defense to install a "concrete fantasy" and images of the American Pacific as *South Pacific.*

Postwar inscription of local places and peoples into some "concrete fantasy" of the American Pacific can still generate cultural capital for travel writers of the up-market "tourist gaze," from Simon Winchester to Paul Theroux. In *Pacific Rising* Winchester is delighted that one of the sacred sites for tour guides on Kaua'i is "where Mitzi Gaynor washed that man right out of her hair."[11] For a postmodern audience, driven by pastiche and simulacra, such an allusion could almost count as a historical deep memory binding consciousness to place and self to history.

But, for the Macintosh- and Toyota-driven vision of Winchester's Pacific, Hawai'i (like the "Pacific Basin") figures in as "vanishing wilderness" and people-emptied landscapes of wilderness sublimity that once "had mystic associations with long-vanished Hawaiian cultures"—in short, as the charming flora and fauna of "the Old Pacific."[12] There are no sentiments of Hawaiian nationhood or possession, no cultural nationalists to disturb Winchester's "concrete fantasy" of Old Pacific paradise for the *Conde Nast Traveler.* No micropolitical thematics of the Hawaiian sovereignty struggle disturb the tourist spread of Rimspeak.[13]

In *The Happy Isles of Oceania,* an archive of white cultural (by no means *first*) possession, Paul Theroux reveals a condescension (if not ego-centered contempt) toward the cultures of the Pacific, as in his comments on the novelist Somerset Maugham as his Euro-American precursor in Samoa: "Maugham was another writer who had sanctified a place by using it as a setting; he had done the islands a great favor—made them seem [*sic*]

Pacific, ed. Lenor Mandeson and Margaret Jolly (Chicago: University of Chicago Press, 1997), 99–122; and Carolyn O'Dwyer, "American Identity across the Pacific: Culture, Race, and Sexuality in *South Pacific* and *Tales from the South Pacific,*" *Antithesis* 7 (1995): 123–37.

11. Simon Winchester, *Pacific Rising: The Emergence of a New World Culture* (New York: Prentice Hall, 1991), 368.

12. Ibid., 366–71.

13. For a summary of recent configurations between state and nation, see Chieko Tachihata, "The Sovereignty Movement In Hawai'i," *The Contemporary Pacific* 6 (1994): 202–10; *Ka Leo O Ka Lāhui Hawai'i: A Compilation of Materials for Educational Workshops* (Honolulu: Ka Lāhui, 1993); and Hawaiian Sovereignty Advisory Commission, Final Report, 18 February 1994.

exotic and interesting."[14] Without "sanctification" by the cultural capital and mythology of Western writers, painters, anthropologists, travelers, and moviemakers, these "places without history" in the Pacific do not exist—that is the mind-boggling claim. At best, the Pacific beckons these writers as a submissive woman of color waiting to be inscribed/awakened into Edenic trope, engendered into submission, inculcated into English as in the pedagogy of Gauguin's French Tahitian travelogue, *Noa Noa*. Such writers are searching to find what Vilsoni Hereniko and Teresia Teaiwa debunk in *Last Virgin in Paradise*.[15] Theroux desires "the apotheosis of the South Seas: distant, secluded, empty, pristine—ravishing in fact."[16]

At a time when ethnography as a social science grows increasingly skeptical of its own ability to objectify, trope, describe, and salvage non-Western cultures in any redemptive way, it is shameful to see Theroux rescue the literary genre of travel writing for this belated project of self-discovery and snobbery from Patagonia to the Solomon Islands. Such attitudes link Louis Bougainville's Venus-struck *Voyage* to Theroux's pioneerlike kayak, with its dog-eared copy of Malinowski's *The Sexual Life of Savages* and self-pitying male hunger for paradise-on-earth, figured as some "happy island" (troped as a dark submissive woman) in the vast vacancies of Oceania.

Given this lineage, it may not appear so strange that most American movies made in or about Hawai'i, from the First World War's *Martin Eden* (1914) to the postwar *South Pacific*, "took place aboard aircraft, ships, boats, or submarines," as Robert Schmitt outlines in *Hawai'i in the Movies, 1898–1959*.[17] This perspective from the ocean toward the native shore presupposes the militarization of local space from the cold war American gaze: an aesthetic-commercial "sanctification" of Pacific Ocean localities from within defensive optics and codes of representation.

Blue Hawaii (1961), a movie that popularized the "paradisal interpretation" of Hawai'i as a mass-tourist garden of exotic/erotic delight in the "South Pacific," at least tried to turn Elvis Presley into a place-bound

14. Paul Theroux, *The Happy Isles of Oceania: Paddling the Pacific* (New York: Putnam, 1992), 350.
15. Vilsoni Hereniko and Teresia Teaiwa, *Last Virgin in Paradise* (Suva, Fiji: Mana Publications, 1993).
16. Theroux, *Happy Isles*, 398.
17. Schmitt, *Hawai'i in the Movies*, 6.

Pacific resident.[18] Elvis's detailed knowledge of local custom and idiom (expressed in a mildly Southern pidgin accent) allows him to drop out of his wealthy family's Great Hawaiian Fruit Company and pineapple production into the key business of the fiftieth state's future, mass tourism. Chad Gates gets a job as tour guide for Hawaiian Island Tours, escorts and croons five haole women around the islands, and finally marries his half-Hawaiian, half-French sweetheart, Maile, at a wedding on Kauaʻi fit for a (rock) king. To the dismay of his racist mother (played by Angela Lansbury), Elvis hangs out with native beach boys, speaks scraps of pidgin, surfs, and longs to waste his fortune crooning *aloha* to Maile and his knee-slapping friends in a grass shack at Hanauma Bay (*sic*). Elvis at least gets close to, if circling around, the local culture of Bamboo Ridge. As tour guide, he gets to guide a bunch of giddy teenagers "who have more than scenery on their minds" as they become "wahines" (movie ad).

For the most part, the photogenic landscape of Hawaiʻi, as in an array of postmodern TV series starring Hawaiʻi-as-place from *Hawaiian Eye* (1959–1963), *Hawaii Five-O* (1968–1980), *Big Hawaii* (1977), *Magnum P.I.* (1980–1988), *Aloha Paradise* (1981), *Hawaiian Heat* (1984), *Jake and the Fat Man* (1988–1990), *Island Son* (1989), and *Raven* (1991), to the most recent drama, *The Byrds of Paradise*, figures as Edenic backdrop to some *imagined ethnoscape* of racialized, exoticized, blatant orientalizing-of-the-local plots (local Japanese usually play shifty-eyed Yakuza, and Hawaiians and Samoans, nightclub bouncers or gophers).[19]

This "tourist gaze" on Pacific locality as exotic/erotic site of tourist fulfillment is palpable in the tackiest Elvis-croons-in-Hawaiʻi movie ever

18. "*Blue Hawaii*, a [1961] film that was never intended as serious commentary [on Hawaiʻi] but one that attracted huge audiences because of its star—Elvis Presley—and its evocative title, had a greater impact upon popular impressions of the island than any other film ever made. In a sense, this is regrettable, as its portrayal of Hawaiian society, while blandly complimentary, is a blurred amalgam of Hawaiian, Samoan, and Tahitian culture overlaid with borrowed Southern notions of hospitality, aristocracy, leisure, and race. Despite these shortcomings, however, it does project an essentially paradisal interpretation and stands, thus, as a major factor in the popularization of this view of the islands." See Paul F. Hooper, *Elusive Destiny: The Internationalist Movement in Modern Hawaiʻi* (Honolulu: University of Hawaiʻi Press, 1980), 22.

19. Ibid., 22–28. Also see Ed Bark, "Isle 'Byrds' Worth a Look" [includes catalog of TV series set in Hawaiʻi], *Honolulu Advertiser*, 3 March 1994, B1; and Ed Rampell, "The Tackiest Films Ever Made about Hawaiʻi," *Honolulu Weekly* 2 (15 April 1992): 4–5.

made, *Paradise, Hawaiian Style* (1964), which uses a soporific plot about Elvis and the plight of his tourist shuttle company and banal calypsolike music but features primal Pacific events such as Samoans, Tongans, and Tahitians playing ever-smiling Hawaiians dancing the hula. This takes place at the just-opened Polynesian Cultural Center, the real star of the show. Perspective on place and culture is rendered through the gaze of United Airlines and tourist company helicopters (piloted by a singing Elvis) sweeping over vast native-emptied rain forests of Kaua'i and over the tourist-thick resort hotels and azure Pacific waters from the Royal Hawaiian to the Kahala Hilton: tourist heaven as "paradise, Hawaiian style."

Twentieth Century-Fox's motion picture, *South Pacific*, directed with escapist exaggeration and those at times ludicrous, "ever-present [colorizing] filters" by Joshua Logan that drench the yellow Pacific in red, white, and blue hazes, premiered at the height of the cold war when U.S. military hegemony across the Pacific had solidified into nuclear normality and the "insistent mushrooming discourses" (Soaba) were doing their anti-Soviet work.[20] Circulation of *South Pacific* through the cultural arteries of the American imaginary was aggravated with the advent of another technology, the LP album of *South Pacific*, which proved to be a blockbuster as well. The VCR and Ted Turner's television network's penchant for singalong musicals in the American grain have prolonged this musical's afterlife into the 1990s, even as the Johnston atoll (Kalama Island) in the far-flung "South Pacific" is used to incinerate chemical weapons left over from North Atlantic struggles.[21] As cinemascope spectacle, cultures of the North Pacific and *South Pacific* fuse into a fantasy of Edenic enchantment, boundary blurring, and Asian/Pacific otherness here figured as that broker of local beauty and commercialization of native custom, Bloody Mary. Mary's broken-English slogan for this emerging Asian-Pacific lifestyle is "Native Skirts fo'Dollah."

South Pacific is far more than a *heterotopia* of "escapism" and harmless space of cross-cultural otherness, as some critics have claimed of the genre.[22] Mythology of racial and cultural superiority was concretized to

---

20. Rick Altman, *The American Film Musical* (Bloomington: Indiana University Press, 1987), 197.

21. See William A. Callahan and Steve Olive, "Chemical Weapons Discourse in the 'South Pacific,'" in *Asia/Pacific as Space of Cultural Production*, ed. Rob Wilson and Arif Dirlik (Durham, NC: Duke University Press, 1996), 57–79.

22. Altman, *The American Film Musical*, 62.

ratify the American presence in this musical appropriation of the South Pacific and to assuage the labor of Asian/Pacific boundary negotiation the music mystifies. Cultural domination takes place in dreamscapes of blue and red suffusion on so-called Bali Ha'i.

This labor of territorial possession that "takes place on two islands in the South Pacific during the recent war" seems harmless enough in its symbolic-fantasy fusion of transnational bodies across racial, class, and national divides.[23] While the pidgin-speaking, bootlegging go-between character, Bloody Mary, negotiates the marriage of local culture and the body of her Tonkinese/Tonganese daughter to a swooning marine lieutenant from Princeton, Joseph Cable, Emile De Becque joins his French colonial presence as landed aristocrat ("Is all this yours?") and antifascist hero to the cockeyed, smarmy New World optimism of Nurse Nellie ("He's a cultured Frenchmen— / I'm a little hick").[24] Dominating the Japanese and subordinating Pacific peoples to commercial and military enterprise from Papua New Guinea to the Bikini atoll, American and French administrators work together to represent, construct, and install *their* "South Pacific" into an enchanted Bali Hai playground fit for Euro-American romance, commodity worship,[25] sexual contamination, danger, passion, and (above all) military might.

These colonial innocents "have to be taught" to savor Proust's novels of landed gentry and sip cognac on "some enchanted evening" in a white settler's manor. But they also have to overcome a three-hundred-year legacy of racial prejudice that Ensign Nellie Forbush brings with her from Little Rock to categorize the peoples of Polynesia by racial color. In Michener's short story, American racism is overt, as Nellie (played with nervous charm by Mitzi Gaynor in the musical) muses on the sexual contamination of the French émigré, who (like his colonial predecessors from the time of Bougainville) had been enchanted by "the Venus of Tahiti": "Emile De Becque, not satisfied with Javanese and Tonkinese women, had also lived with a Polynesian. A nigger! To Nellie's tutored mind any person living or dead who was not white or yellow was a nigger. . . . Her entire Arkansas upbring-

23. Oscar Hammerstein and Joshua Logan, *South Pacific: A Musical Play* (New York: Random House, 1949), 1.

24. Ibid., 10.

25. See Lamont Lindstrom, *Cargo Cult: Strange Stories of Desire from Melanesia and Beyond* (Honolulu: University of Hawai'i Press, 1993), on the fantasy of the "cargo cult" as universalizing the commodity fetish to Melanesian natives.

ing made it impossible for her to deny the teachings of her youth. Emile De Becque had lived with a nigger. He had nigger children."[26]

Like many an uneven exchange within colonial contexts of commercial dependency and metropolitan administration, a global/local bargain does get struck; Nicholas Thomas argues that "local appropriation for local ends" in the Pacific "must all ultimately be seen in the global context of European dominance."[27] Natives of the South/North Pacific from the Solomon Islands to Guam will have to be taught the market system, modern warfare, geopolitics, and, above all, the militarization of local space and identity by global powers from polities of Europe, America, and Japan. Americans, for their part, will have to be taught to sing along with the U.S. Department of Defense, and the U.S. Pacific Command Center, and take up the burden of French plantation colonialism done over in Nellie's lesser key of *innocent disavowal*.[28]

James Michener, prolific mythographer of national settlement as democratization into the narrative of "Golden Man" assimilator, has become a whipping boy for the "local literature" movement emerging in Hawai'i—not so much for *South Pacific* as for his novel *Hawaii*, which came out in 1959 as if to legitimate, in one panoramic gaze of triumph, Hawai'i's march from primordial emptiness through missionary culture to the imagined community of a liberal statehood. This proves relevant to mapping the "real nexus" of cultural labor and national imagining such popular literature is involved in. As the *New York Herald Tribune* blurb on *Hawaii* has it, "James A. Michener tells the whole story of the people, Polynesian, American, Portuguese, Chinese, Philippine, Japanese, who have mingled to make our fiftieth state."[29] Dedicated to "all the people who came to Hawaii," including indigenous ones in a grand telos of Hawaiian modernity as prolonged Americanization, Michener's *Hawaii* narrates the

26. James A. Michener, "Our Heroine," in *Tales of the South Pacific* (New York: Fawcett Crest, 1974), 138.

27. Nicholas Thomas, *Entangled Objects: Exchange, Material Culture, and Colonialism in the Pacific* (Cambridge, MA: Harvard University Press, 1991), 184.

28. On the desublimating of American imperial acts of possession, see Amy Kaplan and Donald Pease, eds., *The Cultures of United States Imperialism* (Durham, NC: Duke University Press, 1993).

29. James A. Michener, *Hawaii* (New York: Random House, 1959). For local idolatry of Michener as national hero, see Melissa Sones, "Portrait of an 'Average' Guy [James Michener]," *Honolulu Advertiser* 27 January 1986, D1–2.

movement of Asian/Pacific cultures into what I would call the *melting-pot sublime* and, as such, proves inadequate to describe the Asian/Pacific dynamics of the local literature movement in Hawai'i. Given Michener's commonsense liberal view, multicultures will mix and amalgamate races and customs into the fusion of the nation-state.

"Local" culture critics have been less sanguine about *Hawaii* as "masterpiece" of historical production and would unsettle such fantasies of place and offshore tactics of cultural representation. Michener's "contrived pidgin English" in *Hawaii*, as Stephen Sumida contends, has served to mystify the dynamics of local culture and indigenous possession, if not denigrate local perspectives as substandard, minor, and insufficient to grasp the dynamic of historical progress or articulate their own values and place in the metropolitan system. "The inference is that Hawai'i's pidgin vernacular is the identifying mark of a savage, a fool, or a simpleton," Sumida cautions.[30]

Bloody Mary represents such a transnational body who merges Tonganese superstition and Tonkinese Chinese venality into a toxic Asian/Pacific brew of bad English, stinking body, and clownish manners. With her crass, fawning pursuit of the "saxy Lootellan" from "Philadelia" money and Princeton cultural capital for her younger-than-springtime daughter, Liat, Bloody Mary plays the disfigured Asian/Pacific body of mangled English and opportunistic hybridity. She integrates native costumes and customs (a mélange of hula skirts, betel nuts, shrunken heads, and boar's teeth) to capitalist absorption into the wartorn world system: "Look, Lootellan, I am rich. I save six hundred dolla' before war. Since war I make two thousand dollah."[31] As enchanted native eager to commoditize all social relations, including her own French-speaking Catholic daughter, Bloody Mary will have to be taught to smooth and lighten "her skin as tender as DiMaggio's glove," but, above all for a residually Puritan white culture, to "use Pepsodent":

> *Men [singing Seabees]:*
> Bloody Mary's chewing betel nuts,
> She is always chewing betel nuts,
> Bloody Mary's chewing betel nuts—
> And she don't use Pepsodent.

30. Stephen H. Sumida, *And the View from the Shore: Literary Traditions of Hawai'i* (Seattle: University of Washington Press, 1991), 81.
31. Hammerstein and Logan, *South Pacific*, 120.

(*She grins and shows her betel-stained teeth.*)
Now ain't that too damn bad.[32]

The makings of this Pacific racial hierarchy and neocolonial division of labor in *South Pacific* are articulated in Michener's short story "Fo' Dolla," which provides the musical its political structure: "It was only proper that as a Tonkinese [from French Indochina] she [Bloody Mary] should exercise her endowed rights over the inferior Melanesians. Like a true *grand dame*, she cleared the way for the greater nobility, a white lieutenant, to step ashore."[33] If Melanesian savage in blood, Liat would be unacceptable; if Chinese, the cultural and racial border in the Pacific becomes negotiable through sexual contact and, the extreme of Eurasian contract, marriage (Cable must die before such a Hollywood-taboo marriage can be consummated): "Were Bali-hai and all its people merely a part of the grim and brooding old cannibal island? Were Liat and her unfathomable mother merely descendants from the elder savages? No! The idea was preposterous. Tonkinese were in reality Chinese, sort of the way Canadians were Americans, only a little different."[34]

Even as the violence of war by outsiders destroys and displaces Pacific space and uproots whole cultures in the name of military necessity, as later at the Bikini atoll, the Lono-like Cable (in his first appearance to Bloody Mary, he descends from the clouds) still fears that Miss Liat is too close to *cannibal* blood, too *Tonganese*, "too far away from [movie stars of] Philadelphia, PA" with their Ivory Soap skin.

South Pacific, like Michener's blockbuster epic of Hawaiian locality, *Hawaii*, worked as spectacles circulating in the American pop tropological grain. The people of the Pacific are enlisted into Western mores and the history of Hawai'i is inscribed into Michener's myth of "Hawaii" as multiracial heaven. *South Pacific* comprises part of a tropological intertext through which the local North/South Pacific, displaced and disfigured into subjugated local knowledge, circulates and tries to affirm (if belatedly within metropolitan markets of cultural capital) counterclaims to identity, language, community, nation, and place. If the seamless makings of the *South Pacific* nation can be called into question as *cold war cultural artifact*,

32. Ibid., 18–20.
33. Michener, "Fo' Dolla," in *Tales of the South Pacific*, 184.
34. Ibid., 191.

the transnational production of Hawai'i into ex-primitive icon, from Hollywood to APEC, can be challenged and undone.[35]

Antonio Gramsci urged that to grasp the function of "culture" in any formation of "national-popular" hegemony,[36] as well as the makings of subaltern resistance, we have to look to what he calls "the real nexus," that is, to the contexts of a work's social creation and reception as well as its absorption in cultures, spaces, and histories.[37] Such a *real nexus* between representations and the apparatus of material power, soliciting consent in contexts of monetary and military coercion, is suggested in the opening sequence of *South Pacific,* which contains this paragraph superimposed over the swaying palms of a spectacular tropical sunset emptied of prior

35. During the postwar era, when the Asia-Pacific region became the U.S. Pacific Command Center's staging ground for phobias of communism in Russia, China, North Korea, and Vietnam, the American "territory" of Hawai'i had to be taught the dangers of international communism as threat to labor, trade, and freedom. In *Big Jim McLain* (1952), John Wayne played the un-American hunting agent sent out from Washington, D.C., to Honolulu on "Operation Pineapple" to ferret out communist labor organizers, secret agents, and fellow-traveling University of Hawai'i professors: "An island espionage ring [international communists seeking to block trade and communication to the 'Far East' via poisoned Pearl Harbor waters and labor blockages in Honolulu] has Duke seeing red!" reads the Warner Brothers blurb (see Schmitt, *Hawai'i at the Movies,* 60; and Rampell, "The Tackiest Films Ever Made about Hawai'i," 5). *Big Jim McLain* was released just as the Hawaii 7 labor leaders were going to trial for violations of the Smith Act as communist threats to the U.S. government. House Un-American Activities Committee agent McLain flies to Hawai'i to uncover international machinations and expose communist takeovers of Hawaiian labor, shipping, and trade; Wayne does so, but the worldwide network of left-wing terrorist criminals get off via Fifth Amendment pleas to McCarthy's panel. "Duke" does end up marrying a lovely haole divorcée (Nancy Olson) and bops around the ethnoscape with Korean war hero James Arness, from the Royal Hawaiian Hotel to the prememorial USS *Arizona* site to the leper colony on Moloka'i to Hotel Street dives and a communist meeting place at what looks to be, what else, Hanauma Bay!

36. For an unpacking of this crucial Gramscian concept, see David Forgacs, "National-Popular: Genealogy of a Concept," in *The Cultural Studies Reader,* ed. Simon During (London: Routledge, 1993), 177–90. As applied to American national-popular contexts, see Donald Pease, introduction to "New Americanists: Revisionist Interventions into the Canon," *boundary 2* 17 (spring 1990): 1–37.

37. Antonio Gramsci, *Selections from Cultural Writings,* ed. David Forgacs and Geoffrey Nowell-Smith, trans. William Boelhower (Cambridge, MA: Harvard University Press, 1985), 356.

peoples: "The Producers thank the Department of Defense, the Navy Department, the United States Pacific Fleet, and the Fleet Marine of the Pacific for their assistance in bringing this motion picture to the screen." Militarization of the Pacific Ocean puts infrastructural demands on the environment and disrupts local place and vision. Geopolitical possession remained intact twelve years after the war as *South Pacific* moved from novel to play to movie and went global. Natives have to be taught to rethink their Pacific spaces as "off limits" and "Navy property." Natives have to be taught to take part (even if they play only silent, goofy, or, at best, smiling backdrop to the complications of Western romance) as warriors (and cargo carriers) in the global battle for "enemy-held islands" (there are counter-mappings of the Pacific war in poems and songs by island peoples).[38]

By the "tropological sway" of *South Pacific* in the imagined nation-state community, I would imply something like what Gramsci theorizes as the workings of "concrete fantasy" within the "national-popular" imaginary: a collective interpretation of national community, which, in times of organic crisis and micropolitical struggle, can give way to alternative interpretations and, in our specific case, allow for changes in the self-representation of U.S. culture and its role in the Pacific.

Racial torment in Michener's Nurse Nellie toward Pacific peoples is no anomaly coming from the Eisenhower-era bigotry of Little Rock. Through his Peeping Tom narrator, Tommo, Melville, as interpreter of the early American Pacific, associated the Polynesians of Hawai'i with "Negroid" blood and the woolly-headed Fijians in *Typee*. This 1843 romance turned Melville's phantasmatic Pacific native Fayaway into an olive skinned, blue-eyed, smooth and lovely goddess who stepped out of the Greco-Roman mythologies rather than out of Marquesan culture.[39]

As Paul Lyons has argued, a racial binary structured American fears of being tattooed and cannibalized by Pacific natives (like the one-eyed chief Mow-Mow) reverting into black "savages."[40] Lamenting the "fatal impact" of Western civilization on indigenous Pacific cultures and the arrogant

38. For debunking counterviews of the Pacific war in various genres of oral circulation, see Lamont Lindstrom and Geoffrey White, "Singing History: Island Songs from the Pacific War," in *Artistic Heritage in a Changing Pacific*, ed. P. Dark and R. Rose (Honolulu: University of Hawai'i Press, 1993), 185–96.

39. Herman Melville, *Typee* (New York: Penguin, 1972), 133–36.

40. See Paul Lyons, "The Figure of the Tattooed Cannibal and Its Deconstruction: Herman Melville's *Typee*," unpublished manuscript.

violence of national agents such as U.S. Navy Captain David Reynolds, Melville nonetheless described King Kamehameha III in 1843 as "a fat, lazy, negro-looking blockhead, with as little character as power," while he separated the more "voluptuous Tahitians" and "European cast" Marquesans from "the dark-haired Hawaiians and the woolly-headed Feejees [who] are immeasurably inferior to them."[41] By the turn of the nineteenth century, after the monarchy of Queen Liliʻuokalani toppled, Jack London (with true Anglo-Saxon delight) still found "niggers" everywhere his white characters gazed across the colonies of Melanesia (see, for instance, "The Inevitable White Man").[42] "Melanesians. Polynesians. Tonks! They're all alike," as one of Michener's American sailors simplifies the complex cultures of the Pacific in "Fo'Dolla," as he dreams of repossessing his white "hot number in cold Minneapolis."[43]

Given the four-hundred-year-long imperial outreach by Western powers to cross and claim the Pacific Ocean for metropolitan purposes, island geography is not a physical given but a cultural projection. From conquest to contest, the Pacific is a contested space inscribed with power, class struggle, and polity, overrepresented by outside powers, encoded with (white/native/multicultural) mythology, and circulated through the "mimetic technologies" of global capital as *South Pacific*—the movie, not the place.[44]

To invoke the cultural politics of Gramsci, for whom complications of place, location, and class alignment are always crucial to the formation of

41. Melville, *Typee*, 258, 252. On *imperialist* dynamics of the U.S. presence in the Marquesas and commercial outreach into the Pacific as relating to racial injustices at the Jacksonian national core, see John Carlos Rowe, "Melville's *Typee:* U.S. Imperialism at Home and Abroad," in *National Identities and Post-Americanist Narratives*, ed. Donald E. Pease (Durham, NC: Duke University Press, 1994), 255–78.

42. Jack London, "The Inevitable White Man," in *South Sea Tales*, ed. A. Grove Day (Honolulu: Mutual Publishing, 1985), 235–55.

43. Michener, "Fo' Dolla," 193–94.

44. Stephen Greenblatt, in *Marvelous Possessions: The Wonder of the New World* (Chicago: University of Chicago Press, 1991), argues that "engaged representations . . . are relational, local, and historically contingent" (12), and that "in the modern world-order it is with capitalism that the proliferation and circulation of representations (and devices for the generation and transmission of representations) achieved a spectacular and virtually inescapable global magnitude" (6). In other words, the global systems of representation, by this very magnitude and the far-reaching power of circulation, took dominion over more local systems of representation.

national-popular identity, "East and West are arbitrary and conventional, that is historical constructions, since outside of history every point on the earth is East and West at the same time."[45] Pacific geography, and the taken-for-granted orientations of "East" and "West" as binary terms, are driven, in Gramsci's skeptical view, "from the point of view of the European cultured classes, who, as a result of their world-wide hegemony, have caused them to be accepted everywhere." The result has proved formative for peoples affected by this (orientalizing) self-knowledge: "Japan is the Far East not only for Europe but also perhaps for the American from California and even for the Japanese himself, who, through English political culture, may then call Egypt the Near East."[46]

As geopolitical meaning gets sedimented into binary geographic terms such as "East" meeting "West" or into that contemporary signifier of all-purpose indeterminacy, "Asia/Pacific," and the subordination of "Pacific Basin" to "Pacific Rim," these historically burdened signifiers come to occlude what Gramsci would track as "specific relations between different cultural complexes."[47] Given the "real nexus" of global power and struggle for international as well as internal hegemony over its own peoples, the USA's representations of the "South Pacific" as an enchanted yet inferior place would absorb Pacific space, both North and South, into the workings of its own imaginary geography and geopolitics.

If only in the reimagined genres of culture as "minor literature," colonial binaries are breaking down, the codes of capitalist space-time can get scrambled, and a third or *in-between* space emerges, as Deleuze imagines the nomadic movement of "lines of flight" across continent and ocean as a *deterritorialization*: "American literature operates according to geographical lines: the flight towards the West, the discovery that the true East is in the West, the sense of the frontiers as something to cross, to push back, to go beyond."[48] Deterritorializing geography back into countermythology, Deleuze can conclude that, in the watery reaches of Pacific space, "Captain Ahab has a whale-becoming," just as the "fugitives" from European (De

45. Antonio Gramsci, *Selections from the Prison Notebooks,* ed. and trans. Quintin Hoare and Geoffrey Nowell Smith (New York: International Publishers, 1971), 447.
46. Ibid.
47. Ibid.
48. Gilles Deleuze and Claire Parnet, "On the Superiority of Anglo-American Literature," in *Dialogues,* trans. Hugh Tomlinson and Barbara Habberjam (New York: Columbia University Press, 1987), 37.

Becque) and American (Nellie) binaries of race and national fantasy may find new life in the Eurasian hybridity of the postwar Asian/Pacific.[49]

Seeking to undermine these constructions of local Asia/Pacific cultures by people of liberal will such as Michener, Theroux, and Winchester—which I have troped into the genre of *South Pacific*—with interior constructions of place and dynamics of multicultural identity, my aim has been to posit the makings of *an oppositional regionalism* in the Pacific. Such "minor literature" fractures the settler nation-state imagination and reclaims location as ground of place and vision. Enacting "critical regionalism" and minority languages that refuse to be assimilated into or explained by myths of multicultural "American" identity, the Pacific local has emerged as a distinctive place, ground of commitment and identity and language. Hawai'i, as I have claimed, stands for some Trojan horse of Asian/Pacific localism imploding within the national imagination of the United States.

Bamboo Ridge, as place and cultural symbol, sits in the middle of one of the most heated real estate markets in the world, on a Pacific island named O'ahu where, since the days of King Kamehameha I (who, in the military wake of Cook and Vancouver, first unified the islands into nation status), governing groups have drawn power, legitimacy, and structure from possessing (in contracts and symbols) the land, the *'āina*. This ground is contested within various symbolic heritages and affiliations of power. Adhering to the nexus of locality at Bamboo Ridge posits a way of *reimagining* relationship among region, nation, and globe in which difference is not negated nor reified but constructed, negotiated, and affirmed. In effect, the local has materialized into alternative narratives and counterclaims on the "American Pacific."

At another politicized extreme, Native Hawaiians seek to possess and preserve the land as locus of cultural identity. These Hawaiians' claim would fracture the myths and legal status of sovereign territory—the imagined unity—of the U.S. nation-state. For example, Dana Naone Hall's protest poems of place are forceful in their evocation of Hawaiian mythology and Hawaiian "signs" mobilized against transnational resorts and golf courses bent on taking over the beachscapes of Maui.[50] Any stance of

49. Ibid., 44.
50. See Dana Naone Hall, "Ka Mo'olelo o ke Alanui" (The story of the road), which recovers Hawaiian history of a Maui road as a means to resist its closure for tourist

"critical localism" has to struggle with/against forces of transnational simulation. In a poem fracturing her Chinese Hawaiian American identity as
a diasporic Chinese into more Hawaiian claims of counter-American alle-
giance, Carolyn Lei-LaniLau writes: "in spite of the plantations and pineapple fields, / the tourists / and military, / Hawai'i never became the
50th state."[51]

Caricature of Pacific values, sense of place, and embodiment (as in the
squatting body of Bloody Mary, named after a semitoxic Western drink) are
being replaced by the interiorized, grounded, and tension-packed Hawaiian Creole English of Lois-Ann Yamanaka, that "transcendent tita"
whose Bamboo Ridge Press book *Saturday Night at the Pahala Theatre* has
caused a sensation in Hawai'i.[52] This book has brought local poetics into
sharper focus, especially in relation to Hawaiian thematics and Asian
American norms (her work has been avidly anthologized and honored on
the mainland).[53] As in some *Spoon River Anthology* of pidgin personae, in
Yamanaka's Pahala, sister and sister clash for domination; males intimidate, exploit, and initiate women; titas rule; mother abuses daughter; races
clash and mix and fuse into the working-class community of a Big Island
plantation. Pidgin expression is not the exception but the rule, in love, in
family, in ethnic interaction. Suggesting ties to the Hawaiian uncanny as

resort usage), in *Ho'omānoa: An Anthology of Contemporary Hawaiian Literature*, ed.
Joseph P. Balaz (Honolulu: Ku Pa'a, 1989), 34–36. Haunani-Kay Trask, in "Coalitions
between Natives and Non-Natives," in *From a Native Daughter: Colonialism and Sovereignty in Hawai'i* (Monroe, ME: Common Courage Press, 1993), disqualifies all non-
Hawaiians from claims to being "Hawaiian in spirit" or practicing and expressing an
ethic of *mālama 'āina*: "Immigrants to Hawai'i, including both *haole* (white) and Asians,
cannot truly understand this cultural value of *mālama 'āina* even when they feel some
affection for Hawai'i. Two thousand years of practicing a careful husbandry of the land
and regarding it as a mother can never be and should never be claimed by recent arrivals
to any Native shores. Such a claim amounts to an arrogation of Native status" (248).
51. See Carolyn Lei-LaniLau, "Ha'ina 'ia mai ana ka puana" (Let the story be told), in *A
North Pacific Rim Reader*, special issue of *Chicago Review* 39 (1993): 168–74, and her
neo-Nativist and creolized autobiography, *Ono Ono Girl's Hula* (Madison: University of
Wisconsin Press, 1997), as well as Haunani-Kay Trask, "Ko'olauloa," in *Light in the
Crevice Never Seen* (Corvallis, OR: Calyx Press, 1994), 80.
52. David K. Choo, "Fishing for a Local Voice: Bamboo Ridge and the Search for an
Island Literary Identity," *Honolulu Weekly* 3 (20 October 1993): 7.
53. Yamanaka's work is anthologized in Jessica Hagedorn, ed., *Charlie Chan Is Dead: An
Anthology of Asian American Fiction* (New York: Penguin, 1993).

lurking in the wilderness and wilds of the psyche, the plantation space of Yamanaka's Pahala opens out to mountain ("Haupu Mountain") and ocean ("Glass").[54]

In desublimating personae of crazed Deleuzian pidgin English, as in poems such as "Tita: Japs" and "Tita: The Bathroom," local Japanese identity is viewed as hardly one of purity or ethnic wholeness but one of self-division, self-hatred even, a longing to be othered into haole cultural styles (from Cher to Judy Garland) and, at another extreme, the deeper Hawaiian place-values and resonance in poems such as "Pueo" and "Glass." In "Yarn Wig," the range of voices is acute, the humor devastating toward local style as a mixture of aspiration and abuse, custom and mass mediation (as in the title poem, which details the disruptive effect of mainland pornography on gender relations in the plantation town of Pahala on the Big Island).

In one of the quasi-Hawaiian poems of place, "Glass," pidgin becomes symbolic vehicle for a probing into place-as-history and into reaches of the numinous world of the sacred as incarnated by the "glass floater" given up by the Pacific Ocean, "light blue and cool in the shade of the naupaka bushes" (107). Bernie, the *kupuna*-like taxidermist, becomes an older initiator of the main female character, Lucy, not into sexual domination but into the wild animal and spiritual energies of the place that he respects and knows intimately (as in the trip out of the plantation smallness to the greater natural world of Haupu Mountain) and reveals in the trip to the ocean:

> Us get in the Jeep and pass the cow pasture
> by the just burn sugar cane field.
> Then us pass Punaluʻu and Honoapu Mill.
> Bernie go slow through Naalehu
> then Waiohinu by the Mark Twain monkeypod tree.
> Bernie tell me stories about every stone wall,
> every old graveyard, every stream,
> and even the monkeypod tree. (107)

Tapping into deeper memories and ties to place as enriched by layers of indigenous and settler cultures, Yamanaka is no *purist*, but postmodern and fluid in her Asian/Pacific/American identity tactics. Not only in the

54. Yamanaka, *Saturday Night at the Pahala Theatre*, 94–96, 106–7.

quality of crazed pidgin voice but in the mongrel range of lower culture, meaning the "My Eyes Adore You" playing on the 8-track in WillyJoe's yellow Datsun, eating corn beef patties with rice in front of the *Ed Sullivan Show*, vanilla cokes, Sonny and Cher looks, and Donny Osmond and Captain and Tenille tapes (111–15). "Tita: User" offers a cornucopia of local appropriations and circulation of American pop culture in the Asian/Pacific community of the Pahala Theatre. "I was encouraged [by Faye Kicknosway, Eric Chock, et al.] to write in the voice of my place without shame or fear," Yamanaka claims in her biographical statement for *Charlie Chan Is Dead*.[55]

Yamanaka vanquishes Michener's slobbering Bloody Mary with a vision of compassionate interiority, voices ranging from Tita and Kala to the pathos of the WillyJoe character, whose lack of standard English does not disable him from emotional depth, complexity of insight into place, family. His loved one, Lucy, gives him another language, finally, in the lyric memorialization of her poem "Name Me Is," where both find voice and affirm it in its own peculiar and distinctive Hawaiian Creole English: "I is. / Ain't *nobody* / tell me / otherwise."[56] Like Milton Murayama, John Dominis Holt, Gary Pak, Zack Linmark, Michael McPherson, Juliet Kono Lee, Haunani-Kay Trask, and others, Yamanaka has learned, with a Deleuzian vengeance along a line of flight from Pahala to Honolulu to New York City, "to write in the voice of [her] place without shame or fear."

Until the of rise of decolonizing literature in the Pacific during the late 1960s in Papua New Guinea and Maori New Zealand, and in the 1970s as centered around the University of the South Pacific in Fiji and such writers as Albert Wendt, Subramani, Patricia Grace, and Vilsoni Hereniko, various genres of Western discourse coordinated, fantasized, and measured the cultures of the Pacific. As I have tried to show, a literature of the Asian/Pacific community of Hawai'i did not emerge until the late 1970s and is still coming into self-conscious expression. Another "literature of Hawai'i" can be seen to have operated, since the 1940s, in the American

55. In Hagedorn, *Charlie Chan Is Dead*, Yamanaka also claims, "I write in the pidgin of the contract workers to the sugar plantations here in Hawai'i, a voice of eighteenth century [*sic*] Hawai'i passed down to now third- and fourth-generation descendants of various groups" (544). But Japanese contract laborers were not recruited and transported to Hawai'i until 1868. See Ronald Takaki, *Strangers from a Different Shore: A History of Asian Americans* (New York: Penguin, 1989), 43.
56. Yamanaka, "Name Me Is," in *Saturday Night at the Pahala Theatre*, 140.

Pacific to produce quite a different (nonlocal) vision of the "South Pacific" as seen by settlers, tourists, and explorers in the American missionary lineage.

The operation of such national narratives can be enduring, as is apparent in the so-called first anthology of Hawaiian literature that is still on sale in contemporary Hawai'i and evokes, for culture-browsing tourists, what Hawai'i was and is as an exotic branch of U.S. (especially New England) culture. Browse through Borders or the ABC discount store on a stay in Hawai'i; amid the works of Twain, Maugham, and London, you will hit upon *A Hawaiian Reader* in the tropical rack. This anthology of what its editors name "the best writings on Hawai'i" was first published in 1959 to cash in on (and culturally confirm) Hawaiian statehood and has gone through numerous reprintings.[57] According to the historical framework of this anthology, the literature of Hawai'i begins with the journal of Captain James Cook as he initiates barter in 1778 with what he calls the "naturally well bred"—but occasionally pilfering—natives of this small, undiscovered "nation." "As soon as we landed," Cook writes, "a trade was set on foot for hogs and potatoes, which the people of the island gave us in exchange for nails and pieces of iron formed into something like chisels."[58]

Aiming to chart "an informal history of Hawai'i from primitive times to the present," as the anthology proclaims, this literature of Hawai'i continues through the private journal of James Burney, first lieutenant on the British *Discovery*, who records the death of the Lono-like Cook at the hands of these Pacific "Indians."[59] This literature of Hawai'i materializes again

57. A. Grove Day and Carl Stroven, eds., *A Hawaiian Reader* (Honolulu: Mutual, 1984). The book was first published in 1959 by Appleton-Century-Crofts. For a critical appraisal of Day's Pacific scholarship that foregrounds its Americanizing, racial, and tourist-friendly dynamics, see Paul Lyons, "Pacific Scholarship, Literary Criticism, and Touristic Desire," *boundary 2* 24 (1997): 47–78.

58. James Cook, "The Discovery of the Hawaiian Islands," in *A Hawaiian Reader*, 7; reprinted from James Cook and James King, *A Voyage to the Pacific Ocean* (London: G. Nicol and T. Cadell, 1784).

59. James Burney, "The Last Days of Captain Cook," in *A Hawaiian Reader*: "The boats soon after came off with an account that Captain Cook and four of the marines were killed and their bodies in possession of the Indians" (16). "Indians" was a common Euro-American misnomer for peoples of the Pacific; as Bernard Smith explains in *Imagining the Pacific: In the Wake of the Cook Voyages* (New Haven: Yale University Press, 1992), "[From] the time of Columbus's misconception that he had reached India, the term 'Indian' developed a generic usage for all non-European peoples, apart from a few

through an entry portraying the encounter of George Vancouver with King Kamehameha I, who "begged a plate, knife, and fork" of the British captain, Thomas Manby writes, and wanted one of his "domestics" "to learn the art of cookery" so that the Hawaiian monarch could begin to "live like King George."[60] The theme of island literature seems to be the mimicry of European taste, a hybrid desire, a longing for the culture of the metropolitan capital. The local is measured from the gaze of the first white men on the scene who claim semantic possession and confer imaginative interest.

This narrative of first contact with Pacific primitives—who can only emulate and look with pathetic longing on the mores and artifacts of European cultivation—continues in the viewpoint of Otto Von Kotzebue, a captain in the Russian Imperial Navy who sketches Queen Namahana in 1824 as one of the first chiefs to be Christianized; when offered a bottle of fine wine by the captain, she said she must also have fine wine glasses to drink the same, and so "seiz[ed] without ceremony the glasses that stood on the table."[61] The New England missionary apparatus then appears, in full flesh, through the writings of Hiram Bingham enforcing chastity on the unwilling sailors aboard a warship in port in Honolulu in 1826, and continues through the perceptions of displaced New Englanders in Laura Fish Judd and James J. Jarves, who portray the ongoing battle "between heathenism and missionaryism."[62]

By such a binary terminology of savagery and redemption, you know what side of this historical struggle these writers were on. After a portrayal of Hawai'i by Victorian writers such as Charles Warren Stoddard and Isabella Bird, we fall into the company of Anglo-American notables and "liter-

---

old-time exotics such as Arab and Chinese. In his journal of [Cook's] *Endeavour* voyage, Joseph Banks calls the natives of Tierra del Fuego, the Tahitians, the Maori, and the Australian Aborigines all Indians, though he is at pains to distinguish their physical and social differences" (173). Edgar Allan Poe simplifies this schema of Indian hating further in the wildly fantastic American Pacific of *The Narrative of Arthur Gordon Pym of Nantucket* (1838), by calling all these peoples "savages."

60. Thomas Manby, "With Vancouver at Kealakekua Bay," in *A Hawaiian Reader,* 35.
61. Otto Von Kotzebue, "A Queen of the Sandwich Islands," in *A Hawaiian Reader,* 46; reprinted from *A New Voyage round the World* (London: Henry Colburn and Richard Bentley, 1830).
62. James J. Jarves, "Between Heathenism and Missionaryism," in *A Hawaiian Reader,* 69–76; reprinted from *Why and What Am I? The Confessions of an Enquirer* (Boston: Philips, Sampson, 1857).

ary greats" such as Twain, Stevenson, London, Rupert Brooke, Maugham, J. P. Marquand, William Meredith, and May Sarton, each of whom was "a sojourner, a traveler, or a tourist" but will have their literary sway.[63]

Displaced to the back of the book, as it were, Native Hawaiians do have a *small* chance to say something about what constitutes the literature of "Hawai'i." Even in this Euro-American narrative, there lurks some trace of "ancient Hawai'i" tucked into the back of A Hawaiian Reader voicing the native gods and *menehunes* and what Michener calls the quaint "folklore of the islands."[64] A sermon welcoming statehood for Hawai'i in 1959 by Reverend Abraham K. Akaka is included *as Hawaiian literature!* Nowhere is the literature of resident citizens included, nowhere does the multicul-ture of Hawai'i enter into history from the point of view of Asian-Pacific Americans, Hawaiians, or other "locals" who constitute the history and culture of this nation/state in its struggles.

Michener, whose underedited novel *Hawaii* was published to mark statehood in 1959 and, as fat book and bare-breasted movie, constitutes what Katherine Newman has called "an obstacle to the recognition of any indigenous, synthesized, Hawaiian-American literature," wrote an intro-duction to A Hawaiian Reader.[65] If Michener acknowledged the history and value of these nonwhites to the making of Hawai'i, he justified their exclu-sion on the grounds that, though they worked hard, they wrote no litera-ture. (There were already haiku and tanka clubs on the Big Island in 1903, and dramatic and novelistic works were written in Hawai'i throughout the twentieth century by Asian Americans.)[66] Because locals could not yet represent themselves, they had to be represented by outsiders and other national parties: "It was the Chinese who gave the islands much of their nineteenth-century color. It was the Japanese who did the heavy work in building the great plantations, and it has been the Filipinos who have kept the sugar cane and the pineapple growing," Michener admits.[67]

Michener's pluralism wavers and grows phobically white: "Having ar-rived in the islands as laboring peasants, these Orientals did not produce a

63. Sumida, *And the View from the Shore*, 88.
64. James A. Michener, introduction to *A Hawaiian Reader*, xvi.
65. Katherine Newman, "Hawaiian-American Literature: The Cultivation of Mangoes," MELUS: The Journal of the Society for the Study of the Multi-Ethnic Literature of the United States 6 (1979): 71.
66. Sumida, *And the View From the Shore*, 306.
67. Michener, introduction to *A Hawaiian Reader*, xiv.

literature of their own, but Professors Day and Stroven have included important passages [by others, that is] that give them representation."[68] In a later anthology, *The Spell of Hawaii* (1968), Day and Stroven do include a short story by Milton Murayama, one of the real innovators of local literature, but they begin their anthology of "the exotic literary heritage of the Hawaiian islands" not just with Captain Cook but with the opening pages of Michener's *Hawaii*.[69] This passage, repeated in the sweeping opening vistas of the movie *Hawaii* (1966), evokes the primordial emptiness of a biblical oceanic space shorn of Hawaiians, yellows, and whites: "Raw, empty, youthful islands, sleeping in the sun and whipped by rain, they waited."[70] Hawai'i waited, that is, for James Michener to come down the path of William Ellis, James Jackson Jarves, and Pierre Loti and represent, for the metropolitan world, Hawai'i's history as polity of "the Golden Man" in lordly cinemascope over the "South Pacific."

There is a tacit silence administered in anthologies of the American Pacific produced by an earlier generation of University of Hawai'i English professors as they worked in the aptly named "Kuykendall Hall" (named at statehood after the white historian Ralph Kuykendall, the building was almost named after Herman Melville). Such works by Cook, Michener, Day, and others can give a sense of exactly what "local literature" *is not*. These works evoke, instead, the apparatus of white mythological imagery, sentiment, and a discourse of nation making (white settler imaginary) rooted in the colonial heritage of "the largest of the white-settler states of the Pacific."[71] It is against contexts of historical omission that the "local literature" movement that emerged in the late 1970s and flourished in the 1980s needs to be understood. The "local literature" movement at Bamboo Ridge would produce, in effect, a countermemory to such whitewashed histories of this Pacific place and its literary and cultural productions. Whatever the beauty of Hawai'i, "So much death, / so much blood /

68. Ibid.

69. Milton Murayama, "I'll Crack Your Head *Kotsun*," in *The Spell of Hawaii*, ed. A. Grove Day and Carl Stroven (Honolulu: Mutual, 1968), 323–35. This collection also interestingly includes writing by a prolific Native Hawaiian trained in history at Lahainaluna Seminary, Samuel M. Kamakau, author of *The Ruling Chiefs of Hawai'i* (Honolulu: Kamehameha Schools Press, 1961), and *The Works of the People of Old: Na Hana a ka Po'e Kahiko* (Honolulu: Bishop Museum Press, 1976).

70. James A. Michener, "From the Boundless Deep," in *The Spell of Hawaii*, 10.

71. Gerald Segal, *Rethinking the Pacific* (New York: Oxford University Press, 1990), 371.

is a part of this place" in its history of colonial entanglements, racial negotiations, vanquished spirits that refuse to go away.[72]

Dispossessed from the land since the Great Mahele of 1848, which the common people opposed to no avail, the Hawaiian culture and language has been threatened with extinction.[73] Against all odds, and part of the struggle to demilitarize Kahoʻolawe Island in the 1980s, this Hawaiian sense for place and prior ecology of spirit and the land has reasserted itself. "*Mālama ʻĀina*, cherishing the land, is a foundation of the movement to stop the U.S. military's bombing of Kahoʻolawe island."[74] Respect for the land and culture is captured in a poem by Joe Puna Balaz, a part-Hawaiian poet who has moved from composing generic, delocalized English sonnets in the early part of his career to embrace the Hawaiian part of himself and express the ethic of *mālama ʻāina*.[75]

If colonialism is taken as a "process of erasing and replacing and reor-

---

72. McPherson, "Mālama," in *Singing with the Owls,* 20.

73. An outline of the seizure and cession of Hawaiian lands to American custody and the legal battles underway to reclaim them is offered in Michael McPherson, "*Trustees of Hawaiian Affairs v. Yamasaki* and the Native Hawaiian Claim: Too Much of Nothing," *Environmental Law* 21 (1991): 453–97. Also see McPherson, "Vanishing Sands: Comprehensive Planning and the Public Interest in Hawaiʻi," *Ecology Law Quarterly* 18 (1991): 779–844, on the use of zoning laws to preserve some kind of special Hawaiian relationship to nature and the ocean.

74. Lilikala Kameʻeleihiwa, *Native Lands and Foreign Desires: Pehea Le E Pono Ai?* (Honolulu: Bishop Museum Press, 1992), 48. This history of the land division of 1848 shows how disruptive "private ownership of ʻĀina" (11) proved to Hawaiian metaphors of reciprocal care and transpersonal benefit that had seemingly governed prior models of land and nation based on social equilibrium (*pono*).

75. Joseph P. Balaz, "Moeʻuhane," in *Hoʻiʻhoʻihou: A Tribute to George Helm and Kimo Mitchell*, ed. Rodney Morales (Honolulu: Bamboo Ridge Press, 1984), 91. In *Hawaiʻi Review* 20 (1986), edited by Morales (a fellow Hawaiian activist and "local" author who is not Hawaiian by blood although similarly committed to the decolonization of Hawaiʻi), Balaz—not to get too *purist* about his cultural identity as "Hawaiian" poet—describes himself in these postcolonial hybrid terms: Joseph P. Balaz is "part-Czechoslovakian, part-Hawaiian, part-Irish, partly crazy, and he likes to part his hair right down the middle" (106). For works in Hawaiian cultural poetics written in English and Hawaiian mixtures, see Joseph P. Balaz, ed., *Hoʻomānoa: An Anthology of Hawaiian Literature* (Honolulu: Ku Paʻa, 1989). This anthology (with Hawaiian glossary) includes writers as diverse as Trask, McPherson, Naone, Holt, Puanani Burgess, Tamara Wong Morrison, and Balaz (discussed below) under the thematic of promoting a "thickening" of Hawaiian culture "by blood, consciousness, and purpose" (vii).

dering the memories of the colonized to suit the colonizers," as Albert Wendt puts it, Balaz's poem remembers the Pacific otherwise.[76] As Balaz writes in "Moeʻuhane," evoking through its title some dream messengers and set in his birthplace on rural Oʻahu, the past lives on as alternative space and countermemory in the American Pacific:

> I dream of
> the ways of the past—
> I cannot go back.
>
> I hike the hills
>   and valleys of Wahiawa,
> walking through crystal
>   streams
> and scaling green cliffs.
> I play in the waves
>   of Waimea,
>
> and spear fish
>   from the reefs of Kawailoa.
>
> I grow bananas, ʻulu,
>   and papayas
>   in the way of the ʻāina.
>
> I cannot go back—
> I never left.[77]

Cultivating Hawaiian identity in the Pacific, Balaz's work posits the Pacific not only as a local but as an indigenous space of cultural production. This *indigenous Hawaiʻi*, with its textured use of *mele* (chants), sacred hula, and poems with layers of island genealogy and mythology, can be posed against tourist simulations of place as those "huge sluttish pleasures of its Nipponized beach front hotels."[78] Hawaiian historian Samuel M. Kamakau captured this Hawaiian archive of poetry of Pacific places in the pages of *Ruling Chiefs of Hawaiʻi*, in his chapter "Hawaiʻi before

76. Albert Wendt, "Novelists and Historians and the Art of Remembering," in *Class and Culture in the South Pacific*, ed. Anthony Hooper et al. (Suva, Fiji: University of the South Pacific Press, 1987), 87.

77. Joseph P. Balaz, "Moeʻuhane," *Hoʻiʻhoʻihou*, 91.

78. Theroux, *Happy Isles of Oceania*, 473.

Foreign Innovations." "The composing of meles," Kamakau observes, "was a skilled art in old days in which some people became famous. They composed chants about the sky, space, the ocean, the earth, sun, moon, stars, and all things. Many had secret meanings woven into them. They were composed of symbolic phrases (*loina*) and hidden meanings (*kaona*)."[79] Such poems can be found in the Mary K. Pukui and Alfons Korn anthology of Hawaiian chants and poems, *The Echo of Our Song*. In "Hula Mano no Ka-lani-'ōpu'u," Kamehameha's fierce uncle, Ka-lani-'ōpu'u, takes possession of the waters off the Big Island by claiming kinship and symbolic affiliation with the white-finned shark; in "He Mele He'e Nalu," the ruling chiefs of Kona show their royal prowess with feats of courage and art in treacherous waters of the Pacific; in "He Inoa no Ka-lā-kaua," rings of fire blaze around the various sites of Honolulu from Fort Street calico shops to the Church of Mary of Peace to form a fire lei of loyalty to honor the coronation of King David Kalākaua in 1874.[80] Such *meles* bespeak detailed knowledge of Hawai'i as place and, in their own way, take symbolic possession of the local terrain.

79. Kamakau, *Ruling Chiefs of Hawai'i*, 240. This passage is based on Kamakau's writing for the Hawaiian newspaper *Ka Nupepa Ku'oko'a*, 21 December 1867.
80. Mary K. Pukui and Alfons L. Korn, eds. and trans., *The Echo of Our Song: Chants and Poems of the Hawaiians* (Honolulu: University of Hawai'i Press, 1979). The poems I refer to are (in English): "Shark Hula for Ka-Lani-'ōpu'u" (4–8); "A Surfing Song" (37–41); and "Fire Chant for King Ka-Lā-kaua" (134–49), composed by David Malo II.

CHAPTER 6

Shark God on Trial:

Invoking Chief Ka-lani-ōʻpuʻu in the Local / Indigenous / American Struggle for Place

HAWAIʻI: CULTURAL POLITICS AND THE PLOVER

How much meaning can a little *plover* bird be made to bear? Plenty, if that sea-crossing shorebird who winters in the Pacific and summers in Alaska gets caught up in the cultural politics of literatures made in Hawaiʻi, with their complex and contested tangle of U.S., Asian / Pacific, transnational diasporic, and indigenous strands. For Albert Saijo in his lyrical memoir, *Outspeaks: A Rhapsody,* the plover is an admirable figure of "ANIMAL CIVIL-ITY" living on edges and borders, embodying nomadic movement, improvisation and risk, jazzy flights between solitary foraging and communal roosting: anarchic and poetic existence on a small budget.[1] For Haunani-Kay Trask in a place-claiming poem of island mappings called "Hawaiʻi," the plover is figured into the decolonizing binaries, racial imaginary, and "fatal contact" narrative of her collection, *Light in the Crevice Never Seen;* the Pacific golden plover (*kōlea*) becomes an icon of haole plunder, "thickened by the fat / of our land," embodying generations of land-grabbing settlers, island developers, and tourists who exploit natural and native resources and move on, "rich," fat, and "beautiful," both colonizer (the settler) and colonized (nature, land).[2]

1. Albert Saijo, *Outspeaks: A Rhapsody* (Honolulu: Bamboo Ridge Press, 1996). In Juliana Spahr's review for *Tinfish,* that "journal of experimental poetry with an emphasis on work from the Pacific region," Saijo's plover thus figures as "a utopic model for dealing with contradictions" (*Tinfish* 6 [March 1998]: 54).
2. Haunani-Kay Trask, *Light in the Crevice Never Seen* (Portland, OR: Calyx Books, 1994). In the poem itself, the "haole plover" is the white colonialist who plunders, whereas in

In a traditional Hawaiian hula *mele* miming the bird's head-bobbing movements and erotic motions called the *hula kōlea,* to the contrary, the plover bird is not so much a fat haole colonizer as a tender little food "morsel," flighty lovemaker, and heroic "wayfarer" whose sea journey is linked in this poem to a brave flight from Kahiki, land of mythic origins and bounty from heaven, and thus serves as a metaphor for the Hawaiian quest for beauty, royal protection, and love.[3] Not so much a colonial settler (as in Trask) or a diasporic border-hopper living on margins (as in Saijo), the plover figures in this hula poem as *both* native settler and diasporic ocean crosser, although the diaspora in this latter Nativist case is linked to claims for connections to a Polynesian and royal "homeland" (Kahiki/Tahiti), both rooted and routed across the vast Pacific as genealogical heritage and erotic knowledge subjugated by the colonial education system.[4] Diasporic Hawaiians have long spread their customs and mixed their genealogies across the vast Pacific.[5]

Trask's explanatory footnote, the plover is itself plundered by "plover-shooting white men," as suggested by Mary Kawena Pukui's Hawaiian dictionary expression, *haole ki kōlea.* On the bird's Pacific habitats and three-thousand-mile nonstop flights across the Pacific twice a year, see Marion Coste, *Kōlea: The Story of the Pacific Golden Plover* (Honolulu: University of Hawai'i Press, 1998).

3. Nathaniel B. Emerson, *Unwritten Literature of Hawaii: The Sacred Songs of the Hula* (Rutland, VT: Tuttle, 1982), 219–20. This important work was originally published by the Bureau of American Ethnology in 1909, which in 1906 had broadened the scope of research on "American Indians" to include the natives of the Hawaiian islands and their cultural forms, seen as under threat of disappearing from the impact of modernity and thus in need of ethnographic reconstruction.

4. For an argument that contemporary versions of "diaspora discourse" in our transnational and postcolonial moment "are caught up with and defined against (1) the norms of nation-states and (2) indigenous, and especially autochtonous, claims by 'tribal' peoples," see James Clifford, "Diasporas," in *Routes: Travel and Translation in the Late Twentieth Century* (Cambridge, MA: Harvard University Press, 1997), 250.

5. Sea-faring "Kanaka" worked in the fur trade and sawmills for the Hudson Bay Company from 1812 on and helped to turn British Columbia into "the home base for what was probably the largest single group of Hawaiians ever to congregate outside their native islands"; see Tom Koppel, *Kanaka: The Untold Story of Hawaiian Pioneers in British Columbia and the Pacific Northwest* (Vancouver: Whitecap Books, 1995), 12–20. Hawaiian, Northwest Coast Indian, and Anglo-Canadian customs and blood have mixed into a new settler identity, although the ties to the Hawaiian homeland have amplified since the early 1970s via jet travel and technologies of space-time shrinkage that interlink the Pacific as did the outriggers and steamships of old (122–32).

This distinct type of *hula kōlea* is discussed in Nathaniel B. Emerson's classic commentary on Hawaiian hula in *Unwritten Literature of Hawaii*. In this context-rich and textually uncanny study of the oral poetry of nineteenth-century Hawai'i, Emerson ends his analysis of Hawaiian genre (and worldview) by lambasting an unidentified white historian (the Christian historian and Lahainaluna Seminary teacher Reverend Sheldon Dibble, writing his *History of the Sandwich Islands* in 1843), who had disqualified Native Hawaiian "heathens" from realms of spirituality and high literary culture by contending that they lacked all sense of *the sublime*. This latter aesthetic sense was capable of being felt by New England Christians such as the Lahainaluna Seminary historian himself, of course, who best appreciated (and could write about) the wondrous sublimity of waterfalls and Pacific Ocean vistas, whereas the Native Hawaiian islander could only think of finding a calabash of poi or the nesting place of crabs, stuffing his belly with food, and cavorting in his leisure. Indicting Dibble's racist inability to understand the native mind and its complex "disposition toward nature" (as evinced in the epic chants and hula poems, for example), Emerson quotes the following passage from Dibble as a bad anthropology "tied to a false theology":

> To the heathen the book of nature is a sealed book. Where the word of God is not, the works of God fail either to excite admiration or to impart instruction. The Sandwich Islands present some of the sublimest scenery on earth, but to an ignorant native—the great mass of the people in entire heathenism—it has no meaning. As one crested billow after another of the heaving ocean rolls in and dashed upon the unyielding rocks of the iron-bound coast, which seems to say, "Hitherto shalt thou come and no farther," the low-minded heathen is merely thinking of the shellfish of the shore. As he looks up to the everlasting mountains, girt with clouds and capped with snow, he betrays no emotion. As he climbs a towering cliff, looks down a yawning precipice, or abroad upon a forest of deep ravines, immense rocks, and spiral mountains thrown together in the utmost wildness and confusion by the might of God's volcanoes, he is only thinking of some roots in the wilderness that may be good for food.[6]

Schooled in the American romanticist taste for "sublimest scenery" as evidence for theological justification as well as an endorsement (at a

6. Quoted in Emerson, *Unwritten Literature of Hawai'i*, 262.

deeper ideological level) for a century's Manifest Destiny politics of frontier settlement, Dibble ascribes to himself "the commanding view" of the first white man on the scene, at once mastering aesthetic pleasure and theological meaning, as well as asserting physical and historical supremacy over the scene the native (shorn of his own metaphors and narratives of place as mana-laden) cowers before like an unthinking, pre-Kantian animal.[7] As Emerson scathingly remarks, "There is not a poem in this volume that does not show the utter falsity of this view."[8]

Nathaniel Emerson, himself the second-generation product of U.S. missionary settlers on Maui and an active proponent of the Annexationist cause,[9] is here indicting prior generations of missionary ideologues, such as his hula-denouncing father, who failed to grasp "the truth and the poetry" of the Hawaiian mind and "cosmogony" as embodied in the Hawaiian language and cultural forms like the hula they had sought to denigrate if not eradicate via a process of colonial exclusion, "debasement," and a "recurring nomination of the abject" as all that is filthy, profane, and native.[10] In the (purported) absence of history and meaning for this "sublime" Hawaiian landscape, Dibble will teach a generation of Native Hawaiians such as David Malo, Moku, and Samuel Kamakau to compile a history of Hawaiian events and legends (as in Dibble's ten-author compilation into "one true and connected account" of *Ka Moolelo Hawai'i*, published by Lahainaluna School Press on Maui in 1838) in which they must situate themselves as fallen into pagan idolatry (especially so in the

7. On this imperialist angle of vision, see David Spurr, "Surveillance," in *The Rhetoric of Empire: Colonial Discourse in Journalism, Travel Writing, and Imperial Administration* (Durham, NC: Duke University Press, 1993), 15. On "the sublime" as an aesthetic-political genre of American and Australian white settler appropriation, see n. 32 below.

8. Emerson, *Unwritten Literature of Hawai'i*, 262.

9. The Reverend John S. Emerson and his wife, Sophia, Nathaniel's parents, served in the missionary company for twenty-six years at Waialua and four years at Lahainaluna; in 1858, they signed a denunciation of the hula as a "great and increasing evil" in a two-page request for suppression of it to King Kamehameha V. See LaRue W. Piercy, *Hawai'i Truth Stranger Than Fiction: True Tales of Missionary Life and Historic Characters Fictionalized in Michener's 'Hawaii'* (Honolulu: Mutual, 1985), 52.

10. Spurr, *The Rhetoric of Empire*, 78: racialized debasement and abjection of the native by the settler serving "both as a justification for European intervention and as the necessary iteration of a fundamental difference between colonizer and colonized." Dibble classified Hawaiians as "low, naked, filthy, vile and sensual, covered with every abomination and stained with blood" (quoted in Piercy, *Hawai'i Truth*, 42).

case of Malo), and thus write themselves into an Enlightenment narrative of their own people's displacement by a teleology of progress on the American Congregationalist model.[11] Nonetheless, as in Kamakau's rich and relentless newspaper writings from 1842 to 1876, compiled into such works of self-ethnographic sway as *Ruling Chiefs of Hawai'i* and *Ka Po'e Kahiko,* Native Hawaiian historians deformed this genre of Christian historiography and made it tell of counterclaims and rival mythologies of place, submerged aesthetics, geographical complexity, and a subaltern historical memory of colonial dispossession.[12]

SHARK GOD ON TRIAL IN THE U.S. COLONIAL SYSTEM:
REALITY AS REAL ESTATE

From plovers of the air to sharks of the sea, our way of imagining a relationship to these creatures, and by extension forging a sensibility for Pacific places and "place-based politics," is fraught with the contradictions of Hawai'i's history as long rooted in colonial conflicts, uneven globalization, and racialized misapprehensions.[13] My analysis will move toward

11. On this complicated situation of both learning from and rejecting the narrative predispositions of Enlightenment history via Dibble's training, see Gary Pak, "E Ala Mai Kakou E Na Kini Na Mamo (We, the multitudes of descendants, are waking up): 19th Century Hawaiian Historiography and the Historical Novel of Hawai'i" (Ph.D. diss., University of Hawai'i, 1997), esp. chap. 3 on the emergence of Native Hawaiian historiography in David Malo, Samuel Kamakau, and John Papa Ii. Also see Ben F. Finney, Ruby K. Johnson, Malcolm Chun, and Edith K. McKinzie, "Hawaiian Historians and the First Pacific History Seminar," in *The Changing Pacific: Essays in Honor of H. E. Maude,* ed. Niel Gunson (Melbourne: Oxford University Press, 1978), 308–35.

12. To counter Dibble's sense of the nonaesthetic Hawaiian, consider Kamakau's evocation of a (precolonial) countersublime in his narrative on the death of Kamehameha III in *Ruling Chiefs of Hawai'i,* rev. ed. (Honolulu: Kamehameha Schools Press, 1992), 416: "To a people living happily in a pleasant land with purple mountains, sea-girt beaches, cool breezes, life long and natural, even to extreme old age, with the coming of strangers, there came contagious diseases which destroyed the native sons of the land." In the same passage, Kamakau writes of native dispossession and goes on to evoke this stunning image of pastoral lament, land loss, and spiritual pathos, like something out of Oliver Goldsmith's "Deserted Village": "The old villages lie silent in a tangle of bushes and vines, haunted by ghosts and horned owls, frequented by goats and bats."

13. On the turn to making a place-based politics as a way of fending for locality and resources in the globalization system, see Arif Dirlik, "Place-Based Imagination: Globalism and the Politics of Place," *Review* 22, no. 2 (1999): 151–87, and his important

establishing a more postmodern—and polyglossic—notion of justice in the contemporary Pacific by challenging the seamless workings of the U.S. literary nation-state with the uncanny return of a shark god hula poem on Ka-lani-ōʻpuʻu from early nineteenth-century Hawaiian literature. The aim is to promote a keener global sensibility toward local and indigenous identity in Hawaiʻi as this can be rooted (and routed) in multitongued spatiality, competing symbolic systems and language games, and the clashing traditions and heritages of Pacific, Asian, and American makeup that demand a postmodern hearing. The attempt, implicitly, is to refigure the whole notion of a "poetry of place" and, by extension, to determine how we would conceptualize the ground of "local literature" as such. The shark god, as it were, puts the local and U.S. state apparatus on trial in ways that affect contracts, genres of poetry, and the notion of place-bound identity and cultural community in the Pacific.

Enduring as an island of "local representations and beliefs" in the Pacific as a noncontiguous territory positioned within yet outside the U.S. mainland cultural hegemony, Hawaiʻi has become a postmodern island microstate of global cultural flows and local encounters.[14] Inside this contemporary Hawaiʻi of "local motions," to invoke the logo of a North Shore surf shop, distinctive cultural articulations and political-economic entanglements into the transnational marketplace of global tourism and Asia/Pacific exchange are intermixed in person, code, and habit. It makes sense to speak of these Hawaiian islands, then, not so much as a seamlessly confederated U.S. *state*, but as a site of heteroglossic spatiality. Hawaiʻi is an island space, that is, like Sir Thomas More's countercapitalist *Utopia*, captured by yet outside capitalist regimes of knowledge and power where other stories of place, self, and belonging go on being circulated, imagined, contested, and sold.

If an Americanized version of Hawaiʻi has blasted off "from the Stone

---

critique of transnational diasporism in Asia-Pacific, "Bringing History Back In: Of Diasporas, Hybridities, Places, and Histories," *Review of Education/Pedagogy/Cultural Studies* (forthcoming).

14. On indigenous locales, see Michel de Certeau, "The Politics of Silence: The Long March of the Indians," in *Heterologies: Discourse on the Other,* trans. Brian Massumi (Minneapolis: University of Minnesota Press, 1989): "The land, serving as a reference point, in addition to preserving local representations and beliefs (often fragmented and hidden beneath the occupiers' system), is also a ballast and defense for the 'own' against any superimposition" (229).

Age to the Atomic Age in two hundred years," as two noted white scholars of history and literature once boasted of the fiftieth state, some "little" histories of communal belonging have *not* been blasted away from the place.[15] This is the case even as alternative symbol systems have been suppressed, and the damages to the locals and locale are often sublimated in a haze of tourist fantasy and Michener-like master narratives of democratic progress from indigenous tyranny to shopping mall luxury.[16] The U.S. language games of Hawaiian representation (mostly rooted in "offshore" Hollywood fantasies of "South Pacific" still) multiply and compete to take semiotic possession of this (globally enchanted) locale, "Hawaiʻi." These language games are being generated inside and outside Hawaiʻi's porous island boundaries. In the transnational calculus, Hawaiʻi still beckons as the "Blue Hawaiʻi" of tourist dreams: aloha shirts, dreamy beaches, mai tais, and native girls conjured like rent-a-cars. As the pidgin-speaking Hawaiian comedian-poet Bu Laʻia undercuts the commodity-sexy allure of a Hawaiʻi forever calling *Aloha!* with lovely hula hands to the agencies of global tourism, "Thank you for visiting Hawaiʻi, brah, but don't forget to go back home!"[17]

For the two tongues of English (*ka ʻōlelo haole,* "the strangers' tongue" as it is called in Hawaiian) and Native Hawaiian were never allowed to be equal in status and to coexist in public spaces of education and acculturation in modernizing Hawaiʻi. Enforcing American cultural sway and commercial hegemony with the coming of the New England Congregational missionaries to Oʻahu in 1820, the English language superseded the Hawaiian language, which was banned as a language of public school instruction in 1898 upon annexation into organic U.S. territory.[18] Only

15. Ralph P. Kuykendall and A. Grove Day, *Hawaii: A History, from Polynesian Kingdom to American Statehood* (Englewood Cliffs, NJ: Prentice Hall, 1976), foreword to the first edition (1948), v.

16. See Kuykendall and Day, *Hawaii: A History.* "It was in this position, as a territory on the road to [U.S.] statehood, that the people of Hawaii usually thought of their island home" (214).

17. Bu Laʻia, *False Crack???* CD, Pig Poi Records, Honolulu, 1995. For a scathing critique on indigenous grounds of cultural dispossession, see Haunani-Kay Trask, "Lovely Hula Hands: Corporate Tourism and the Prostitution of Hawaiian Culture," in *From a Native Daughter: Colonialism and Sovereignty in Hawaiʻi* (Monroe, ME: Common Courage Press, 1993).

18. See Larry Lindsey Kimura, "The Revitalization of the Hawaiian Language," *Hawaiʻi Review* 13 (1989): 74–76.

as recently as 1986 was this state-imposed *injustice* reversed, with the Hawaiian language officially adopted by law as the "second language" by the state of Hawai'i under its Hawaiian governor, John Waihe'e. Since the 1980s, Hawaiian immersion programs such as Pūnana Leo have been implemented to further the education of Native Hawaiians interested in growing up bilingual and immersing themselves in Hawaiian cultural mores. At the strongest extreme, Hawaiian has proven to be the basis of a cultural flourishing in the literary and performing arts, has served as the means of ongoing cultural rehabilitation and pride of symbolic and mythical identity, and supports the ongoing struggle for *self-determined national sovereignty* underway and gathering concrete political form into, perhaps, an indigenous "nation within a nation."[19]

Everyday lives/subjects and the stories of identity inside the creativity and chaos of the Pacific Rim are being shaped, coded, marketed, and organized under an Asia-Pacific transnational banner, with unforeseen consequences good and bad. This drive for regional coherence is no longer just Euro-American-centered but is being mobilized under the capitalist dynamism of APEC.[20] This hegemonic framework around an Asia-driven Pacific demands situated critical interrogation of the Pacific *local/locality* if we are to acknowledge and, in effect, adjudicate the competing language games of symbolic representation, local/indigenous emergences, and "cultural identity discourse" that seek to evolve within modern nation-state apparatuses across the region.

SHARK GOD VERSUS THE POLITICAL ECOLOGY OF *JAWS* AND *MOBY-DICK*

To show the disruptive potential of "local mythology" within the global economy of the postmodern/postcolonial world (with its stress on enacting the situated strategies and language games of the local), I want to tease

19. See Trask, *From a Native Daughter*, on struggles of decolonization and cultural nationalism; and Candace Fujikane, "Between Nationalisms: Hawai'i's Local Nation and Its Troubled Paradise," *Critical Mass: A Journal of Asian American Cultural Criticism* 2 (1994): 23–57, on the makings of a nonindigenous but coalitional Asian/Pacific "local nation."

20. For cultural genealogies and situated critiques of this, see Arif Dirlik, ed., *What Is in a Rim? Critical Perspectives on the Pacific Region Idea* (Boulder, CO: Rowman and Littlefield, 1998).

out the poetics and politics of place, as these can be generated out of a nineteenth-century Hawaiian poem (composed in the genre of the *hula manō,* or "sitting dance imitative of sharks")[21] in which a shark god takes possession of a Hawaiian harbor in the name of the Big Island king the poem/chant/hula exists as "sacred" language to honor and endorse. This so-called pagan/barbaric song of sharks never really existed in oblivion, but it was put out of circulation by the American religious and commercial hegemony and speaks the suppression of another history, another ethos of the land, as well as an intimate and *different* knowledge/mythology of the Pacific Ocean and the local community tending the island shores.[22] I want to invoke the precolonial imaginary of place, first, to contest the gods of reality as U.S. real estate as well as, beyond this, to suggest other ways of coalescing a politics and poetics for the place-based imagination of Hawai'i. I will read the poem not so much as ontology as cultural-political strategy.

This name-chant poem is called, in English translation, "Shark Hula for Ka-lani-ō'pu'u."[23] This hula poem praises the high chief of the outer Hawai'i island as well as his high-blooded genealogy as linked to the *'aumākua,* "ancestral sharks" who served as protectors and as ties to the past.[24] These Hawaiian guardian-spirit shark gods have, so the poem

21. Mary Kawena Pukui and Samuel H. Elbert, *Hawaiian Dictionary* (Honolulu: University of Hawai'i Press, 1986), 88.

22. "Basically, minorities are not social ensembles, they are territories of language. Every one of us belongs to several minorities, and what is very important, none of them prevails. It is only then that we can say that our [postmodern] society is just. Can there be justice without the domination of one [language] game upon the others?" See Jean-François Lyotard and Jean-Loup Thebaud, "Majority Does Not Mean Great Number but Great Fear," in *Just Gaming,* trans. Brian Massumi (Minneapolis: University of Minnesota Press, 1985), 95. Also see n. 57 below.

23. Mary K. Pukui and Alfons L. Korn, eds., *The Echo of Our Song: Chants and Poems of the Hawaiians* (Honolulu: University of Hawai'i Press, 1979), 3–8.

24. See Samuel Mānaiakalani Kamakau, *Ka Po'e Kahiko, the People of Old,* trans. Mary Kawena Pukui (Honolulu: Bishop Museum Press, 1991), 73–81. In addition to the native mythologies of shark and ocean archived in the cultural narratives of David Malo, *Hawaiian Antiquities (Moolelo Hawai'i),* trans. Nathaniel B. Emerson (Honolulu: Bishop Museum Press, 1951), John Papa Ii, and Kamakau, for contemporary Hawaiians who still hold to such beliefs and on such grounds opposed the shark-hunting expeditions implemented by the Hawai'i Shark Task Force after a resident was killed by a tiger shark in the waters off Maui in 1991, see Jim Borg, *Tigers of the Sea: Hawai'i's Deadly Sharks* (Honolulu: Mutual, 1993).

claims in memorable oral language, given Ka-lani-ō'pu'u not only his royal name (*O kou inoa ia,* runs the generic formula of the refrain), heavenly influx, and mandate of sacred mana (power), but also his claim to the land and harbor he rules over as Big Island chief. "Ka-lani-ō'pu'u, the right to impose the kapu [sacred laws/taboos] on the land [island] is yours" [by] "the right of a shark with arched dorsal fin to bare teeth," as the opening lines so starkly put it. The royal names mentioned in the poem also connect him to genealogies that rule on Kauai and Maui, perhaps suggesting a broader claim to rule more than one island.

Later in the poem, the king is described as not so much descended from the water-ruling sharks: he has become one, as the community "we" voice urges its subject:

> Now answer us, Ka-lani-ō'pu'u, fierce Island-Piercer!
>   This is your name chant:
> You are a white-finned shark riding the crest of the wave,
>   O Ka-lani-ō'pu'u:
>   a tiger-shark resting without fear.

After invoking various images of natural power and heavenly energy to ratify the sacred mana and incarnate the royal prowess of this Big Island high chief, the shark hula poem ends with this *quasilegal claim* for Ka-lani-ō'pu'u to possess and rule over the island of Hawai'i. Such a claim comes down from the kapu chiefess, Ke-aka-mahana, his powerful great-grandmother who had royal blood claims to the island polities of Hawai'i and Kauai. She was descended from the much-honored king Lono-i-kamakahiki, whom Samuel M. Kamakau made so much of as legitimate genealogical origin in his tragicomic history of the Hawaiian nation up to the time of Kamehameha III in 1854:

> Your sovereign sway surveys this island and beyond
> over the multitudinous children of [Great-grandmother] Ke-aka-
> mahana,
> by whose name you do inherit and wear by right
> the shining feather cloak.

This chant of twenty-five lines was written for the high chief of the island of Hawai'i, Ka-lani-ō'pu'u (d. 1782), the powerful uncle of King Kamehameha I, who first unified by force the islands of Hawai'i into the centripetal makings of a modern and internationally recognized nation-kingdom after fateful contacts with the European nation-state and juridical models of the British sea captains James Cook and George Vancouver. Called the "Tereoboo," Ka-lani-ō'pu'u it was who, dressed in feather capes and helmets and surrounded by priests and offerings, welcomed Captain Cook to the Big Island in 1779 during the navigator's second visit to the so-called Sandwich Islands, the one that resulted in Cook's self-apotheosis, wrath, and death.[25]

Indeed, the reign of this Big Island chief is associated, in a plethora of historical and dramatic accounts, with the death of Captain Cook. For it was Ka-lani-ō'pu'u whom Cook took hostage on the *Resolution* in retaliation for acts of theft on 14 February 1779—thus (in Greg Dening's words) violating "all the rules he had set his crew for cross-cultural encounters"— and this act of mutual misunderstanding and mounting hostility led to the attack by the chief's warriors in which Cook was slain.[26] Although "the business of war" was the principal occupation of Ka-lani-ō'pu'u's reign and he was known for his club beating of heads and abuse of common people, even urinating in the eyes of defeated foes on Maui (as described by Kamakau), this fierce uncle of Kamehameha who tried unsuccessfully to conquer Maui several times also "delighted in the hula dance" and loved to watch old and young perform it in the Kailua region as well as to dance it himself until old age.[27] The arts of hula and war found a strong ally in him.

To enforce a lineage drawn from the Kamehameha line and ratified by forces of nature as well as to shape communal history into an image of legitimacy compelling place-bound belief, the "Shark Hula for Ka-lani-ō'pu'u" was performed as a "sitting hula" with totemic movements and symbolic gestures that enforced its layered symbolism of place into the body and resonated into the community of (pagan) believers for whom a powerful class of *kupua* beings could magically shift from human form to plants, animals, and back to gods with political-sexual implication.[28]

25. See Gananath Obeyesekere, *The Apotheosis of Captain Cook: European Mythmaking in the Pacific* (Princeton, NJ: Princeton University Press, 1992).

26. Greg Dening, *The Death of William Gooch: A History's Anthropology* (Honolulu: University of Hawai'i Press, 1995), 140–41.

27. Kamakau, *Ruling Chiefs of Hawai'i*, 79, 84, 105.

28. Thus (like the pig god Kamapua'a) the shark god/shark-man linkage can be read as symbolically mimicking the linkages of human behavior to the mandates of the gods/rulers and the free play of animals/commoners. For a historically sophisticated un-packing of one such Hawaiian oral narrative in the context of antimissionary beliefs

Calling such a *sacred* hula song one of those myriad Hawaiian "animal dances," Emerson claimed in the salvage ethnography of cultural preservation he compiled for the Bureau of American Ethnology Bulletin in 1909 that "the last and only mention of [the shark hula's] performance was in 1847," when King Kamehameha III made a tour of Oʻahu and was feted with chants and hulas by his Hawaiian subjects in the island kingdom.[29] The shark hula would have been a way of honoring the Kamehameha lineage; but, with the land divisions of the Great Mahele under Kamehameha III, such a hula poem and its symbolic claim to the lands (like a premodern real estate deed) would fall into disuse or be discredited by haole settlers enforcing the claims of English.

For the time and space markings of the shark chant was fast dying out in the Christian and capitalist scheme of things that was taking over the island polity. This was so after the Great Mahele of 1848 divided up the island and linked spaces of indigenous tenancy into the capitalist geometry of real estate and English-language contracts as fee-simple tenure deeds took possession of the islands and limited native access to the lands.[30] The shark god poem was not just "bad" poetry, it evoked threatening symbols of another way of life, narrated another way of taking possession of the landscape, the language, and the sea—it imaged forth another history of the place and its polity that the literatures of the white settlers wanted to forget.

Mary Kawena Pukui, that treasure trove of Hawaiian language knowledge, vernacular proverbs, and native wisdom, working along with Alfons L. Korn, a Victorianist member of the English Department at the

and prohula sentiments after King Kalākaua's coronation of 1883, see Lilikala K. Kameʻeleihiwa, *A Legendary Tradition of Kamapuaʻa, The Hawaiian Pig-God* (Honolulu: Bishop Museum Press, 1996), xi–xii and afterword.

29. Emerson, *Unwritten Literature*, 221. Helen Roberts, *Ancient Hawaiian Music* (New York: Dover, 1967), 169, confirmed this in her survey of the hula in 1923–1924, saying that the *hula manō* was last performed in 1847 at Waimea, Oʻahu, on a tour made by Kamehameha III.

30. Land and sea access for natives is still under contention in state courts. On this far-reaching alienation and redistribution of the land into the contract law system as well as native resistance and acceptance, ironically giving rise to such land-rich trusts of Hawaiian capitalism cum Christian instruction as the Bishop Estate, see Lilikala Kameʻeleihiwa, *Native Land and Foreign Desires: Pehea La E Pono Ai?* (Honolulu: Bishop Museum Press, 1992).

University of Hawai'i who took his residence in Hawai'i seriously as a scholarly mandate to listen to the cultural others in the Pacific as well, have made the shark poem/chant/sacred song available for interpretation and cultural circulation at the local and global levels. The afterlife of the shark god demands a postmodern hearing in contexts where the master narratives of Euro-American colonization no longer inspire complete credibility and social sway. Translation can help disturb the normative codes, converting little into big and contesting the sublime into the pompous and irrelevant. If the language game is little, its import can be social and cosmic.

From the transcendental hermeneutics of whiteness in Melville's *Moby-Dick* to the ecological melodrama of terrorized New Englanders in Peter Benchley's novel/Steven Spielberg's film *Jaws,* the creatures of the briny deep have served as a focus of U.S. unconscious projection and ideological need to express some of the deepest capitalist longings and spiritual phobias of the national-popular imagination.[31] Whales and sharks have not just been plundered for oil, sperm, skin, bones, and food, they have been *demonized and transcendentalized* into sublime objects of dread and wonder: wondrous beings part commodity and part godhead, at once alienated and dangerous, endangered by Ahab and his state police and naval apparatus force but laden with the phobic mythologies of American sublimity challenging the national will to dominate the frontier wilderness and turn the God-given natural resources of the material earth (following the Emersonian Protestant capitalist poetic) from sublime symbol to global commodity.[32] Sharks and whales are not so much antagonists or oceanic coresidents as they are ancestors for the aboriginal Hawaiians, some of whom

31. When a white-tipped reef shark recently took residence in Hanauma Bay, a snorkel shop salesman tried to explain to a Japanese tourist why the waters were closed: "I made a gesture of a fin moving through the water, and the man said, 'Ah, Jaw-zu!'" ("Shark at Hanauma Beaches Snorklers," *Honolulu Advertiser,* 13 May 1998, B1). Thus, *Jaws* is an example of the American imaginary going global and mediating the local and even the indigenous belief systems (see my analysis below of a short story by Rodney Morales on Hawaiian sharks).

32. See Rob Wilson, *American Sublime: The Genealogy of a Poetic Genre* (Madison: University of Wisconsin Press, 1991), tracking the Puritan and Romantic origins of this "sublime" poetics of U.S. national domination over "empty" wilderness frontiers. On the sublime as a genre of white settler colonialism marshalled against the aboriginal peoples and vast wilderness spaces of Australia, see Meaghan Morris, "White Panic or Mad Max and the Sublime," in *Trajectories: Inter-Asia Cultural Studies,* ed. Kuan-Hsing Chen et al. (London: Routledge, 1998), 239–62.

tamed and rode sharks and claimed them as family protectors.[33] At a more fearful extreme, "The shark is a ravaging lion of the sea whom none can tame," wrote Kamakau.[34] For New Englanders, as representative capitalist Americans on their whaling ship factories, the "unpitying sharks" are figured as atheistic demons of wilderness antagonism and lethal devils of white racial animosity that need to be sacralized (via symbolic textualization) into Leviathan or, in the worst-case scenario, liquidated from anxious corners of the earth, whether a resort harbor full of vacationing tourists in Massachusetts (as in *Jaws*) or the splendors of the Pacific from Honolulu to Canton (as in Ahab's whaling ship factory quest in *Moby-Dick*).[35] "Queequeg no care what god made him shark, wedder Feejee god or Nantucket god," Melville writes in the pidgin English voice of the Polynesian native harpooner on the *Pequod*, "but de god wat made shark must be one dam Ingin."[36]

The shark god was offensive to American beliefs and customs. Consistent with his early conviction as a visiting journalist that Christian, commercial, and democratic forms had improved the "untaught and degraded race" of Hawaiians, Twain derided their "lascivious hula-hula dance" for a Sacramento newspaper in 1866, and went on in the best-selling *Roughing It* (which made his American reputation) to poke fun at the "christianized Hawaiian's" holding a "latent loyalty to the Great Shark God," which came out when Kilauea volcano erupted or there was an earthquake or when he superstitiously feared, at any odd moment, "he had sinned against the Great Shark God."[37] The shark, associated by Hawaiians with powerful warriors who can devour the island and, more terrifyingly, with high chiefs

---

33. Kamakau, *Ka Poʻe Kahiko*, 88–89.

34. Ibid., 73. In addition to Kamakau's detailed native recall, see Leighton R. Taylor, *Sharks of Hawaiʻi: Their Biology and Cultural Significance* (Honolulu: University of Hawaiʻi Press, 1993).

35. Herman Melville, *Moby-Dick* (New York: Signet, 1980), 531. A notice in the *USA Today* best-selling books list from the summer of 1995 says it all, announcing *White Shark* by Peter Benchley: "Something more dangerous than a white shark is in the water," meaning the geopolitical phobias of a declining nation-state ready to take the threat out of the postwar Pacific Ocean.

36. Melville, *Moby-Dick*, 295, chapter on "The Shark Massacre" as sharks attack whales and native crew alike.

37. Mark Twain, *Letters from Hawaii*, ed. A. Grove Day (Honolulu: University of Hawaiʻi Press, 1975), 70–71, 254; *Roughing It* (Berkeley: University of California Press, 1995), 459–60.

who can rule over them (as in the saying "The Chief is a shark that lives on land"), the shark is also associated with lovemaking prowess;[38] thus, according to hula-loving King David Kalākaua, every species of shark "was tabu to women."[39] Of course, Hawaiians did distinguish between a benevolent or "patron shark" that protects and aids the family that worships it as ancestral god, and a malevolent shark that injures, kills, or eats human beings, but the point is that the shark was associated with a different signifying system that baffled the sensibility, interpretive codes, and legal system of austere Calvinists.[40] As Greg Dening has written of the British astronomer William Gooch, amazed and baffled by Hawaiians as "priest-ridden as catholics" as they caught sharks bare-handed in the waters off Kealakekua Bay for a fierce new king named Kamehameha, who (like his uncle) was associated with the tiger shark, "Gooch could no more see what the Hawaiians did when they caught sharks than he could see the Hawaiian culture that contexed this 'priest-ridden' society."[41] The beaches of the Pacific where the indigenous and Euro-American cultures would meet, in Dening's metahistorical reckoning, remained frontiers, boundaries, and marginal places of disorder, danger, and risk where the interpretive codes could entangle, clash, and (mis)translate across the divide of incommensurable terms: "[Gooch] could not know the metonymies Hawaiians made of sharks as gods and chiefs and strangers."[42]

To be sure, this little Hawaiian shark hula chant for Ka-lani-ō'pu'u is written in that dreaded *hula manō* genre of an "obscene" dance form so

38. Pukui and Elbert, *Hawaiian Dictionary*, entry for *holopapa*, 78; entry for *manō*, 229, figurative for "passionate lover" pursuing women. For contemporary transformations of these shark mythologies, fears, and legends, see Fred Barnett, *Hawai'i's Shark Stories* (Kailua, HI: Orca Press, 1996).

39. David Kalākaua, *The Legends and Myths of Hawai'i* (Honolulu: Mutual, 1990), appendix, 529.

40. I draw on the Hawaiian ethnographic research of Martha Warren Beckwith, Joseph Emerson, and Dennis Kawaharada as compiled and reprinted in Emma M. Nakuina et al., *Nanaue the Shark Man and Other Hawaiian Shark Stories*, ed. Dennis Kawaharada (Honolulu: Kalamaku Press, 1994), 5, 66.

41. Dening, *The Death of William Gooch*, 144–46. In Dening's account, Gooch was en route to Waimea, O'ahu, where he would be slain on 12 May 1792 by Hawaiians who took his "sparkling eyes" for the god Lonoikouali'i (152).

42. Gooch's last written words were "Sharks, sharks," suggesting to Dening a Westerner's bafflement, estrangement, and sense of mounting despondency before "the metonymies Hawaiians made of sharks as gods and chiefs and strangers" (ibid., 148).

206 Reimagining the American Pacific

despised by the commercial-missionary oligarchy that it took umbrage against King David Kalākaua, who sought to revive native forms such as the hula at his coronation ceremony in 1883.[43] Its *wild chanting* occurs in a throaty, wailing, poetic language bellowed out in praise of the shark gods and their kindred king. It is thus voiced in a subaltern Hawaiian language filled with those "hideous noises at night" that the New England Calvinists hated as signs of nerve-wracking paganism and that had been outlawed from cultural production in the islands by a converted Hawaiian queen, Ka-'ahu-manu. It may still strike the rational ears of moral capital as pagan and wrong, as a symbolism of royal violence forever outside the proper codes of poetry and the law of the Greco-Roman father. Even today in Hawai'i, the Roman Catholic Church has banned all forms of hula being performed as part of church services.[44] The hula is more than a dance, it is a Hawaiian cosmology, an expressive miming of place and body in symbolic conjunction.

As a diasporic New Englander and a state-salaried professor of American literature in the New Pacific, I have long been fascinated and haunted by this shark poem since I first read it in the dual-language anthology (Hawaiian/English) translated by Mark K. Pukui and Alfons L. Korn, *The Echo of Our Song: Chants and Poems of the Hawaiians* and had begun teaching it in my poetry classes at the University of Hawai'i at Mānoa in the 1980s as an example of the "local poem." I called this shark poem an uncanny example of "local literature" because, like the works of Asian/Pacific "local literature" that were emerging since 1978 around Bamboo Ridge Press and in more indigenous-based collections such as *Ho'omānoa: An Anthology of Contemporary Hawaiian Literature* edited by Joseph Puna Balaz, it gave voice to the symbolic narratives, myths, hidden languages, and ancestral cultural mores of the "local" island and, as distinctive language, took possession of the Hawaiian locality in a way that was frighten-

43. The printed hula program was declared obscene and charges were brought against one of Kalākaua's aides and the printer. See Albert J. Schutz, *The Voices of Eden: A History of Hawaiian Language Studies* (Honolulu: University of Hawai'i Press, 1994), 348. Suppression of Hawaiian language practices and cultural forms ("The Kahuna is the deadly enemy of Christian civilization," wrote Sereno Bishop, editor of *The Friend* newspaper, in 1892) increased during the U.S.-led Annexationist era, when monolingual policies came in dominance.
44. Melissa Tanji, "Bishop Seeking to Lift Ban on Hula: Vatican Prohibits Dance in Church," *Honolulu Advertiser*, 13 July 1998, A1.

ing in its sublime power, poetic layering, cultural authenticity, and direct-
ness of claim.[45]

The shark god beliefs live on in altered forms in contemporary Hawaiian local literature, adding a dimension of awe and respect to attitudes
in relation to the ocean as well as revealing a hybrid in-mixing of other
cultures that makes for respect. In "When the Shark Bites," which won the
Honolulu Magazine fiction prize in 1994, Rodney Morales tells a tale of two
part-Hawaiian brothers on the Waiʻanae Coast whose experience of surfing and fear of shark attacks on surfers has been given a "chicken skin"
dimension by learning from their Grandmother Wong of the shark-man,
Kawelo, with a shark's mouth hidden on his back.[46] (Kawelo is a warrior
hero from Kauaʻi who is alluded to in "Shark Hula for Ka-lani-ō'puʻu" and
whose family shrine is dedicated to the king of the shark gods.)[47] The boys
project their fears of a predatory shark in the guise of a trickster human on
a mysterious new lifeguard, Manny, an overtattooed, scarred, "spooky-
looking guy" in an outsized '62 Impala who keeps warning them to stay
away from the deep water, all the more to entice them into it as he sings his
favorite karaoke tune, Bertolt Brecht's "Mack the Knife" as sung by Bobby
Darin: "When the shark bites with his teeth, dear, / Scarlet billows start to
spread." Indeed, as in the special mix of Hawaiian ancestral and mass
media influences that mark the fiction of Morales,[48] the boys' shark god
belief is mediated by an array of other American pop cultural shark icons:
UNLV basketball coach Jerry "The Shark" Tarkanian, a video game called
"Shark Attack," Japanese and haole real estate "sharks," the *Jaws* sound-
track. The fear of a shark-man attack on the leeward coast, real or pro-

45. Joseph P. Balaz, ed., *Hoʻomanoa: An Anthology of Hawaiian Literature* (Honolulu: Ku
Paʻa, 1989).

46. Rodney Morales, "When the Shark Bites," *Honolulu Magazine*, 27 (April 1994): 34–
72. These images and the fearful narrative of Morales's shark-man draw on and trans-
figure Native Hawaiian sources: see Nakuina et al., *Nanaue the Shark Man*, 8, 21, 51, 66.
Dennis Kawaharada has edited several important collections of the native mythologies
and narratives of place and ocean, including *Hawaiian Fishing Traditions* (Honolulu:
Kalamakū Press, 1992) and *Ancient Oʻahu: Stories from Fornander and Thrum* (Honolulu: Kalamakū Press, 1996).

47. Pukui and Korn, *The Echo of Our Song*, 7.

48. See Rodney Morales, *The Speed of Darkness* (Honolulu: Bamboo Ridge Press, 1988),
for example, "Daybreak over Haleakalā/Heartbreak Memories (A Two-Sided Hit)," on
Hawaiian and American cultures colliding in the character of Bud Newman as he
becomes reindigenized on Kahoʻolawe.

jected, leads the boys to bond more closely to each other, to undergo a heroic encounter with the sea, to learn from an array of cultural elders an attitude of respect and awe toward the ocean.

In Kathleen Tyau's nostalgia-drenched novella of Hawaiian Chinese localism and the charms of pidgin English, *A Little Too Much Is Enough*, a chapter called "Family Shark" recounts how the narrator's father, Kuhio, is so drenched in Chinese and Hawaiian superstitions that he thinks he encounters his family's shark god off the moonlit waters of Waikīkī, when it is actually his future Chinese father-in-law coming into his life: "I wondered, How can the aumakua speak hakka? Who was this calling me stupid and blind? Then I thought maybe he was a Chinese ghost, the gui, coming to take me back to China."[49] Again, as in the mixed cultural languages of Morales, local, Asian/Pacific diaspora, and Hawaiian premodern beliefs mingle to enchant the scene and deepen the languages and beliefs that link people to place and mixed cultural groups to each other.

In *Shark Dialogues*, Kiana Davenport's outsized and swashbuckling romance of a Big Island family, the Kealohas, Pono, the Hawaiian matriarch and kahuna of a Kona coffee farm, rules over four upper-middle-class granddaughters who are the products of mixed-mongrel marriages and Asian/Pacific beliefs. Pono bears a special relationship to the shark god and ʻaumakua of her family, whom she dreams about and even transforms into in visions of transmigration. (This image is influenced not only by Hawaiian beliefs but by Davenport's reading of stories by Kobo Abe.)[50] Pono is dreaming of being a shark when she meets her husband, Duke, in the ocean; she and he later drown themselves in Shark Bay in a mutual suicide, their suffering compounded by his leprosy and her hatred of the haole-driven and hybrid new world of violence and consumption the offspring are products of. Even Vanya's far-fetched embodiment of terroristic violence as a tactic in the Hawaiian sovereignty struggle, however irresponsible or wildly "offshore" it seems as fantasy, is given a ratification to "move forward" by the vision of a shark (the reincarnation of Pono) in the waters off the Kona coast at the end of this magical-realist saga. Although the Hawaiian beliefs at times seem forced and overdone as a sensa-

---

49. Kathleen Tyau, *A Little Too Much Is Enough* (New York: Norton, 1996), 168.
50. Kiana Davenport, author's note, in *Shark Dialogues* (New York: Atheneum, 1994), 492.

tionalized reworking of what Mudrooroo Narogin calls dream-based and racialized "aboriginality,"[51] they coexist in a network of Asian/Pacific images and connections that the daughters and their offspring embody, linking Chinese opium smokers, Japanese Yakuza, Filipino nationalists, Australian aborigines, and American veterinarians and mercenaries into a strange compound as "hybrid products of the new world." Different heritages and metaphoric systems clash and collide in strange ways, blood and history amalgamating in ways the characters cannot control or the author cannot fully mediate into a compelling and credible image of place and cultural-political community.[52]

The great author John Dominis Holt's life as hapa-haole Hawaiian was deeply associated with shark gods and their conflict with the beliefs of Christian modernity. In his memoir, *Recollections,* Holt tells of a Hawaiian caretaker, Kaiʻa, who, like a native mentor, taught him respect for the "aliʻi makua—the old sharks who had been living in the bay for centuries."[53] But he also tells how his own father led "shark hunts" and gruesome slaughtering of the sharks with rifles, until Kawela Bay was filled with blood during "the massacre of [Kaiʻa's] ʻaumākua," which the adolescent Holt was forced to watch in the interest of "developing [his] macho instincts" as well as to drive the homosexual inclinations out of the sexually ambiguous son.[54] At the end of Holt's prescient novel, *Waimea Summer,* as the young Mark Hull is about to leave for Honolulu and return to the modern world of science, Christianity, and urban illumination, the waters of Kawaihae harbor fill up with the blood of bulls and cattle attacked by sharks. The kahuna of Puu Kohala shrine soon explains to the young part-Hawaiian that this is a fit "small sacrifice" to the shark gods of the Pacific, "they who protect those who are theirs," as he recalls how the youthful Kamehameha demonstrated his royal prowess by single-handedly destroying an enemy shark named Keoua Kuahuula: "The Great One stunned the shark with blows, opened its jaws and tore them asunder until the shore was red with

---

51. Mudrooroo Narogin, *Writing from the Fringe: A Study of Modern Aboriginal Literature* (Melbourne: Hyland House, 1990), 27.

52. For a demanding critique of Davenport's reconstructed and market-tuned indigeneity, see Paul Lyons, review of *Shark Dialogues, Mānoa* 7 (1995): 265–67.

53. John Dominis Holt, *Recollections: Memoirs of John Dominis Holt, 1919–1935* (Honolulu: Ku Paʻa, 1993), 9.

54. Ibid., 12, 204.

the blood of the enemy."[55] Holt's protagonist is shown the force and power it will take to be a leader of the islands, and in a chanted genealogy that awakens a vision of gathering chiefs in some eternal present of vision, Hull is connected to the lineage of the Great One, Kamehameha, just as the shark god hula had connected Kamehameha's uncle to the royal lineage in its takeover of Hawaiʻi and other islands.

POSTMODERN JUSTICE IN THE PACIFIC

Postmodern justice demands, I am urging here, a different way of hearing comparative literature and, a fortiori, imagining place and history: the *little stories* of the shark god et al. can at least be heard, preserved, and circulated for the alternative knowledge of the sea, earth, and ecosphere they can present in these days of late capitalism when earth and ocean seem on the verge of irrevocable ecological degradation. There is *another* knowledge of the Pacific and its complex local communities out there; citizens of APEC and the New Pacific would do well to listen to these counternarratives and countervisions of what constitutes a proper and decent knowledge of the earth and sea. Postmodern justice demands that these minor language games of the local and the little, the mythic and the communal, be listened to in some "heterological" way that does not presume to judge and adjudicate their wisdom in some all-mastering Hegelian kind of way. That language game of philosophy and truth, that dialectic of absolute enlightenment and will to mastery over non-European others is intolerant, moribund, and terroristic. Such arrogant language games have gotten us into the endgame the late-capitalist Earth is in.

The odds are stacked against such a shark chant as repository of native beliefs being heard in the U.S. legal system. In "Pele in a Christian Court," Joseph Chang (in a *Hawaiʻi Review* essay aligning a non-Hawaiian local with the preservation and usage of non-Hawaiian ecological beliefs) shows that Native Hawaiian claims to disrupt the Geothermal Project in the Puna rain forests of the Big Island are doomed to defeat in a U.S.-based court where nature is presupposed to be a desacralized commodity and for whom Pele worship by Hawaiians can only be validated, not by the communal force of native animism, but by truth claims of Western material

55. John Dominis Holt, *Waimea Summer* (Honolulu: Topgallant, 1976), 193–94.

archaeology and cultural anthropology proving some unbroken continuity since the coming of Captain Cook.[56]

If such language games remain *incommensurable,* like a lyric poem and a legal will, this kind of comparative analysis would challenge the naturalized way such a symbolic act of language possession can be suppressed and disavowed by the U.S. legal and military courts. (For some Hawaiians, can we not say that this oral chant constituted a communal contract?) If we examine the expressive range of the Pacific as cultural locality within APEC, these different cultural literatures can help provide *different mappings of the Asia-Pacific region* and, as such, can help to circulate alternative mappings and subjugated knowledge of modernity and the spaces/times and future directions (capitalist telos) of postmodern history inside the Pacific.

Perhaps, at least in the dialogical genres of cultural criticism and the circuits of international literature, Chief Ka-lani-ōʻpuʻu and his courtly poets of the Hawaiian name chant can get another hearing of the little story by the big. Subjugated knowledges may be given a different hearing in the dialogical courts of postmodern justice, so to speak. For ours is an age that has grown incredulous of the domineering master narratives of dialectical progress via the will to negation, as well as the drive to speculative totality claiming view-from-nowhere universality, as Jean-François Lyotard claims in *The Postmodern Condition.* Such a theory of competing language games and suppressed (pagan) "driftings" beyond the philosophical rationales of the state can at least provide a space—or opening—where, against all the instrumentalized odds of the marketplace, the "little stories" of alternative mythology, unorthodox belief, indigenous knowing, and subaltern mapping can be given the *justice* of a renewed postmodern hearing.[57]

I have tried to counter the reigning *master narrative* of capitalist teleology and nature as real estate in the APEC-coded Pacific with another story: a *local story,* a little story with its own abiding claims to make on Pacific

56. Joseph Chang, "Pele in a Christian Court," *Hawaiʻi Review* 36 (1993): 42–55.

57. On master narratives of speculative knowledge and social liberation from superstitions and tyrannies of the past as these contend with subaltern local stories, see Jean-François Lyotard, *The Postmodern Condition: A Report on Knowledge,* trans. Geoff Bennington and Brian Massumi (Minneapolis: University of Minnesota Press, 1948); *The Differend: Phrases in Dispute,* trans. Georges Van Den Abbeele (Minneapolis: University of Minnesota Press, 1988); and Lyotard and Thebaud, *Just Gaming.*

identity and these Hawaiian harbors. If the indigenous volcano goddess of Pele goes on trial in the court system of the Big Island, she will always already lose to the powers and ruses of the state's geothermal lawyers, as the U.S. court cannot recognize another language and alternative language game—however compelling such a shark chant or Pele myth is to the Hawaiian community of believers, however continuous its genealogy down from the past and the cultural unconscious of its symbolic adherents who believe in and would still recognize the reality of its real estate claims. The stories do not match; the gods of Adam Smith and U.S. contract law have seemingly blown out the shark gods of King Kamehameha's terrible uncle.[58]

The U.S. court is not the *only* framework in which peoples and subjects of history can take possession of place and tell stories of the past. The shark god on trial in the U.S. system and hunted down by the Hawai'i State Task Force to mollify tourists loses, as does the volcano goddess Pele on the Big Island, because the belief system and modes of legitimated knowing are stacked against hearing another belief system, dealing with a different pragmatics, and understanding an alternative language game, such as the sacred poetry and wisdom of the shark hula.[59] *Postmodern*

58. American Congregationalist missionaries, from the time of their settlement under funding from the American Board of Commissioners for Foreign Missions in 1820, despised and denigrated Hawaiian hula as a form of cultural expression and "heathen" dance (in the words of Hiram Bingham) "designed to promote lasciviousness." As Mary Zwiep writes in *Pilgrim Path: The First Company of Women Missionaries to Hawaii* (Madison: University of Wisconsin Press, 1991), "Captain Vancouver [in 1794 in Waimea, O'ahu] objected when he watched a hula *mai*, traditionally composed to honor the genitals and reproductive power of a chief. But he was otherwise appreciative; the [American] missionaries condemned all the dances impartially" (164).

59. I do not want to sound too *fatalistic* about the capitalistic legal system of the white settler states in the decolonizing Pacific; in Australia, the *Mabo* High Court decision of June 1992 has powerful implications for the adjudication of aboriginal land claims and the potential redistribution of national/indigenous geography. See the special issue of *Race and Class* edited by Peter Poynton (April–June 1994). On the ongoing struggle by Native Hawaiians against the Shipman plantation estate to gain access to the site where hula is said to have originated on the Big Island, "where the goddess Pele turned hula dancer Hopoe into stone," see Ed Rampell, "Incident at Kea'au," *Honolulu Weekly* 8 (6– 12 May 1998): 6–8. In a related case of cultural-political struggle in the Pacific, Patricia Grace's novels, such as *Potiki* (Auckland: Penguin, 1986) and *Baby No-Eyes* (Honolulu: University of Hawai'i Press, 1998), record efforts by Maori people and lawyers to enter their oral stories and myths into law courts as evidence in disputed land cases in

justice demands that we try to hear something else besides the drone of contract law and the language games of transnational capital adjudicating the story of "corporate real estate" taking dominion over what a place-based Pacific community takes to be the real, the beautiful, and the good.

"bicultural" New Zealand. On ongoing land struggles among customary claims, zoning laws, and development interests, see Michael McPherson, *"Trustees of Hawaiian Affairs v. Yamasaki* and the Native Hawaiian Claim: Too Much of Nothing," *Environmental Law* 21 (1991): 453–97, and "Vanishing Sands: Comprehensive Planning and the Public Interest in Hawai'i," *Ecology Law Quarterly* 18 (1991): 779–844.

CHAPTER 7

Good-Bye Paradise:

Theorizing Place, Poetics, and Cultural Production

in the American Pacific

A frightening type of *papalagi* architecture is invading Oceania: the super-stainless, super-plastic, super-hygienic, super-soulless structure very similar to modern hospitals; and its most nightmarish form is the new-type tourist hotel—a multi-story edifice of concrete, steel, chromium and air-conditioning.
　　—Albert Wendt, "Towards a New Oceania"

(Ever wonder why there is a McKinley Street and a McKinley High School, but no Cleveland *anything* in Hawai'i?)
　　—H. K. Bruss Keppeler, "Native Hawaiian Claims"

Our visitors [tourists] come here with a perception of what Hawai'i is to them—Paradise.
　　—Visitors Experience Task Force, 1993 Tourism Congress[1]

CYBORGS ACROSS ASIA/PACIFIC?

Retoolings of neocapitalism as a global system, associated with the rise of postmodernism into cultural dominance and the mixed languages of postcolonial contentions, has been driven by various forces that, at a macro-

1. The first epigraph is taken from a key reassertion of Pacific regional identity against liberal modernity by the Samoan novelist Albert Wendt, reprinted in *Writers in East-West Encounter: New Cultural Bearings*, ed. Guy Amirthanayagam (London: Macmillan, 1982), 210. The second depends on the knowledge that U.S. President Grover Cleveland and his Blount Commission *opposed* and considered illegal the overthrow of Queen Lili'uokalani by an oligarchy of American businessmen in 1892, and is taken from the only article on cultural politics in *The Price of Paradise: Lucky We Live Hawaii?*, ed.

level of analysis, would include the following: a telecommunications revolution in media, globalization of production and rise of the transnational corporation as the locus of economic activity, and the change of the modernist nation-state from manipulator of internal conflict and territorial border keeping over NATO and the Pacific to just-in-time manager of what Kenichi Ohmae pronounces is a new "borderless interlinked economy."[2] Accelerated during the creative-destructive dynamics of the 1980s, cybernetic technologies and global modes of production/representation have generated what cultural critics and management gurus alike now recognize as "the globalization of capitalism" on a sweeping scale of global/local interaction that is the source "at once of unprecedented unity globally, and of unprecedented fragmentation."[3] These transformations, like some broken Bob Dylan record of *Blood on the Tracks*, run through this study as the material ground for theorizing local cultural production and a kind of place-based poetics in the American Pacific.

We are only beginning to come to terms with the postnational geopolitics and "transnational imaginary" of this global/local interface, the neolocalization of community and power into mobile forms of place-bound identity, and the consequences of what Arjun Appadurai has called "the global production of locality." The United States of America is a refiguring cold war nation in the last phases of military hegemony in the Pacific region, yet it spreads and struts, at times of APEC, across the Asia/Pacific ocean like some Old World (Fordist, military-industrialized) Godzilla rising from the nuclear waters.[4]

Randall W. Roth (Honolulu: Mutual, 1992), 198, which I use throughout this chapter to access the dominant discourse of Hawaiʻi-as-Pacific-paradise. The third expresses the position of the third tourism congress sponsored by the Hawaiʻi Department of Business, Economic Development and Tourism and is quoted in Stu Glauberman, "Tourism Congress to Seek Solutions," *Honolulu Advertiser*, 13 December 1993, C1.

2. Kenichi Ohmae, *The Borderless World: Power and Strategy in the Interlinked Economy* (New York: Harper, 1990).

3. In my reading of this global/local interface, I again draw on speculations of Arif Dirlik, who argues that "the transnationalization of production" has given us a capitalist postmodernity at once "of unprecedented unity globally, and of unprecedented fragmentation." See Arif Dirlik, *After the Revolution: Waking to Global Capitalism* (Middletown, CT: Wesleyan University Press, 1994), 50.

4. The local, as ground and space of cultural identity, is being integrated into—if at times remaining resistant to—global agents and forces across this new Pacific in ways that, I will claim, challenge and undermine the imagined community of the settler nation-state.

Given the rise of Asian/Pacific interzones, "global cities," and *global/ local* export zones fusing transnational technologies to local customs, as, for example, in the rearticulation of Confucian spiritualism to the labor of microchip production and fashion semiotics from Singapore to Taiwan and Seoul, or Masahiro Mori's *technoeuphoric* claim that cyborgs "have the buddha-nature within them,"[5] not to mention ongoing transformations of Asia-Pacific into a region of *dematerialized cyberspace* linking the coast of California to postmodern Hong Kong and Japan (as foreshadowed in transnational spectacles such as *Blade Runner*), Pacific Rim nations are tooled to play a vanguard part in this global/local restructuring and, in effect, are helping to disturb settler countries such as the United States, Canada, and Australia from narratives of national identity that would look back to Western-Europe-as-Old-World capitalism model. *Globloc* is the latest coinage in postmodern Japan; the permeability of any locale in the age of global economy makes for the world shopping mall culture of a consumption-oriented novel rooted in brand-glutted subjectivity, such as Banana Yoshimoto's *Kitchen* or Douglas Coupland's North American world drifters and global "mcjob" hunters in *Generation X*.

As one cultural premonition, recall that in Philip K. Dick's vision of San Francisco in the year 2018, *Do Androids Dream of Electric Sheep?* (1968), the Rosen Association, which engineers and produces the Nexus-6 android, has spread across the Pacific Coast of the United States to Russia, as well as to an offworld colony on Mars called New America. This trans-global corporation is so flexible and mobile in its high-tech feats of generating temporary contract cyborg labor that the transnational police forces of these city-states cannot prohibit (or even locate) them. If agency of production has been mystified, as in *Blade Runner,* the colonial dynamics of global capital remain all but intact: "Legally, the manufacturers of the Nexus-6 brain unit operated under colonial law, their parent autofactory being on Mars."[6] This Asia-Pacific, in other words, is located not so much offshore as *offworld*.

Rick Deckard's quest in Dick's novel to find and police the boundary between the human and technological subjectivity depends on his prior

5. Masahiro Mori, *The Buddha in the Robot: A Robot Engineer's Thoughts on Science and Religion* (Tokyo: Kosei, 1981), 13.
6. Philip K. Dick, *Blade Runner (Do Androids Dream of Electric Sheep?)* (New York: Ballantine, 1991), 24.

search to locate the agents, corporations, and instruments of global capital in its latest transnational and supralegal mode. These bioengineered cyborgs of the Asia/Pacific that Deckard searches for in the heart of late-capitalist desire would serve, as the TV ads for Rosen Inc. announce, to duplicate those "halcyon days of the pre–Civil War Southern states" as "body servants or tireless field hands." Short of this racial humiliation so dear to right-wing America, feminized cyborgs can be turned (like the Rachel Rosen prototype) into pleasure machines for scopophilic desire like so many postpastoral sheep chewing on the grasses in a transnational limbo.[7]

As John Naisbett and Patricia Aburdene hector the case for transnational coprosperity in *Megatrends 2000* while preparing the U.S. post–cold war imaginary for "the rise of the Pacific Rim" and strategies of compulsory globalization, "In the fast-paced Pacific Rim, the economic advantages belong to the swift."[8] Given capitalization of the Asian/Pacific local, power belongs to the conquest of space by time, dissolving the local into the movements of hypercapital and information highways across the Pacific. Commodity chains diffuse across regions and change nation and globe into a cybernetic matrix of speed and profit. Still, given this global restructuring of local spaces of identity and prior community, multiplex Pacific Basin cultures inside the Pacific Rim do not factor in as agents nor as locations of resistance so much as sites of tourist simulacrum and rest (or vacant spaces for weapons disposal) for Pacific Rim profit, image production, and pleasure. As postnational subject, Deckard moves from servomechanism of the American nation-state to become that diasporic new lackey, a Pacific Rim transnational agent.

Later down the superhighway toward *transnational postmodernity* and "jacking" himself into the disembodied rush of space-become-information-matrix, Deckard will be superseded by the cyborg cowboy, Case, in William Gibson's *Neuromancer,* another U.S. macho cyborg for whom the whole world has become a Chiba City of global information. Turning the American Pacific into dread-ridden cyberspace, Gibson's heroes of transnational expansionism can leap across the Oriental dangers of cybernetic infinitude, uncritically in the hire of an ever more dematerializing corpo-

7. Ibid., 14.
8. John Naisbitt and Patricia Aburdene, *Megatrends 2000: Ten New Directions for the 1990s* (New York: Avon, 1990), 198.

ration: "With his deck, [Case] could reach the Freeside decks as easily as he could reach Atlanta. Travel was a meat thing."[9] Labor is a *meat thing*, too, as feminist critics have shown of the transnational exploitation of women and poorer peoples that goes on in "peasant Asia" and the maquiladoras of Mexico. From Tokyo to the trans-American Sprawl, the North/South dynamic of the Pacific Rim (from one view in Vancouver) has all but dissolved into what Gibson has called "the bodiless exultation of cyberspace," as the wired-up cyborg promises to redeem the local Pacific from isolation if not the race and class contradictions of material history as in a new, post-U.S. transnational sublime.[10]

The neo-eclecticism of postmodern philosophies and tastes to consume and mimic cultural difference and nomadic flux—what James Clifford and others would now theorize and embrace as so many "discrepant cosmopolitanisms" routing and rerooting across spaces of local mixture[11]— cannot be dissociated from this by-now-advanced "eclecticism in labor practices" and an international division of labor such that sweatshops and family labor systems can coexist in the same urban space with spectacular telecommunications networks that would dematerialize local earth and sweatshop into the capitalist logic of time-as-money.[12] Clifford's invoca-

9. William Gibson, *Neuromancer* (New York: Ace, 1984), 77. On Japan as "panic" site of changed subjectivity (sublime cyborg), exotic othering, and dismantlement in the Pacific, see David Morley and Kevin Robins, "Techo-Orientalism: Futures, Foreigners and Phobias," *New Formations* 16 (1992): 136–56.

10. Gibson, *Neuromancer*, 6.

11. James Clifford, "Borders and Diasporas," unpublished lecture for Borders/Diasporas Conference, Center for Cultural Studies, University of California at Santa Cruz, 3–4 April 1992. Subsequent references to Clifford will be to this analysis, but also see "Traveling Cultures," in *Cultural Studies*, ed. Lawrence Grossberg, Cary Nelson, and Paula Treichler (New York: Routledge, 1992), where Clifford warns against a "local/ global dialectic [that may tip] a little too strongly towards 'external' (global) determinations" (100). For a mixed-blood poetics of "critical creolism" as a phenomenon of emergent "counternations" such as the Hopi Nation and the Chicano Southwest, see Keijiro Suga, "Critical Creolism Stands by Chicanos in Their Endless Journey from/to Aztlán," *Meli-Melo* no. 9 (1992): 98–108.

12. David Harvey, *The Condition of Postmodernity: An Inquiry into the Origins of Cultural Change* (Cambridge, MA: Blackwell, 1990), 187. Also see Harvey, "From Space to Place and Back Again: Reflections on the Condition of Postmodernity," and Mike Featherstone, "Global and Local Cultures," both in *Mapping the Futures: Local Cultures, Global Change*, ed. Jon Bird, Barry Curtis, Tim Putnam, George Robertson, and Lisa Tickner (London: Routledge, 1993).

tion of a "hybridity" discourse, which has all but achieved normative status in postcolonial studies, aims to articulate a third or *in-between* space of "borders/diasporas," such that modernist binary oppositions of global capital posed against local culture are resisted and represented even as to-and-fro transcultural flows are praised: "Too often we are left with an awkward gap between levels of analysis: generic global forces/specific local responses," as Clifford stages the opposition to resist any easy or tired binary of the colonized world system.

Riding some *diasporic* global/local interface of an ever creolizing cultural poetics emanating from the "Black Atlantic" to the frontier U.S.-Mexican border, Clifford would resist both a capitalist "globalism" that is self-defined as progressive and dynamic as well as any easy "localism" that remains too " 'rooted' (not routed) in place, tradition, culture, or ethnicity conceived in an absolutist mode." This latter warning against local entrenchment and in praise of global hybridity may, by now, give us regional pause, especially in an Asia/Pacific region where "cultural politics" and not just "global megatrends" would trouble the "postcolonial" horizon with alternative spaces and subaltern claims; aboriginal claims at the local level (resurgent in Hawai'i, Australia, Taiwan, and New Zealand, to be sure) can become subordinated, in such a "transcultural" analysis of the *ethnoscape,* to more flexible/impure/creolized articulations of transformation at the border. Without being romanticized or nativized in some quasi-fascist new way, the local needs to be worried into existence as the potential site of critical regionalism and what Raymond Williams called "the bond to place" as articulated ground of resistance to transnational capitalism.

The dynamism of capitalism as a global system has been tied to the plot of a technoeuphoric poetics of "creative destruction" in which, as Marx noted at the outset of technological modernity, "all that is solid melts into air" and those Chinese walls of tradition, region, and local identity are relentlessly battered down by commodity exchange, cultural interchange, and forces of technological innovation.[13] This bashing of the "Asiatic mode of production" and "neocapitalism" has reached such an advanced state within cultures of Pacific Rim capitalism, that Takayuki Tatsumi, reflecting

---

13. Karl Marx and Friedrich Engels, *The Communist Manifesto* (London: Penguin, 1967), 83–84: "In place of local and national seclusion and self-sufficiency, we have intercourse in every direction, universal inter-dependence of nations. And as in material, so in intellectual productions."

on the spread of cyberpunk culture across the region during the hyper-capitalist 1980s, can claim, in science fiction visions of global space in *Neuromancer* (1984) and *Mona Lisa Overdrive* (1988), that William Gibson circulated "the signifier of Japanese language—like 'Chiba City' or 'Gomi no Sensei'—as its 'semiotic ghost' " without ever having visited Japan it-self.[14] Gibson's "semio-tech" perception of some matrix of cybernetic in-finity from a transpacific Apple PC in Vancouver, Canada, has been able to feed back into formations of "Japanese postmodernism" itself to refashion local styles and techno-identity and to prefigure Japanese custom.[15]

Rim visions of "flexible labor production" and the global mishmash of styles spreading across the Asia/Pacific reaches a level of world intensity and global spectacle in Ridley Scott's *Blade Runner,* where the Babel-like Tyrell Corporation pyramid rises up out of the filthy Third World mix of Los Angeles streets to dominate all prior modes of production ("I just make eyes," says old Chun in his refrigerated sweatshop in late-capitalist Chinatown) and to intimidate urban subaltern agents ("He knows every-thing, he big genius"). Like some global-corporate version of William Blake's anti-God of British industrialization, Urizen, Tyrell reigns over space, time, capital, and body and enchains worker-subjects from a Tower of Babel looming over the mixed-race city.

Although, as Roy Baty, the Blakean-liberation cyborg confesses to Ty-rell, before bashing out the corporate head's eyes with de-oedipalizing glee, "You're a hard man to see." Today's grimy-chic "blade runner look" of postindustrial ruin and mixed-blood sublimity now rises, as in Los Angeles and Vancouver—fusing with Tokyo and Hong Kong into "the 'capital of capital' in the Pacific Rim"—and threatens to turn into the cultural dominant of contemporary urban design. The "look" resurfaces in Ridley Scott's *Black Rain* (1989) as the trademark postindustrial skies hovering over Osaka.[16] Given global technologies of representation and

14. Takayuki Tatsumi, "The Japanese Reflection of Mirrorshades," in *Storming the Reality Studio: A Casebook of Cyperpunk and Postmodern Fiction* (Durham, NC: Duke University Press, 1991), 367–72.

15. Japan's Ainu, needless to say, do not figure in these technoeuphoric visions of Japanese postmodern identity as cyborgian "technoscape," as the feminist fiction of Tsushima Yukio has recalled in uncanny fictional works of feminist subjectivity such as *Woman Running in the Mountains* (New York: Pantheon, 1991).

16. Edward Soja, *Postmodern Geographies: The Reassertion of Space in Critical Social Theory* (London: Verso, 1989), 192. On the "blade runner look," see Norman M. Klein,

image exchange, Hollywood can generate and control, in such blockbusters, emerging spaces and subjects of this Asian/Pacific transnational sublime as a space of sheer cultural immensity (Rim city gone offshore if not offworld) and of labor domination (the cyborg-human now starring as transnational subject).

Given modes of global production flowing into older spaces of local culture, as well as more hybrid confusions of technology and organic agent into "buddha-nature," then, the difficulty facing postmodern cultural production is the contemporary problematic of time-space *unrepresentability,* that is, the inability to map, recognize, or aesthetically represent even at a local level what Fredric Jameson calls our "whole world system of present-day multinational capitalism" as this "offshore" social totality impinges on disparate locales.[17] Because the local, refigured in disciplines from cultural geography to ethnography to urban studies as some innovative and mobile global/local interface, has to think and feel the power of global capitalism in its full spatiality, the aesthetics of region, place, and location are very much back on the postmodern agenda. "In clinging, often of necessity, to a place-bound identity, however," David Harvey warns within contexts of global/local marketing propagated by Kenichi Ohmae, Robert Reich, et al., "such oppositional movements become a part of the very fragmentation which a mobile capitalism and flexible accumulation can feed upon."[18] The reassertion and coalition-based construction of "place-bound identity," as I have detailed through a meandering focus on the Bamboo Ridge culture in Hawai'i, nonetheless has become crucial to the preservation of cultural difference for many locals given the spread of cyborgs across the Asia-Pacific zone. In the case of indigenous Hawai'i, this transnationalization of local space and identity threatens cultural sur-

---

"Building Blade Runner," *Social Text* 28 (1991): 147–52: "The film *Blade Runner* has achieved something rare in the history of cinema. It has become a paradigm for the future of cities, for artists across the disciplines" (148).

17. On this *sublime* problematic facing the postmodern subject as inability to grasp the "whole world system of present-day multinational capitalism," articulated through Jameson's "cognitive mapping" of cultural objects as well as the matrix-quests of cyberpunk science fiction, see Peter Fitting, "The Lessons of Cyberpunk," in *Technoculture,* ed. Constance Penley and Andrew Ross (Minneapolis: University of Minnesota Press, 1991), 310–11. See Fredric Jameson, *Postmodernism, or, The Cultural Logic of Late Capitalism* (Durham, NC: Duke University Press, 1992), 37.

18. Harvey, *The Condition of Postmodernity,* 303.

vival itself and puts their national struggles on tourist hold. But the anti-imperialist words of U.S. President Grover Cleveland, in his message to Congress on 12 December 1893, should not be dissolved into the magical waters of the transnational Pacific: "By an act of war, committed with the participation of a diplomatic representative of the United States and without authority of Congress, the Government of a feeble but friendly and confiding people has been overthrown. A substantial wrong has thus been done which a due regard for our national character as well as the rights of the injured people [Native Hawaiians] requires we should endeavor to repair."[19]

DISLOCATING "PARADISE" IN THE AMERICAN PACIFIC

Expressed against the onslaught of these transnational technologies of late-capitalist spectacle, local orientations have reasserted themselves at least since the mid-1970s in Hawai'i, despite the fact (as Noel Kent has observed) that any such " 'localism' is all too easily equated with parochialism in this metropolitan age."[20] Paradoxically, the most local works of postmodern cultural production in Hawai'i are already affected if not *invaded* (to use the novelist Albert Wendt's anticolonial verb from "Towards a New Oceania" to resist the disruptive effect of hotel-style architecture

19. On the Apology Bill of U.S. President Bill Clinton and a Joint Resolution of the One Hundred and Third Congress on 17 January 1993 and relevant documents by Cleveland and others from 1893, see Richard J. Scudder, ed., *The Apology to Native Hawaiians on Behalf of the United States for the Overthrow of the Kingdom of Hawai'i* (Honolulu: Ka'ilimi Pono Press, 1994). Because of this U.S. Apology Bill and mounting historical evidence of injustice, a United Nations report filed in Geneva on 30 July 1998 recommends that Hawai'i be returned to the UN's list of "non-self-governing territories," and thus be eligible for "decolonization" and a UN-sponsored plebiscite to redetermine its political form. For a U.S.-centered state reaction to this, see "U.N. Can't Nullify Hawaii's Annexation," editorial, *Honolulu Star-Bulletin*, 12 August 1998. On 12 August 1998, over five hundred Hawaiians raised the Hawaiian national flag over Iolani Palace to the sounds of Queen Lili'uokalani's anthem "Hawai'i Pono'i" to protest and "denounce 100 years of U.S. control over these tropical islands"; see "Hawaiians Gather to Protest U.S. Annexation," *Los Angeles Times*, 13 August 1998.
20. Noel Kent, "To Challenge Colonial Structures and Preserve the Integrity of Place: The Unique Potential Role of the University," in *Restructuring for Ethnic Peace: A Public Debate at the University of Hawai'i*, ed. Majid Tehranian (Honolulu: Spark M. Matsunaga Institute for Peace, 1991), 119. For a related analysis, see Eric Yamamoto, "The Significance of Local," *Social Process in Hawai'i* 27 (1990): 12–19.

on the "faa Samoa" in Western Samoa) by this global problematic; the global/local interface remains a predicament Pacific authors have to work through in order to affirm some enclave of "local culture."

This has most strongly been the case, as we have seen, with the emergence of the "local literature" movement at Bamboo Ridge journal and press, which, since its founding in Honolulu in 1978, has resisted the metropolitan assumption that writers in Hawai'i "are subordinate to the mainland" or the national belief that "we [in Hawai'i] are really no different here and can even be *like* the mainland if we try hard enough," as the local poet Eric Chock remarked.[21] It is within these contexts of "global localism" that I will discuss the local culture articulated in the movie *Good-Bye Paradise* (1991), which, not surprisingly given Hawai'i's *peripheralization* to the Pacific Rim economy of California since the 1850s and into the era of tourist simulacrum, is the first feature-length movie to be produced entirely in Hawai'i.[22] Kayo Hatta's *Picture Bride* (1994), set in the troubled ethnic plantation culture of Waialua Sugar Company in 1915, is only the second locally produced independent feature film to be made in Hawai'i; combining the work of Asian American artists with such transnational superstars as Toshiro Mifune from *Black Rain, Picture Bride* explores the ethnic markings, discrepancies, and tensions of local culture in Hawai'i from the point of view of a localizing (and Americanizing) Japanese woman named Riyo, who breaks her ties to Japan, touches upon shores of indigenous culture, and becomes a local mother caring for her future generation of children on O'ahu. Hawaiian cinema still has to be invented, from such subaltern points of view. For, as Ackbar Abbas has remarked of postcolonial Hong Kong cinema in the 1990s, caught up in the tensions, disappearances, and paradoxes of globalization in an Asia/Pacific island space, such cinematic practices of a "new localism" have to forge images and terms by which to investigate "the dislocations of the local, where the

21. Eric Chock, "On Local Literature," in *The Best of Bamboo Ridge,* ed. Eric Chock and Darrell H. Y. Lum (Honolulu: Bamboo Ridge Press, 1986), 8.

22. See Philip Damon's review, "Appealing 'Paradise' Goes Far Beyond Its Island Home," *Honolulu Advertiser,* 29 May 1992, C2. "Peripheralization" implies the (ongoing) global process of uneven geographical development; see Gareth Evans and Tara McPherson, *Watch This Space: An Interview with Edward Soja,* working paper no. 9, 1990–1991, Center for Twentieth Century Studies, University of Wisconsin at Milwaukee.

local is something unstable that mutates right in front of our eyes, like the language itself."[23]

Good-Bye Paradise, even in its sad little title, recalls earlier fall-from-Eden narratives of Hawai'i as a lingering Asian/Pacific paradise in the South Seas. These tropes of gardenlike embodiment in the forever-out-of-history Pacific retain material legitimacy in the postmodern American imagination even while prior master narratives of the United States as "utopia achieved" bite the deregulated dust of late-capitalist expansion.[24] Paul Theroux, wandering as voraciously as Henry Adams across the Pacific (his "happy isles of Oceania" real estate) in an inflatable kayak with a stack of late-imperial Euro-American texts, broken male heart, and dog-eared copy of *Sexual Life of Savages,* does not find "the happy isles of Oceania" he craves until he is back in his comfortable home in Honolulu. "It often seemed to me that calling the Hawaiian Islands 'paradise' was not an exaggeration, though saying it out loud, advertising it, seemed to be tempting fate," Theroux confesses, just before ending his tourist romance-quest for Pacific paradise in the $2,500-a-night Orchid Bungalow at the Mauna Lani paid for by the tourist industry.[25] Hawai'i novelist Armine von Tempski put

23. Ackbar Abbas, *Hong Kong: Culture and the Politics of Disappearance* (Minneapolis: University of Minnesota Press, 1997). Films such as Wong Kar-wai's *Chungking Express* (1994) have been exemplary in this respect, finding spatial and temporal "practices of the image" by which to capture the global and local dynamics (and romances) of one little food stand in Hong Kong. On the ongoing attempt at "writing Hong Kong" in a literature expressive of the local and banal and antimonumental, see Abbas, chap. 6: "addressing the local, which is one of the most distinctive signs of writing Hong Kong" today (112).

24. Jean Baudrillard traverses the freeways, deserts, and commercialized simulacra of America as some neoprimitive "utopia achieved" in *America,* trans. Chris Turner (London: Verso, 1988). For postnational movements in the USA that would "expose national identity as an artifact rather than a tacit assumption" of homogeneity within the American imaginary, see Donald Pease, ed., *New Americanists 2: National Identities and Postnational Narratives,* special issue of *boundary 2* 19 (1992).

25. Paul Theroux, *The Happy Isles of Oceania: Paddling the Pacific* (New York: Putnam, 1992), 482. For a polemic against U.S. neo-imperial attitudes toward Pacific peoples, see Rob Wilson, "Paul Theroux's Venomous Views," *Honolulu Advertiser,* 8 January 1994, which resulted in a small storm of controversy and several defenses from tourist industry employees (including the Hawai'i coffee-table book writer Jocelyn Fujii) of Theroux's Pacific writings in *Happy Isles* as "honest," "truthful," and "accurate" representations of the Pacific.

this claim for paradise in the American Pacific even more ostentatiously, as befits the granddaughter of Polish nobility and heir to a sixty-thousand-acre Haleakalā Ranch on Maui; as she writes in her 1940 autobiography, *Born in Paradise*, "Attaining Paradise in the hereafter does not concern me greatly. I was born in Paradise."[26]

Not to be outdone by von Tempski's materialization of literary-biblical trope of paradise as a chunk of Americanized real estate in the Pacific, the interdisciplinary team of legal, social, and economic policy theorists charting the materials costs of inhabiting the contemporary state of Hawai'i, in the cost-benefit analysis *The Price of Paradise: Lucky We Live Hawaii?*, along with Sumner J. La Croix do answer a qualified yes to affirming life in this tax-ridden "Eden." La Croix, a professor of economics at the University of Hawai'i at Mānoa, assesses (in this local best-seller) that, despite the highest housing and cost of living expenses in the USA, Honolulu has clean air, clean water, warm winters and moderate summers, beautiful forests and mountains, spectacular views, a culturally diverse ethnic population tied into Asian and Pacific culture, good food, and a varied night life. He proudly concludes, "No place is right for everyone but, aside from the high cost of living, Hawai'i is most people's idea of paradise."[27] *Most people's idea of paradise,* unless you are a sovereignty-seeking Native Hawaiian whose culture has been transformed into tourist simulacra and whose land has been alienated into military and state profit and for whom the struggle for national sovereignty is gathering juropolitical force.

Can "Paradise" be recuperated and natives pacified in the ecotourism of the American Pacific, even in a cost-benefit analysis? Yes, claims the U.S. tourist-knowledge apparatus of *The Price of Paradise*, "as long as Honolulu retains its unique beauty, environment and cultural attractions"[28] and local citizens can endure a tourist-driven economy in which "we get less for more," as runs the general market refrain in that book.[29] "Paradise," despite threats of overgovernment and international flux and tourist stagnation, is here—if only as a lurking regional trope—to stay.

Eric Chock has titled one of his well-respected Bamboo Ridge Press

---

26. Quoted in Stephen H. Sumida, *And the View from the Shore: Literary Traditions of Hawai'i* (Seattle: University of Washington Press, 1991), 91.

27. Sumner J. La Croix, "Cost of Housing," in *The Price of Paradise*, 136.

28. Ibid., 138.

29. Michael A. Sklarz, "High Rents," in *The Price of Paradise*, 144.

collections *Last Days Here* to suggest the imminent phasing out of local Hawaiian culture, language, and customary difference in and around Honolulu's Chinatown. If certain ties to place-bound identity and community are strong, as in mixed-ethnic poems such as "Tutu on Da Curb" ("Her hair all pin up in one bun, / one huge red hibiscus hanging out / over her right ear") or "Chinese Fireworks Banned in Hawai'i" ("cousins eat jook from the huge vat / in the kitchen"), Chock's title poem to his Pacific-local-oriented collection more ominously shows a fished-out and polluted river near Honolulu Chinatown, where an old Chinese man fishes if only to keep his old customs and preserve his ghostly memories of place and keep local identity intact:

> The empty bucket stares a moment
> toward his brain, so he closes
> the closet door, hums
> the ashes off his cigar,
> and goes in to dinner.
> He will never forget his days here
> In the dirt under the mango tree
> prints of chicken feet
> go every which way[30]

Given such costs of social displacement and downsizing, "Paradise" (minus the chicken prints, ethnic smells, rotting tilapia, and sulking Hawaiian natives) remains a white mythological trope by which to integrate Hawai'i into the transnational tourist flow. Paradise tropes and images belatedly project a U.S. vacation space of Pacific culture that, despite much evidence to the contrary (such as the American-backed overthrow of the Hawaiian monarchy in 1893), must remain outside the workaday labors of Euro-American history. Can "Paradise" ever write back to challenge the fantasies of this American empire? One of Stephen Sumida's strongest claims about the local literature movement in Hawai'i that has flourished since the late Talk Story conferences of 1978 and 1979 is that, by resisting the sway of U.S. national culture, "the facile image of Ha-

---

30. Eric Chock, "Last Days Here," in *Last Days Here* (Honolulu: Bamboo Ridge Press, 1989), 71. On Chock's Pacific localism and innovative use of pidgin (Hawaiian Creole English) in his poetry, see Gayle K. Fujita Sato, "The Island Influence on Chinese American Authors: Wing Tek Lum, Darrell H. Y. Lum, and Eric Chock," *Amerasia* 6 (1990): 17–35.

wai'i's as paradise, everywhere associated with pop literature, music, film, and travel poster-graphics of Hawai'i, is contradicted by nonfiction and fictional works [of local literature such as Milton Murayama's *All I Asking for Is My Body*] that may serve as prototypes in the development of Hawai'i's literature beyond the simple pastoral."[31] Circulated through the pastoral haze of national authors such as Twain, London, and Michener and rehashed as popular culture, "the facile image of Hawai'i as paradise" has been challenged as dehistoricizing fantasy expanding its hegemonic terrain and telos of development-driven prosperity—at whatever cost to indigenous or local culture—into the Asian/Pacific.

During this process of tourism-driven transnationalization, the island of Maui risks becoming a suburb for Hollywood scriptwriters; post-hurricane Kaua'i is doing everything it can to attract more Steven Spielbergs to come over from the Rim, film more *Jurassic Park*s, and turn the wilderness and ecohistory of Hawai'i into a theme park; and the backside of Diamond Head on O'ahu has been reconstructed by the Waihe'e and Cayetano administrations into a state-funded film studio. But this self-orientalizing production of Hawai'i into a "paradise of the Pacific" needs to be placed in politicized quotation marks and undermined as a trope of the dominant discourse helping to naturalize the American idea of the Pacific as a dreamspace both within and outside (as oriental other) the dynamic workings of national/transnational capital in its globalizing outreach.

Crucial to the entry of the state of California if not the Pacific Northwest into the dynamism of the world system as located in the Pacific Rim in 1848 was communication with, labor from, and representation of Hawai'i. In brief, Hawai'i served as the mediating space in the creation of an "American Pacific," transmitting the cheap labor and abundant resources of the Asian/Pacific region to mainland America via the West Coast. As mediating link to the markets of Canton, the whaling waters off Japan, and the furs of Alaska, Hawai'i was linked within seventy years (from the arrival of New England Calvinist missionaries in 1820 to the overthrow of the Hawaiian monarchy in 1893) to American national self-interests. As I

31. Sumida, *And the View from the Shore,* 38. On the complex cultural-political vision in Murayama's novel, see Rob Wilson, "The Languages of Confinement and Liberation in Milton Murayama's *All I Asking for Is My Body,*" in *Writers of Hawaii: A Focus on Our Literary Heritage,* ed. Eric Chock and Jody Manabe (Honolulu: Bamboo Ridge Press, 1981), 62–65.

have claimed (see chapter 3), the twin strategies of discourse (apparent in the Sacramento journalism of Mark Twain) developed during the course of the nineteenth-century process of modernization on the American capitalist-democracy model: *commercialization* via the imposition of the plantation economy and all but total alienation of native lands by 1848, and *pastoralization* into a Pacific "paradise" outside of Euro-American time and space, that is, outside the dynamism of history.

The space of Hawai'i could be said to lead American patriots and citizens, as in James Jones's novelistic metaphor, *from here* (plantations, racial troubles, military battles) *to eternity* (paradise as a multicultural fusion in the Asian/Pacific little bars and dance clubs of River Street).[32] As American outpost into the Asia/Pacific at Pearl Harbor since the early 1880s, the space of Hawai'i had to be linked to economic domination and military surveillance and yet preserved, by sublimating tropes of heaven-on-earth as a region of fantasy (*Fantasy Island* was restaged for a new TV series set on Maui in 1998) immune to destruction and ecological damage. Hawai'i must remain what Twain rhetorically boasted (in what became a key line for the tourist industry) were "the loveliest fleet of islands that lies anchored in any ocean."[33]

GOOD-BYE PARADISE AS GLOBAL/LOCAL COMMUNITY

Good-bye Paradise, produced and directed by Dennis Christianson and Tim Swage (released by Pacific Focus Inc./Axelia Pictures International, 1991), made its premiere at the International Film Festival at the East-West Center in Hawai'i that features Asian/Pacific films. This movie portrays the upscale gentrification of Honolulu Chinatown as represented through the closing of an old bar, called the Paradise Inn, and its abrupt transformation

32. James Jones's World War II novel *From Here to Eternity* became an Academy Award–winning movie in 1953, with outdoor shots of Schofield Barracks, Kuhio Beach, Halona Cave, and Waialae Golf Course, though the multiculturalism of Hotel and River Streets was filmed in Hollywood and "faked"; see Robert C. Schmitt, *Hawai'i in the Movies, 1898–1959* (Honolulu: Hawaiian Historical Society, 1988), 60–62.
33. Mark Twain, *Letters from Hawaii*, ed. A. Grove Day (Honolulu: University of Hawai'i Press, 1975), vi. See Sumida, *And the View from the Shore*, 38–56, on Twain's troubled vision of a race- and class-divided "Pacific paradise"; and Susan Gillman, "Mark Twain in Context," in *Dark Twins: Imposture and Identity in Mark Twain's America* (Berkeley: University of California Press, 1989), on U.S. race anxieties.

by Pacific Rim management into Katrina's in Chinatown. Focusing on the last Saturday in the business life of this multiethnic bar and a small upstairs business complex operating since the 1930s, the film traces the uneasy conversion into a site for the consumption of "California cuisine" and an upscale art gallery. The half-million-dollar movie thus traces, on a small and contradictory scale of place-bound sentimentality to be sure, the threatened fate of Hawai'i's local culture/literature/film within a global context of cultural reinvention and economic displacement.

Through the yuppie gaze of the Chinese American owner of the Paradise Inn bar, John Young, for whom "public opinion is a commodity you buy and sell like anything else," *Good-bye Paradise* shows that the Hawaiian local must put itself on the pathways of transnational capital to prosper, as is clear in a tourist-driven economy where more visitors mean surplus value for everybody from university professors to hotel busboys since the "jumbo jet age and mass tourism" came to Hawai'i in 1970 and boomed into a global/local necessity even as the poetics of place began to be reconstituted into an "ex-primitive" or user-friendly tourist landscape.[34]

This process of global modernization has already become a recognizably postmodern process of mimicking, simulating, and in effect uneasily displacing local style and indigenous customs, as in the commercially transformed hula of the Kodak Hula Show or the Mormon-sponsored performance of South Pacific cultures as Hawaiian at the Polynesian Cul-

34. James Mak and Marcia Sakai, "Tourism in Hawai'i: Economic Issues for the 1990's and Beyond," in *Politics and Public Policy in Hawai'i*, ed. Zachary A. Smith and Richard C. Pratt (Albany: State University of New York Press, 1992), 187. On any day, there are some 170,000 tourists in Hawai'i: "In 1989, nearly 6.6 million tourists visited" (193), a figure subject to fluctuations in the economies of the United States, Japan, and Europe. Given intensified global flows, the authors accurately note that "in recent years, there is a growing local resentment against nonresident ownership of hotels, golf courses, residential real estate, and other real assets" (193). On this issue of global tourist culture and Pacific accommodations and indigenous resistance, from the Polynesian Cultural Center to IMAX, see Andrew Ross, "Cultural Preservation in the Polynesia of the Latter-Day Saints," in *The Chicago Gangster Theory of Life* (London: Verso, 1994). For a Native Hawaiian view tied to Polynesian models of space, time, and identity and yet sympathetic to cultural tourism in the globalizing Pacific, see George Kanahele, "Tourism: Keeper of the Culture," in *Ecotourism: Business in the Pacific Promotes a Sustainable Experience*, conference proceedings, ed. John E. Hay (University of Auckland and East-West Center, Honolulu, 1992), 30–34; and George Kanahele, *Kū Kanaka, Stand Tall: A Search for Hawaiian Values* (Honolulu: University of Hawai'i Press, 1986).

tural Center: "See all of Polynesia! All in one place!" proclaims one of their sweeping 1993 ecotourist center advertisements. Inputs from global culture, technologies of the video image from Betamax to IMAX, and commodity forms would disrupt (and enlist) the mixed community of locals who once took care of one another during the postwar era (oversentimentalized in the film through the pidgin-speaking pathos of Pat Morita, playing Ben, a former pineapple cannery worker turned street person and drunk).

Locals and locales, such as those around Honolulu's Chinatown (or Hawaiian communities such as Waianae on the leeward coast of Oʻahu), are confronting the transformation of the Pacific region into the site of a simulated transnational ethnicity that goes under the user-friendly rubrics "ecotourism" or "cultural tourism." As Haunani-Kay Trask argues this binary anticolonial scenario, while eloquently defending resurgent claims of the Hawaiian sovereignty struggle one hundred years after the McKinley-endorsed American annexation of the native kingdom and land by imperial logic: "Burdened with commodification of their culture and exploitation of their people, Hawaiians exist in an occupied country where hostage people are forced to witness (and, for many, to participate in) their own collective humiliation as tourist artifacts for the First World."[35]

Indigenous Hawaiians (20 percent of Hawaiʻi's population, by the most expansive count of mixed-blood quantum) do not necessarily want to be absorbed into the great American multiculture, as Trask has argued of the *kanaka maoli* (people of the land) and, in fact, are forging a strong Pacific version of cultural nationalism tied to the preserving of language, custom, and land. Big Sharon, the big-hearted Hawaiian waitress in *Good-bye Paradise,* nostalgically dances with Joe and Tiny to the awesome Gabby Pahanui's slack-key "Moonlight Lady" to signify the threat of global foreclosure from the Pacific Rim to the multiethnic proletarian culture in Hawaiʻi of those "who work in the fields by day" and would still party in the Paradise Inn at night.

Good-bye Paradise warns that the ethos of contemporary tourist-driven Hawaiʻi (as the hospital warns Joe, who gets behind on his payments for Ben) has become one of "just doing business" and following the economic

35. Haunani-Kay Trask, "*Kūpaʻa ʻĀina* (Hold fast to the land): Native Hawaiian Nationalism in Hawaiʻi," in *Politics and Public Policy in Hawaiʻi,* ed. Zachary A. Smith and Richard C. Pratt (Albany: State University of New York Press, 1992), 246.

mandates of turning place into space and both into accumulated powers of time and money. (As Hawai'i property law expert David Callies glibly claims of the resort takeover of local landscapes, "Golf courses tend to be good neighbors," whatever the shape or size of the water-drained neighborhood that is left.)[36] As the movie in its nonglamorous style intimates— the constrained image scheme and image practice recalling in a lesser key Nagisa Oshima's refusal to use the color green or "characters sitting and talking on *tatami*"—"Paradise" seen as a Pacific space and location of Hawaiian culture may be phased out piece by piece, neighborhood by neighborhood, in the name of California cuisine and the rise of transpacific profits.

In a contentious narrative twist, the agent of change in *Good-bye Paradise* is no global outsider from Japan or Hong Kong (as in the reiterative orientalism of TV's *Raven* series, with its endless supply of inscrutable Yakuza, Samoan bouncers, and slimy Japanese businessmen invading a calmly photogenic Hawai'i), but the yuppie architect son of the owner, Waichee Young, who as a second-generation Chinese worked his way up from his father's plantation life on Maui to owning business and real estate in Honolulu. This older Mr. Young hovers over the movie like a genius loci, his calming voice-over of decency and paternalistic good cheer recalling the haole bar manager, Joe Martin, to an ethic of care, compassion, and humor that his architect son is helping to phase out. Transnational capitalism of the "Pacific Rim cuisine" variety demands that proponents and agents express the TNC-class interests, and here a local Chinese rises to fill the role.

This Asian American MBA-wielding son, John Young, has married a vulgar capitalist haole from California (who, in true postmodern intertextual fashion, looks and acts like the Ivana Trump of Chinatown), who embodies a cool blonde style of selfishness and profit and local indifference. She feels no ties to the old compassionate ethic and community loyalty to the locale that his father felt for his workers and tenants: a local multiculture comprised of Cook, the thrifty and scurrilous Chinese who plans to open his own Thai restaurant ("It's just Chinese food with peanut sauce and curry"); Tiny, the huge Hawaiian with a heart of gold and scraps of Hawaiian wisdom about mahus and the moon; Big Sharon, Little

36. David L. Callies, "Development Fees," in *The Price of Paradise*, 170.

Sharon, Billy, even Lieutenant Nomura; and Evelyn and Elmira Lymon, the old Catholic sisters who are coolly being evicted.

The Chinatown neighborhood around the Paradise Inn, personifying the mix and endurance of local identity, "has survived disease, fire, war, and even tourism," as old Mr. Young quips, but the attack of California cuisine on local favorites like Spam masubi seems ever more dangerous to the fate of Hawaiian hybrid/indigenous identity. The movie is thus riddled with a recognizably postmodern nostalgia for what David Harvey calls (after the affirmative rearguard "critical regionality" theorized by British architect Kenneth Frampton) cultivating and amassing the oppositional force of a "place-bound identity."[37] Tiny's affirmation of Hawaiian local identity as the upbeat (essentialist) claim that "Chinatown is always going to be Chinatown, Joe," does not match the global/local circumstances, nor does Joe's one-man charity organization to expend a thousand points of socialist-Christian light on Hotel Street. Even nostalgia must have some critical edge to it, becoming grounded and politicized as a mobilizing vision of place.

Given an economy in which it costs 34 percent more to live than on the mainland and in which state and local government collect 30 percent more taxes per person than the U.S. average, the movie is correct to suggest that one tends by economic necessity (as much as by local tradition) to build an ʻohana (extended family) of mothers, fathers, uncles, aunts, grandparents, friends, "or other reluctant but cooperative souls" in order to survive.[38] This results in a watered-down parody of residual Hawaiian values in

37. Kenneth Frampton, "Towards a Critical Regionalism: Six Points for an Architecture of Resistance," in *The Anti-Aesthetic,* ed. Hal Foster (Port Townsend, WA: Bay Press, 1983), 16–30; and Kenneth Frampton, "Place-Form and Cultural Identity," in *Design after Modernism: Beyond the Object,* ed. John Thackara (London: Thames and Hudson, 1988), 51–66. David Harvey, *The Condition of Postmodernity,* 303.

38. Leroy O. Laney, "Cost of Living," in *The Price of Paradise,* 29. It is worth recalling the argument of Raymond Williams, who saw "bonds to place" increasingly serving as a local strategy of transnational resistance given the new international division of labor and production: "But *place* has been shown to be a crucial element in the bonding process—more so perhaps for the working class than the capital-owning classes—by the explosion of the international economy and the destructive effects of deindustrialization upon old communities. When capital has moved on, the importance of place is more clearly revealed." See "Decentralism and the Politics of Place," in *Resources of Hope: Culture, Democracy, Socialism,* ed. Robin Glade (London: Verso, 1989), 242.

Good-bye Paradise, here captured through the hearts of gold in Tiny (a huge Hawaiian bouncer) and Billy (the half-Hawaiian, half-Chinese bartender), who finally, with saintly Joe, decides to "stay in the neighborhood" for food and bonds of local affection after the bar is closed.

Transnational tourism has become the "primary export" of Hawai'i (like the casino economy of Nevada)[39] and, in this process of liberal-consensual displacement, the state's natural beauty and landscape sublimity has seemingly been changed into its primary "asset."[40] The language of Pacific Rim economism can conclude that supply-and-demand dynamics will keep the cost of living in Hawai'i high but the standard of living "admirable." Still, the claustrophobic and semi-impoverished spaces of Honolulu Chinatown cannot compete with the scenic and sensual allure of hotel-heaven Waikīkī or the "fearful beauty" of the wilderness in Hawai'i Volcanoes National Park. To invoke the panjudgmental "tourist gaze" of Paul Theroux, in its full orientalist and exotic splendor, "The two most obvious facts of Hawai'i are the huge sluttish pleasures of its Nipponized beachfront hotels and, in great contrast, its rugged landscape of craggy volcanoes and its coastal headlands."[41]

Hawaiian nationalism, in such a calculus, is never even mentioned as a real or emergent threat to tourist reveries of a native-emptied resort or volcano. Cultural nationalism in the new Pacific cannot be marketed as ex-primitive tourist delight—at least not yet.

In a theme that resonates with social dynamics driving the contemporary "local literature" movement in Hawai'i, *Good-bye Paradise* helps show (through the synecdochic allegory of the bar as space of local culture) that a once pastoral ethic of mutual care and multicultural unity in Hawai'i is fast giving way in contemporary Honolulu to an ethic of profiteering and a fake, delocalizing style of image- and self-promotion. If, in the imaginary polity of *Good-bye Paradise,* this restructuring hurts the old residents and scrappy citizens like old Ben and the white Christian ladies who have

39. James Mak, "Tourist Taxes," in *The Price of Paradise,* 97.
40. David McClain, "Hawai'i's Competitiveness," in *The Price of Paradise,* 10.
41. Theroux, *The Happy Isles of Oceania,* 473. On the British lineage of Theroux's "tourist gaze" that prefers the emptiness of wilderness scenery to the turmoil of history, see John Urry, *The Tourist Gaze: Leisure and Travel in Contemporary Societies* (London: Sage, 1990): "Travel [remains] the marker of status" (5), and *disgust* toward Pacific natives (especially Melanesian peoples and Samoans) functions as his sign of a globally threatened late-imperial superiority.

dwelled over the bar, the costs to indigenous Hawaiians are barely measured. Local TV news celebrity Joe Moore plays (and, saintlike, overplays)
bar manager Joe Martin, who holds onto a Christian socialist ethic of
neighborhood care and concern (*aloha spirit* affirmed as local core) like
that of the old Mr. Young, who had years ago taken him in as a stepson
after his dog soldier days in Vietnam landed him across the Pacific in
Hawai'i—feeding stray cats, sending drunks home in taxi cabs, caring for
street people and the elderly. Although *Good-bye Paradise* gets excessively
sentimental through Moore's unselfish unconcern for money and waxes
nostalgic for the multiethnic *all-in-the-'ohana* Hawaiian way of life in old
Honolulu that is being phased out from the inside by transnational transformations of the inner city into upscale real estate, it does show the
process and cost of cultural displacement at work in downtown Honolulu.

   Good-bye Paradise, humorously by turns, reveals the creolized community that has come about over years of coexisting on the plantation as in
the bar, mixing Chinese cook, Hawaiian bouncer, Chinese owner, Japanese cop, white manager, and half-Chinese, half-Hawaiian hostess with incoming haole waitress from the American South even as this local community is now being disrupted, phased out, molested from local space.
Threatened is that very complex of Hawaiian values, still much touted at
the core of local culture, called *aloha 'āina* (love of the land), which, even
transformed from its agricultural origins in taro farming, implies (in
Sumida's multicultural rephrasing) "symbols and metaphors integral to
the Hawaiian language [and that] bind love of the land (i.e., if you love and
cultivate the land, the land will return by feeding you), family, sustenance,
and culture itself into a rich complex of values—values involving reciprocity among people and between people and nature."[42]

   Like the starry-eyed localist hero Ben Knox, who squats on the Scottish
beach in Bill Forsyth's *Local Hero* (1983) and muses on how to resist the
encroachment of an oil refinery from Texas and Aberdeen on the community at Furness Bay, Joe Moore, local news anchor, plays *local hero* of a
resistant multiculture and agent of this uncanny *aloha spirit* of "reciprocity

42. Sumida, *And the View from the Shore*, 108. For a finely theorized place-based treat-
ment of Asian-Pacific American identity in Hawai'i, see Stephen H. Sumida, "Sense of
Place, History, and the Concept of the 'Local' in Hawai'i's Asian/Pacific Literatures," in
Reading the Literatures of Asian America, ed. Shirley Geok-lin Lim and Amy Ling (Philadelphia: Temple University Press, 1992), 215–37.

among people." Martin labors to build up and preserve local charms and local mores from the damages of historical molestation and that American commonsense narrative called "progress." That this localized and working-class haole who came to Hawai'i by way of Vietnam, across Asian/Pacific space, loses politically but gains a moral-sentimental victory of love over time and money offers little consolation. Two capitalist ethics here compete, a paternal national one and a more brutally transnational one; the former wins only at the symbolic level as the bar gets closed and is redone into California cuisine art. Both *repress* the presence of the Hawaiian sovereignty movement that is refusing such accommodations to state-driven future planners and economist knowledge-workers from the University of Hawai'i calculating their own "price of paradise."

At least since 1988, it has become apparent that the majority of Hawai'i's multicultural citizens have opposed the influx of overblown foreign investment in general, and Japanese investment in particular.[43] Almost two-thirds of the hotel rooms in the state are owned by foreign investors, especially Japanese, so this retrenchment in the local economy and place can be read as a reaction to the makings a borderless transnational economy that peaked across the decade of the 1980s and is dismantling place and culture of the very distinctiveness that makes Hawai'i attractive. This new Pacific of hotel resorts and microchip factories is the dream of the Pacific Rim, the paradise of APEC. But the loss of land and property imparts a sense of lost control and cultural displacement from Honolulu to Vancouver and works to dismantle dreams of home ownership; even the former governor of Hawai'i (a Hawaiian by blood) recognizes this.

Yet the postmodern context of hypercapital mobility is such that the local is affected by the invasion and retreat of global capital, in this instance the very mobility of the Japanese yen in foreign real estate markets such as upscale Kahala or Indonesian capital from the transnational big spender, Sukarman Sukamto, developing place into capitalized space at "Landmark Waikīkī."[44] The local is driven up, down, and out by fluctuations in the

---

43. James Mak and Marcia Y. Sakai, "Foreign Investment," in *The Price of Paradise*, 33.
44. Ibid., 36. Throughout 1993, the Indonesian national Sukarman Sukamto became the focus of local controversy concerning the site, form, and funding of a Hawaiian Convention Center, which he wanted to place on the Aloha Motors site along with an array of resort hotels and shops to be owned and run by his Indonesian conglomerate. Other "local" holdings of Sukamto include the Waikīkī Landmark luxury condominium adjacent to the convention center property (which he sold to the state for $136 million in

global financial system, as neighborhoods such as Kahala in Honolulu experience the influx and out-flight of Tokyo yen given the dynamics of repatriated capital that burst in 1991. "Local assets," in what seems to be the makings of a deregulated global economy reorganized and energized around the Pacific Rim from NAFTA to APEC, are threatened by capital from Japan, Australia, Taiwan, Canada, and California. Much like a country or a company, further, the local economy of Hawai'i is instantly affected by global events and downturns (in economics and politics), such as the 1985 United Airlines strike, Operation Desert Storm in 1991, and the national recession as it affects the tourist flow from Pacific Coast states such as California. The Japanese transnational economy, its export-driven bubble burst, had repatriated much of its capitalist investment in Waikīkī Beach and Hawai'i by 1997 and 1998.

As a *tourist microeconomy,* the little state of Hawai'i must compete with countries and city-states such as Bermuda, Fiji, Hong Kong, Las Vegas, and the Bahamas for tourist capital and market its local soul as the stuff of fascination and redemption. Also, given transnational dynamics of knowl- edge flow and productive employment, "Hawai'i may very well have a brain drain problem [of out-migration] like that commonly found in third- world countries."[45] This is so, in postindustrial terms, given the global shift toward developing a tourist-driven local economy that is riddled by low-wage and low-skill service industries. In Hawai'i, this means that pineapple production and sugar plantations are being phased out and tourist resorts and golf courses are being phased in, as is happening with Hamakua Sugar on the Big Island and, on a near-total scale, to the Dole- run island of Lāna'i.[46]

According to one professional advocate for transnational restructuring of the local, the local market of 1.1 million people is quite "unsophisti- cated" compared to Asian citizens and those of the West, because "related and supporting industries for anything but travel and tourism are not world class" and cannot compete with Pacific Rim countries that manage

---

1993); he also owns the Bank of Honolulu. By 1997, Indonesian currency was in a crisis that would ramify throughout the Asian-Pacific region, halting the flow of such massive investment and inter-Asia tourism.

45. Walter Miklius, "Out Migration," in *The Price of Paradise,* 243.

46. Given the spread of tourism into the major global industry, cultural criticism must now stand and measure the costs and claims of this transcultural/transnational flow on local place-bound identity, in Hawai'i as in England.

and evaporate the interior Pacific with their APEC-like gaze from Hong Kong to Los Angeles.[47] In social science terms, this free-market discourse establishes that, with an entrenched elite who can benefit from restricted competition, the state of Hawai'i resembles a "one-export-commodity developing country model, with an overdeveloped public sector that adversely affects entrepreneurial activity and an entrenched elite trying to maintain its privileges"; such factors prevent Hawai'i's long-delayed emergence into the "Capital of the Pacific."[48]

The "Pacific Basin" is being bypassed, if not all but ignored, in Pacific Rim mappings of capital's megatrends; this Pacific "finanscape" center can be better located in Hong Kong, Tokyo, Los Angeles, Vancouver, or Sydney.[49] With a sense of national decentering as Australia turns toward transnationalizing its links to Asia-Pacific and overcomes its own Asia-bashing heritage, Meaghan Morris has described the belated metamorphosis of the Sydney Tower into a technological icon of Pacific Rim domination from down under, as if for once undoing the tyranny of northern space and Atlantic time: "Inside the Tower, electronic communications were repeatedly invoked as enabling Australia's integration into the age of global simultaneity: no more time lag, no more 'isolation' by vast space from the rest of the world and from each other."[50] With uncanny cultural

47. McClain, "Hawai'i's Competitiveness," 10. Most of APEC's countries are located on the Pacific Rim from South Korea to New Zealand to Canada to Indonesia. "Pacific Basin" island states, sites, and countries are viewed as tourist sites, not as global agents.
48. For Hawai'i's pretensions to being a major Pacific Rim player, see Noel Jacob Kent, "The Pacific Rim Strategy," in *Hawai'i: Islands under the Influence* (New York: Monthly Review Press, 1983), 95–103.
49. See Arjun Appadurai, "Disjuncture and Difference in the Global Economy," *Public Culture* 2 (1990): 1–23, on "the five dimensions of global cultural flows," which he terms ethnoscapes, mediascapes, technoscapes, finanscapes, and ideoscapes. Hawai'i, like Vancouver in the Pacific Northwest, is as much an *ethnoscape* as a *finanscape* for the inrush of Asian capital and transpacific tourist flow. On the global/local interface, see Katharyne Mitchell's study of transnational disruptions via Hong Kong capital of place-bound identity in Vancouver on the Pacific coast of Canada, "Multiculturalism, Or the United Colors of Capitalism," *Antipode* 23 (1993): 263–94. As Mitchell shows, transnational capitalism across the Pacific Rim is not a nameless or faceless totality, but a system driven by local agents with specific interests and their own strategies for linking up locales and cities such as Vancouver to the transnational flow of profit and pleasure.
50. Meaghan Morris, "Metamorphoses at Sydney Tower," *New Formations* 11 (1990): 9. Internet and fax networks, to some extent, have overcome the tyranny of metropolitan

politics, Morris is again thinking through the sway of Euro-American cultural technologies over Pacific cultures and remote spaces in her finely transnationalized reading of the Australian film *Crocodile Dundee* (1986) as an *"export-drive* allegory" in which a Pacific wilderness space and alien white culture settling in the outback "manages to export its crocodile-poacher and, with a little help from the American media, market him brilliantly in New York."[51] The *Mad Max* series, for Morris, becomes a global/local allegory of eradicating the aboriginal peoples and claiming vast desert spaces for technological takeover.

If the grimy transnational cyborg promises to redeem the Ancient Pacific of sleepy gardens and casual patriarchy from any lingering sense of global isolation, meanwhile, local Pacific space is being reconstituted (in Sydney and Honolulu) into a tourist landscape (as outback Eden) on the transcultural flow from Tokyo and Indonesia. An *aloha* to local culture, *Good-bye Paradise* was barely shown in Honolulu, never mind Sydney or Los Angeles; these pastoral politics do not circulate well in the reaches of cyberspace. Still, a cultural politics of place and newly forged identity, from Bamboo Ridge to Suva to Papua New Guinea, surges up elsewhere and otherwise to challenge the U.S.-dominated global flow of representations and the glut of cargo-cult culture from an American system of image production that can always "incorporate exotic elements from abroad— samurai culture here, South African music there, John Woo films here, Thai food there, and so forth."[52]

According to the multicultural-liberal idealism that drives the localized plot of *Good-bye Paradise,* then, to return to that ill-fated local bar and

---

distance in the Asia/Pacific region, not to mention such effects as the globalization of cultural studies that renders Morris or Kuan-Hsing Chen key agents of the new knowledge formations affiliated paradoxically with both Birmingham and these "Asia/Pacific" and "inter-Asia" locales.

51. Meaghan Morris, "Tooth and Claw: Tales of Survival, and *Crocodile Dundee,*" in *The Pirate's Fiancée: Feminism, Reading, Postmodernism* (London: Verso, 1988), 248. On *Mad Max* films as phobic allegories of national, local, regional, and global interactions, see Morris, "White Panic or *Mad Max* and the Sublime," in *Trajectories: Inter-Asia Cultural Studies,* ed. Kuan-Hsing Chen et al. (London: Routledge, 1998), 239–62.

52. See Fredric Jameson, who argues for "the fundamental dissymmetry between the United States and other cultures" via English and mass popular culture in the global system: "Globalization as Philosophical Issue," in *The Cultures of Globalization,* ed. Fredric Jameson and Masao Miyoshi (Durham, NC: Duke University Press, 1998), 63.

small-scale movie, racial and ethnic jokes can fit in an economy of mutual exchange, in which "the rules down here" specify that you "make one joke and take one joke." Despite the multicultural mix and mixed-blood match (Joe quits as Young's manager and goes off with the Asian local, Billy), the movie, like the ever-popular TV series *Hawaii Five-O,* does preserve a racialized hierarchy of roles coming down from plantation days of the Big Five: with native Hawaiians kept in lowly physical service positions (Big Sharon, Tiny), Japanese in middle management positions (Lieutenant Nomura), the charitable white as paternal luna managing the plantation (Joe Martin plays the role of Jack Lord here), and the Chinese scraping to rise from farmer rags and stigmatized pidgin (like Ben's) to yuppie riches (like John "Junior" Young's) in two generations. The movie does not invent a new image practice, as does recent Hong Kong cinema, to challenge and express deeper social realities of Hawai'i.[53]

Despite the contradiction-ridden nature of "local culture," ethnic customs and ways of life do linger on and somehow collage and endure across time and memory. About each local Hawaiian character in *Good-bye Paradise,* with the crucial exception of the transnational "Greater Chinese" operator, John Young, it could be said, as Juliet Kono Lee claims in "Yonsei" of her American pop fourth-generation son moved so far from prior

53. Still, in the words of Luis I. Reyes and Ed Rampell, from their comprehensive and interesting study, *Made in Paradise: Hollywood's Films of Hawai'i and the South Seas* (Honolulu: Mutual, 1995), *Good-bye Paradise* represents a move in the right direction toward representing the Pacific local (and not just locale): "Locally produced, written, and directed, with a cast of mainly Hawai'i residents, *Good-bye Paradise* illustrates the difference in sensibility and sensitivity between a Hollywood vision of Hawai'i as just another pretty backdrop, and a more mature, insightful view of the problems confronted by the 50th state" (180). They also note of *Hawaii Five-O,* which ran on CBS from 1968 to 1980 and is still popular in global circulation, that it conveyed a "representative image of Hawai'i, its beauty, its racial mixtures and way of life" (320), despite its transnational Oriental specter of Wo Fat as an inscrutable Red Chinese spy from out of the U.S./Asian cold war binary of *The Manchurian Candidate* (1962). Jack Lord's state police force hunts for Wo Fat (oddly named after a popular local Chinese restaurant) from Honolulu to Singapore and Hong Kong as global agent of local crime and labor disturbances in Hawai'i, in tune with *Hawaii Five-O's* overall strategy of seeing crime and social unrest as something introduced *from the outside* and aggravated by regional and mainland gangs into the perilously Asian/Pacific fiftieth state. I thank Professor Bruce Stillians, long-time *kama'āina* resident of Hawai'i (who once played a diamond thief captured by Lord on this show), for the latter insight into the prolocal ways of *Hawaii Five-O.*

generations of Japanese who worked the sugar plantations on the Big Island,

> Your blood runs free
> From the redness of soil.
>   But you are mired
> Into this locality.[54]

As Rodney Morales urges his own postmodern yet Pacific-oriented claim for place-bound identity, in a colorful short story about a surfer with a mystical attachment to the Pacific Ocean and the mix of Hawaiian/local/ U.S. pop culture, *"Me and the Pacific have this thing, see?"*[55] Or, to invoke the localist claim of Joe Balaz, as enunciated in his beloved Hawaiian Creole English (pidgin), "Eh, like I told you, / dats da continent— / Hawai'i / is da mainland to me."[56]

DIGGING DOWN INTO "PARADISE"

During a recent excavation in Honolulu's downtown Chinatown, where the old Wong Building was being demolished to make way for a new housing project, archaeologists for the city were astonished to find layers of local and Hawaiian culture reaching back to a seventeenth-century Hawaiian settlement. Just ten feet of soil provided a chronological history of Honolulu Chinatown from the mid-seventeenth through the eighteenth and nineteenth centuries. The eighty-seven-year-old Wong Building was the last wooden structure in Hawai'i and had housed the old Cebu Pool Hall, a local male Filipino hangout fallen into decrepitude in the 1970s.

Like some deeper cultural unconsciousness rooted to place and memory, beneath the Wong Building were three burn layers pointing to three separate Chinatown fires. Radiocarbon dating further suggested a precontact Hawaiian settlement called Kikihale (supposedly named after a daugh-

---

54. Juliet S. Kono, "Yonsei," in *The Best of Bamboo Ridge*, ed. Eric Chock and Darrell H. Y. Lum (Honolulu: Bamboo Ridge Press, 1986), 52. Kono's claim that her *yonsei* (fourth-generation) Japanese American son is "mired into this locality," which I have used as a celebratory signifier of Bamboo Ridge localism, is later concretized into the ethnic signifier of *"zoris . . .* caked with mud," in *Hilo Rains* (Honolulu: Bamboo Ridge Press, 1988), 103.

55. Rodney Morales, "The Speed of Darkness," in *The Speed of Darkness* (Honolulu: Bamboo Ridge Press, 1988), 127.

56. Joseph P. Balaz, "Da Mainland to Me," *Chaminade Literary Review* 2 (1989): 109.

ter of Kou, a former chief on Oʻahu) where Kamehameha the Great had later quartered his lieutenants and retainers after the conquest of Honolulu on his way to uniting Hawaiʻi into a new nation comparable to the states of Cook, Vancouver, and the missionaries from Boston.

Other findings included objects of Hawaiian material culture that ranged from a drilled shark's tooth to bits of shell necklaces, Chinese porcelain from the 1700s, ale bottles from Glasgow, champagne bottles from Paris, and samples of English creamware.[57] Globalized into American space, Honolulu covers up, just barely, another history of local spaces and cherished modes. "Honolulu," Samuel Kamakau records, "was originally a small place at Niukukahi [at the junction of Liliha and School streets] which some man turned into a small taro patch. Because of their aloha for him, his descendants gave this name to the whole *ahupuaʻa* [a land section extending from the mountains to offshore reefs]."[58]

Honolulu is a space of transnational flows and creative mixtures: routes of flight out, across, and back into the Asia Pacific. Joan Didion has remarked, with her weary liberal taste for exotic remoteness and postimperial U.S. mask of "Pacific distances," "This leaning towards Asia makes Honolulu's relation to the rest of America oblique, and divergent at unexpected points," as much tied to Hong Kong and Taipei as it is to the ancient Hawaiian past and customary ways of feeling.[59] By the traffic of Honolulu Harbor, buried beneath the ethnic space of the Paradise Inn, *local* culture was *global* in a complex Asian/Pacific/European mix that expresses the history of Hawaiʻi as a place amalgamating the debris of the future. (No android's limb was found.)

As if to counter my own glibly transnational reconfiguration of the Pacific into "Asia-Pacific" in places of neocolonial influx, I would like to end this

57. June Watanabe, "Dig Turns up Best Look Yet at Old Hawaiʻi," *Honolulu Star-Bulletin*, 5 November 1992, A1. Watanabe quotes from Joseph Kennedy, head of Archaeological Consultants of Hawaiʻi.

58. Samuel M. Kamakau, *The Works of the People of Old (Na Hana a ka Poʻe Kahiko)*, trans. Mary Kawena Pukui (Honolulu: Bishop Museum Press, 1992), 7. Kamakau recorded this impression on 11 November 1869, after the Great Mahele, he lamented, had forever disturbed this Hawaiian sense of space as running smoothly from mountain to sea.

59. Joan Didion, "Pacific Distances," in *After Henry* (New York: Simon and Schuster, 1992), 132.

chapter on a more hopeful, place-bound note, with this comment from Mililani Trask, a leader of Ka Lāhui Hawaiʻi, a major Hawaiian sovereignty group, as she evokes the genius loci of the Hawaiian locale in these neo-indigenous (and mixed up) terms: "In our constitution we do not use Jesus, Jehovah, Pele or any of that, we just use the generic terms *Akua* (Spirit). Personally, I consider that my religious practices are appropriate to all of my bloodlines [Catholic and Native Hawaiian, as well as the later path of Tibetan Buddhism]." She continues to tap into symbolic resources in an inventive, global and local way: "In Ka Lāhui, we believe that the first element of sovereignty is a strong and abiding faith in the Akua, and that is in the constitution. It's very culturally appropriate for us to anchor ourselves in spiritual practice. In the traditional [Hawaiian] way it [Spirit/Akua] governed everything, including your diet, your social life, all of that."[60]

60. See "Trask on the Task," Mililani Trask interviewed by Derek Ferrar, in *Honolulu Weekly* 4 (12 January 1994): 6. Also see *The Waiʻanae Book of Hawaiian Health: The Waiʻanae Diet Program Manual* (Waiʻanae, HI: Waiʻanae Coast Comprehensive Health Center, 1993), for the development of a pre-Cook taro-based diet as counterregimen to the junk food diet that has given Hawaiians the worst health profile (overweight, diabetes, heart attacks) of any so-called ethnic group in the United States. Ka Lāhui's eight-point master plan ("Hoʻokupu a Ka Lāhui Hawaiʻi") for the achievement of Hawaiian sovereignty is outlined by Mililani B. Trask, "Hawaiians Must Come Together on Proposals," *Honolulu Advertiser*, 14 August 1998, A18, based on aims to "build consensus through a culturally appropriate mechanism," to "terminate the state policy of wardship," and to "restructure a political relationship with the United States through a reconciliation process pursuant to the congressional apology bill." Trask is the first *kiaʻāina* (governor) of the group, which has been in the vanguard of articulating the Hawaiian sovereignty struggle in state, U.S. government, and United Nations forums, even as many other advocate groups for Hawaiian sovereignty remain divided as to what form sovereignty should take ranging from complete independence to some form of being a state-within-a-state, OHA-like agency. See the sociological overview by Dana Takagi, "Forget Post-Colonialism!" *ColorLines Magazine* 2 (1999): 5–8, who is working on a book-length study of this struggle. Also see the superb studies geared to attune citizens to deeper indigenous resonances of place and value in Cristina Bacchilega, "Notes towards an Understanding of 'Place' in Adaptations of Folk Narratives in Hawaiʻi," speech delivered at UH Mānoa, 18 November 1998; and "settler discourse" studies of Alex Calder from the University of Auckland, whose "Land and Literature in F. E. Maning's *Old New Zealand*" (forthcoming) shows the complex and unevenly "bicultural" exchanges of language values and land sales being represented in Maning's *Old New Zealand* (1862) and, even more deviously and utopically so, in Jane Campion's 1993 Pacific-based movie, *The Piano*.

Honolulu, too, was once the site of taro ponds and fresh water, the site of roots and flows—a place where good-bye means hello, where love of the land came to be embodied in a site and was expressed in chant, film, or poem, and where paradise seems literal and disappearing, just around the corner from King's Bakery.

CHAPTER 8

Becoming Global and Local in the U.S. Transnational Imaginary of the Pacific

Capital is becoming more and more cosmopolitan.
　　—John Stuart Mill, quoted in the OED to define "cosmopolitan"

It will not be long before such a mighty tide of wealth will roll between California and the Orient as shall render the Pacific the "highway of nations" on a grander scale than the Atlantic is now. . . . in a short time [Honolulu] will rank only second to San Francisco among the towns of the Pacific. . . . Annexation [of Hawaiʻi] to the United States would be of definite benefit . . . for the protection of American interest firmly established there.
　　—George Washington Bates, *Sandwich Island Notes: By a Haole* (1854)

MAPPING THE GLOBAL/LOCAL: MIXED BLESSINGS OF "THE GLOCAL"

If the call of *global culture* has cosmopolitan appeal to the booming countries of the Asia-Pacific region, so does the no-less-resonant *nostalgia for the local* that is figured—in an unevenly intensified "global cultural economy"—as space, tactic, or metaphor for particularized survival.[1] In this

1. The shoring up of "the local" as one source of Hong Kong identity, in the face of the 1997 return to China, is theorized in Ackbar Abbas, *Hong Kong: Culture and the Politics of Disappearance* (Minneapolis: University of Minnesota Press, 1997), 11–15, 81–82. In the overstuffed, transnational space of Hong Kong, Abbas calls this "the fallacy of the local" or "the merely local" as a kind of nativist backlash against (both) the global cosmopolitan and the British colonial. On the invention of the local in Wong Kar-wai's

chapter, I link "the local" as such with the cultural semiotics of *particularized survival* in the Asia-Pacific because, in the United States, where (not surprisingly, along with the United Kingdom) "globalization discourse" is being widely propagated, the form that this transnational restructuring of finance, labor, information, technology, media, ethos, and culture will take comes down to a process of "rendering of the world as a single place."[2] Worrying the fate of ethnic/racial difference under the present U.S.-led globalization forms, Stuart Hall has warned that "what we call 'the global' . . . is the self-presentation of the dominant particular," meaning, in this "U.S. postmodern" case, the superpower location from which a sociologist of transnational flows such as Roland Robertson theorizes his voluntary, upbeat, free market model of "globalization."[3]

This globalization process underway from London to Taipei is by no means an *even* one and generates myriad contradictions and tensions in its spread across borders. Except perhaps in the "Internet Gold Rush" gaze of Bill Gates in *The Road Ahead,* who sees what he calls the rise of a "friction-free capitalism" spreading across a globe (unconsciously echoing those heliocentric tropes of the British Empire) where *the sun never sets on Microsoft,* or those American end-of-history idealists of democratic market forms (such as Francis Fukuyama) whom Derrida views as philosophers of pragmatic delusion and unfreedom in *Specters of Marx,* globalization is by no means just a euphoric information highway.[4]

---

films as estranged and "upside down," see especially *Happy Together* (1997), which sets the Hong Kong local in gay Argentina.

2. This is the claim of Roland Robertson, using his much repeated formulation from *Globalization: Social Theory and Global Culture* (London: Sage, 1992), in "Social Theory, Cultural Relativity, and the Problem of Globality," in *Culture, Globalization, and the World-System: Contemporary Conditions for the Representation of Identity,* ed. Anthony King (Minneapolis: University of Minnesota Press, 1997), 87; essays from this collection will be cited throughout this chapter. On more recent claims for "globalization," see below.

3. See Stuart Hall's fine essays, "The Local and the Global: Globalization and Ethnicity" and "Old and New Identities, Old and New Ethnicities," in *Culture, Globalization and the World-System;* this quotation is from p. 67 of the latter essay: "I think the global is the self-presentation of the dominant particular."

4. For Derrida's take on the "virtualized" economy of global capital and his return to Marxian problematics within poststructuralist analysis, see Vincent B. Leitch, *Postmodernism: Local Effects, Global Flows* (Albany: State University of New York Press, 1996),

Even given the will to an affirmative reading of "global popular culture" as it links up to and helps to circulate and energize "the local" into forms of the neolocal or reindigenous, globalization will still need to be viewed more critically as a process that goes on collapsing space into time and money, disrupting nations and localities, polarizing economies, and raising neocolonial fears of domination if not "postmodern panic" attacks over capitalist speculation and a disappearing material ground.[5] Consequences of impoverishment, injustice, uneven development, ecological disaster, and the saturation of local culture by economic forces are being drawn out at many points of global/local contact. The local is going not so much offshore as it is offworld.[6]

Perhaps at this point in the century's end the local will be outflanked, mimed, and consumed by forces of transnational capital ("the global") and the market-driven state, as many cultural critics in the United States now contend. If so, then there is little room for the local to create counter-discourses, to forge nomadic enclaves and coalitions, to struggle to express alternative linkages, movements, and regional concepts of transnational forces, in short, to survive the overwhelming impact of the global and transnational on spaces and identity forms of the local.[7] Calls for "critical

---

chaps. 1 and 12. See also Jacques Derrida, *Specters of Marx: The State of the Debt, the Work of Mourning, and the New International,* trans. Peggy Kamuf (New York: Routledge, 1994).

5. In one month of "global financial instability" alone—March 1995—foreign institutional stock investors repatriated close to U.S. $4 billion out of Taiwan. See "Foreign Investment in Taiex Plunges," *China News,* 6 April 1995, 7. On the U.S. globalization process, see Richard Walker, "California Rages against the Dying of the Light," *New Left Review* 209 (1995): 42–74.

6. With area studies being downsized and refigured in the post–cold war era from the University of California to the Social Science Research Committee and East-West Center, the impact of the global on the local has to be retheorized to fit the strangely "cosmopolitan" and postnational terrain. See the essays in Pheng Cheah and Bruce Robbins, eds., *Cosmopolitics: Thinking and Feeling beyond the Nation* (Minneapolis: University of Minnesota Press, 1998).

7. It is this attitude of negative-dialectical dismay toward transnationalization that, in many ways, comes across as the dominant note in the collection of essays edited by Fredric Jameson and Masao Miyoshi, *Cultures of Globalization* (Durham, NC: Duke University Press, 1998). It is no small achievement that, in a time when the dynamics of the "global economy" are being rephrased in euphoric terms from the White House to

regionalism" and, in fact, any return to an *uncanny localism* seem in these cognitive mappings of globalization and culture, always already defeated, just so many symbolic acts of "compensatory ideology" circulating within and against the logic of commodity culture. "Is global difference the same today as global Identity?" Jameson asks at the end of *The Seeds of Time* while trying to figure in the forces of the "neoregional" and "the neo-ethnic" as so many postmodern nostalgias for belonging to the present.[8]

Still, overextended applications of "colonial" logic or even a Fanon-inflected dialectics of "postcolonial subjectivity" are no longer adequate to describe what is going on, for example, in complex global/local cities such as Hong Kong.[9] In Taipei, as a Taiwanese literary scholar told me in 1995 while explaining the impact of the global system on dazed, hyperflexible citizens and visitors (like myself; see chapter 1) residing in a maze of commerce, semiotic and ecological overload, and neoculture, "The global overwhelms the local and annihilates the ego." "Well, yes," I responded defensively, "but the local can fight back in this global city, as in one of those noisy funerals in Taipei that take over a city block with microphones blaring on pickup trucks, hired mourners, Taiwan beer can wreaths, and even short-skirted cheerleaders! Not to mention the anarchistic traffic habits, or the mixed tongues of the Taiwanese/Chinese/aboriginal Pacific island feeding at once into this global city." Such "global cities," we now realize, are becoming fluid forms and consolidation points for refracting and scaling down the local into a cultural fit. "In the distance [of a global city], tumult, power, creation, luxury—and poverty as well," as Henri

---

post-Maoist China, such theorists dissent from this liberal capitalist common sense by elaborating the workings of the world system otherwise. Oddly, the *nation-state* has become the site where global technologies and impacts of transnationalization can still be managed and socially adjusted in local-yet-global policy.

8. Fredric Jameson, *The Seeds of Time* (New York: Columbia University Press, 1994), 205. As Jameson skeptically remarks of the current movements of critical regionalism and dirty realism, "Neoregionalism, like the neo-ethnic, is a specifically postmodern form of reterritorialization; it is a flight from the realities of late capitalism, a compensatory ideology, in a situation in which regions (like ethnic groups) have been fundamentally wiped out—reduced, standardized, commodified, atomized, or rationalized" (148). On space-place dialectics, see Neil Smith, *Uneven Development: Nature, Capital, and the Production of Space* (Cambridge, MA: Basil Blackwell, 1990).

9. See Abbas, *Hong Kong: Culture and Politics of Disappearance*, and the special issue of *Hong Kong Cultural Studies* 5 (1997), ed. Stephen Chan, on Hong Kong as "global city" where McDonalds and AIDS impact on the biopolitics of the local post-Chinese culture.

Lefebvre saw in Paris in the global/local dialectics of *Critique of Every-day Life*.[10]

We need not get too optimistic about small-scale neighborhood victories, rock spectacles, e-mail enclaves of the popular-democratic, the taking back of the streets for populist ritual and transient occupation. Still, these streets are where, as Lefebvre memorably urged in *The Production of Space,* spatial tactics of the local can do battle to swerve, mobilize, challenge, and survive: "No space disappears in the course of growth and development [via capitalist modernity]: *the worldwide does not abolish the local.*"[11] Given the reign of capitalist modernity, transnational cultural studies can move to articulate and affirm spaces and grounds of local poetics and communities within uneven (at times, unjust) changes of capital reforming economies, nations, localities, and regions in these postcommunist 1990s of the Pax Americana.

What I am getting at is this: Intensified global/local contact is a mixed blessing at best, and creates what can be called *third spaces* of interaction in between/against capitalist dynamics of *the global-sublates-the-local.* We can call this third space of creation, echoing both "postcolonial" ambivalence discourse and that buzzword of "multilocal" global businesses, "the glocal" culture. *Glocal* can be used to suggest some mobile, inventive, and synergistic sense of *global/local interaction* that we will try further to unpack along the Honolulu–Taipei flight into the transnational waters of Asia-Pacific.[12] If to become "cosmopolitan" means to become a mobile citizen of the floating world, loosened from the prejudices of the national or stick-in-the-mud mentality of the local, as Bruce Robbins has urged, then these newer modes of "cosmopolitan culture" have to come to terms with the impurity and synergy of the global/local.[13] As we enter this

10. Henri Lefebvre, *Critique of Everyday Life,* trans. John Moore (London: Verso, 1991), 43.

11. Henri Lefebvre, *The Production of Space,* trans. Donald Nicholson-Smith (Oxford: Basil Blackwell, 1991), 86. On differences between capitalist space and the tactics of forging "place-bound identity" within dynamics of global postmodernity, see Arif Dirlik, "Place-Based Imagination: Globalism and the Politics of Place," *Review* 22, no. 2 (1999): 151–87.

12. On "third spaces" of global/local culture, see Mike Featherstone, "Global Culture: An Introduction," in *Global Culture: Nationalism, Globalization and Modernity,* ed. Mike Featherstone (London: Sage, 1990), 9–11.

13. See Bruce Robbins, ed., *The Phantom Public Sphere* (Minneapolis: University of

heated-up era of globalization, a new kind of *cosmopolitan* knowledge is being called for, one conscious of global/local discrepancies and theorizing a range of situated interrelationships in the "single-space economy" of global capital.[14]

AMPING UP "THE LOCAL"

The models of globalization emerging across disciplines, from urban geography to cultural studies, try to counter the unidirectional world-system assumption of centers dominating peripheries with a more situated and localized sense of cultural heterogeneity and the will to plural forms as possible outcomes and sources of creative static inside the system. We need not follow a liberal free market globalist like John Naisbett down the route of high-capitalist euphoria in *Asia Megatrends* to deduce that some "global paradox" of large meeting small can, at times, intensify the power and creative potential of the local, subnational, ethnic, and tribal to alter workings of global domination and transnational forms. Inside the global economy, as global/local encounters intensify and "lines of flight" fight against the stability and power of territory and state identity, by some David-meets-Goliath-and-wins paradox, *the local counts even more as the global ground of creation and invention.*[15]

Ruptures of economy from politics and cultures may allow for open-

---

Minnesota Press, 1993), and, above all, see his move toward a "critical cosmopolitanism" in *Secular Vocations: Intellectuals, Professionalism, Culture* (London: Verso, 1993).

14. See the Gramscian speculations in Paul Bové, afterword to *Global/Local: Cultural Production in the Transnational Imaginary*, ed. Rob Wilson and Wimal Dissanayake (Durham, NC: Duke University Press, 1996), 372–85.

15. See John Naisbett, *Global Paradox: The Bigger the World Economy, the More Powerful Its Smallest Players* (New York: Avon, 1994), and *Megatrends Asia: Eight Asian Megatrends that Are Reshaping Our World* (New York: Touchstone, 1997). Naisbett offers a transnational embrace of the "thinking globally, acting locally" paradigm he sees driving the economies of "the Asia-Pacific," which, especially through an expanded "Global China" region, will lead the world into what he boasts will be the Pacific Century. Needless to say, his books are widely translated and popular in Asia-Pacific markets, as are the more phobic works by Samuel Huntington warning of "civilizational" standoffs between "East" and "West"; see Kuan-Hsing Chen, "Watch Out for Civilizationalism: Huntington and Nandy," in *History and Theory of Cultural Studies*, ed. Lee Yu-cheng (Taipei: Institute of Academia Sinica, 1997).

ings, feedback, and inventions of altered public spheres and democratized mass media in what Arjun Appadurai claims has become "the global cultural economy." Without resorting to overcheery models of global/local space and flexible identity, the local has to be factored into our globalization models via multiple modes of situated analysis, if only potentially as the site of resistance, flight, and fragmentation of global flows.[16] For, in a strong sense, globalization implies that the decentering of Euro-American cultural schema, master narratives, and media have to be taken into account and those modernist binaries of center-periphery mapping seen again in situated ways related to forces of class, place, race, and gender.[17] The "world system" model itself is dissolving in Asia-Pacific, as in other sites of global/local interchange from London to Taipei.

"I describe China more as Europe," John Farrell, president of Coca-Cola's China division in Hong Kong, told *Newsweek*, lured on as such big transnationals are by the late-capitalist sublimity of 1.2 billion consumers on the postcommunist mainland chiming in "Let's Coke" or "Let's buy a motor scooter today!" Farrell's palpably "Go-China" mandate to such transnational companies sounds as though he has been studying cultural studies readers in Melbourne and Urbana, as he calls for heightened localization, a process of getting your transnational feet on the ground, and connecting with networks of transmission and step-by-step exchange (gathering so-called Chinese mothers-in-law). "Every region has distinct

16. The collection coedited by Rob Wilson and Wimal Dissanayake, *Global/Local: Cultural Production and the Transnational Imaginary* (Durham, NC: Duke University Press, 1996), aims to be an analytical step forward in this regard. For the proliferation of related works, see the bibliography in King, "Preface to the Revised Edition" and "Introduction: Spaces of Culture, Spaces of Knowledge," in *Culture, Globalization, and the World-System*, vi–xii, 1–18.

17. See the essays gathered in Inderpal Grewal and Caren Kaplan, eds., *Scattered Hegemonies: Postmodernity and Transnational Feminist Practices* (Minneapolis: University of Minnesota Press, 1994). Attempts to rephrase migrant movements, nomadism, and cultural intermixtures across national borders and class lines as a philosophical utopia of linguistic displacement and decentering can begin to sound like so much postcolonial utopianism; for a philosophical example, see Iain Chambers, *Migrancy, Culture, Identity* (London: Routledge, 1994). For a trenchant critique of the euphoria of dislocated hybridity, see Benita Perry, "Problems in Current Theories of Colonial Discourse," in *The Post-Colonial Studies Reader*, ed. Bill Ashcroft, Gareth Griffiths, and Helen Tiffin (London: Routledge, 1995), 36–44.

groups. You need local knowledge to get by," as the man selling soda in Hong Kong insightfully said.[18]

Global + local = glocal is how a new marketing series puts the global/local synergy formula in the Great Future series filling upscale Taipei and Hsinchu bookstores like Eslite. This synergy model premises its vision of a Great Future coming to Taiwan on the grounds of envisioning a "common future" rooted in pancapitalist globalization: "Although people do not share a common past," the series epigraph says, "yet it is possible to live in a common future. The core idea of a common future is the unified life community of the world. However, before humanity's selfishness can progress into this non-existing wonderland, the concept of localism remains. Thus, the initial stage of a common future is the globalization of localism; that is the idea of 'GLOCAL.'"[19] The local promises to be compounded into the capitalist elixir of global modernity.[20]

The *glocal* dialectic is even more complicated, fluid, uneven, and flexible than this Pacific Rim vision suggests. The Great Future is not just a *win-win situation* for local culture(s), modernist nations, or the unevenly globalizing economy along the Pacific Rim. Indeed, *Globalize or die, Globalize or your locality will fade into political-economic oblivion* would be a blunt way of putting the transnational mandate in the Asia/Pacific region as shaped by the APEC forces of today.[21] The cultural and economic news is not all upbeat and uncritical.[22]

18. *Newsweek*, 20 February 1995, 12; and Robert Young, *White Mythologies: Writing History and the West* (London: Routledge, 1990), chap. 7, "Disorienting Orientalism."

19. See Zhi-hong, *Dominators in the 3rd Millennium*, Great Future series no. 3 (Taipei: Shu-hua Publishers, 1994). I thank Sho-hua Liu for help translating and understanding this work.

20. As such, it may be that the global/local dialectic ("the glocal") is a looser, more spatially fluid if not ideologically complicitous way of describing and encoding these binary structures and dialectics of the capitalist world system, which haunts the new global/local thinking, such as here.

21. One of the main organizing frames for the current use of "Asia-Pacific," APEC refers to Asia-Pacific Economic Cooperation. Increasingly endorsed as a liberalizing market mechanism by the Clinton administration and a bubble-burst Japan now following the U.S. model of segmented "deregulation," APEC was formed in 1989 to help ease trade barriers and systematically liberalize and integrate markets in the region (see chap. 1). ASEAN struggles to maintain some measure of regional autonomy within APEC's "Asia-Pacific."

22. See the variously situated essays in Kuan-Hsing Chen, ed., *Trajectories: Inter-Asian*

If it is a semiotic coinage reflecting the class position of cosmopolitan hybridity, as used for example in Japanese postmodernity, "glocal" is floated throughout a global marketing book like *Global Vision: Building New Models for the Corporation of the Future* (1994), cowritten by John and Caroline Daniels of IBM and the London Business School.[23] "Glocal" is used profusely to express the transnational drive of big corporations to secure marketing in multiple and incommensurable locales, as if reflecting the reciprocity of the global to the local.[24] ("Greater China" remains a huge, daunting, if not threatening example of this, a point I shall return to; also see chapter 1.) For the Danielses, "glocal" is an analytical concept that implies the risky attempt of transnational capital "to balance and constantly adjust global and local activities."[25] For, under changing business conditions, as *Forbes* magazine pointed out in 1990, *globalization* has become the structural mandate for executives and the rallying cry for U.S. universities in their research agendas and multicultural programs. *Becoming glocal*, in effect, has become the fate of cosmopolitan capital (and capitalist culture) in ways that would amuse John Stuart Mill (see the first epigraph to this chapter).[26]

The local, as ground of cultural production and technological invention, in other words, has become a David-like strategy of interface with the heated-up global cultural economy. The local, in reconfigurations in the Asia-Pacific region, now installs, particularizes, and amalgamates this media / capital / cultural input in odd, fluid ways not fully answerable to the

---

Cultural Studies (London: Routledge, 1998), and David Morley and Kuan-Hsing Chen, eds., *Stuart Hall: Critical Dialogues in Cultural Studies* (London: Routledge, 1996). Based in Taiwan and connected to the forces of "Inter-Asia" emergences, as I have earlier suggested, Kuan-Hsing Chen has articulated a powerful global / local perspective and critical internationalism within the emergence of cultural studies and the Asia-Pacific region.

23. See John L. Daniels and N. Caroline Daniels, *Global Vision: Building New Models for the Corporation of the Future* (New York: McGraw-Hill International, 1994).

24. Also see Roland Robertson, "Glocalization: Time-Space and Homogeneity-Heterogeneity," in *Global Modernities*, ed. Mike Featherstone, Scott Lash, and Roland Robertson (London: Sage, 1995), 25–44.

25. Daniels and Daniels, *Global Vision*, xxx.

26. "Global Brand, Local Touch" has now become the advertising slogan of Acer Computers, the fast-rising Asian information technology company, using a timely global / local strategy that proclaims: "We're a multinational corporation that enjoys strong brand-name recognition, yet keeps each business localized in order to be as responsive as possible to local business environments" (ad in *China News*, 5 June 1995).

monolithic logic of "colonization."[27] We can recall here the rise of trans-national studies of the Pacific Rim Little Dragons as a feat of global/local synergy, a multiplier effect of global meeting local, as in Thomas Gold's *State and Society in the Taiwan Miracle* or works on the Little Dragons and neo-Confucian capitalism by Ezra F. Vogel, where dependency and development are said to meet and energize in complex new ways under "party-state" leadership and culture into something expansive, booming—an outcome more like Tokyo's than Detroit's or Brasilia's.[28]

"Nation-states *are* eroding as economic actors. Region-states [such as Taiwan, Singapore, and Guangdong province] *are* taking shape" that recognize that their primary linkages are now with the global economy; to survive, such places (Hong Kong may be in some vanguard position) must "put global logic first" to thrive globally and reshape their conceptual and social geography to fit the contours of a more transnational region. So says Kenichi Ohmae, arguing in defense of a "borderless economy" of global production in which it is not the nation-state but the "region-state" that has become the agent of political-economic change. Exemplary of these changes, Taiwan has in effect become a leading agent of such forces and thus comprises "a new Commonwealth of China"; by this strategy of global/local regionality, Taiwan may emerge as "one of the most important and autonomous agents in the world."[29]

27. For wary speculations on transnational colonialism and the amplification of uneven profits in Asia-Pacific, see Masao Miyoshi, "Sites of Resistance in the Global System," *boundary 2* 22 (1995): 61–84. Also see Miyoshi's cautionary look at the transnationalization of U.S. academic spaces and forms in "Ivory Tower in Escrow: Ex Uno Plures," essay forthcoming in the university special issue of *boundary 2* being edited by Paul Bové; and the powerful critiques of diasporic opportunism, transnational and denational delinkage, and ethnic professionalism in Arif Dirlik, "Asians on the Rim: Transnational Capital and Local Community in the Making of Contemporary Asian America," and Sau-Ling C. Wong, "Denationalization Reconsidered: Asian American Cultural Criticism at a Theoretical Crossroads," both in *Amerasia Journal* 21 (1995).

28. Thomas Gold, *State and Society in the Taiwan Miracle* (Armonk, NY: M. E. Sharpe, 1986), and Ezra F. Vogel, *The Four Little Dragons: The Spread of Industrialization in East Asia* (Cambridge, MA: Harvard University Press, 1991). This might be called articulation within the discourse of Asian-Pacific "Rimspeak" (see chap. 1). Also see Denis Fred Simon and Michael Y. M. Kau, eds., *Taiwan: Beyond the Economic Miracle* (Armonk, NY: M. E. Sharpe, 1992).

29. Kenichi Ohmae, "Putting Global Logic First," *Harvard Business Review* 73 (1995): 125.

As transnationals globalize, they need to localize as well. This is the paradox that Naisbett, Acer Computer Products, Sony, Coke, Ohmae, the Danielses, et al. can see: as the regions of contact and expertise multiply, rules change into learning a more grounded and situated pragmatics of exchange, often incommensurable language games, cultural networks, and legal systems. These corporate forms have to localize to survive in China, not to mention that diasporic "Greater China" that would include Hong Kong, Taiwan, and Northern Pacific Chinatowns in Vancouver and San Francisco.[30] The discourse of international locality is in the air of Asia-Pacific; it deforms the citizens, rivers, and streets: a sublime "China" now confronts transnational corporations like some strange new Europe. It is a terrain of multiple localities, several languages, and cultural peculiarities where global standardization of products and cultural goods will no longer work, and Euro-American models have to be scaled down and refashioned for the better.

"GLOBAL HOMOGENEITY"

"Globalization" is not just an advertisement slogan, not just *pomo* consciousness, style, or attitude. Globalization is, after all, *expensive* to install and circulate in its workings; by one account, an American multinational corporation now spends over $300,000 per year on each expatriate employed in setting up firms abroad. Global restructuring means the risk and promise of expanding investment abroad and luring foreign investment at home, as capital moves in both directions across national borders as fast as computerized light. Not the "boat people" but the "yacht people" of Hong Kong are seen as the diasporic threat of some transnational Yellow Peril to the middle-class local mores and urban real estate of Vancouver, who want the influx of global capital but would resist the impact of Chinese culture and power crossing over into *their* post-England/post-France region of the Pacific Rim.[31]

30. See Ien Ang, "On Not Speaking Chinese: Postmodern Ethnicity and the Politics of Diaspora," *New Formations* 24 (1994): 1–18, on the disparate and uneven diaspora of over thirty million "Overseas Chinese" ethnic subjects dispersed to some 130 countries. Also see Jon Stratton and Ien Ang, "On the Impossibility of a Global Cultural Studies: 'British' Cultural Studies in an 'International' Frame," in *Stuart Hall: Critical Dialogues in Cultural Studies,* ed. David Morley and Kuan-Hsing Chen (London: Routledge, 1996), 361–91.

31. See Katharyne Mitchell on Vancouver and its Hong Kong and Taiwan influx, "The

In scenarios mapping *postmodernity* as spread of space-time compression, the threat lingers of homogenization via the transnational spread of the commodity form. The end result is explained as one of saturating everyday culture with global capitalism, as in Marxian explanations, to map this borderless postmodern culture as a reflection of "global capital."[32] Despite claims for "disjunction" and an amped-up cultural poetics of *quirkiness at the borders* of our so-called global cultural economy, globalization raises ethical and political issues of center/periphery domination and the production of structural imbalances and class and gender exploitation at home and abroad, all along "the global assembly line." It does not do to use "transnationalization" in a strictly affirmative sense, to express some neologism for cosmopolitan "internationalization" taking place apart from the market. Much as we might love and admire the redneck counterculture of Elvis Presley, strange things are happening to him in the process of global and self-commodification in his twenty-year afterlife as profane illumination.

Ulf Hannerz has called the more pessimistic neocolonial models of globalization "the global homogenization scenario," which recalls lopsided cultural flows, saturation of everyday space, and the commercial takeover of the local. Such quasi-Marxian mappings are being countered by looser, flexibly articulated mappings of "global/local" interaction developing in *Public Culture* and the cultural criticism of Paul Gilroy, James Clifford, Benjamin Lee, Naoki Sakai, Mary Louise Pratt, and others. These models emphasize localization, translation, and "peripheral corruption," some particularized and proliferating interplay of cultural and political disjunction in expanding and multiple public spheres. In effect, this kind of global/local thinking affirms the *mishmash creole creation* of metro-

---

Hong Kong Immigrant and the Urban Landscape: Shaping the Transnational Cosmopolitan in the Era of Pacific Rim Capital," in Rob Wilson and Arif Dirlik, eds., *Asia/Pacific as Space of Cultural Production* (Durham, NC: Duke University Press, 1995), 284–310.

32. See Arif Dirlik, *After the Revolution: Waking to Global Capitalism* (Hanover, NH: Wesleyan University Press, 1994). On the post-Gramscian dynamics of the global/local dialectic, see David Harvey, "Militant Particularism and Global Ambition: The Conceptual Politics of Place, Space, and Environment in the Work of Raymond Williams," *Social Text* 42 (1995): 69–98, and Fredric Jameson, "On 'Cultural Studies,'" *Social Text* 34 (1993): 17–52.

politan products, theories, and forms that would attempt to overwhelm local, marginal, and minor knowledge and symbols.[33]

Homogenization scenarios and fears of injustice do hover around the spread of the market, as Derrida put it, like Marx's ghost returning with nineteenth-century class wisdom. "The spectacle is *capital* accumulated to the point where it becomes image": this is the "homogenization scenario" proposed by Guy Debord amid the social upheavals of Paris in the 1960s.[34] Debord's skeptical analysis of commodity culture via "the spectacle" has been reissued amid the *global* structures reigning ever more supreme on into the 1990s. Debord retells a postmodernized yet Marxian scenario of global market forces saturating the everyday life-world via an "ideology of democracy," which ironically has the opposite effect of *disempowering the urban subject*. Colonization of the "free" subject here takes place via a quite public process of *image-commodity fetishization* and media spectacle. In this grim logic, commodity becomes image, image becomes spectacle, and thus becomes the power to separate, disconnect, and delocalize the viewer from real agency—"the world of the commodity ruling over all lived experience," in the mass media as in city space.[35] In effect, the social life of the global city is day-by-day colonized as the commodity becomes "spectacle" of capitalist advertisement.

In a booming Pacific Rim city such as Taipei, to apply the overgrim dialectic of Debord, the commodity can contemplate itself and its own spectacles in another "global city" of capital. Everyday life is lived in thrall to the commodity/image/spectacle and its global/local rounds. The city is a space of flows, disappearing locales, semiotic overload. There is little room for the creativity of flight and in-mixture. It becomes another site of the global city where "God is dead." And yet the global city is also where the dead gods remain hidden in the uncanny and surreal textures of the local: the global city where the neon signs glow, the global city of Taipei where commodities can clot and multiply, speed and flow. Cultural studies

33. See Ulf Hannerz, "Scenarios for Peripheral Cultures," in *Culture, Globalization, and the World-System*, 107–28.
34. See Guy Debord, *The Society of the Spectacle*, trans. Donald Nicholson-Smith (New York: Zone Books, 1994), 24. "Situationist" media tactics and surrealism of the signifier may still be called for to resist the spectacles of Evita culture or Elvis sightings in Tanzanian shopping malls, not to mention the spread of the "sublime Patriot" missile.
35. Ibid., 26–29.

at times stands bewildered, feeble, enchanted before this global fate. Still, in Ackbar Abbas's cautionary reading of Hong Kong as space of transnational flows and local glut, the cultural-political options seem gleefully grim: "The Merely Local is no longer there; the Placeless has never been there. Does the transformation of the Anonymous provide a model [of urban architecture] for other Asian cities to follow?"[36]

In her critique of the globalization models of Immanuel Wallerstein, Roland Robertson, et al. at SUNY Binghamton in 1989, Barbara Abou-El-Haj has warned that our attempts to map these global/local dynamics may still depend on inadequate analytical vocabularies and tidy "binary oppositions" that go on repeating colonial and imperial linkages of older knowledge formations (Abbas's work on Hong Kong is certainly cautious of this). At worst, such models reactivate a Eurocentric dialectic in which the global sublates the local and the peripheral is beholden to the power of the center: "Our ambition to do equal justice to global and local is limited at the outset by our failure to generate a comparative language beyond the set of tidy binaries which reproduce the global regime in the very attempt to eviscerate it: center/periphery, core/periphery, western/non-western, developed/developing, etc. . . . Beyond our primary categories, global/local, we have yet to find a language capable of describing equal exchange in a world of unequal exchange."[37] Still, as she notes with that telling G/L slash, by disrupting tidy conceptual hierarchies, rendering fluid older spatial boundaries, and dealing with unequal distributions of power and capital within as well as between national and regional categories, "Global/local is a qualitative step forward."[38]

Other cultural critics of the transnational and postcolonial interface, such as the coeditors of *Scattered Hegemonies*, have faulted global/local knowledge formations for merely repeating imperial dynamics and neocolonial binary codes in which the global always already structures and sublates the local.[39] More to the point, the coeditors of *Cultures of United States Imperialism* go to the opposite extreme: they would fault "global/

36. See Abbas, "Building on Disappearance: Hong Kong Architecture and the City," in *Hong Kong*, 81–90.
37. Barbara Abou-El-Haj, "Languages and Models for Cultural Exchange," in *Culture, Globalization and the World-System*, 142.
38. Ibid., 143.
39. Grewal and Kaplan, introduction to *Scattered Hegemonies*, 11–12.

local discourse" for overemphasizing or romanticizing the local as site of resistance to the global and, thus, for inadequately confronting structures of *imperialism* latent in the globalizing powers, especially the U.S. area formation, with its ongoing Open Door policies. Such a perspective, Donald E. Pease and Amy Kaplan warn, risks repeating that "paradigm of denial" that allows Americanists once again to sublimate and disavow political and economic imperialism at home and abroad under the guise of a more flexible "global-localist discourse."[40]

Still, under conditions of postmodernity, nations are going local and global in ways that render our residual, Debord-like descriptive vocabularies (tied as so many are to mapping the *modern* nation-state and the industrial workings of capitalist culture) inadequate, belated, insufficiently porous and flexible. As regimes of accumulation, production, and consumption go on changing, those Fordist industrial-age master narratives that guided the formation of the modern nation-state and consolidated into the comparative literatures of national identity may no longer fit the global/local terrain, where innovation (and not just domination) does occur. This reality is the *post*modern moment for the postnational and postcolonial forms, as "identity" is reshaped by the global/local interaction in culture as in the political economy. As I have been attempting to document along the Honolulu–Taipei flight to Asia-Pacific, the cultural production of local identity takes place inside a transnational imaginary that deforms local/national agents even as we map, express, and belatedly try to explain the process.[41]

40. Donald E. Pease and Amy Kaplan address these issues in separate introductions to *Cultures of United States Imperialism* (Durham, NC: Duke University Press, 1993). See Kaplan, 3–19, and Pease, 26, where he argues, "The emergent discourse of 'global-localism' proposes the most challenging critique directed against the pre-constituted categories anchored in the discourse of anti-imperialism. . . . The discourse of global-localism should not be ignored, but neither should it displace the critique of [American] imperialism."

41. To his credit, Frederick Buell attempts to provide such a postnational mapping of "Asian America," for example in *National Culture and the New Global System* (Baltimore: Johns Hopkins University Press, 1994). His reading of localities, ex-colonial and otherwise, as globally produced spaces of "postmodern boundary violating and syncretistic cultural intersections" remains far too euphoric and monolithic, his notion of globalization too idealized and uncritical as he disavows and posts "world system" and "Third World" analysis (5–34).

MAKING CULTURAL POETICS INSIDE A
"GLOBAL/LOCAL" NATION

The United States, as I have been urging in this study via discussing Hawaiʻi as site of Asia/Pacific contradictions, has become an unstable entity of global/local deformation during these decades of globalization at the state core. We are entering a brave new world of ascending and descending nationalism. The nation-state, as theorized in Stuart Hall's talk "The Local and the Global: Globalization and Ethnicity," is being undone above and below its own structures of modernity by transnational relations and local ("ethnic") forces making contradictory claims on time, place, and community.[42] In effect, "Germany's problems are becoming less German," as Habermas expresses the racial and economic saturation of European nations within global problems and global/local flows.[43]

The cultural politics of the local are brought to bear against the global in sites in the Asia-Pacific region, arousing what Stuart Hall has called the weight of "a lot of little local politics."[44] Theorizing Great Britain's postimperial decline as global industrial power, given these postwar decades spreading "postmodern global culture" from the USA, Hall goes on to warn that the erosion of the nation-state, national economies, and national cultural identities represents a dangerous moment: the gobbling up of the local by the national can lead to dismantling those remnants of the local and critical resistance via a process of offshore transnationalization. More affirmatively speaking, as the black (in its fully global coloration and multi-

42. Stuart Hall, "The Local and the Global: Globalization and Ethnicity," in *Culture, Globalization, and the World-System*, 18–39.
43. See the interviews on a transnationalized/relocalized Western Europe with Jürgen Habermas, who ponders postunification and the impact on the German national imaginary of the UN/U.S.-led Gulf War, post-Soviet struggles, immigrant and subaltern migrations raising racial phobias, postcommunist danger, and other global problems: Habermas interviewed by Michael Heller, *The Past As Future*, trans. and ed. Max Pensky (Lincoln: University of Nebraska Press, 1994). A German word expresses the mood of cynical reason and depoliticized gloom that seems to reign before the triumph of the market and impotence of critical theory to intervene: *Theoriemudigkeit* ("weariness with theory"). See Paul Bové on this mood in the USA and its professionalization into "New Historicism" California-style at *Representations* journal, for example, in *In the Wake of Theory* (Middletown, CT: Wesleyan University Press, 1991).
44. Stuart Hall, "Old and New Identities, Old and New Ethnicities," in *Culture, Globalization and the World-System*, 41–52.

ple locations) is being put back into the Union Jack,[45] the core of national identity can be reshaped and creolized in contexts of ethnic difference, both locally and globally, from Birmingham to the ex-British colony of Hong Kong (where a new cultural identity rallying around a poetics of the local has begun, against the apocalyptic odds of 1997, to assert itself).[46]

The identity of "Englishness"—which in its spread through a global empire made "English English" into *the* world language of commerce, culture, and law—was formed in the prior epoch of international finance when the world market was dominated by nation-states and upper-class culture at the imperial core. This notion of national identity is being undone in a "postimperial" outreach, when London is just one of the global cities consolidating the transnational flows of culture, migrancy, and finance in "regimes of representation" emanating from the metropolitan center. (The minority-driven historicizing of the U.S. literary canon is a related global/local effect.) Hall declares that this "new kind of globalization is not English, but American" in its mass spread, linguistic impurity, and pop culture–driven cultural hegemony; this time around the empire, the core culture of American globalization is called "the global postmodern" and comes booming out of Hollywood, Duke University Press, Rout-

45. For an inventively "transcultural" reading of the Black Atlantic and UK interface, see Paul Gilroy, *Black Atlantic: Modernity and Double Consciousness* (Cambridge, MA: Harvard University Press, 1993); *"There Ain't No Black in the Union Jack": The Cultural Politics of Race and Nation* (Chicago: University of Chicago Press, 1991); and *Small Acts: Thoughts on the Politics of Black Cultures* (London: Serpent's Tail, 1993).

46. See *Northbound Imaginary: Relocating Post-Colonial Discourses in Hong Kong*, special issue of *Hong Kong Cultural Studies Bulletin* 3 (1995). In "The New Hong Kong Cinema and the Déjà Disparu," *Discourse* 16 (1994): 65–77, Ackbar Abbas registers this intensified *localism* occurring in Hong Kong under the threat of disruption and disappearance since the Joint Declaration rejoins a more transnational and nostalgically obsessed Hong Kong to Mainland China in 1997: "The new localism, on the other hand, investigates the dislocations of the local, where the local is something that mutates right in front of our eyes, like the language itself. Hong Kong Cantonese is now sprinkled with snatches of Mandarin, English, and barbarous sounding words and phrases—a hybrid language coming out of a hybrid space. It is by being local in this way that the new Hong Kong cinema is most international." For a different take on this postcolonial trauma of doom and boom, see Rey Chow, "A Souvenir of Love," *Modern Chinese Literature* 7 (1993): 59–78, as well as the essays and poems on Hong Kong culture in *West Coast Line* 21 (1997), and Gregory B. Lee, *Troubadours, Trumpeters, Troubled Makers: Lyricism, Nationalism and Hybridity in China and Its Others* (Durham, NC: Duke University Press, 1996).

ledge, MTV, and Wall Street offices (and garages) dressed in "global mass culture" garb.[47]

If there is an uneven feedback loop circulating mass imagery and mass communication from a high-tech core, this new U.S. hegemony, as Hall notes, takes place and spreads via "a peculiar form of homogenization" that seeks to amplify alliances with local forms of culture and multiplies linkages of capital, and hence embraces the proliferation of contradictions and ethnic/peripheral/marginal difference.[48] This is crucial for the workings and particularized survival of the local. As such, the emergence of a "global/local critical vocabulary" may reflect so many attempts to come to terms with this *looser* U.S.-driven situation, one in which the peripheral and local have more autonomy and cultural difference drives the imagery and fashion machines of postmodern global capital.

American dominance via MTV and the cultural capital of the Billboard 100 and *Rolling Stone* cannot be taken for granted along the Pacific Rim. At Tower Records outlets from Taipei to the world's biggest in Tokyo, East Asian pop culture dominates interest in a network that spreads from Hong Kong to Tokyo and Shanghai; in March 1995, for example, the best-selling compact disc at Taipei's Tower Records was not Madonna's *Bedtime Stories* but Sandy Lam singing *Love, Sandy* followed by Faye Wong's *Sky*. According to a recent survey in the *China Labor Daily*, primary school children in mainland China can tell you more about Hong Kong pop singer Andy Lau—his birthday, names of movies he has starred in, his hit songs—than they can about Mao Zedong. On Mainland China, consumer-driver pop culture has become the ground of market-socialist hegemony over populist desire as well as something potentially other to the system.[49]

---

47. Hall, "The Local and the Global," 27. I think Hall is being a bit too British-empire-gazing when he claims that this "global mass culture" remains Western-centered and once again speaks the same old hegemony-seeking, if rudely Americanized, English. Asia-Pacific may work otherwise, in other languages and flexible codes. See Hall's trenchant discussion with Naoki Sakai on the possibility of cultural studies in postimperial Japan, "A Tokyo Dialogue on Marxism, Identity Formation and Cultural Studies," in *Trajectories: Inter-Asia Cultural Studies*, ed. Kuan-Hsing Chen (London: Routledge, 1998), 360–78.

48. Hall, "The Local and the Global," 28.

49. "Lau Is in, Mao Is Out," *China News*, 12 March 1995. See Leo Ching on Taiwan and its attraction to the commodity culture of Japan and Hong Kong that undermines assumptions of U.S. culturalist hegemony in the region, in "Imaginings in the Empires

LOCATING CULTURAL STUDIES ALONG THE ASIA-PACIFIC RIM

Throughout the Asia/Pacific region, we can find evidence of a "counter-politics of the local" surging up and affirming locality in contexts of international influx. Places driven by "Asian-Pacific" dynamics, such as Taiwan and Hawai'i, are reshaping themselves into counternational and subnational entities at the same time, ascending and descending into something transnational and indigenous/local.[50] Given dynamics of high-tech-driven globalization, we can now see unpredictable outcomes, managing chaos and strange weather along the Pacific Rim. Australian cultural critics, confronting the global/local interface of cultures down under in the Pacific, are finding their own evidence to undermine the commonplace view that the transnationalization of media empires leads to a strengthening of U.S. hegemony.[51] The spread of cultural studies, as it localizes in differing national and regional contexts, has seen the proliferation of "schizoid" global/local logic and *nonbinary* explanations to map this uneven, fragmentary, and nomadic flux along certain lines of flight.[52]

of the Sun: Japanese Mass Culture in Asia," in *Asia/Pacific as Space of Cultural Production,* ed. Rob Wilson and Arif Dirlik (Durham, NC: Duke University Press, 1995), 262–83.

50. Some writers in post–Bamboo Ridge Hawai'i, disgruntled with sentimental forms of ethnicity and the nostalgia for place-bound identity, see Bamboo Ridge Press as operating, at times, more like that Taiwanese syndicate, the Bamboo Gang, which echoes the Chinese name for the Taiwan city of Hsinchu, or New Bamboo, where this first generation of ex-mainlanders settled. See the postmodern and cyborgian version of "the local" Hawai'i in the poems of Barry Masuda in Walter K. Lew, ed., *Premonitions: The Kaya Anthology of Asian North American Poetry* (New York: Kaya Production, 1995), 178–84, for example, "Cybercarp: Pastoral Ala Moana."

51. For example, Ien Ang has claimed of the widespread genres of media globalization, "There are, by contrast, contradictory and simultaneous processes of internationalization and localization of media production; centralization and decentralization of media power, homogenization and fragmentation of media consumption." See "Global Media/Local Meaning," *Media Information Australia* 63 (1991): 4–8.

52. If there is an "Asian-Pacific" imaginary driving political-economic reshaping of the region, there is as yet no Asian-Pacific cultural studies to deal with these transformations in any adequate critical way (see related materials on this in chap. 1). See Jon Bird, Barry Curtis, Tim Putnam, George Robertson, and Lisa Tickner, eds. *Mapping the Futures: Local Cultures, Global Change* (London: Routledge, 1993); and Valda Blundell, John Shepherd, and Ian Taylor, eds., *Relocating Cultural Studies: Developments in Theory and Research* (London: Routledge, 1993).

Some *surreal* mix of local, national, and global inputs and styles seems a fact of life in London as in Taipei, Honolulu, and Seoul. As the media euphoria of McLuhan meets the world-system logic of Wallerstein, this "global culture" of mishmash postmodernity can look a lot like Hong Kong, Bloomingdales, and the Ginza after all, that is to say, an integrated nexus rendering the local/national more open to the sexy culture of the commodity form and the financial weather reports of the *Asia Wall Street Journal*.[53]

From a survey of the *China Post* and *China News* in 1995 and 1997, it is clear that "Asia-Pacific" is a much-used signifier to express Taiwan's regional location in a globalizing contemporary economy. What it means is peculiar to the Pacific Rim vision of the Pacific: "Asia-Pacific" means the capitalist culture of Asia for the most part, and dominantly Hong Kong and Southern China, perhaps Japan; but there is no mention of any internal or island Pacific country or location, and the USA seems to figure in only as one huge export zone. The slogan "Go South," used earlier in the decade by the transnationalizing government of Taiwan to mobilize Asian/Pacific investment strategies (in places such as Vietnam, where Taiwan leads foreign developers), takes on weight as expressing an unfulfilled linkage with the other Pacific, and not just the migrant labor of the Philippines, and can have disturbing potential.[54] Exemplary of "Asia-Pacific" dynamics reforming the Pacific Rim, Taiwan is envisioned (by political policy and in its own English press) as a regional hub of Asia-Pacific transport, business, media, and exchange.[55] Liberalization and deregulation in the 1990s have led to a freer flow of goods and people into and out of the island, as Taiwan competes with business hubs such as Hong Kong and Singapore for regional primacy as a center of global/local interaction and exchange.

53. Surrealism, in which "urban elements are mixed up and hybridized without regard for historical contexts," though intensified in postmodernity, is just one type of urban space as theorized by Arata Isozaki and Akira Asada in their own poetics of local disappearance into "Anywhere"; see Abbas, "Building on Disappearance," 76–77.
54. On repressed aboriginal Pacific elements of Taiwanese cultural/national identity, see Chiu Yen Liang, "From the Politics of Identity to an Alternative Cultural Politics: On Taiwan's Primordial Inhabitants' A-Systemic Movement," in *Asia/Pacific as Space of Cultural Production*, ed. Rob Wilson and Arif Dirlik (Durham, NC: Duke University Press, 1995), 120–44.
55. See chap 1.

Perpetually under construction, open to the creative forces of popular democratization in global and local ways, postmodern Taipei, to zoom in on the maze, barrages the senses as an impure, dynamic, unevenly interwoven mixture of the traditional and modern, postmodern and primitive, high-tech and agrarian residual. In Pacific Rim guise, this means the expressive synergy of the global meeting the local, incarnating the unstable global/local dialectic. Beyond zoning, beyond rules, postmodern if not postcolonial Taipei swarms and creeps, amalgamates, grungy and grimy and full of signs and textures, mixes business and pleasure, life and cash. This neosublime of mixed commercial-residential uses makes Tokyo and Seoul seem as tame as Hilo.[56]

Consider this multilingual global/local item: "The Taipei City Government is considering adopting English as a third 'common language' alongside Mandarin and Hokkien (Taiwanese) as part of efforts to become a world-class metropolis and a major business hub in the Asia-Pacific region. . . . [The goal is] to expand the use of English into all levels of society to come in line with the city's development into a more international city."[57] Thus, in one move, the triple pulls of the local (Taiwanese) and the *transnational* (World English) on the *national* (Mandarin) would be pragmatically legitimated and brought by the city government into mixed-tongue circulation and public ratification, as they already are to some degree in the global/local city of Taipei.

The complex *Asian/Pacific locality* that is Taiwan, reformulated under the state gaze of the PRC since 1947, which has again become a global power and reclaimed Hong Kong in July 1997, looks at once forward to the high-tech and commodified market of Japan and backward to its own primordial Pacific inhabitants whose languages and tribal visions make new claims on the Han-based nation that emerged in differential defiance. In this sense, the island of Taiwan is truly Asia/Pacific in its tension: torn between Hong Kong and Tokyo and Beijing, as well as called back by the conjuring of primordial memories older than the modes of modernity and the nation-state the KMT represented as collective common sense to its tribal inhabitants from mountain and sea.

56. Recall that ICRT radio ad for Pacific Rim survival (in English and partly in Mandarin) when it's summer in the city: "It's gridlock in Taipei. Oh no, I have another headache. Take Bufferin!"

57. *China Post*, 5 April 1995, 15.

Taiwan: with its distinctive Asian-Pacific history of taking into its own island makeup all kinds of refugees and pirates, traders, runaways, and migrants from more confining terrain to the north in the PRC and Hong Kong and God knows where else. Ambiguously tied to the motherland yet maintaining quasi-autonomy of cultural-political identity, Taiwan is seeing companies relocating from Hong Kong to the Singapore city-state to keep developing and investing in Mainland China without being absorbed as of 1997, when China took over the former British colony. Some twenty thousand Taiwanese have registered headquarters in Hong Kong to do business on the mainland. "China" is thus a multiple signifier of unresolved tensions and global/local contradictions. Whatever its relationship to the mainland, Taiwan functions as a regional entity, both local-national and offshore transnational (would-be "hub of the Asia-Pacific region"). Many people in different walks of life in Taiwan are beginning to wonder about— and protest—the social and ecological consequences of this "all for export" mentality at the core of Taiwan's transnationalization given the proliferating politicization of civil society in Taiwan since the end of martial law in 1987.[58]

"Taiwanese identity" is an open question, or a threat, a promise: refiguring the past, challenging the literature and art of the present with nativist and cosmopolitan tensions, opening what has been called "the Pandora's Box of the island's political future."[59] On the one hand, the "Taiwanization" of political power that has culminated in the presidency of Lee Teng-hui has corresponded with the rise of a "nativist literature" and "homeland literature" in the arts and a caustic fiction riddled with rural nostalgia and urban gloom; on the other hand, the influx of postmodernist style continues to complicate any simple "nativist" or tradition-oriented mix.[60]

Working as cultural icons both internationally and locally, Ang Lee's two Oscar-nominated Taiwanese films, *The Wedding Banquet* (1993) and *Eat Drink Man Woman* (1994), span the diasporic spaces of these Tai-

---

58. See Stevan Harrell and Huang Chun-chieh, eds., *Cultural Change in Postwar Taiwan* (Taipei: SMC Publishing, 1994), 8.

59. See Thomas B. Gold, "Civil Society and Taiwan's Quest for Identity," in ibid., 47–68.

60. See the essay on the hybrid elements of Taiwanese aesthetic identity by Jason C. Kuo, "Painters of the Postwar Generation in Taiwan," in *Cultural Change in Postwar Taiwan*, ed. Stevan Harrell and Huang Chun-chieh (Taipei: SMC Publishing, 1994), 246–74.

wanese global/local identities. If nostalgic for Chinese patriarchy and aligned to the nation-state pathos of contemporary fathers, the films do portray the reconstituted Taiwanese family as a cosmopolitan mixture of Confucian and postmodern norms. The postnational space of Taipei connects and intermixes with the gender norms, expressive values, and technologies of New York City, Stockholm, and Sydney, and the genres merge Hollywood screwball comedy with Hong Kong textures of capitalist good fortune, risk, and kung fu mastery surviving in the vision of the displaced mainlander father (the general, the master chef) living within displacement. With such a mixed background, it makes postmodern sense that Hollywood would turn to Lee to film Jane Austen's *Sense and Sensibility* (1995) to express tensions between capitalist prudence (global sense) and romantic excess (local sensibility and custom), as if (working between the colonialisms of Japan, China, and the USA) Lee could express a "British" ex-colonial subject.[61]

Asking at once for recognition from the Chinese mainland as "political entity" and for international legitimacy from the UN, GATT, and the World Trade Organization, Taiwan is torn internally between the calls of Asian motherland and Pacific homeland. Or is it simply that "world as a single place" of transnational capital calling? In contexts of heightened globalization, the emergence of a new and uncanny localism, grounded in distinctive culture and languages and claiming other histories to simplistic "Chinese" claims, can represent a threat to hegemony—to "rival nations" on both sides of the Taiwan Strait.[62]

A scholar in the National Taiwan Normal University library, poring over an essay in *Telos*, gets up to ask me the meaning of the italicized phrase *homo economicus*. Is this the Asian-Pacific cyborg we have already become,

---

61. Lee's "Father Knows Best" films are read much more skeptically as doing nation-state work by Kuan-Hsing Chen, "Taiwan New Cinema'" in *Oxford Guide to Film Studies,* ed. John Hill and Pamela Church Gibson (Oxford: Oxford University Press, 1998); and Shu-mei Shih, "Globalization as Minoritization: Ang Lee and the Politics of Flexibility," *New Formations* (forthcoming). For a related study, see Rob Wilson, "Korean Cinema on the Road to Globalization: Tracking Global/Local Dynamics, or Why Im Kwan-Taek Is No Ang Lee," in a collection of essays (Wayne State University Press, forthcoming) on Korean cinema coedited by David James and Hyun-Ock Im.

62. As Abbas writes of the Hong Kong "local" as it interfaces 1997, "In many cases newfound interest in local culture and politics appear at the moment when catastrophe, real or imagined, threatens" (*Hong Kong,* 70).

homo economicus as Pacific Man? Later, I read a headline that suggests much about the flexibility of Taiwan as "Asian-Pacific" hub: President Lee Teng-hui says "chaos only temporary" (*China News,* 3 March 1995). Another headline around the same time in the *China Post* best allegorized for me the David-versus-Goliath battle of Taiwan island in all its global hopefulness as island power: "Locals Conquer Mount Everest."

Tracking lines of flight, as I have urged in this study, the global/local interaction has become a mixed blessing and foreshadows an uneven yet hopeful future inside the "Asia-Pacific region," sites in which globalization has intensified commitments to the local and the regional in a new way. Every generation of Americans since the Civil War, as F. Scott Fitzgerald once warned, shares the "sense of being somehow about to inherit the earth."[63] But, in the ever flowing Asia-Pacific, what we inherit is made out of the ocean and the salts of labor and poetry, and the magical waters and "lines of flight" may just flow from your hands. As cultural critics, as citizens with lingering commitments to justice, community, and place, we need to measure the damages and chart the dreams of local sensibility and national imaginary as these practices emerge within the brave new world that is late-capitalist globalization.

63. F. Scott Fitzgerald, undated letter to Frances Scott Fitzgerald, in *The Crack-Up,* ed. Edmund Wilson (New York: New Directions, 1945), 306.

CHAPTER 9

Postmodern X:

Honolulu Traces

Since Copernicus man has been rolling from the center toward X.
—Friedrich Nietzsche, *The Will to Power*[1]

Once there were "neighborhoods," like Kaimuki.

Explain yourself in plain English. *Art House. Artwear.*

Deployed as news or fashion, postmodernism was beginning to feel like a problem of discursive overload, too much information coding the individual head.

"I, author-function."

"I" "was" "suffering" "from" "a" "case" "of" "semiotic" "overload."

Location became a question of continuity, like how do I get from one day to the next, that was not a function of lyric mood. The problem of living within nonnarrative was gleefully read as decentered pluralism, first-person-singular "rooms with a view."

Some were attacking "theory" for premature totalizing: "Jameson's Restaurant" (North Shore), "Lentricchia's Bar & Grill" (Durham). Some were fed up with the will to theory: "We have a hunger for examples."

1. Friedrich Nietzsche, "European Nihilism," in *The Will to Power*, trans. Walter Kaufmann and R. J. Hollingdale (New York: Vintage, 1968), 8.

"I, author-function" was suffering from a case of semiotic overload, so I headed home to the Island Colony to drink some Japanese beer with Hawaiian labels (surf scenes of Waikīkī Beach minus the hotels).

The assembling and disassembling of a poem was related to a helicopter hitting the beaches of Nicaragua, though this was my own projection.

Eventually the question of postmodernism came around to the wonders of dining at McDonalds, though I tried to point out that the pseudovernacular styles spelled the death of regionalism in simulacrous copy, the emptying out of local creolization: koa wood counters for Waikīkī, Peggy Hopper prints for Moiliili, pastel sailboats for Hawaiʻi Kai, Elvis posters for Bamboo Ridge.

The Kodak Hula Show, which has existed in Honolulu since 1937, could now begin to function nicely as a postmodern art form, phasing out so-called real hula, or at least desacralizing it in the context of mass images, a trillion copies, flashbulbs popping from Pearl City to Rochester. So the postmodern became a function of image displaced from prior context, force severed from history, sign floating in the free market of commodity exchange. A kind of sublime infinitude.

It was simply, the man said, a matter of imperial burlesque, *not* a matter of choice, tone, or mood. You were both exhilarated and weirded out, overamped and emptied, filled with a million exchangeable signs with the inability to do anything about it except keep on exchanging them, even in a Mānoa zendo.

"Products from all over the world lie available to you on the shelves [of the Waikīkī Duty Free Shop]. What do you reach for? Do you think about climbing on board your jetliner with a newly purchased six-pack of Coke? No. But what about a Gucci bag? Yes, of course. In a sense, duty-free shops are the precursor to what life will be like in a genuinely borderless environment."[2]

2. Kenichi Ohmae, *The Borderless World: Power and Strategy in the Interlinked Economy* (London: Fontana, 1991), 34.

The "ontological hunger" you felt for the sacred displaced itself into a search for private truth. She became your signifier/signified, "Hiroshima Mon Amour." "She" alluded to an infinite range of lexical possibilities, metaphors, cottage industry truths, site of tropological production.

My fellow Americans, you had a nostalgia for master narratives, a longing for mountain grandeur and paternal households across the prairies of Iowa, so the political unconscious invented Pat Robertson ("I, Pat Robertson, do solemnly swear . . .").

Her anger was not cold war paranoia, simply an accurate consciousness of events. As for "reification," why do these people have to use such foreign-sounding words to talk about such simple things?

The bottom line is.

"India and Pakistan have fought two of their three wars [since 1947] over the Himalayan state and continue to skirmish daily along the 'line of control' that [since 1971] divides Kashmir [between the two]. . . . The airstrikes, the first in Kashmir in 20 years, have escalated tensions between the two nuclear powers in South Asia and alarmed world leaders."[3]

Eric Chock. Robert Chalk.[4]

I filled my cramped study walls in the Island Colony with postcards and pictures of Emerson, Kenzaburo Oe, Robert Johnson, and Montgomery Clift, and a gleaming photo of a red '57 Chevy convertible I had coveted as a

3. "Pakistan Claims Two Fighters Downed," Associated Press wire story, *Honolulu Advertiser*, 27 May 1999, A1.
4. Eric Chock is the coeditor of Bamboo Ridge Press and author of the cautionary collection of poems on the death and rebirth of the Honolulu local, *Last Days Here* (Honolulu: Bamboo Ridge Press, 1990); "Robert Chalk" is another name for Rob Sean Wilson, author of this mongrel essay/poem on the disappearance of the Honolulu local as a fate of postmodern desacralization. On this global/local fate, also see Rob Wilson, *Ananda Air: American Pacific Lines of Flight* and *Automat: Un/American Poetics*, both forthcoming; and "Seven Tourist Sonnets" on the Internet journal from Australia and England *Jacket* 7 (1999) (www.jacket.zip.com.au/jacket07/index07), edited by the innovative poet/editor John Tranter.

kid back in the downsizing Brass Valley of western Connecticut. I longed for time to stand still, back up, leap, rewind, fast-forward.

Father Marx. Father Freud. Mother Nature. Mother Goose.

My disgust at sublime commodification was based on a lapsed-Catholic abhorrence toward a desacralized world.

"They alarmed me."

Whatever happened to the Kuhio Bar & Grill?

Wallace Stevens's "Anecdote of the Jar" began to look like an air-raid drill on slovenly, Third World natives. Haiku read like suicide dives into the Pacific, ethnic pacification.

The aura must die and be reborn as signs. The aura of a billboard for designer jeans. As for the symbol, what would be left to symbolize?

Each day postmodern English deployed itself in expanding territories. Time was wrapped in clear plastic at Liberty House in Ala Moana, readying the planet for Easter clearance sales. Space was a detailed regret for the billing lading.

We locals fondly called the thirteen nuclear submarines the "old blues" and "old salts" of Pearl Harbor. How many Hiroshimas squared? The state had plans to evacuate the citizens of Honolulu to the kahuna-laden "friendly island" of Moloka'i. There would probably be a traffic jam on the H-1 freeway going out to the airport. Remember the last tsunami scare?[5]

5. I dedicate this little mongrel poem/essay to Eric Chock, who for twenty years, from 1979 to 1999 in Hawai'i, has supported my poetry and cultural criticism in the journal *Bamboo Ridge*, and made this transplant from Connecticut/California feel a part of something emerging and evolving, something bigger than self or career; given the huge obliviousness of the U.S. lyric poetry scene, this support meant a lot to me and still does.

Part Italian, Part Many Things Else:

Creating "Asia/Pacific" along a Honolulu – Taipei
Line of Flight

In Pirandello we have, moreover, the critical awareness of being simultaneously "Sicilian," "Italian," and "European" . . . Pirandello is critically a Sicilian "villager" [local] who has acquired certain national and European traits, but who feels these three elements of civilization [local, national, global cosmopolitan] to be juxtaposed and contradictory in himself. From this experience has come his attitude of observing the contradictions in other people's personalities and then of actually seeing the drama of [postmodern] life as the drama of these contradictions.

—Antonio Gramsci, "Theater of Pirandello"

ON DE-BECOMING A HAOLE

Settled amid the long-rooted identity struggles on this most fluid and contentious of Asian-Pacific islands, haoles are all sort of lumped together into one crude category, cast as the death-dealing Hegelian white other: half-affectionately and with historically justified outrage bashed and blessed as the hostile "white stranger" profiteering in the indigenous terrain of this tourism-driven island microstate, Hawai'i. "Once a haole, always a haole" runs the simplistic refrain, as if race is destiny and culture is the fate of birth and bounded belonging. Within such colonial frameworks, there is no place to create or move along a line of flight.

To Rob Martone (Hoashi) Wilson, given my semiwretched experiences of growing up half-Scottish and half-Italian in ethnic and class enclaves, my historical trajectory westward from mill towns in Connecticut to the Asian-Pacific region, as well as a scholarly poetic career writing inside the complicated terrains of Hawai'i, South Korea, and Taiwan, this *undifferentiated* category for "white people" as Eternal Haole masks the impurity of how self-divided, culturally schizophrenic, and full of domination/subordination, lines of invention and flight, and class injustice white groups have lived in relation to one another. American culture is not just given by family or nation, but quested for and contested into being through strategies of mixture and risk, in places such as Waterbury, Connecticut, in WASPish New England USA, where I grew up in the postwar era of the Baby Boom. As earlier claimed (see introduction), my flight westward was never meant to enact a miming of the Manifest Destiny "frontier" project, but to express (as in Jack Kerouac's "dharma bum" quest for wilder freedoms in California and disorientation via Asian belief systems such as Buddhism and Tao) a way across and out of American common sense at the shopping mall of the soul. It traced a different, more mixed, haphazard way of "becoming global."

Embracing "deterritorialization" and "becoming minor," Deleuze saw the promise of American literature, its madness and quest for experimentation and release, in these words from F. Scott Fitzgerald in the "depression trilogy" from *The Crack-Up*, written as he was undergoing a breakdown of his powers as a writer and his country was making its way through a massive depression and clash of ideologies in between the two World Wars. "The ones who had survived," Fitzgerald told himself as his gifts fell apart, "had made some sort of clean break. This is a big word and is no parallel to a jail-break when one is probably headed for a new jail or will be forced back to the old one. The famous 'Escape' or 'run away from it all' is an excursion in a trap even if the trap includes the South Seas, which are only for those who want to paint them or sail them."[1] Of course, as I have tried to show, these South Seas do not exist just as backdrop for white people to write about, paint, or sail around in, to forget their sense of worthlessness and modern unease in exotic travel pieces for the *Saturday Evening Post:* Asian-Pacific peoples have inhabited these sites as places of sweat, creation, and belonging. At the edge of empires, Americans must tread warily in places where their binary machines fall apart into otherness and they can begin to learn the ways of silence, inaction, and wonder.

Still, Fitzgerald points to the creative potential of the *flight westward:* the

---

1. F. Scott Fitzgerald, "Pasting It Together," in *The Crack-Up*, ed. Edmund Wilson (New York: New Directions, 1945), 81.

discovery that the U.S. self is a mobile flux, becoming *disoriented* at the frontier and crossroads; letting go of land, the idle chatter of standard English, comfortable moorings in convention, preformed ideology, the lineage of habit. "A clean break is something you cannot come back from; that is irretrievable because it makes the past cease to exist," Fitzgerald continues, as he relegated his old selves and manic anxieties, midcareer, "to the junk heap of the shoulder pads worn for one day on the Princeton freshman football field and the overseas cap never worn overseas."[2]

So what, one might ask? Why care about this Jazz Age writer sinking into alcoholism, authorial tycoon seeking some will to oblivion and self-forgetting as if in a "clean break" from the past? It is exactly *crazed speculations* such as these that Gilles Deleuze takes as expressions of the will to nomadic flight and "geographical becoming" that is at the heart of "American" literary culture, as it creates the future along "lines of flight to the orient," where East is calling out to the West and the West can be left behind. To leave, to escape, to unsettle is to *trace a line of flight:* becoming a force of imaginative rupture and assemblage, becoming one of those experimental producers and forces for minority expression "who create their line of flight, who create through a line of flight."[3]

A writer not writing becomes a kind of used maniac, an automaton; for to write is to create a nervous line of flight into otherness, to shape a process of *becoming-other,* like Ishmael becoming Queequeg; or Ahab becoming the white whale of his own deepest national-personal demons; or, in our century, the quirky Italo Calvino becoming Gary Cooper or Jimmy Stewart by projecting himself into American spaces in a remote seacoast town in prefascist Italy. Such a "minority" project creating social transformation does not exist ready-made, but has to be nurtured into expression like some Robocop war machine writing within/against a dominant language (working over the "island English" of Imperial England) or creating group formations of identity, along lines of flight "which are also ways of advancing and attacking."[4]

2. Ibid., 84.
3. Gilles Deleuze and Claire Parnet, "On the Superiority of Anglo-American Literature," in *Dialogues,* trans. Hugh Tomlinson and Barbara Habberjam (New York: Columbia University Press, 1987), 36–37.
4. Ibid., 43. On the will to deform "imperial English" via minority islands of experimental languages within/against it, also see Charles Bernstein, "Time out of Motion: Looking ahead to See Backward," in *A Poetics* (Cambridge, MA: Harvard University Press,

At the U.S. origin of this "becoming that is geographical," we might recall the white-ethnic conflicts of transatlantic sender countries such as Ireland, England, Scotland, Germany, Yugoslavia, and Poland. Or the "Northern and Southern conflict" that still tears Italy between the cultural capital of Romans to the north and the passionately localized traditions of the island of Sicily to the south. This remains just one example of internal division, class and regional conflict, split between islands and mainland as not just a function of place rivalry but of country and city oppositions, clashes of custom and cultural capital. Such regional hatreds are aggravated by the injustices of the global system spreading across the landscape its cars and malls of Fordism, blockbuster fantasy films that changed the shapes and codes everyday life. In places like San Remo, Italy, for example, where Calvino grew up nourishing his singular imagination on the American cinema of the thirties, glutting his own counterlife on those American films "that have something absolutely novel to tell us: and always that novelty has to do with the highways, the drugstores, young faces or old, the way one moves through spaces, the way one passes one's life."[5]

This is what that mentor figure of cultural studies in the twentieth century, Antonio Gramsci, born to a lower-middle-class family in Ghilarza, Sardinia, in 1891, imprisoned for ten years by the fascists of Mussolini for his communist activism and will to justice on earth, until his death in prison in 1937—this is what Gramsci called the problematic of "The Southern Question."[6] "What Italy has given to the world" is not only authors such as Pirandello and Quasimodo from Sicily, the god-poet Dante from

---

1992), 117–20; Susan Schultz's journal of experimental Pacific-based writing, *Tinfish;* the "War-Machine" series of works in cultural politics by the *Isle Margins* journal collective in Taipei; and Rob Wilson, *Automat: Un/American Poetics* (forthcoming) on cultural and poetic dynamics of becoming in Asia-Pacific as linked to the uprooting of New England seen as a site linked to China and Hawai'i.

5. Italo Calvino, "A Cinema-Goer's Autobiography," in *The Road to San Giovanni*, trans. Tim Parks (New York: Vintage, 1994), 63–64.

6. See Antonio Gramsci, *Selections from the Prison Notebooks*, ed. and trans. by Quintin Hoare and Geoffrey Nowell Smith (New York: International, 1985), 67, 70–74, 92–99. This is a problematic from the 1920s that raises enduring questions (and cultural-political strategies) on regional conflict, national hegemony, and the power of the global political economy as class exploitation. We might recall it in any discussion of "local"/ "southern" island identity. For example, the "southbound imaginary" of Taiwan to Southeast Asia and the "northbound imaginary" of Hong Kong to China have proven to be important research agendas for cultural studies in these sites.

Florence, Fellini, and Calvino from postmodern chambers of cinema-going along the Mediterranean, as well as pizza from Naples and those Gucci bags of Asian-Pacific fascination. Italy has given us Antonio Gramsci from the universities and prisons of Sardinia. Anybody who knows transnational cultural studies these days, as it spreads and changes from Birmingham to Melbourne to Honolulu and Taipei, knows how important Gramsci has proven to contesting ("reimagining") the production of twentieth-century cultural identity in commonsense conditions of subaltern domination, popular duping, and media resistance, conditions of cultural capital that continue ripping off the unwary, the undereducated, racially stigmatized creatures of this late-capitalist shopping mall world from Kalihi and Watts to Auckland and Mars.[7]

Recently, in the political ferment that is Italy, while Japanese, European, and U.S. tourists gloated and watched, immigrants from such places as Senegal, Ghana, Nigeria, and Morocco marched down the monument-littered streets of Rome. These stigmatized others carried protest banners saying "We Want a World Made Up of All Colors" and "Down With All Racists!" This march, organized by Italy's three main labor federations, drew some fifteen thousand citizens to protest a series of violent attacks on immigrants in Italy (the same thing is happening in Germany and France, given our border-hopping transnational economy, as within the white backlash against "Southern" (Mexican/Asian) immigrants in anti–affirmative action California). What a way for "the country of Benetton," with its multicultural, multicolored ads, to act. I could not help recalling how Italian immigrants into the working cities of New England were discriminated against, treated as scum, derided, beaten only fifty years ago by a different configuration of labor unions and race and class politics.

For I grew up in the mixed-ethnic part of Connecticut: not the Gold Coast of WASP normality, but the Brass Valley of industrial labor, grim Yankee work ethic, Catholic school pedagogy, and ethnic interaction/intermarriage. A place where each new ethnic group (coming from Italy or Puerto Rico) was marked as inferior, outsider, colored, shiftless, lazy, for the sin of not having come over to New England with the forebears of John

7. For a retooling of this Gramscian heritage to fit the global/local conditions of contemporary cultural studies and the transnational/postcolonial moment, see Stuart Hall, "The Problem of Ideology: Marxism without Guarantees" and "Cultural Studies and Its Theoretical Legacies," both in *Stuart Hall: Critical Dialogues in Cultural Studies,* ed. David Morley and Kuan-Hsing Chen (London: Routledge, 1996), 25–46 and 262–75.

Winthrop and Betsy Ross on the *Mayflower*—as if those "black-hearted Protestants" (as my father called them) had done so. Given that my mother's immigrant family, the Martones, had uprooted themselves from Naples and Fagenta, Italy, to move to New York City and parts north in the early twentieth-century labor diaspora, I was both one of those marked creatures of lazy erotic passion, dirty smells, and beastly hairiness and sloth, as well as, through Scottish ancestors on my father's side, one of those grim little wasp-hearted subjects. Robert Sean Wilson, my great-grandfather, grew up in Collingwood, Ontario, and became an English schoolmaster after his family settled there in 1852 after taking the ship *Ann Harley* from Glasgow as a "line of flight westward" from the island of Jura, Scotland, and later traced a movement toward Montreal and Everett, Massachusetts, in quest of work. Thus, I could (and did) play both sides of the ethnic/nonethnic streets of myself, like a pragmatic flower child who believed in democracy and read Walt Whitman's e pluribus unum catalogs as literal description of the U.S. cultural polity.

HOUSE UNAMERICAN ACTIVITIES:
TAKING FLIGHT TOWARD ASIA/PACIFIC

Coming from this non-wasp tradition and growing up in the punk-ethnic streets of lower-middle-class New England, it is a good fate, at times, to be stigmatized, scorned, marked (in reverse) as a minority, outsider, as "resident alien" local, as they say in Taiwan. I came to be what I am as Rob Wilson hailing from Waterbury, Connecticut, and education into High English at the University of California at Berkeley, minor experiences, as when I got to Honolulu in 1976 and was not chosen for pickup basketball games because the teams were Japanese or Samoan or Micronesian or University of Hawai'i at Mānoa dorm. Nobody knew me at the Kanewai courts and all looked on me with mute suspicion as nonlocal. This was a learning experience of xenophobia and racial/ethnic stigmatization: maybe to know a bit what Dave Sakai felt as the only Japanese student in his high school in Kennedy-era Connecticut.[8]

8. *Xenophobia*, I realized, can be a local's defense against a long heritage of orientalism and an American brand of (disavowed) colonialism in the Pacific, sublimating its economic and military operations into the freedom of free market idioms and conversion to its liberal self-beliefs.

Later, I played forward on a Roy Sakuma Production team in the Pearl City over-thirty basketball league with a bunch of local players: Roy, with his magic ukulele hands playing swift-moving guard and shooting money shots from all angles, and our quiet, powerful center Kali Watson (since become the director of Hawaiian Home Lands), who turned up late from his Bishop Street law offices but could turn the game around with his domineering presence on the court. We hung out together on Sunday near Cook Field courts and got along well in the mix and flow of "local culture" at its best. Since the mid-1970s, having experienced the mix and muck of the local literary scene and culture, I have become engaged "organically" (to use the Gramscian term) both as writer and poet-scholar to express and dignify the plight of Asian/Pacific ethnicity on the mixed-tongue islands of Hawai'i and Taiwan. I can only assume that such an affiliation grows out of prior experiences of having a mixed-blood heritage in New England, as well as out of respect for the subaltern cultures of Italy, Ireland, and Scotland.

In 1995, a literary scholar at National Tsing Hua University in Taiwan, just back from an upscale conference on "cultural identity" in Vienna, informed me, "They say in Italy that an Italian first identifies with his local region ('I am a Milano'), then with Europe ('I am a European in spirit'), and only third with the modern nation of Italy ('I am an Italian')." If the local might take precedence (in this maxim of Italian identity) over the global and the national, this identification would only thicken in blood, language, and cultural commitment. Although I was a bit drunk from Taiwan beer, my ears perked up at this global/local maxim: Was this a way to clarify connections among the cultural politics of Italy, Taiwan, and Hawai'i? Was "Taiwanese" at once a localist, internationalist, and nationalist coding, in that order? (Taiwan is not even recognized internationally as a nation, though it functions as one; see chapters 1 and 8.)

Questions multiplied. What about a Sicilian or Sardinian, like Gramsci? What about the multiple peoples of Hawai'i, Asian/Pacific/European settler peoples versus Hawaiian indigenous ones? How would this formula work to express island identity for the diverse and contradictory groups here? Was each island grouping, in odd ways, both inside and outside some domineering mainland national hegemony? Was it content to be "merely local" in some nomadic, unaccountable sense that kept on moving while standing still in the huge ocean? Island: nation unto itself where things flowed in circles and came back around to nurture the community and the is/land? Or forces of fleeting power came and went across the island body, to rip it off?

What kind of new "pidgin cuisine" identity-speak was I cooking up here—part Italian, part Taiwanese, part Korean, part Hawaiian—as the Bamboo Ridge novelist Gary Pak asked me via e-mail, from Honolulu to Taipei, across our words of local greeting, *e mālama pono, take care da body.* (Wasn't the famous Honolulu mayor, Johnny Wilson, perhaps a distant Scottish-Hawaiian relative of mine?[9] What about that Sicilian politician from Hartford who looked like a more suave version of my Uncle Peter, Mayor Frank Fasi? Now I must be hallucinating in my own Pacific!)

To supplement this push toward doing cultural theory of Asian-Pacific islands as sites of migrant mixture, I offer a few final examples of my own cultural schizophrenia expressed and affirmed as a good thing: culture experienced as a process of stylistic and biological impurity, as well as the embrace of translocal mixture and spiritual adventure as "dharma bum." I again invoke a poem from the *Best of Bamboo Ridge* of 1986 "Anita Sky": "I marinated her heart / Oh Italian artichoke."[10] This was written by Rob (Martone) Wilson at a thirty-something moment when the scapegoated and feminized Italian part of myself, my mother's side of the family, was coming to the forefront after I felt burnt out by a WASP ethic of work and grim self-mastery that I identified with the Scottish side of my family, which had driven me to get a doctorate in English in my twenties: Italianicity that I identified with emotional depth (heart), iconography of Catholicism (Mary worship), operatic self-display of emotion (confession), food and forgiveness (beyond revenge), recipe for pasta.[11]

There are passages, by way of looping back, that I would like to quote

9. The part-Hawaiian engineer and Democratic mayor of Honolulu for fourteen years from 1920 to 1954, Johnny Wilson, who has a tunnel and lake on Oʻahu named after him, first brought ward politics from Chicago to Honolulu and thus helped shape the Democratic bloc vote that wrested power from the Republican sugar oligarchy. See Bob Krauss, *Johnny Wilson: First Hawaiian Democrat* (Honolulu: University of Hawaiʻi Press, 1994), 41–52, 70–77.

10. *Best of Bamboo Ridge,* ed. Eric Chock and Darrell Lum (Honolulu: Bamboo Ridge Press, 1986), 111.

11. An earlier work of poetry and mixed-language prose, *Waking in Seoul* (Seoul: Mineumsa Press, 1988), tracks my flight "waking to global capitalism" in postmodern East Asia and moving away from fixed categories of American selfhood into crossroad situations of flux and reinvention; ethnicity and forms of nationalism keep coming back at the transnational border where identity struggles are being carried on and amplified.

from an oral history study of life in the Connecticut Brass Valley that show how fiercely separated ethnic communities were from one another back in the Northeast, as well as how marked, stigmatized, and subordinated these U.S. immigrant groups were to the dominant WASP culture. As Sarah Cappella puts it, "The Irish married the Irish. I'm Italian, I marry the Italian. That's the way it was in those days. Now no more. Now it's a mixed world."[12] Frank Keane recalls the reign of ethnic tensions in the Brass Valley: "There was no melting pot. When you came into town, if you were Italian, you moved up to Town Plot or way up to the North End. They were Italian people, and it was Little Italy. If you were French, you moved down to the South End. That's where the French church was and all the French-speaking people."[13] If you tried to go to an Irish church like St. Patrick's, you were told, "You don't belong here; you're Italian."[14] A shop foreman named H. Hickman recalls a dispute he had with a "Mick" in an Ansonia mill, in which he argued (in terms miming imperial logic), "The English are the dominant people in the world—aren't they? You admit that. That's what God made 'em for. They dominate over Ireland don't they? Well, that's why I was sent over here [to Connecticut] from England to dominate over you."[15] Times may have changed, through in-mixture and intermarriage, into something better.

My mother's story (Katherine Martone Wilson, who taught me that Mary worship and mutual respect were at the core of existence) suggests how, as a second-generation Italian from Naples, she was snubbed and treated poorly by my father's smugly superior Scottish sisters in Connecticut, who looked down on Italians (EYETALIANS) as not fully fit for belonging in New England, as dark and dirty, erotic peasants, and so on. But my father, Robert John Wilson III, became a Catholic to marry my Italian mother, and this will to transformation became a key motif in my life as will to spiritual existence and subaltern cultural politics. Culture seen as quest for states and mixtures not of identity but self-transcendence, impurity, outreach.

12. Quoted in *Brass Valley: The Story of Working People's Lives and Struggles in an American Industrial Region*, The Brass Workers History Project, compiled and edited by Jeremy Brecher, Jerry Lombardi, and Jan Stackhouse (Philadelphia: Temple University Press, 1982), 92.
13. Quoted in ibid., 21.
14. Comment by Caroline Nardello, ibid., 22.
15. Quoted in ibid., 22.

I grew up in a city where the once-blue rivers flowed with the prosperity, muck, and industrial filth of hard labor in the brass and copper mills and other industries that never slept during the wars and postwar buildup. Slowly, ethnic barriers and borders broke down in Connecticut via social interaction, intermarriage, willy-nilly coalition, risk-taking flights toward "paradise" like the cross-country journey in the Eagles' song "The Last Resort." In the course of mobility from Fitzgerald's 1930s into Reagan's 1980s, we find the push toward articulating ethnic concerns and cultural themes of third and fourth generations who by now are *tired* of market homogenization and a creeping sense of cultural loss. Falling down and breaking out, we see the return of "white ethnics" into the house of sub-altern/local culture, in works of autobiographical fiction such as those of Frank Lentricchia, Michael Ondaatje, and Michael Stephens.[16] America is not just will to domination but an energy of invention and flight, "becoming ethnic," to put this in hopeful Deleuzian terms of minority flux and nomadic risk.

Postmodern morals we could now draw from this, although others will see different themes in the muck of my life and the cultural politics I have presented here around Bamboo Ridge. A now defunct Kyoto journal of postmodern ethnography/poetry called *Melimelo* followed its own pro-impurity vision, which makes a lot of sense to me, given the mixtures of heritage, the trajectories I have made in my life: "Look to the offshoots, not to the roots."

This is where I want to live, work, and love amid the makings of culture and poetry during my coming years on earth: inside those "borderlands" and space of flows where two or more cultures can clash and mix, abiding on islands where different races can occupy the same territory in peace, respect, and coalition; where different classes can touch, flow, and move;

16. See Frank Lentricchia, *The Edge of Night: A Confession* (New York: Random House, 1994), and Michael Stephens, *The Brooklyn Book of the Dead* (New York: Dalkey Archive, 1994). On performative dimensions and dangers of such works, see Kit Wallingford, "The Theater of the Self," *American Quarterly* 49 (1997): 423–28. Also see the powerful critique of this self-performative genre of academic memoirs of cultural identity by Cynthia Franklin, "Turning Japanese/Returning to America: Race and Nation in Memoirs by Cathy Davidson and David Mura," which will form part of her forthcoming study of this genre. My colleague's shrewd comments, however, have not deterred me from writing this devious little memoir of a coda, nor from linking my scholarly works in theorizing poetics to the "lines of flight" and dharma-bum movements in my own life.

"where two or more cultures edge into each other . . . , where the space between two individuals shrinks with intimacy."[17]

For if this is an uncomfortable "place of contradictions," a *disorienting* space of flows and impure mixtures of rival codes and powers, it is also where something fresh and promissory of transpacific culture might be created. Sicily, Taiwan, and Hawai'i are island places of intimate identity and wacky mixed tongues where binary colonial selves like Caliban and Prospero can turn into one another, and, in their rage, bliss, and mixed tongues, can have lovely kids named Calibanos Prosperity Scorsese-Chung.[18] We can only give back what we can to these places and sites of Asia/Pacific: the respect, creative flux, and cultural wonders they have given us as island communities in which "to work and to love" and to flow back into the dirty, magical Pacific.

17. Gloria Anzaldúa, preface to *Borderlands/La Frontera* (San Francisco: Aunt Lute Books, 1987), vii.

18. This is my own cultural deformation of Aimé Cesaire's (postcolonial) deformation of Shakespeare's *The Tempest* in *Une Tempest* (Paris: Editions du Seuil, 1969), set in the tormented West Indies, which I have taught over and over in the interlinked region of Asia-Pacific as a way of undoing the "white magic" of Master Prospero and his bag of English Department tropes of excolonial possession and cryptic will to redemption. See Rob Wilson, "Another Tempest," *Tinfish* 1 (1995): 11.

Takaki, Ronald, 22
Talk Story (conferences), 119, 126n, 131,
140, 143, 227. *See also* Bamboo Ridge;
Sumida, Stephen
Teaiwa, Teresia, 168
Thailand, 29
Theroux, Paul, xvi, 12, 65, 72, 102, 225,
234; *Happy Isles of Oceania*, 73n, 77,
113–14, 167–68, 225
Thomas, Nicholas, 12n, 172
Tinfish (journal), 120
Tonouchi, Lee, 142
Tourism, xvii, 70n, 71; in Hawai'i, xiv–xv,
xvii, 93n, 111, 137, 197, 229–31, 269–
72. *See also* Hawai'i; Polynesian Cul-
tural Center; Kodak Hula Show; Sense
of place; Waikīkī Beach
Transnational capitalism, 245–68; in
America, 8, 44, 161; Asian way of, 7, 13,
14–15, 23, 29, 42–43, 98, 107. *See also*
APEC; Globalization, Localization;
Marx, Karl; Pacific Rim; Williams,
Raymond
Trask, Haunani-Kay, 74n, 77, 103, 122,
129n, 149, 180n, 231; *Light in the Crev-
ice Never Seen*, 191–92. *See also* Native
Hawaiians
Trask, Mililani, 243. *See also* Native
Hawaiians
Tupou, Taufa'ahau, King, 12–13
Turner, Ted, 170
Twain, Mark, 23, 79, 124, 147–48, 166,
181, 204–5; anti-imperialism of, 94;
journalism of, 95–103; *Letters from
Hawaii*, 95–103, 229; on plantation
economy in Hawai'i, 93–103; *Roughing
It*, 95, 97, 100n, 204. *See also* Hawai'i;
Native Hawaiians; United States
Tyau, Kathleen, 208; *A Little Too Much Is
Enough*, 208

United Airlines, xv
United Nations, 105
United States: cold war dynamics of, 31,

32, 63, 90n, 108–9, 112, 165, 170–72,
175n; globalizing dynamics of, 1–24,
98–103, 108, 197–99, 215–44, 245–
68; national identity of, 5–8, 16–24,
120–24, 159–62. *See also* American
studies; American Pacific; American
sublime; Bamboo Ridge; Hawai'i;
Heath Anthology of American Literature;
London, Jack; Manifest Destiny;
Melville, Herman; Michener, James;
Monroe Doctrine; Multiculturalism;
Native Hawaiians; Open Door Policy;
Pearl Harbor; Twain, Mark; Whitman,
Walt
University of Hawai'i, 104, 105, 206
Utopia, vii

Vancouver, George, 184, 201
Vespucci, Amerigo, vii
Vietnam, 52n, 63, 65, 112, 236
Vogel, Ezra F., 254
von Tempski, Armine, 226–27; *Born in
Paradise*, 226

Waihe'e, John, 198
Waikīkī Beach, xi–xii, xiv–xv, xvii, 110,
126, 131, 142, 144, 234, 236–37, 270.
See also Hawai'i; Tourism
Watson, Kali, 279
Weinberger, Casper, 89
Wendt, Albert, 13, 67, 70n, 104, 138, 187–
88; "Towards New Oceania," 69, 105,
138–39, 215, 223–24. *See also* Oceania;
Samoa
Werbach, Adam, xviii
Whitman, Walt, 17, 62, 278; "Passage to
India," 102
Whitney, Henry M., 102
Wilkes, Charles, 71
Williams, John, 77
Williams, Raymond, 164, 220. *See also*
Critical regionalism; Transnational
capitalism
Williams, William Carlos, 150

Rob Wilson has published poems in various journals, including
*Tinfish, Taxi, Bamboo Ridge, Mānoa, Central Park, New Republic,
Ploughshares, Partisan Review,* and *Poetry.* He teaches in the English
Department at the University of Hawai'i at Mānoa and Korea
University in Seoul, and is an advisory editor for the journals
boundary 2 and *Inter-Asia Cultural Studies.* His works of poetry and
cultural criticism include *Waking in Seoul, American Sublime,
Asia/Pacific as Space of Cultural Production,* and *Global/Local:
Cultural Production and the Transnational Imaginary.*

Library of Congress Cataloging-in-Publication Data
Wilson, Rob.
Reimagining the American Pacific : from South Pacific to Bamboo
Ridge and beyond / Rob Wilson.
p. cm.—(New Americanists)
Includes index.
ISBN 0-8223-2500-4 (cloth : alk. paper)—ISBN 0-8223-2523-3 (pbk. :
alk. paper)
1. Pacific Area—Civilization. 2. Public opinion—Pacific Area.
I. Title. II. Series.
DU18.w55 2000
909'.09823—dc21   99-056924